Child
Advocacy

Child Advocacy

New Professional Roles for Helping Families

Jack C. Westman

 THE FREE PRESS
A Division of Macmillan Publishing Co., Inc.
NEW YORK

Collier Macmillan Publishers
LONDON

The Free Press
A Division of Macmillan Publishing Co., Inc.
866 Third Avenue, New York, N.Y. 10022

Collier Macmillan Canada, Ltd.

Library of Congress Catalog Card Number: 78-24762

Printed in the United States of America

printing number
1 2 3 4 5 6 7 8 9 10

Library of Congress Cataloging in Publication Data

Westman, Jack C
   Child advocacy.

   Includes index.
   1. Children's rights--United States. 2. Child
development. I. Title.
HV741.W37 362.7'0973   78-24762
ISBN 0-02-934540-5

Copyright Acknowledgments

Excerpt from H. Schuchman, "Towards Assuring Confidentiality of Records in Large-Scale Assessment Programs," in *American Orthopsychiatric Association Newsletter*, August 1975, vol. 9, 4–5. Reprinted with permission of the American Orthopsychiatric Association, Inc. See pages 352–353.

Excerpts from Joseph Goldstein, Anna Freud, and Albert J. Solnit, *Beyond the Best Interests of the Child*, The Free Press, 1973, pages 108–111. Reprinted with permission of Macmillan Publishing Co., Inc. Copyright © 1973 by The Free Press, a Division of Macmillan Publishing Co., Inc. See pages 255–256.

Excerpt from James H. Lincoln, "Model Statute for Termination of Parental Rights," in *Parental Justice*, November 1976, vol. 27, no. 4, 3–8. Reprinted with permission of the National Council of Juvenile and Family Court Judges. This statute is the work of the Neglected Children Committee of the National Council of Juvenile and Family Court Judges, 1975–1976, under the leadership of Honorable James H. Lincoln, chairman. The writing of this statute was made possible by a grant from the Edna McConnell Clark Foundation of New York, New York. See pages 281–283.

Excerpt from H.H. Foster, Jr., *A Bill of Rights for Children*, Charles C. Thomas, Publisher, 1974, page xv. Reprinted with permission of Charles C. Thomas, Publisher. See pages 258–260.

Excerpt from Nicholas Hobbs, *The Future of Children*, Jossey-Bass, Inc., Publishers, 1975, pages 3–4. Reprinted with permission of Jossey-Bass, Inc., Publishers. See pages 224–225.

To our sons
Daniel, John and Eric

Contents

Preface

The aim of this book is to assemble information about what children need in order to thrive in our complex society. Inevitably it will fall short of that objective. Certainly, all the answers are not known, but what is known suffers from the lack of dissemination and application. Some may prefer to magnify the unknowns, thus excusing themselves from responsibility for the tragic neglect of millions of American children. This book takes the opposite position. It holds that problems are undetected and remedies unused simply because a particular child lacks an advocate who can identify that child's needs and ensure that they are met.

I have drawn upon the knowledge of many people who work in different disciplinary territories and speak different professional languages. Because we share a commitment to children, we desperately need to know more about each other. At the risk of naivete in the depth of each discipline concerned with children, I hope that the breadth of this book will stimulate others to surmount the barriers that stand in the way of the healthy development of too many children.

This book deals with young people who have yet to attain complete responsibility for their lives and experience the full measure of satisfaction, and frustration, of adulthood. Those of us who have reached it know too well that adulthood falls short of the hopes and dreams of our childhood. For the young, however, the future remains full of possibilities. Throughout this book the word "children" refers to everyone prior to the age of majority, however that state is defined. To those young people who no longer wish to think of themselves as children, or even adolescents, I apologize and appeal for a better descriptive word.

Above all, this book seeks to demonstrate that a useful body of knowledge about the developmental needs of children exists and that there are ways of applying that knowledge to the problems that all children face, especially those who differ from most.

For their helpful comments, I would like to thank William Bolman, Katherine Forbes Buffington, Ross Campbell, Timothy Chybowski, Constance Clune, Norman Fost, James Greenley, Marc Hansen, Richard Immler, Alfred Kadushin, Deborah Kramer, Bruce Miller, William Morse, Joseph Noshpitz, and Andrew Watson. The opinions and conclusions reached in this book are solely mine, however, and I assume full responsibility for them. My appreciation goes to Cyndi Hackett for her diligent and painstaking work on the drafts of the manuscript. I am especially grateful to my wife, Nancy, for her forbearance and advocacy during the gestation of this book.

Madison, Wisconsin

Introduction

In many parts of the world, children are seen everywhere in community life. They mingle freely with adults and other children. In industrialized countries, however, they have largely disappeared from public view. The relative lack of visibility of children in the United States—in many ways—is the reason for this book.

The disappearance of children from the mainstream of adult life as a civilization modernizes results from the shift of responsibility for children from families to specialized child caring systems which deal with parts of their lives. In the process, large numbers of children are lost in the mazes of modern societies to the ravages of fragmented lives.

Strikingly, children reach public view in America when something goes wrong and they become problems as underachievers, delinquents or dropouts. Even more important is the fact that many children's problems do not surface until later life. It is the tracing of the roots of later problems to the early lives of children that makes it possible for a book like this to appear today.

Some say that Americans do not care about their children. More accurately, Americans are perplexed about what to do for children and paralyzed in acting, less because of indifference and more because of uncertainty. Most adults are worried about children, particularly their own; they may feel helpless, but they are not indifferent. Awareness that the early years of childhood are so critical makes many adults reluctant to act because of the possibility that they might do more harm than good. Certainly, past experience in attempting to solve children's problems suggests that often we do make things worse. The history of children who have not fit into their life situations has been that of removal from their homes, removal from their schools, removal from child caring institutions, and ultimately removal from society to custodial institutions. Our record in ameliorating the problems of children is bleak.

This does not mean that all of our children are in jeopardy. Although insufficient in strength, there have been a number of currents flowing in the direction of improving the lot of children and, specifically, of helping children in need of special care. One purpose of this book is to call attention to what can be learned both from our mistakes and from our efforts that have served children well. We do not need to wait for major social changes to improve the lot of our children. It can be done now through sensitizing parents, professionals, and social planners to their roles as advocates for children. In truth, we cannot afford to wait because of the financial, social, and moral benefits that would accrue from promoting the development of our children and from preventing and detecting problems at an early stage.

Most important, child advocacy furthers the recognition of children as coequal partners with adults and care-givers. Parenthood can become more of a mutual growth experience for parents and children, rather than a pathway of duty and sacrifice. In the process, it will become more difficult to classify children who differ from others as deviant and more possible to recognize and accept individual differences and variations in children.

Reflecting the evolution of our society toward recognizing the importance of the individual, the civil rights movement provided impetus to child advocacy through popularizing advocacy as a means of helping minority groups to achieve status until they were able to pursue their own ends. Through that experience, the complementary ingredients of advocacy both for individuals and for classes of people were recognized and developed.

This book will assess the general importance of children in our society and what is known about their developmental needs. Because child advocacy is at once both a powerful and an elusive concept, we will identify its critical issues, specifically touching on the need for advocacy in the areas of education, law, welfare, health, mental health, and social policy. In so doing, we will identify child advocacy skills that can be learned by professionals and lay persons, obviating the necessity for adding new advocacy people, places, and administrations to an already crowded and bewildering array of disconnected programs and services for children. Although parents are the natural advocates of children, our thesis is that all professionals bearing some form of responsibility for children should learn advocacy skills, and in concert with others influence child caring systems to serve children more effectively.

Professionals have an important, often unrecognized, role to play in helping parents to identify and meet the special needs of their children. This can be done through sensitizing existing child caring systems and personnel to the individual needs of the children they serve without the creation of new and separate advocacy systems. Simultaneously, there is a need to influence social policies so that the interests of children and their families can be furthered rather than ignored or undermined, as is presently the case. In fact, one of this book's premises is that social policy can be influenced most effectively by bringing the problems that children and their parents face into public awareness.

Contrary to the belief of some, advocacy for children does not threaten parents, adults, or child caring agencies. It is not a megaphone for children's wishes but is addressed to determining and furthering children's developmental needs. Parents are aided in carrying out their roles as advocates and in negotiating the often bewildering paths to assistance for their children. Agencies are aided in identifying as-yet-untapped needs for their services and in finding new ways to reduce duplication of effort and increase interagency collaboration.

Without an advocacy stance, professionals tend to focus on what is wrong with children and to differentiate, separate, and isolate them. With child advocacy, we are forced to recognize the determinants of children's problems and to identify ways to ameliorate them. This means that attention is focused on strengthening existing child caretakers and exercising caution in removing children from them to impersonal institutions.

Early in this century, Maria Montessori called attention to what she called universal prejudices against children. Most important was the attitude that adults know what is best for children and always "act for their good." As examples, she cited the assumptions that children must be taught to learn, overlooking their insatiable thirst for learning; that children's minds are empty, overlooking their rich imaginations; and that children cannot work, overlooking the fruits of creative play and the contributions of children to the lives of adults. In order to promote a more objective approach to children, this book calls attention to "agism" as a form of prejudice akin to racism and sexism. As an antidote, uniquely American values and customs can be identified and used to guide methods and objectives of child rearing rather than simply relying upon the power adults wield over children.

The children whom we have already failed are obvious, and those whom we are failing can be identified if simple criteria are followed by people knowledgeable in the development of children. When needful children are identified, individual case advocacy can find appropriate services and ensure that help is obtained. As the following pages will show, the challenge for parents and professionals is to know when individual children are not thriving, and how and where to help them. The challenge for our society is to place a high priority on policies that further the developmental well-being of our children.

Part I
Reasons for Concern About Children

In the little world in which children have their existence, whosoever brings them up, there is nothing so finely perceived and so finely felt as injustice.

Charles Dickens

This section introduces the concept of child advocacy as the missing ingredient in our past thinking about all children, particularly those with special requirements.

The first chapter explains why children merit special national attention today. Although small in size, children are large in numbers and in economic cost. Evidence is reviewed to demonstrate the importance of early life for all children in generating or preventing later social, emotional, and intellectual problems. For the surprisingly large number of children at risk, the concepts of vulnerability and invulnerability are described. Because children cannot be considered apart from the irreducible parent-child unit, the concept of *vulnerable parent-child unit* is suggested as having more powerful predictive value than vulnerable children or vulnerable environments.

1

In Chapter 2 the relative well-being of children today is contrasted with the extreme forms of "agism" seen in the cruel oppression of children in previous times. The evolution of "child savers," and now "child advocates," in the United States is traced. Special attention is devoted to the reports of the six White House Conferences on Children since 1909 as synopses of trends in attitudes toward and hopes for children. The failure of most programs for children is attributed not to a lack of desire to help them but to a lack of coordination and continuity of services.

Chapter 3 defines the concept of child advocacy and shows how assuming degrees of parenting responsibility for children's lives is an appropriate, and sometimes essential, function for professionals and society. The central features of child advocacy are then described: bridging child caring systems, knowledge of child development, conflict resolution, fact finding, interdisciplinary teamwork, and protecting and promoting the legal rights of children. Through applying these principles, the interests of children can be furthered, both at the levels of class advocacy for groups of children and case advocacy for individuals.

Chapter 1
Children at Risk

Adults are simultaneously drawn to and frustrated by children. A child's appealing face on a fund-raising brochure touches the hearts and pockets of most people; however, the behavior of a disturbed child is bewildering, if not repugnant. Contradictory feelings also surface in America as we are told that our children are neglected when we sense that they are overindulged. Because of this ambiguity, this chapter is devoted to placing the problems of American children in perspective.

Frequently heard arguments for increasing concern about the welfare of children include pleas for pity, preparing better citizens, preventing crime and mental illness, fulfilling our duty to the young, and conserving children as a national resource. All of these views assume that adults are responsible for protecting and nurturing their young. Overlooked, however, is the fact that beyond their obvious dependency children deserve attention simply because they are people, comprising 30 percent of the

3

population. Strangely enough, it is a novel idea that children merit attention simply because they are members of society and require representation as do adults. In spite of the decline in birthrate in the 1970s, children will continue to be our largest minority, as reflected in the projection that 32 percent of the population will be under 18 in year 2000 (Bureau of the Census, 1975, 1977).

In America children are valued by adults as sources of happiness, companionship, pride, and personal development. In developing nations, as they once were in this country, children are also valued for their economic value and as a source of security in the later lives of their parents (Espenshade 1977). Counterbalancing these assets are formidable costs in the forms of both direct out-of-pocket child rearing expenses and indirect loss of parental earning power, particularly for mothers. Of even greater importance for some are the emotional and psychological burdens of child rearing.

From a strictly economic point of view, children are a short-term financial drain on society and families. In 1977, the cost of raising one child through high school in the United States was between $35,000 and $53,000—between $77,000 and $107,000, if the income lost by a nonworking mother was taken into account (Espenshade, 1977). The prospect of this cost leads many young American couples to pause before embarking on parenthood. On the other hand, the cost of rearing a child is more than recovered by society through a child's later tax payments and lifetime earnings. In monetary terms, society recovers much more from investing in children than the cost of rearing them.

The economic importance of children is further reflected in the fact that approximately 20 percent of the Gross National Product is spent on or by the young. On the other hand, less than 10 percent of the federal budget is devoted to programs serving children, reflecting their lack of visibility in the political process (NCOCY, 1976). This disparity between the economic prominence of children and their relative insignificance in federal expenditures calls attention to the question of whether or not more time, effort, and money should be devoted to them.

The Influence of Childhood on Later Life

In order to address the question of whether or not children deserve greater attention in America, we will first examine evidence of the ways that early life experiences influence later life.

We know that many eminent people were the products of difficult and stressful childhoods. We know that stress can promote, as overindulgence weakens, strength of character, and that efforts to make children's lives easier might erode character development (Sperling, 1974; Chiriboga, 1978). We also suspect that efforts to educate or inform parents about child rearing have done as much to undermine as to bolster parental self-confidence by unduly emphasizing the delicate nature of early life. Many parents have been excessively worried about their parenting ability. More recently, many young people feel that the responsibilities of parenthood are too great for them. Following these lines of thinking, it might be better if society did not worry about its young.

A closer look at these ideas is in order. First, a number of thoughtful studies have been devoted to the backgrounds of creative people. Three of the books, *Cradles of Eminence, Three Hundred Eminent Personalities* and *Lessons from Childhood*, bring out the ways in which the early lives of many leaders could be regarded as pathogenic. Of eminent persons studied, most were from backgrounds that included poverty; broken homes; rejecting, overpossessive, estranged, or dominating parents; physical handicaps; or school failures (Goertzel, 1962, 1978). Furthermore, many eminent people were disappointments to their parents, and some were given up by teachers as beyond hope (Illingworth, 1969). On the other hand, there were few instances of frank parental neglect and, although sometimes experienced as rejecting, one or both parent figures showed a strong love for learning, often accompanied by physical exuberance and persistent drive. In essence, the "cradles of eminence" were characterized by forceful, if not socially successful, parental personalities.

The question remains unanswered as to whether or not creative people would have been more so if their early home environments had been more pleasant and supportive. Moreover, the constitutional endowment of each one of these persons, most of whom were regarded as geniuses, could override environmental experience. But we must also question the meaning of fame and eminence. Many gifted leaders have done as much to misdirect the progess of society as to advance it. In this light, the burden is on those who argue that the backgrounds of creative people contradict the view that children ought to be provided reasonably supportive early lives. They must prove that mistreatment is not harmful for most children, especially those who lack outstanding talents.

In answer to the argument that more knowledge of early life is not helpful because it will increase worry about children without providing useful answers, a myriad of studies point to the fact that there is good reason to be concerned about large numbers of children. Unfortunately, these studies deal with pieces of a puzzle, each one lacking the impact that results when they are all put together. When viewed as a whole significant information emerges. The research can be grouped as follows: (1) epidemiological surveys of large population samples; (2) studies of special populations of children at risk for such problems as school failure, juvenile delinquency, and drug abuse; (3) studies of the childhood antecedents of mental illness in adults; (4) the literature on the causes of emotional disorders in children and the effectiveness of treatment; and (5) long-term studies of "normal" adults that shed light on the determinants of social adaptation.

EPIDEMIOLOGICAL SURVEYS

One of the most comprehensive prospective epidemiological surveys of children is the National Child Development Study in England, Scotland, and Wales, which demonstrated that marked differences in children's school and community adjustment were apparent by the age of seven in 16,000 children born in 1958 (Davie, 1972, 1975). High risk factors were identified, permitting the early identification of a group of children in whom the risk of handicap was increased because of perinatal and social factors. Among the factors increasing vulnerability were: unwed parent, low social class, overcrowding, high birth rank (fifth or later), abnormal delivery, and abnormal birth weight or gestation. The most striking factor was that children from working-class families were the most vulnerable and had the least access to services. By the age of seven, 13 percent of the children were judged to be at risk for severe physical, mental, or multiple handicaps and 25 percent at risk for educational problems. The criteria used in judging maladaptation were conservative and, other than social class, family factors were not taken into account.

The National Child Development Study supports the concept of a "continuum of reproductive casualty," which postulates a range of vulnerability in early life from death through spontaneous abortion of a defective fetus to educational problems in the later lives of prematurely born infants (Pasamanick and Knobloch, 1966). Of the 5 to 10 million conceptions occurring annually in the United States, 2 to 3 million result in spontaneous abortions due to chromosomal defects or pathogens, and another 1 million are terminated artificially. Of the 4 million fetuses that reach 20 weeks of gestational age, 1.5 percent die before delivery, 1.5 percent die in the first postpartem month, 1.5 percent have severe congenital malformations, and 10 percent will have learning disorders that range from mild to severe retardation (Babson and Benson, 1971; Butler, 1963).

Another extensive survey was carried out of all the 3,000 children born in 1954 on the Hawaiian island of Kauai (Werner, 1971). More detailed information was gathered in this study on the social and psychological state of families. By the age of 10, nearly one-third of the children were judged to be in need of remedial education, mental health services, or health care. The factors relating to social and family conditions were found to be 10 times more contributory to school and behavioral problems than perinatal trauma, which in itself was confirmed as predisposing to vulnerability, adding the concept of a "continuum of environmental casu-

alties" to the "continuum of reproductive casualties." The Kauai study indicated that perinatal complications were related to later physical and
psychological impairment only when combined with persistently adverse
environmental circumstances. These findings were confirmed by a study
of 1,000 North Carolina first-grade children whose psychological and
educational status were predicted from demographic information available solely from their birth certificates (Ramey, 1978).

Even under favorable socioeconomic circumstances, a follow-up study
of a nursery school population disclosed a relationship between maladaptation during the early years of childhood and later school achievement
and performance (Westman, 1968). This study demonstrated that problems did not disappear as children grew older. Those children had access
to optimal health care, and 30 percent of the sample received mental
health or special educational services prior to the age of 18.

STUDIES OF SPECIAL POPULATIONS

Information on special populations considered to be at risk is illustrated by a follow-up study disclosing that prematurely born children at
seven years of age showed more symptoms of behavioral disturbance in
school than did matched controls (Drillien and Wilkinson, 1964). Other
studies have highlighted the importance of family factors in determining
whether or not prematurely born children show later maladaptation
(Neligan, 1976). The presence of mental illness in mothers was found to
be associated with adverse influence on the perinatal condition of infants,
including birth weight and mortality (Zax, 1977).

In another study, Stott (1976) found that school age children with
chronic physical ill health showed a greater liability to develop behavioral
disturbances than did healthy children. Furthermore, in another follow-
up study, Stott found that children whose mothers had been subjected to
emotional tension during pregnancy suffered more physical illness, physical abnormality, neurological dysfunction, behavioral disturbances, and
developmental lags than did controls. In general, the study showed that
mothers' prenatal and perinatal illness, physical stress, household moving, financial strain, personal tension, emotional traumata, unwanted
pregnancy, and illness of relatives and friends were correlated positively
with later physical and emotional morbidity in the children. In a similar
vein, Grunebaum (1975) found that the adverse impact on young children
of mental illness in their mothers could be alleviated by joint admission of
both mothers and babies to a psychiatric hospital.

An extensive literature exists on the effects of maternal or psychological deprivation on child development. At least one-third of children receiving inadequate parental stimulation during the first year of life suffer
developmental, mental, and interpersonal impairment related to the de-

gree of deprivation (Langmeier, 1975). Similar findings have resulted from experimental drive and stimulus deprivation in animals (Bronfenbrenner, 1968). Most critically, the failure to form an attachment with parent figures during the first year of life may jeopardize an individual's capacity to form intimate relationships in later life. Furthermore, the severing of that early attachment through parental death predisposes that person to depression when separation and loss occur in later life (Bowlby, 1973).

Other sources of information on special populations include the extensive studies on the family backgrounds of juvenile delinquents (West, 1977). Sociologists, psychologists, and penologists agree that delinquency is not simply the result of poverty, culture, or social class. It is clear that delinquents are not normal children gone astray. There are also cultural supports for delinquency and, for some, passing through a delinquent phase is a developmental rite. Much is known about the crucial importance of the antisocial peer group in drawing vulnerable youngsters into lives of crime. More fundamentally, however, longitudinal studies, such as the classic work of the Gluecks, have established the role of families in spawning delinquent behavior through their influence on the personality development of children (Westman, 1977; Offord, 1978). Furthermore, potential delinquents can be identified by the age of nine through their behavior and family characteristics (West, 1977).

Clinical studies of delinquent populations consistently demonstrate that at least one-third have significant psychopathology (Lewis, 1976; Westman, 1977). A recent analysis (Lewis, 1976) of the parents of a population of delinquents disclosed that 72 percent showed significant impairment or incapacitation in overall mental health functioning, using the criteria of the Midtown Manhattan Study (Srole, 1962), in which 24 percent of a survey of a randomly selected population were so classified.

The adverse influence of poverty on children depends upon more than economic disadvantage (Brill, 1978). Research has generally shown a relationship between high psychiatric impairment and low socioeconomic status in children. When compared with middle-class children, welfare children in New York City were found to encounter more problems in adaptation, particularly in long-term welfare families. The degree of maladaptation, however, was correlated positively with maternal physical and emotional illness, unhappy marriages, and punitiveness (Eisenberg, 1976). Other studies have indicated that poor single-parent families have the highest risk of social and psychological maladaptation for their children (Kellam, 1977).

While there is widespread agreement that alcoholism is linked to familial factors, the debate continues over the relative importance of genetic and environmental influences. Evidence assembled to date supports both views, indicating that the answer lies in a combination of genetic and environmental factors. One-fourth to one-half of all alcoholic persons have had an alcoholic parent or close relative. The children of alcoholic parents are twice as likely to become alcoholic and have a higher incidence of personality, behavioral, and emotional problems than those of nonalcoholic parents (Booz, 1974; Cork, 1969; Chafetz, 1961; El-Guebaly, 1977). Alcoholic mothers tend to produce babies that are underdeveloped and malnourished (Davie, 1972). Furthermore, alcoholism is implicated in child abuse (Hindman, 1977; Browning, 1977).

In a related vein, the babies of drug-addicted mothers tend to be born developmentally disadvantaged and addicted. Later, they are prone to school adjustment problems and to be placed in foster care (Fanshel, 1975). Furthermore, heavy cigarette smoking of a mother during pregnancy is correlated with later developmental problems in her child (Davie, 1972).

Numerous studies conducted in several different countries have demonstrated that malnutrition coupled with socioeconomic deprivation during the first two years of life is associated with retarded brain growth and mental development that persist into adult life (Lloyd-Still, 1976). On the other hand, studies of such malnourished children raised in affluent adoptive homes after the second year of life show remarkable recovery, emphasizing the importance of the quality of life in determining the long-range effects of malnutrition (Winick, 1975).

All of these special problem areas overlap and point to the especially high risk involved when they converge in the poor, alcoholic, delinquent, educationally disadvantaged population.

CHILDHOOD ANTECEDENTS OF ADULT MENTAL ILLNESS

Another source of information on the importance of childhood is the growing literature that relates childhood bereavement and the experience of excessive separations during early life to depression in later life (Videbech, 1975). Traumatic environmental events in childhood play a role in later manic-depressive psychoses as well. The most powerful predisposing factor is parental deprivation, through death or admission to a psychiatric hospital of a mother or father during one's childhood. These findings do not detract from the importance of genetic factors in manic-depressive psychosis; however, they point to the correlation of home conditions with the expression of the disorder, either in a causal or aggravating role.

Studies of the children of mentally ill parents disclose that growing up in homes with a schizophrenic parent increases the risk of later schizophrenia. Although the hypothesis that pathological communication in families is a causative factor in schizophrenia is being challenged, it is also known that abnormal communication patterns exist. Even though the anomalies of parents and their schizophrenic offspring have a genetic basis, life circumstances play significant ameliorating or aggravating roles. Furthermore, the sufferings that these children endure continue to affect their lives even when they do not interfere with their health or vocational attainment (Bleuler, 1974, 1978). The children of one schizophrenic parent have a 10 percent—and of two, a 33 percent—chance of becoming schizophrenic, probably based on genetic, colored by environmental, factors (Wender, 1977). The children of psychotically depressed mothers have an even higher rate of psychiatric impairment (Grunebaum, 1975). Experimental evidence also is appearing identifying a deficiency in positive affect and excessive rigidity in interactions between mothers who have been psychotic and their young children (Gamer, 1977).

The literature also supports a relationship between maladaptation in childhood and schizophrenia (Kupfer, 1975). A Danish study found that adult schizophrenic persons had more pregnancy and delivery complications, suffered more early separation from parents, showed more disciplinary problems in school, and displayed more emotional sensitivity to stimuli than did controls (Mednick, 1977).

Another source of data is the growing number of follow-up studies on childhood neurosis. A controlled study disclosed that more than 75 percent of neurotic children were at least mildly ill at follow-up during adulthood, compared with only 15 percent of a control group (Waldron, 1976). The findings were that children with neurotic difficulties sufficient to bring themselves to professional attention have a less favorable prognosis for adult mental health than do control subjects. The study also indicated that neurotic children require effective treatment in order to achieve adult mental health.

The follow-up studies conducted by Robins (1966, 1977) demonstrate that antisocial children are at high risk for later social maladjustment. Failure in elementary school led to school absence, which was followed by dropout, leaving the family home before 18, and early marriage. Teenage drinking was followed by the use of marijuana, amphetamines, and arrests. When non-antisocial child guidance clinic patients were compared with controls, no differences were found at adult follow-up, indicating that the treatment of neurosis was effective. For antisocial children, however, 71 percent were involved in later arrests, indicating that predelinquent behavior in childhood is a strong predictor of adult maladjustment. The antisocial behavior of the father through desertion, alcoholism, chronic unemployment, failure to support the family, and arrests was the most powerful predictor of antisocial behavior in the children.

Roff's (1974) controlled study of normal, neurotic, and antisocial adults revealed that children headed for adult antisocial conduct can be identified by the age of nine on the basis of the child's behavior and the behavior of the parents. The typical family background was one of serious lack of parental affection and care, coupled with the parents' physical violence, in an attempt to assert control which had not been acquired because of inadequate parenting. The typical mother did not want the child; her handling was characterized by neglect, inadequate control, a wish to be rid of the child, physical cruelty, and abandonment.

The evidence is that adult mental disorders have early manifestations in childhood, in addition to identifiable family patterns. Intervention during childhood, then, offers the possibility of either preventing or minimizing the extent of adult illness.

LITERATURE ON THE CAUSES AND TREATMENT OF CHILDREN'S EMOTIONAL DISORDERS

An extensive literature on emotional disorders in childhood points to the causative interplay of genetic, temperamental, intellectual, interpersonal, family, and social factors (Rutter, 1975).

Emotional disorders in childhood are associated with parental mental illness, parental death, and parental divorce. In Rutter's series, emotionally disturbed children were three times more likely to have experienced parental death than controls (Rutter, 1966; Kalter, 1977). In other studies, Rutter (1966) found six family variables to be strongly associated with child psychiatric disorder: severe marital discord, overcrowding, large family size, parental criminality, maternal psychiatric disorder, and admission into the care of local authority. More specifically, evidence is accumulating on the role of mother–infant relationships in childhood psychoses (Massie, 1977).

The groundbreaking New York Longitudinal Study revealed the importance of temperament in influencing parent–child relationships and later behavioral disturbances in children. Thomas and Chess (1977) described a temperamental constellation in what they called the "difficult child" of a low threshold of arousal, intense reactivity, poor adaptability, and irregularity in biological functioning. If the parents were able to accommodate to the child's "difficult" temperament, a good behavioral outcome was likely. If not, the difficulties were exacerbated and behavioral disturbance often resulted. This study has demonstrated that temperamental conflicts between parents and children contribute to childhood emotional disorders and family problems.

Of greatest significance, however, is the likelihood that many troubled children are not "ill," but are making efforts to adapt to their lives in ways perceived as noxious to adults. The intriguing point has been made that children's behavioral symptoms may be adaptive, not really pathological (Burton, 1968). This point of view extends the concept of child abuse into the emotional and psychological realm by highlighting the "victim" aspect of childhood psychopathology. There is evidence that the absence of a positive maternal perception of the newborn infant is associated with a high rate of subsequent psychopathology (Broussard, 1976). Initially, conflict may arise with parents when their children are unable to communicate their needs adequately. Another form of conflict may occur when children, though able to express their needs, are unrewarded due to the indifference or opposition of those around them. When parent–child conflict is sustained, the children's thoughts and behavior are affected. Bizarre behavior may result, and the children may fall back on socially inappropriate methods of communicating their wants. As a result, "problem" behavior may occur. Far from being "maladaptive," it may represent attempts by the children to wrest satisfactions necessary for their growth from their environments.

In this view, children with behavior disorders have not submitted with a sense of failure and helplessness, but are fighting to save themselves as individuals despite the odds against them. From this standpoint, their behavior is not "maladjusted." The behavior disorder keeps them from retreating from the world. Several examples of children whose behavior disorders are unique responses to their environments are described in one study (Burton, 1968).

> Accident prone children were seen as extremely assertive in their behavior and as needing acceptance by adults and children outside their own families. Many of the mothers were subjected to intense environmental and physical stress and preoccupied with their own problems, leaving them less able to assist their children in their own development. The children through their pranks and escapades sought parental attention and strove to assert their independence.
>
> Another group of sexually assaulted children displayed an exaggerated need for approval and acceptance. The home circumstances contributed to the children's insecurity, and their sexual involvement represented an attempt on their part to gain acceptance and approval from adults.

An important question is whether or not treatment for problems that can be detected during childhood is effective. The experience of child guidance clinics can be used to answer this question. For complicated reasons, child guidance clinics have been criticized because their interventions were limited in benefit. Actually, the evidence is to the contrary. A number of studies show that child psychiatric techniques have been effective with individual children and their families, and that consultation to child caring systems has benefited large numbers of children (Heinicke, 1975; Levitt, 1971).

Child guidance clinics in the past did not fully meet the needs of their communities because the clinics were not large enough to reach all children needing service and because the most important problems in the lives of many of the children were related to racism, poverty, urbanization, and foundering schools. Our still faltering efforts to deal with poverty and minority group problems continue to limit the effectiveness of child mental health techniques, which are stymied by broader social factors.

When troubled children are properly understood and provided with appropriate therapy that includes their families, they have a good chance to surmount problems that previously were overwhelming. Although crisis-oriented and brief therapies have been useful through the years in managing family problems, the emotional and mental disorders of childhood are not comparable to acute, brief physical illnesses. Childhood emotional disorders are more akin to chronic physical illnesses for which intensive and extended treatment is required, often including treatment of the family (Minuchin, 1974). Most of the problems that children present have developed over a long period of time and some may not be susceptible to complete remediation, just as arthritis or diabetes can be treated but not cured. As is the case with physical illnesses, however, the earlier the intervention, the more favorable the outcome.

DEVELOPMENTAL BACKGROUNDS OF NORMAL ADULTS

Another source of information about the influence of childhood experience on later life is from studies of "normal" individuals. Definitions of normality are many faceted and will be discussed in Chapter 4. At this point, the work of the best known students of normal adults will be cited. Their criteria of normality generally include the following: competent performance in the social settings of the home, school, and work, absence of psychiatric symptoms, and presence of high self-esteem.

Studies dealing with the developmental backgrounds of "normal" adults have common denominators. The longitudinal study of Terman's gifted women disclosed that married women with children are more likely to be happy if their own parents' marriage was stable, and if there was an affectionate and warm relationship between them and their parents (Sears, 1975). Follow-up of Terman's gifted men disclosed a positive relationship between affectionate parent relationships in early life and family life satisfaction in later life. These men placed greater importance on achieving satisfaction in their family lives than in their work. The conclusion was that even the most gifted man gets more from his interpersonal than solitary activities (Sears, 1977).

A longitudinal study by Peck and Havighurst (1960) indicated that the level of maturity of children was strongly correlated with mutual trust and approval between children and their parents and also with consistency of family life, which included predictability, in nature and timing, of parents' methods of discipline.

Grinker (1962) conducted a study of male college students who were rated by their teachers to be of good mental health and stability. The typical family background of these students was found to be one in which the mother and father shared responsibilities and interests and were regarded by the children as loving and giving. Their mothers were seen as warmer and more encouraging than their fathers, whose discipline was viewed as being consistent and fair.

Cox (1970) prospectively studied normal college students to relate later psychopathology to childhood experience. She found that the childhood climate need not have been ideal for children to be capable of dealing with their own later lives effectively. She found that childhood homes in which there was anxiety about finances, overattachment of parent to child, occasional dissension between parents, and neurosis in one parent could still produce children who grew into psychological strength. The circumstances correlated with less desirable mental health were: disrupted or alienated parental marriage, distant relationship of parent to child, early and extended mother–child separation, severe neurosis in either parent, and alcoholism of a parent. She concluded that a home relatively free of the above aberrations is more likely to produce an emotionally healthy individual.

In his study of adult men, Vaillant found that, in comparison with normal subjects, those with mental health problems were more likely to have experienced childhoods that were uncongenial to developing basic trust, autonomy, and initiative. The men with emotional problems were seen as less integrated at the end of adolescence, less likely to have used their fathers as role models, and less likely to have mastered the task of intimacy than the problem-free men (Vaillant, 1975, 1977).

Bowlby (1973) summarized the evidence on the development of normal individuals—in his view, self-reliant persons—by pointing to a family background providing strong support for its offspring, combined with respect for their personal aspirations, sense of responsibility, and ability to deal with the world. Far from sapping a child's self-reliance, then, he concluded that a secure base and strong family support greatly encourages it. Recent confirmation of this was found in Brody's detailed longitudinal study (Brody, 1978).

In summary, childhood disorders in development and adult mental illness have been attributed retrospectively to a variety of early constitutional and environmental factors. When these predisposing factors are studied prospectively, whether or not they lead to maladaptation depends upon life experiences. Where the social environment fosters stereotyping and concreteness in thought and rigidity in behavior, early vulnerabilities become resistant to the change implicit in the process of development. Where flexibility, openness, and adaptability are fundamental characteristics of the environment, early vulnerabilities are dissipated as children advance in constructing and organizing their own cognitive, emotional, and social worlds (Sameroff, 1977).

Who is a Psychologically Vulnerable Child?

As can be seen, whether or not a particular child grows into robust physical and mental health depends upon good fortune in a variety of factors, including the child's constitution, family, ecology, culture, social status, economic condition, and community resources. This multiplicity of variables commonly leads to despair about the possibility of ever finding solutions to what seem to be overwhelming global problems of children (Keniston, 1977). Certainly, experience has shown that simple answers do not exist.

On the other hand, when an individual child is understood, specific needs can be discovered and remedies made known. A significant step has been made in the direction of focusing public attention on the plight of children through the concept of the "vulnerable" child. We know that some children are at risk because they are predisposed to developing psychological, emotional, social, and developmental handicaps. Others are already showing signs of maladaptation, but are as yet undetected. Still others have known handicaps but are inadequately served. At each of these levels lie opportunities to prevent or reduce maladaptation. But before anything can be done, we must be aware of what is a vulnerable child and what are the conditions that promote vulnerability.

The "vulnerable" child can be defined, in one sense, as the antithesis of the "invulnerable" child. Heider (1966) describes "invulnerable" children as having strong physiques, good health histories, better-than-average energy resources, and smooth bodily functioning. They have experienced a trustful and confident relationship with parents responsive to their needs. Their environments are supportive and predictable. Observation of their behavior discloses harmony between themselves and their milieus, stable sensory thresholds that are neither too high nor too low, and competence in dealing with everyday difficulties. Observers also perceive them as active, curious, and eager to explore.

Although risking the perils of posing an ideal, unattainable model, the invulnerability concept is useful as a point of departure (Garmezy, 1977). The essential point is that the characteristics of invulnerable children are congruent with their respective environments. Invulnerability, then, is not so much related to innate or acquired superiorities in performance as to harmony between the child's internal bodily and external interpersonal environments and the child's capacity to accommodate to change.

In contrast, vulnerable children have in common personal development that is not proceeding well and environments that are not optimal
for them (Anthony, 1974b). Vulnerable children are at risk for developing
psychological, emotional, social, and developmental handicaps, either
during childhood or later life. The vulnerable child's development through
infancy, childhood, and adolescence is punctuated by crisis and catastro-
phe. It is often difficult to decide unequivocally whether the parent has
let the child down by failing to inculcate basic trust and confidence or
whether the child's constitutional deficiencies would have taxed the resources of an average parent. That the pair are mismatched is generally
obvious to the observer. If one adds to this poor environmental circumstances and inadequate social and cultural opportunities, conditions of
risk are set up to make it ever more difficult for the vulnerable individual
to emerge unscathed from childhood.

At times the environment may be as benign and as predictable as one
could wish, and the vulnerable child still succumbs. Within an adverse
environment in which the average child survives and the invulnerable one
flourishes, the vulnerable child is very likely to break down completely.
The vulnerable individual may malfunction in spite of a good environment, and the invulnerable individual may be unaffected in spite of a bad
environment.

Compounding vulnerable children's problems are their views of themselves and their worlds. It is not surprising to the clinician that vulnerable
children are chronically dissatisfied with their environments, envisage
them as threatening or depriving, and constantly find fault with people
and things in their worlds. Their pictures of the world are colored by disturbing experiences that are the products of distorted tendencies within
each individual (Anthony, 1974b).

> A striking example of the vulnerable child's view of the world can be seen in
> the writings of one of the most vulnerable and creative people in the world of
> literature, Franz Kafka. He recalled as a child opening his eyes after a short
> sleep in the middle of the day and while still drowsy hearing his mother calling
> down from the balcony to someone else in a natural tone saying: "What are
> you doing my dear; it's so hot." A woman answered from the garden: "I'm hav-
> ing tea outside." They spoke comfortably and pleasantly. For the child Kafka
> this was what the world was like, quiet and predictable—until his mind, fear-
> ful and knowing his fear, set to work on it. In this sense the vulnerable child
> creates one's own risks and generates personal fearfulness. In Kafka's words:
> "I am, as it were, specially appointed to see the phantoms of the night."

Who Are the Vulnerable Children in the United States?

The foregoing evidence shows that the process of development of some
children is endangered by known patterns of risk. It is also obvious that

vulnerability usually results from the impact of a constellation of factors, not a single condition or event. Among the most potent factors are genetic predisposition, perinatal trauma, physical, mental and temperamental variances, malnutrition, parental loss, parent–child incompatibility, family disorganization, parent mental illness, and poverty.

A national survey of children in this country is needed to improve statistics on the physical and psychological well-being of American children and to record changes in their development over time (Brim, 1975). A variety of information on nutrition, child abuse, health care, housing, economic status, family structure, educational attendance and achievement, geographic location, and individual physical, cognitive, and emotional development should be collected. Although such an approach risks impersonalization, it is essential in order to develop a national profile that will make the problems of children visible and shed light on their developmental progress or lack thereof. A national profile would refine our understanding of the needs of children, but it is not needed to tell us that many children are in difficulty now.

Although currently employed indices of vulnerability overlap and disclosure of the true extent of problems is often resisted, there are authoritative estimates of the numbers of children in categories of psychological and developmental risk in America today. These estimates are listed in Table 1 and portray a formidable picture:

TABLE 1.   Children in Categories of Risk

28,000,000	Living with Alcoholic Adult (Booz, 1974)
12,500,000	Nutritionally Deficient (NCOCY, 1976)
10,200,000	Living in Poverty (NCOCY, 1976)
10,000,000	Single-Parent Households (Carter, 1976)
7,500,000	Teenage Problem Drinkers (Rachal, 1975)
7,000,000	Experienced Parental Divorce (Carter, 1976)
6,600,000	Severe Perinatal Stress (Werner, 1971)
5,700,000	Experienced Parental Death (Bane, 1976)
2,000,000	Do Not Attend School (Children's Defense Fund, 1974)
1,800,000	"Difficult" Temperaments Under Age 6 (Thomas, 1977)
900,000	Handicapping Chronic Physical Illness (Richmond, 1977)
300,000	Born to Unwed Teenage Mother Annually (DHEW, 1973; NCOCY, 1976)

How many of these children experience actual harm is not known, but they all live under circumstances of risk. In order to identify those children who are vulnerable, a more precise approach is needed.

The evidence is strong that children in these categories are at risk for emotional, educational, and social maladjustment during childhood and later life. Furthermore, these circumstances tend to be more hazardous for ethnic minority groups. Each of these factors in itself, however, is not sufficient to place a child at definite risk. Prospective surveys have shown that perinatal stress becomes vulnerability in response to family and socio-economic factors (Neligan, 1976). Studies of poverty disclose that the critical factors affecting children are those related to family relationships and structure (Dohrenwend, 1969; Langner, 1977; Lawrence, 1977). The high rate of turnover in the population defined as in poverty clouds a true picture of the poor. Thus, between 1967 and 1972, between 8 and 11 percent of the population were classified as poor. However, less than 3 percent were poor in every year, while 21 percent of the population fell into poverty during one or more of these years (Wisconsin Poverty Center, 1977). Malnutrition is associated with poverty and neglect, but its adverse effect upon a child also depends upon parent–child relationships (Lloyd-Still, 1976). In a similar way, disabling illness and constitutional endowment need not produce adverse psychological or social effects in supportive family environments (Rutter, 1966).

With these considerations in mind, neither the concept of "individual vulnerability" nor that of "environmental vulnerability" is adequate. Neither idea fully recognizes the inherent dependency of children who cannot be conceptualized apart from their caretakers. The irreducible unit is parent–child. For this reason, any effort to identify vulnerable children simply through examination, testing, or study of individuals is theoretically impossible (Hobbs, 1975). Moreover, placing the label of vulnerability upon a child runs the risk of inappropriately focusing attention on only a part of the problem, stigmatizing the child and potentially creating a self-fulfilling prophesy. The result may be the creation of the very problem for the child that we seek to ameliorate or prevent.

Parent–Child Unit Vulnerability

The only theoretically sound and ultimately practical solution is to think in terms of children in life situations that engender vulnerability. This means identifying vulnerable parent–child units as a means of taking into account individual, interpersonal, and environmental characteristics that constitute vulnerability to maladaptation for a child. It is the child caring experience and place that determines the fate of most children.

"Parent–child unit vulnerability" is a useful concept since the interaction of individual and environmental stresses occurs within each child's actual caretaking experience (Sameroff, 1977). The parent–child unit is at least dyadic and includes both the care receiver and the care givers. The concept does not imply that one part of the transactional caretaking unit is more or less responsible for the vulnerability. It is a vulnerable parent–child unit that places the child's development in jeopardy.

We have assembled data on two types of parent–child units that produce risk for children: (1) those related to *disruption* of the caretaking unit, and (2) those related to *disturbance* in the caretaking unit. Cutting across these types are poverty, perinatal trauma, disabling illnesses, and constitutional endowment, each of which tends to increase risk. In estimating the numbers of children in each of the two categories, statistical adjustments, using the method of aggregated conditional probabilities, have been made to account for obvious overlaps.

Disruptions of parent–child units include parental divorce, separation, bereavement, and unwed teenage parenting in which biological parent union, however brief, has been disrupted. Bane (1976) estimates that between 20 percent and 30 percent of children growing up in the 1970s will experience parental divorce by the age of 18; 3 percent, separation; and 9 percent, parental death. The total is between 32 percent and 42 percent. Although all of these children might be considered at risk, we have conservatively reduced the divorce figure by two-thirds since there is evidence that there are adaptive and maladaptive divorces and that approximately one-third of children who experience divorce actually suffer ill effects (Brun, 1973; Westman, 1970). An estimated 1.5 percent of children under the age of 18 have been in unwed teenage households. When overlaps between these categories are taken into account, a total of 20 percent of all children under 18 experience clear risk-producing situations due to disruption of their caretaking units.

The second type, *disturbed parent–child units*, includes child abusing and neglecting families, alcoholic and drug-addicted parents, mentally ill parents, and strained parent–child relationships. The American Humane Association reports 466,940 children as being involved in abuse or neglect during 1977. They project that 2 percent of all children are actually subjected to child abuse. One survey estimates that 28 million children live with an alcoholic person (Booz, 1974). An estimated 17 percent of these children, or 4,620,000, and 7 percent of all children, can be conservatively regarded at risk (Cahalan, 1976; Kissin and Begleiter, 1976). In addition, epidemiological studies of mental illness have placed the incidence of severe adult mental illness at 20 percent and incapacitation at 2 to 4 percent (Srole, 1962; Freedman, 1975). It is likely, then, that 5 percent of all children live with one or more mentally ill parent. Another 10 percent of all children are involved in clinically significant strained relations with their parents (Thomas and Chess, 1977), including intact families with disturbed parent relationships and emotional and behavioral problems in their children (Fisher, 1977). When the overlap between each of these categories is taken into account, a total of 21 percent of all children live in disturbed caretaking units.

When overlap between disrupted and disturbed parent–child unit categories is accounted for statistically, we find that 37 percent of all children live in vulnerable caretaking units at the present time and are at risk for childhood or adulthood maladaptation. This figure is conservative, and although seemingly high, is validated by the risk figures of the previously cited National Child Development Study (38%) and the Kauai Longitudinal Study (33%).

Further support for a 37 percent vulnerability estimate can be drawn from a current survey of the prevalence of children with psychological, educational, and social problems. The National Survey of Children, carried out in 1976 by the Foundation for Child Development, tapped a representative sample of 2,200 children between the ages of 7 and 11 (Zill, 1979). Twenty-one percent of the children were already receiving or identified as needing specialized educational services. Furthermore, during the single year preceding the study, 7 percent of the children between 7 and 11 had an emotional, behavioral, mental, or learning problem serious enough so that the parent felt or was told that the child needed professional help. Parenthetically, one-third of these children did not receive service, and an even higher percentage of unserved children is suggested by Kramer (1975).

Even more authoritative confirmation of the magnitude of vulnerability can be drawn from the numbers of children already known to have problems in the public schools. These children are at a risk for maladaptation in adult life if not properly served. The estimates in Table 2 are conservative; they are adjusted for overlap:

TABLE 2.   Children with Problems in Adaptation in U.S. Public Schools

Emotional Disorders	3,920,000 (JCMHC, 1969; Zill, 1979)
Mental Retardation	1,700,000 (OE, 1970)
Juvenile Delinquents	1,252,700 (DHEW, 1975)
Speech and Language Disabilities	1,320,000 (Hobbs, 1975)
Learning Disabilities	700,000 (OE, 1970)
Neurological Disorders	542,000 (Pless and Douglas, 1971)
Hearing Impairment	402,000 (OE, 1970)
Physically Crippled	328,000 (OE, 1970)
Visual Impairment	70,000 (OE, 1970)
Multiple Handicaps	40,000 (OE, 1970)
Total	10,274,700

Thus, we arrive at a conservative aggregate figure of 10,274,700 children, or 15.6 percent of the population under 18, who are currently having problems in adaptation. Because this figure is conservative, the unaccounted for overlap between the categories would probably not lead to a lower empirical number. Furthermore, each child presently has problems that constitute risk for later life maladaptation. This figure coincides with the finding of the National Child Development Study that 15 percent of seven-year-olds were regarded as "maladjusted" (Pringle, 1966).

Another source of data indicating a similar prevalence of handicapped children is the survey carried out by Rutter, Tizard, and Whitmore on the children between 9 and 12 living on the Isle of Wight (1970). It merits special note because of its methodological advantages. The findings were conservatively reported and, because of the island's freedom from the problems of urbanization and the relative availability of health resources, are probably less than would be found in surveys including urban populations (Graham, 1978). The total number of children with significant retardation in reading was 7.9 percent; mental retardation, 2.6 percent; psychiatric disorders, 5.4 percent; and physical handicaps, 5.5 percent. When overlap between the categories was eliminated, the total number of children known to have handicaps was 16 percent. Because of the age of the children, this figure did not include social deviance in the form of delinquency.

A STATE PROFILE

Another perspective on vulnerable parent–child units can be gained by supplementing these national statistics with highlights of a 1974 profile of the concerns of the state of Texas (Texas DCA, 1974):

1. Three of four Texas families with children under six moved in a five-year period.
2. The divorce rate increased 28 percent in five years.
3. Births to unwed parents increased 25 percent in five years.
4. More high school dropouts left school because of marriage, pregnancy, or both, than for any other reason.
5. Households headed by mothers with children under 18 doubled in ten years.
6. The average annual income of families headed by women was half that of all families.
7. Sixty-five percent of one-parent families with children under six were in poverty compared to 28 percent of all families with children under six.
8. Seventy-six thousand children under six were born without any prenatal care.
9. Of children under the age of four, accidents were the chief cause of death.
10. One of three preschoolers was malnourished.
11. For 420,000 children under six whose mothers worked, there were 180,000 child care spaces.
12. Thirty-two thousand children under six were left to care for themselves while their mothers worked.

The Texas study concluded that no one segment of society, no one individual or group of individuals, no one branch or agency of government by itself could accomplish the goal of enabling children to develop into effective human beings under viable and humane conditions of life. In essence, parents and local communities bear the responsibility for deciding what happens to their children. Practical solutions can be achieved only through greater public awareness of the problems and the cooperative efforts of parents, private industry, and public agencies.

Conclusion

There are many pathways open for the growth of each child. All start close together so that, initially, an individual has access to a range of pathways. The one followed at each stage of childhood depends on the interaction between the child and the environment. Thus, after conception, development depends upon the interaction between the newly formed embryo and the intrauterine environment; at birth, it depends upon interaction between the physiological constitution of the neonate and the parenting figures; and at each age, successively, it depends upon the interaction between the child's personality structure and the family and, later, wider social environments.

Personality structure is highly sensitive to environmental influences during the early years of life, diminishing throughout childhood to achieve the greatest stability during the fourth and fifth decades of life. The adverse influences of early relationships, events, and life situations have a bearing on later life, probably not in a direct causative way, but indirectly, through failures at given stages in life to achieve developmentally appropriate objectives (Bowlby, 1973). All of this is indicated by the weight of evidence from extensive studies of the epidemiology of handicaps, special populations at risk, the childhood antecedents of adult mental illness, the causes and treatment of childhood emotional disorders, and the determinants of adult mental health.

Although poverty, genetic predisposition, perinatal trauma, malnutrition, disabling illnesses, and constitutional factors are important contributors to vulnerability in children, whether or not children are vulnerable depends largely upon disruption or disturbances in their caretaking experiences. Disrupted parent–child units include those affected by parental divorce, separation, bereavement, and unwed teenage parenthood. Disturbed parent–child units include child abusing and neglecting, alcoholic and drug-addicted, mentally ill and emotionally strained parents.

The evidence, conservatively viewed, is that at least 16 percent of the children in the United States already have significant physical, mental, developmental, educational, and social handicaps. These children are maladapted now and, therefore, are vulnerable to further difficulty in later life. Even more striking is the likelihood that 37 percent of our children are at risk of maladaptation during childhood or later adult life. Thoughtful reflection on these statistics makes it evident that the argument that we do not know enough today to be concerned about vulnerable children is really an excuse for inaction. If these children possessed a predisposition to a disease such as epilepsy or diabetes, there would be an outcry for intervention. Actually, the 24 million psychologically and socially vulnerable children in this country constitute the largest problem group of any kind, in any age span and in any socioeconomic class. They exceed the number of children who will develop heart disease or cancer, and they can be identified now. The potential benefit of childhood interventions for later adult life is evident.

Because there is no single screening mechanism for identifying the vulnerable child, awareness of the patterns of vulnerable parent–child units should be a part of all public and personal planning of services for children. The global nature and immensity of the problem need not deter us. The real issue is that too many adults are unaware of the nature and effects of adverse conditions and events on our children. Subsequent chapters will be devoted to illuminating the problems that our vulnerable children face and the ways that adults and child caring systems can address them.

References

ANTHONY, E. J. (1974a) "Introduction: The Syndrome of the Psychologically Vulnerable Child." Chapter in Anthony, E. J., and Koupernick, C. (Eds.), *The Child and His Family: Children at Risk*. New York: Wiley.

ANTHONY, E. J. (1974b) "The Syndrome of the Psychologically Vulnerable Child." Chapter in Anthony, E. J., and Koupernick, C. (Eds.), *The Child and His Family: Children at Risk*. New York: Wiley.

BABSON, S. G., AND BENSON, R. C. (1971) *Management of High Risk Pregnancy and Intensive Care of the Neonate*. St. Louis: Mosby.

BANE, M. J. (1976) "Marital Disruption and the Lives of Children." *Journal of Social Issues*, 32:103–117.

BLEULER, M. (1974) "The Offspring of Schizophrenics." *Schizophrenia Bulletin*, 8:93–109, Spring.

BLEULER, M. (1978) *The Schizophrenic Mental Disorders in the Light of Long-term Patient and Family Histories*. New Haven: Yale University Press.

BOOZ, ALLEN, AND HAMILTON, INC. (1974) An Assessment of the Needs of and Resources for Children of Alcoholic Parents. Final Report to National Institute on Alcohol Abuse and Alcoholism, November 30. PB-241119.

BOWLBY, J. (1973) *Attachment and Loss*, Vol. 2, *Separation*. New York: Basic Books, pp. 363–371.

BRILL, N. Q. (1978) "Poverty and Mental Illness in the United States." *Journal of Continuing Education in Psychiatry*, 39:23–34.

BRIM, O. (1975) "Macro-Structural Influences on Child Development and the Need for Childhood Social Indicators." *American Journal of Orthopsychiatry*, 45:516–524, July.

BRODY, S., AND AXELRAD, S. (1978) *Mothers, Fathers, and Children: Explorations in the Formation of Character in the First Seven Years*. New York: International Universities Press.

BRONFENBRENNER, U. (1968) "Early Depression in Mammals: A Cross Species Analysis." Chapter in Newton, G., and Levine, S. (Eds.), *Early Experience and Behavior: The Psychobiology of Development*. Springfield, Ill.: Thomas.

BROUSSARD, E. R. (1976) "Neonatal Prediction and Outcome at 10/11 Years." *Child Psychiatry and Human Development*, 7:85–93, Winter.

BROWNING, D. H., AND BOATMAN, B. (1977) "Incest: Children at Risk." *American Journal of Psychiatry*, 134:69–72, January.

BRUN, G. (1973) *Children of Divorce*. Copenhagen, Denmark: Gyldendals, Boghandel.

BUREAU OF THE CENSUS (1975) Population Estimates and Projections, Series P-25, No. 601, October.

BUREAU OF THE CENSUS (1977) Current Population Reports, Series P-25, No. 643, January.

BURTON, L. (1968) *Vulnerable Children*. London: Routledge and Kegan Paul.

BUTLER, N. R., AND BONHAM, D. G. (1963) *Perinatal Mortality*. Edinburgh, Eng.: Livingston.

CAHALAN, D. (1970) *Problem Drinkers*. San Francisco: Jossey-Bass.

CARTER, H., AND GLICK, P. C. (1976) *Marriage and Divorce: A Social and Economic Study*. Cambridge, Mass.: Harvard University Press.

CHAFETZ, M. E., BLANE, H. T., AND HILL, M. J. (1971) "Children of Alcoholics: Observations in a Child Guidance Clinic." *Quarterly Journal of Studies of Alcoholism*, 32:687–689.

CHILDREN'S DEFENSE FUND (1974) *Children Out of School in America*. Washington, D.C.: Washington Research Project.

CHIRIBOGA, D. A. (1978) "Dimensions of Stress: Perspectives from a Longitudinal Study." *Journal of Psychosomatic Research*, 22:47–55.

CORK, M. R. (1969) *The Forgotten Children*. Toronto: Addiction Research Foundation.

COX, R. (1970) *Youth to Maturity*. New York: Mental Health Materials Center.

DAVIE, R., BUTLER, N., AND GOLDSTEIN, H. (1972) *From Birth to Seven: A Report of the National Child Development Study*. London: Longman Group.

DAVIE, R., AND BUTLER, N. R. (1975) *From Birth to Seven: The Second Report of the National Child Development Survey*. London: Humanities.

DEPARTMENT OF HEALTH, EDUCATION AND WELFARE (1973) NCHS, Monthly Vital Statistics Report. Summary Report. Final Natality Statistics.

DEPARTMENT OF HEALTH, EDUCATION AND WELFARE, Office of Youth Development (1975) Juvenile Court Statistics: 1973. Washington, D.C.: U.S. Government Printing Office.

DEPARTMENT OF HEALTH, EDUCATION AND WELFARE, ADAMAH (1974) "Second Special Report to Congress on Alcohol and Health: New Knowledge." June, p. 50.

DOHRENWEND, B. P., AND DOHRENWEND, B. S. (1969) *Social Status and Psychological Disorder: A Causal Inquiry.* New York: Wiley–Interscience.

DRILLIEN, C. M., AND WILKINSON, E. M. (1964) "Emotional Stress and Mongoloid Birth." *Developmental Medicine and Child Neurology*, 6:140–143.

EISENBERG, J. G. ET AL. (1976) "A Behavioral Classification of Welfare Children from Survey Data." *American Journal of Orthopsychiatry*, 46:447–463, July.

EL-GUEBALY, N., AND OFFORD, D. R. (1977) "The Offspring of Alcoholics: A Critical Review." *American Journal of Psychiatry*, 134:357–365, April.

ESPENSHADE, T. J. (1977) The Value and Cost of Children. Population Bulletin, Vol. 32, No. 1. Washington, D.C.: Population Reference Bureau, April.

FANSHEL, D. (1975) "Parental Failure and Consequences for Children: The Drug-abusing Mother Whose Children Are in Foster Care." *American Journal of Public Health*, 65: 604–612, June.

FISHER, L. (1977) "On the Classification of Families." *Archives of General Psychiatry*, 34:424–433, April.

FREEDMAN, A. M., KAPLAN, H. I., AND SADOCK, B. J. (1975) *Comprehensive Textbook of Psychiatry/II* Vol. 1. Baltimore: Williams and Wilkins.

GAMER, E., GRUNEBAUM, H., COHLER, B. J., GALLANT, D. H. (1977) "Children at Risk: Performance of Three-year-olds and their Mentally Ill and Well Mothers on an Interaction Task," *Child Psychiatry and Human Development*, 8:102–114.

GARMEZY, N. (1977) "Observations on Research with Children at Risk for Child and Adult Psychopathology." Chapter in McMillan, M. F., and Henao, S. (Eds.), *Child Psychiatry Treatment and Research.* New York: Brunner/Mazel.

GOERTZEL, V., AND GOERTZEL, M. G. (1962) *Cradles of Eminence.* Boston: Little, Brown.

GOERTZEL, M. G., GOERTZEL, V., AND GOERTZEL, T. G. (1978) *Three Hundred Eminent Personalities: A Psychosocial Analysis of the Famous.* San Francisco: Jossey-Bass.

GRAHAM, P.J. (1978) "Epidemiological Perspectives on Maladaptation in Children." *Journal of Child Psychiatry*, 17:197–208.

GRINKER, R. R. (1962) " 'Mentally Healthy' Young Males (Homoclites)." *Archives of General Psychiatry*, 6:405–453.

GRUNEBAUM, H. U. ET AL. (1975) *Mentally Ill Mothers and Their Children.* Chicago: University of Chicago Press.

HEIDER, G. M. (1966) "Vulnerability in Infants and Young Children: A Pilot Study." *Genetic Psychology Monograph*, 73: 1–216.

HEINICKE, C. M., AND STRASSMAN, L. H. (1975) "Toward More Effective Research on Child Psychotherapy." *Journal of Child Psychiatry*, 14:561–588.

HINDMAN, M. (1977) "Child Abuse and Neglect: The Alcohol Connection." *Alcohol World*, 1:2–7, Spring.

HOBBS, N. (1975) *The Futures of Children*. San Francisco: Jossey-Bass.

ILLINGWORTH, R. S., AND ILLINGWORTH, C. M. (1969) *Lessons from Childhood*. Edinburgh and London: Livingstone.

JOINT COMMISSION ON THE MENTAL HEALTH OF CHILDREN (1969) *Crisis in Child Mental Health*. New York: Harper.

KALTER, N. (1977) "Children of Divorce in an Outpatient Psychiatric Population." *American Journal of Orthopsychiatry*, 47: 40–51.

KELLAM, S. G., ENSMINGER, M. A., AND TURNER, R. J. (1977) "Family Structure and the Mental Health of Children." *Archives of General Psychiatry*, 34:1012–1022, September.

KENISTON, K. (1977) *All Our Children: The American Family Under Pressure*. New York: Carnegie Council on Children.

KISSIN, B., AND BEGLEITER, H. (1976) *Social Aspects of Alcoholism*. New York: Plenum Press.

KRAMER, M (1975) "Some Perspectives on the Role of Biostatistics and Epidemiology in the Prevention and Control of Mental Disorders." *Health and Society*, Summer.

KUPFER, D. J., DETRE, T. P., AND KORAL, J. (1975) "Relationship of Certain Childhood 'Traits' to Adult Psychiatric Disorders." *American Journal of Orthopsychiatry*, 45:74–80, January.

LANGMEIER, J., AND MATEJCEK, Z. (1975) *Psychological Deprivation in Childhood*. New York: Wiley.

LANGNER, T. S., McCARTHY, E. D., GERSTEN, J. C., SIMCHA-FAGAN, O., AND EISENBERG, J. G. (1977) "Factors in Children's Behavior and Mental Health over Time: The Family Research Project." Chapter in Simmons, R. G. (Ed.), *Research in Community and Mental Health—An Annual Compilation of Research*. Greenwich, Conn.: Jai Press.

LAWRENCE, M. M. (1977) "The Relevance of Psychodynamic, Historical and Cultural Studies of Mother, Family and Extended Family for Infant–Caretaker Interaction Research in an Inner-City Community." Chapter in McMillan, M. F., and Henao, S. (Eds.), *Child Psychiatry: Treatment and Research*. New York: Brunner/Mazel.

LEVITT, E. E. (1971) "Research on Psychotherapy with Children." Chapter in Bergin, A. E., and Garfield, S. L. (Eds.), *Handbook of Psychotherapy and Behavior Change: An Empirical Analysis*. New York: Wiley.

LEWIS, D. O., AND BALLA, D. A. (1976) *Delinquency and Psychopathology*. New York: Grune and Stratton.

LLOYD-STILL, J. D. (1976) *Malnutrition and Intellectual Development*. Littleton, Mass.: Publishing Sciences Group.

MASSIE, H. N. (1977) "Patterns of Mother–Infant Behavior and Subsequent

Childhood Psychosis." *Child Psychiatry and Human Development*, 7:211–230, Summer.

MEDNICK, S. A. (1977) "High-risk Children Identifiable Early in Life." *Psychiatric News*, October 21, pp. 30–31.

MINUCHIN, S. (1974) *Families and Family Therapy*. Cambridge, Mass.: Harvard University Press.

NATIONAL COUNCIL OF ORGANIZATIONS FOR CHILDREN AND YOUTH (1976) *America's Children—1976*. Washington, D.C.

NELIGAN, G. A. ET AL. (1976) *Born Too Soon or Born Too Small*. Philadelphia: Lippincott.

OFFICE OF EDUCATION (1970) Number of Pupils with Handicaps in Local Public Schools: Spring, 1970. Washington, D.C.: U.S. Government Printing Office.

OFFORD, D. R., ALLEN, N., AND ABRAMS, N. (1978) "Parental Psychiatric Illness, Broken Homes and Delinquency." *Journal of the American Academy of Child Psychiatry*, 17(2):224–238.

PASAMANICK, B., AND KNOBLOCH, H. (1966) "Retrospective Studies on the Epidemiology of Reproductive Casualty: Old and New." *Merrill–Palmer Quarterly*, 12:7–26.

PECK, R. F., AND HAVIGHURST, R. J. (1960) *The Psychology of Character Development*. New York: Wiley.

PLESS, I. B. AND DOUGLAS, J. W. B. (1971) "Chronic Illness in Childhood: Part I: Epidemiological and Clinical Characteristics." *Pediatrics*, 45:405–414.

PRINGLE, M. L. K., BUTLER, N. R., AND DAVIE, R. (1966) *11,000 Seven-Year-Olds*. London: Longmans.

RACHAL, J. V. (1975) A National Study of Adolescent Drinking Behavior: Attitudes and Correlates. Research Triangle Institute, April.

RAMEY, C. T., STEDMAN, D. J., BORDERS-PATTERSON, A., AND MENGEL, W. (1978) "Predicting School Failure from Information Available at Birth." *American Journal of Mental Deficiency*, 82:525–534.

RICHMOND, J.B. (1977) "The Needs for Children." *Daedalus*, 106:247–259, Winter.

ROBINS, L. N. (1966) *Deviant Children Grown Up: A Sociological and Psychiatric Study of Sociopathic Personality*. Baltimore: Williams and Wilkins.

ROBINS, L. N., AND WISH, E. (1977) "Development of Childhood Deviance: A Study of 223 Urban Black Men from Birth to 18." Chapter in McMillan, M. F., and Henao, S. (Eds.), *Child Psychiatry Treatment and Research*. New York: Brunner/Mazel.

ROFF, M. (1974) "Childhood Antecedents of Adult Neurosis, Severe Bad Conduct, and Psychological Health." Chapter in Risks, D. F., Thomas, A., and Roff, M. (Eds.), *Life History Research in Psychopathology*, Vol. 3. Minneapolis: University of Minnesota Press.

RUTTER, M. (1966) *Children of Sick Parents: An Environmental and Psychiatric Study*. London: Oxford University Press.

RUTTER, M. (1975) *Helping Troubled Children*. New York: Plenum Press.

RUTTER, M., TIZARD, J., AND WHITMORE, K. (1970) *Education, Health and Behavior*. London: Longmans.

SAMEROFF, A. J. (1977) "Early Influences on Development: Fact of Fancy?" Chapter in Chess, S., and Thomas, A. (Eds.), *Annual Progress in Child Psychiatry and Child Development—1976*. New York: Brunner/Mazel, pp. 3–33.

SEARS, P. S., AND BARBEE, A. H. (1975) "Career and Life Satisfaction of Terman's Gifted Women." Presented at Louis M. Terman Memorial Symposium on Intellectual Talent, Johns Hopkins University, November 6.

SEARS, R. R. (1977) "Sources of Life Satisfactions of the Terman Gifted Men." *American Psychologist*, 32:119–128, February.

SEGAL, J. (1978) *A Child's Journey: Forces That Shape the Lives of Our Young*. New York: McGraw-Hill.

SPERLING, M. (1974) *The Major Neuroses and Behavior Disorders in Children*. New York: Aronson.

SROLE, L. ET AL. (1962) *Mental Health in the Metropolis: The Midtown Manhattan Study*, Vol. 1. New York: McGraw-Hill.

STOTT, D. H., AND LATCHFORD, S. A. (1976) "Prenatal Antecedents of Child Health, Development, and Behavior." *Journal of Child Psychiatry*, 15:161–191.

TEXAS DEPARTMENT OF COMMUNITY AFFAIRS (1974) "The Darker Side of Childhood." Austin: Office of Early Child Development.

THOMAS, A., AND CHESS, S. (1977) *Temperament and Development*. New York: Brunner/Mazel.

VAILLANT, G. E. (1975) "Natural History of Male Psychological Health." *Archives of General Psychiatry*, 32:420–426, April.

VAILLANT, G. E. (1977) *Adaptation to Life*. Boston: Little, Brown.

VIDEBECH, T. H. (1975) "A Study of Genetic Factors, Childhood Bereavement and Premorbid Personality Traits in Patients with Anacastic Endogenous Depression." *Acta Psychiatrica Scandinavica*, 52:178–222.

WALDRON, SHERWOOD, JR. (1976) "The Significance of Childhood Neurosis for Adult Mental Health: A Followup Study." *American Journal of Psychiatry*, 133:532–538, May.

WENDER, P. H. ET AL. (1977) "Schizophrenics' Adopting Parents." *Archives of General Psychiatry*, 34:777–784, July.

WERNER, E. E., BIERMAN, J. M., AND FRENCH, F. E. (1971) *The Children of Kauai*. Honolulu: University of Hawaii Press.

WEST, D. J., AND FARRINGTON, D. P. (1977) *The Delinquent Way of Life: Third Report of the Cambridge Study in Delinquent Development*. London: Heinemann.

WESTMAN, J. C. (1968) "School Career Adjustment Patterns of Children Using Mental Health Services." *American Journal of Orthopsychiatry*, 38:659–665, July.

WESTMAN, J. C. (1977) "Psychotherapy with Juvenile Delinquents." Chapter in Wolman, B. B. (Ed.), *International Encyclopedia of Neurology, Psychiatry, Psychoanalysis and Psychology*. New York: Aesculapius Press.

WESTMAN, J.C. ET AL. (1970) "Role of Child Psychiatry in Divorce." *Archives of General Psychiatry*, 23:416–420, November.

WINICK, M., KATCHADURIAN, K., AND HARRIS, R. C. (1975) "Malnutrition and Environmental Enrichment by Early Adoption." *Science*, 190:1173–1175, December 19.

Wisconsin Poverty Center (1977) "Low Income Population: What We Know About It—Statistical Profile." Paper No. 3. Madison: Wisconsin Poverty Center.

ZAX, M., SAMEROFF, A. J., AND BABIGIAN, H. M. (1977) "Birth Outcomes in the Offspring of Mentally Disordered Women." *American Journal of Orthopsychiatry*, 47:218–230, April.

ZILL, N. (1979) *Happy, Healthy and Insecure: The State of American Children*. New York: Doubleday.

Chapter 2
Society's Concern about Children

That today's children are relatively well off is more evident the farther one goes back in history (Greenleaf, 1978). In a caricaturing mood, de Mause wrote a dramatic portrayal of the evolution of childhood.

In de Mause's (1974) view, between antiquity and the fourth century A.D., an "infanticidal" mode of child rearing prevailed in which parents resolved their concerns about problem children by killing them, a practice with profound effect on the surviving children! Between the fourth and thirteenth centuries, the "abandonment" model appeared as parents began to believe that a child had a soul. A way of handling problem children then was by abandonment to a monastery or nunnery, servitude in the home of a nobleman, or simple emotional abandonment in their own homes. From the fourteenth to the seventeenth centuries, de Mause describes the "ambivalent" mode in which children were viewed as full of amorphous, "dangerous" impulses. The parental task, then, was to mold the formless child.

Later, the eighteenth century saw the advent of the "intrusive" mode. The child was regarded as having a mind that needed to be conquered and an emotional life that needed to be controlled. From the nineteenth to the mid-twentieth century, the "socialization" mode followed. This was characterized by training children through guidance and teaching rather than attempting to conquer their wills. Recently, in the mid-twentieth century, a "helping" mode appeared in which children were seen as knowing better than their parents what they need at each stage of their lives. In this mode, parents work to fulfill their children's expanding needs. The "helping" mode involves parental reasoning and discussion with little emphasis on disciplining the child.

Until the eighteenth century, then, children were regarded popularly as miniature adults, without recognition that their level of thinking, emotions, and behavior were uniquely immature, although medical writings have pointed out stages in child development since Hippocrates and Galen (Demaitre, 1977). The overriding reality that children are physically small and relatively helpless has made them exceedingly vulnerable to the prevailing attitudes and influence of adults. On the other hand, older children can make themselves uncomfortably apparent, as was true during the Middle Ages when bands of predatory children roamed the countryside. Many of the "knights" were actually young adolescents seeking their fortunes. As a result, one of the historical impetuses to strengthening the family unit was to contain, support, and socialize children. Apparently, the development of community schools, beyond those in religious institutions and monasteries, was conceived in part as a means of containing children who otherwise would have been roaming freely (Aries, 1962).

Prior to the eighteenth century, family units were comprised principally of parents and children under seven or eight years of age. Above that age, a child became a working member of society or was apprenticed to a master to learn work skills. During those times adolescence did not exist as we know it today, because of the relatively abrupt transition from childhood to adult status. Compounding all of this was the fact that almost half of the children could be expected to die before reaching maturity.

After the Industrial Revolution, parents increasingly assumed caretaking roles for their children, who stayed with them because society was becoming more complex. It was a new experience for parents to find that the fate of their children no longer depended upon illness and things beyond their control. Parents began to discover that they could influence the lives of their children through better nutrition, immunization, sanitation, medical care, and education. All of this contributed to an increasing emotional investment of parents in their children.

Bremner's three-volume documentary history provides a rich source of details on children and youth in America (1970, 1971a, 1971b). Davis (1976) offers a concise overview. Apparently, eighteenth-century America devoted little attention to reforming offending or offensive adults or children, whether poor, criminal, or insane. Essentially, towns tried to rid themselves of these people by sending them on their way to the next community.

The fate of children without protective parents, in early nineteenth-century New England textile mills, dramatically illustrates the level of popular adult indifference toward children. Poorhouse children as young as four years of age were then used as laborers. Typically, such poor children were leased to textile mills where they worked 16 to 18 hours a day. The younger ones picked up cotton waste from the factory floor. Children of six or seven were put to the spinning wheel or to the loom, where their small, deft, flexible fingers could throw the thread more quickly than adults could. The children usually had half an hour for a frugal breakfast and an hour for a similar lunch. During working hours, they were not allowed to leave their workplace to go to the toilet or to get a drink of water. Children who left their stations were brutally punished by whipping. "Slappers" whipped them when they fell asleep. The lack of sleep, fresh air, rest, and vacations made many of these undernourished children ill. Many died in their teens, literally after being worked to death. This tragic example remains significant to this day, because it illustrates the way in which children can be forced to adapt to harsh environments.

In the 1830s, during the Jacksonian era, an era of popular interest in child nurture began (Wishy, 1968). This was fueled by the threat created by large waves of immigrant children crowded in urban slums, leading to the creation of special environments for such children. This was the period of the establishment of orphanages, institutions for the retarded and the insane, and reform schools for delinquents. As an example, the goal of the newly established Boston Asylum and Reform School was to take children from "abodes of raggedness and want, where mingled with the cries of helpless need, the sounds of blasphemy assail your ears; and from example of father and mother, the mouth of lisping childhood is taught to curse and revile" (Rothman, 1971).

After the Civil War, America was predominantly a country of small farms, businesses, and towns shifting toward urbanization. In the 1880s, however, critical social tension was created by the further influx of millions of immigrants from Europe. They were generally untrained in industrial skills and impoverished. Compulsory education laws were supported by those who wanted to Americanize these strangers and remove the immigrant children from the streets. Furthermore, the Protestant ethic prized industry, thrift, and efficiency, so that there was a lack of sympathy for the poor who did not show these qualities. The state mental hospitals, beginning to have some success during the pre–Civil War era of "moral treatment," were deluged by immigrants who were unable to cope with their new lives, and the quality of state institutional care began its downward trend.

At the same time, the "child savers" became a significant movement for middle-class Americans, particularly feminist groups. Women's traditional functions were affected by the weakening of domestic roles and the rearrangement of family life in large cities. As a result, they reaffirmed the values of the home, parental authority, and rural life (Platt, 1969). In 1875 the New York Society for the Prevention of Cruelty to Children was formed. Its mission was to "rescue children from bad situations," and it opened the first temporary shelter for neglected children (NYSPCC, 1977). The effects of the "child savers" movement were crystallized in compulsory education, which was originally intended to be education for all children, regardless of their needs.

> The Compulsory Attendance Act commands that they shall be placed in schools; if not in regular schools then in other schools provided for them. . . . I therefore call attention again to the necessity of the establishment of a parental school for . . . children who are constantly dropping out of school and become vagrants on the streets. (Harpur Report, 1899)

The popular recognition of childhood as a developmental phase of life with unique characteristics began in the late nineteenth century. Prior to 1880, Americans seldom thought of play as vital for the child's physical and moral development. But the advent of the child study movement in the late 1880s and genetic psychology espoused by G. Stanley Hall revolutionized ideas about childhood. Preceded by the popular writings of Martha Finley, Louisa May Alcott, and Horatio Alger, Jr., by the mid-1890s Hall had succeeded in convincing a good portion of the educated public that the child develops sequentially, passing through definable stages of growth.

At the same time, reformers were becoming increasingly alarmed about the leisure time activities of urban youth and the freedom from constraint that large cities granted. From their perspective, urban industrial society compromised the authority of traditional socializing institutions, and neither the family, the church, nor the school could control and direct a child's instincts in an urban setting. Among other evils spawned by the failure of traditional disciplinary agencies were unprecedented increases in juvenile delinquency and sexual promiscuity among urban youths, leading to the creation of the first juvenile court in 1899 in Chicago.

During the early years of the twentieth century, reformers such as Jane Addams, Lillian Wald, Jacob Riis, and Frederick Howe continued to be concerned about the impact of urban industrial life upon the moral, intellectual, and physical welfare of children. During the Progressive Era organizing play and games for children, particularly children of immigrants, achieved spectacular success through municipally funded and supervised playgrounds in the nation's slums. The efforts of the Playground Association of America culminated in the erection of thousands of playgrounds and parks in congested areas of major cities and in the incorporation of physical education courses in public school (Cavello, 1976).

On the other hand, the failure of most of these efforts is epitomized by the fate of the special classes set up during the 1890s, which quickly became "dumping grounds" for all children who could not be handled in regular classrooms, most of whom were from immigrant families. The following commentary made in 1916 in Cleveland is illustrative:

> At the present time such cases are often handled in a most unsatisfactory manner. The non-English speaking child cannot keep up with his companions in the regular grades. For this reason he is sent to a special class, not because it is the right place for him, but rather because it furnishes an easy means of disposing of a pupil, who, through no fault of his own, is an unsatisfactory member of a regular grade. (Miller, 1916)

The Child Study Movement which Hall led in the 1880s and 1890s created a matrix in which progressive education developed. After World War I efforts to better the condition of children were accelerated by the dismay over the inadequate physical and educational condition of so many army recruits. Well baby clinics and child guidance clinics were established, school health programs were instituted, and mother's pension programs were more widely adopted.

In 1923, Lawrence K. Frank foresaw the need for the systematic and intensive study of child growth and development and envisioned a nationwide plan for such research and parent education. His knowledge of the need for research in human development was accompanied by a vision of programs in homes, schools, and agencies of child care in which the needs of the whole child would be central.

As an executive of the Laura Spelman Rockefeller Memorial, Frank worked to establish research institutes at places such as Harvard, Yale, the University of California, the University of Iowa, the University of Minnesota, Western Reserve, the University of Colorado, the University of Michigan, Syracuse, Antioch, Cornell, Columbia, Vassar, Sarah Lawrence, the Mayo Clinic, Stanford, and the University of Rochester, launching the Child Development Movement. Frank pinned his hopes upon parent education (Senn, 1977).

Subsequently, research in child development proliferated and federal landmarks followed in the form of the 1946 Mental Health Act, which established federal responsibility in the area of mental health, the launching of Operation Headstart by the Office of Economic Opportunity in

1965, the creation of the Office of Child Development in 1969, the Report of the Joint Commission on the Mental Health of Children in 1970, and the signing of the Child Abuse Act in 1974.

The White House Conferences

A broad overview of our society's hopes for troubled children can be gained from a review of the White House Conferences on Children (Beck, 1973). Early twentieth-century social reformers viewed children as a natural resource, shifting concern about child welfare from families into the public domain. The federal government, thereby, was to include the needs of children with its other national interests. These reformers prevailed upon President Theodore Roosevelt to hold the first White House Conference on children in 1909. It was entitled the White House Conference on the Care of Dependent Children and was organized by Jane Addams and Lillian Wald, leaders of the settlement house movement. The immediate result was establishing the Children's Bureau in the federal government to gather information and support scientific research about children.

The second White House Conference on Standards of Child Welfare was held in 1919. The focus was on the statistical reporting of the state of maternal and child health, with recommendations for revising standards rather than advocating more programs. At this point the Children's Bureau had already encountered opposition from other parts of the federal bureaucracy because it threatened special interest groups, and it responded by working narrowly on infant and maternal mortality and health. During that time, the National Committee for Mental Hygiene, founded in 1909, jointly sponsored with the Commonwealth Foundation a national conference on the prevention of juvenile delinquency in 1921. The result was a five-year demonstration project of seven child guidance clinics, spawning a nationwide pattern of child guidance clinics.

The 1930 White House Conference on Child Health and Protection was a radical departure from the previous conferences. It assembled 3,000 participants from all fields touching on the lives of children. Tension between the roles of experts and parents was manifested in the Conference's ambiguous outlook toward the family as the primary child rearing institution. President Hoover summed it up by saying: "Parental responsibility is moving outward to include community responsibility. . . . We have seen what was once charity change its nature under the broader term welfare, and now those activities looked upon as welfare are coming to be viewed merely as good community housekeeping. . . . We must force the problem back to the spot where the child is. This primarily means, and should mean, the home. Our function should be to help parents, not replace them." That Conference urged family change through parent education.

The 1940 White House Conference on Children in Democracy bore the stamp of the international burden of the impending World War II, and stressed rearing children to develop their capacities for exercising the responsibilities of citizenship in a democracy. Stress was placed upon meeting children's needs through a centralized public school system; in so doing, parental responsibilities were limited to the basics: "Giving the child food, shelter and material security is the primary task of the family."

The mid-century White House Conference on Children and Youth in 1950 stressed the importance of professional expertise and research on children.

The 1960 White House Conference on Children and Youth reflected the growing alienation of youth through its concern about the increase in violent crimes committed by adolescents and the growing culture of gangs. The Conference was also concerned about the lack of obedience and the social apathy of youth. Breakdown of the family was seen as a dangerous sign heralding the future breakdown of society. The Conference called for further study of the underlying causes of broken homes and divorce. It held that the family occupies a central place in American society and is essential to a child's development. A large number of recommendations called for education in parenting, beginning in high school to help young people understand the responsibilities of marriage and the privilege of parenthood.

In 1970, the fact the earlier conferences had stressed older children was remedied by holding two conferences, one the White House Conference on Children and the other the White House Conference on Youth. The conferences noted that responsibility for children was shifting away from the family and recommended emphasis on universal comprehensive day care and allied services. With the conviction that the government should not circumvent the family, the conferences urged that developmental, cognitive, and health programs include increasing participation of the family. Income maintenance programs were seen as alternatives for contributing to family support.

This panoramic view of the White House conferences brings out several striking impressions. The first is that, rather than planning for the future, the conferences focused largely on describing the past. They also had a general nostalgic flavor, implying that a return to the "good old days" would be helpful. The conferences also showed a great disparity between their recommendations and what could be implemented; for example, the 1930 Children's Charter was remarkably similar to the 1970 Children's Bill of Rights. The proceedings of the conferences read like a history of adult ideas and hopes about the young, rather than like reports dealing with flesh-and-blood children. Whatever the intentions of the writers, who were well-meaning social reformers, child psychologists, pediatricians, and educators, and whatever their real contact with children, their prescriptions for programs, definitions of needs, and causes for concern somehow lost the child in the process: "In the sweep of seven decades, the image conveyed is one of children, smaller than anyone else, lighter in physical weight and political clout, easily picked up and blown wherever the winds of economic, political and social movement were heading" (Beck, 1973).

As one can see, the White House conferences emphasized social, economic, and educational measures for the benefit of children. Some of the measures advocated for prevention have borne fruit; most have not. This fact was reflected in 1970 in the report of the Joint Commission on the Mental Health of Children, which found that the vast majority of children then needing clinical care were not receving it. As an example, it pointed out that not one community had all the clinical services it needed, and that many communities had no programs at all. Although the weight of the report was devoted to social, economic, and educational measures, there was a recognition that attention must be devoted to individual children. Although poverty was recognized as a devastating experience, unanswered were questions as to why some people live a personally acceptable and nonpathological life at a low income level and others do not. In fact, as had been demonstrated by the phenomenon of juvenile delinquency, it is the individual within a unique environment who must be the focus of attention.

The Status of Children Today

As a means of gaining a perspective on children in modern society, Brim (1971) describes macro, meso, and micro levels of influence on children. At the macrostructural level are the social forces related to technology, law, mass media, and the economy which affect child caring institutions. At the mesostructural level are institutions that serve children specifically, such as the schools, families, and child caring facilities. At the microstructural level are those people who actually take care of children, necessitating a fine-grained analysis of the influence of a particular parent on a child's personality.

A multisystems view of children such as this is necessary because the things that have been done for children in the past have really been done *to* children. This means that the locus of the child's difficulty has been seen as lying solely within the child, ignoring family, community, cultural, and economic factors. This has led to interventions that have focused exclusively on doing to the child, often leading to shifting a child from one place to another. As pointed out by Mead (1976), there is an overwhelming tendency to remove a child from a situation as a way of handling the child's problems. For example, children in difficulty with their families are taken out of their families and placed in foster care. When children have difficulty in foster care, they are removed from the foster homes and placed in child caring institutions. When there is difficulty in child care institutions, they are removed from that place and put into residential hospitals. When that doesn't work, they are ordinarily of sufficient age to be transferred to correctional facilities. The entire approach to children, unlike the way we manage adults, has been to take them out of the circumstance in which the problems arose.

Absent from this line of thinking and action has been the concept that something could be done therapeutically at the first point in which children encounter difficulty, specifically, within their families. It is only in recent years that the possibility of therapeutic family interventions have been conceptually worked through and clinically applied. Children do not exist alone and at the very least are part of dyadic relationships with their parents. If one can think in terms of altering the parent–child unit in a constructive way, the focus of diagnosis and treatment becomes family oriented and more powerful in influencing the child. The most important lesson that history has taught us is that children cannot be viewed outside of their immediate psychosocial and family context. This means that interventions at various systems levels must take into account supporting children's living units and dealing with them within the context of their parents and siblings.

Furthermore, there has been an overriding tendency of our social system to react to children's crises or social problems with temporary "recoil" solutions that either isolate or manage threatening behavior but do not prevent recurrence (Rhodes, 1972). This crisis intervention orientation, which has traditionally been the response of society to children's problems, has led to overlooking the lack of continuity and fragmentation of available services. In some instances there has been an overdevelopment of professional services which deal with a part of the child's problem and in so doing impede an effective, comprehensive, and coordinated approach to the needs of a youngster. The classical example is children who have spent most of their lives in foster homes, institutions, and correctional facilities, literally absorbing millions of dollars of public funds and having contact with hundreds of professional people. All of this might have been averted at the beginning by the ability of the initial foster home to adopt the child. This was prevented by an agency policy which restricted foster homes to temporary care and made it impossible for the child to be adopted. Such grotesque and unthinkable wastage is not uncommon. The fact that this continues at the present time is based upon many social resistances, one of which is that preventive measures require long-range planning, an approach which runs counter to society's short-range, crisis-oriented method of handling social problems.

At this point child welfare, child caring institutions, mental hospitals, juvenile courts, schools, pediatric facilities, and mental health clinics are in a state of ferment, strongly affected by an awareness that some of our programs have been frankly harmful to children and others have been insufficient in number and strength to carry out their missions. We are in the midst of rethinking such things as foster home placement, the isolation of child caring institutions from the mainstream of children's living, and the inability of juvenile courts to function as social agencies. In place of these traditional approaches are mandatory education making it possible for children with emotional and mental handicaps to receive proper education in their communities, pediatric units oriented toward preserving contact between children and their families and reducing the length of hospitalization in accord with a child's developmental needs, increasing availability of family diagnosis and treatment, and children's services in community mental health centers.

Conclusion

From a historical perspective, it is evident that children have come a long way from most extreme oppression to their general state of recognition in modern society. It is also apparent that we have not accomplished enough for children in America. Past reform efforts have waxed and waned. There have been a number of resistances to effective aid for children, based upon the crisis–recoil nature of society and the tendency to deal with the individual child who is too frequently removed from the problem generating situation. Beneath these practices lies the failure to recognize that a child must be regarded as, at the least, part of a two-person unit and the general lack of a family focus. As a result, services that fragment families have been overdeveloped, and services that support and strengthen families are underdeveloped or nonexistent. It is also evident that when adult programs have been established, as in the community mental health system, they have eclipsed preexisting children's programs.

The power of adults through their representation in the political system is reflected in the rapid adoption of policies aimed at reducing sexism affecting adults in recent years. The lack of power of children is seen in the ignoring of their more desperate oppression, justifying such a highlighting term as "agism." Rarely has there been serious introduction of children's points of view in the affairs of the world. An additional complication is that services for children often are carried out largely to serve the interests of those who provide them. Industries—for example, day care—have developed around children without taking their needs into account. This is not to say that there are not large numbers of well intentioned people working with children, but it is to say that the power of adults to control children's lives must be carefully monitored, regardless of intentions.

The United States is regarded by the world as a youthful society and Americans are devoted to preserving youthfulness. These images reflect the preoccupation of adults with extending youth within themselves, however, rather than an interest and commitment to children. The result is that the current preoccupation of adults with their own lives drains their interest in children. Accepting the basic dependence of children, with the implication that they have special needs and rights, means more effort for many adults who already feel overburdened.

At the heart of the problem is the ambivalence toward children that is a part of the human social fabric and must be taken for granted (Rexford, 1969). No longer an economic asset, no longer a comfort in our old age, no longer a continuation of our people in the traditional pattern of our forebears, American children are left without functions beyond those that provide affection and existential meaning for them and their parents. At this time in our civilization, however, these functions may be just what are needed by adults in a society afflicted with loneliness and lack of meaning. The greatest hope for today's children, both with and without special needs, lies not in the creation of special institutions to take care of them, but in their inclusion in the lives and concerns of everyone.

References

ARIES, P. (1962) *Centuries of Childhood*. New York: Knopf.

BECK, R. (1973) "The White House Conferences on Children: An Historical Perspective." *Harvard Educational Review*, 43:653–668.

BREMNER, R. H. (Ed.) (1970) *Children and Youth in America: A Documentary History*, Vol. 1. Cambridge, Mass.: Harvard University Press.

BREMNER, R. H. (Ed.) (1971a) *Children and Youth in America: A Documentary History*, Vol. 2, Parts 1–6. Cambridge, Mass.: Harvard University Press.

BREMNER, R. H. (Ed.) (1971b) *Children and Youth in America: A Documentary History*, Vol. 2, Parts 7–8. Cambridge, Mass.: Harvard University Press.

BRIM, O. G., JR. (1971) "Macro-structural Influences on Child Development and the Need for Childhood Social Indicators." *American Journal of Orthopsychiatry*, 45:516–524, July.

CAVELLO, D. (1976) "Social Reform and the Movement to Organize Children's Play During the Progressive Era." *History of Childhood Quarterly*, 3:508–522.

DAVIS, G. (1976) *Childhood and History in America*. New York: Psychohistory Press.

DEMAITRE, L. (1977) "The Idea of Childhood and Child Care in Medical Writings of the Middle Ages." *Journal of Psychohistory*, 4:461–490.

DE MAUSE, L. (1974) *History of Childhood*. New York: Psychohistory Press.

GREENLEAF, B. K. (1978) *Children through the Ages: A History of Childhood*. New York: McGraw-Hill.

HARPUR, W. (1899) *The Report of the Educational Commission of the City of Chicago*. Chicago: Lakeside Press.

JOINT COMMISSION ON THE MENTAL OF CHILDREN (1969) *Crisis in Child Mental Health: Challenge of the 1970s*. New York: Harper and Row.

MEAD, M. (1976) "Society's Problem with Children." Chapter in Westman, J. C. (Ed.), *Proceedings of the University of Wisconsin Conference on Child Advocacy*. Madison: University of Wisconsin–Extension, Health Sciences Unit.

MILLER, H. (1916) *The School and the Immigrant*. Cleveland: Survey Committee, Cleveland Foundation.

NEW YORK SOCIETY FOR THE PREVENTION OF CRUELTY TO CHILDREN (1977) *100th Anniversary Symposium on Protecting the Maltreated Child*. New York: New York Society for the Prevention of Cruelty to Children.

PLATT, C. (1969) *The Child Savers: The Invention of Delinquency*. Chicago: University of Chicago Press.

REXFORD, C. (1969) "Children, Child Psychiatry and the Brave New World." *Archives of General Psychiatry*, 20:25–37.

RHODES, W. C. (1972) *Behavior Threat and Community Response*. New York: Behavioral Publications.

ROTHMAN, D. (1971) *The Discovery of the Asylum*. Boston: Little, Brown.

SENN, M. J. E. (1977) *Speaking Out for America's Children*. New Haven: Yale University Press.

WISHY, B. (1968) *The Child and the Republic*. Philadelphia: University of Pennsylvania Press.

Chapter 3
Why Child Advocacy?

Our failures indicate that something has been missing in conventional approaches to troubled children. In our view, one of the most important lacks is advocacy. The need for child advocacy has been evident, but rarely achieved, for years. One of the first published examples of child advocacy is Itard's classic work with the "wild boy of Averyon."

In 1800, a naked boy was sighted roaming the woods of central France and finally captured. For six months he remained in the care of a naturalist in Rodez. Mute, shameless, interested only in eating, sleeping and escaping, the boy was housebroken and trained like a dog with a leash. The government then entrusted him to the institute for deaf-mutes in Paris, where he was found to be totally unresponsive and intractable. A committee of experts headed by Philippe Pinel declared the boy an incurable idiot. He would have been placed in an asylum if Itard had not quietly challenged the diagnosis and offered to take charge. For the next six years Itard devoted several hours a day to special training for Victor, as the boy came to be called. Madam Guerin became his foster mother. Although Itard's initial report documented vast improvement in Victor's behavior and intelligence, five years later Itard wrote of slow progress in the boy, failure to learn to speak and major obstacles to further improvement. Victor fell exasperatingly short of becoming a fully human person and died 20 years later in obscurity, still a charge of the state. Although a failure in his habilitative efforts with Victor, Itard established a model for child advocacy by assuming complete responsibility for a young person for whom he had therapeutic objectives. His work could not have been done simply through conventional treatment. (Lane, 1975)

The Itard paradigm captures the image of child advocacy as at once both obvious and elusive. Promoting the welfare of many children with special needs still eludes society's grasp even in modern times. The large numbers of neglected, abused, misunderstood, and unserved youngsters has stimulated government at all levels to develop programs for children throughout the years. As the steadily rising rates of juvenile delinquency and other social indicators attest, however, children continue to suffer from fragmentation and the lack of continuity of a welter of services. Unlike Itard's Victor, troubled children have been handled largely by impersonal institutions that cannot respond to individual needs or, as with Victor, by parent surrogates who came too late. The obvious need of each child for a continuous parent figure and advocate has frequently been ignored.

As shown in Chapter 1, children who are at developmental risk can be identified through vulnerability of the parent–child unit. Even a handicapped child need not encounter serious problems if parenting, education, and service systems can be integrated to promote the child's adaptation. When this occurs, the child's adaptive strengths are maximized and weaknesses are minimized. Under optimal circumstances, then, parents themselves are able to nurture their children and negotiate with other child caring systems to obtain support when necessary. The advocacy inherent in parenting is all that such fortunate children require.

An understanding of child advocacy can be gained from examining the two major aspects of parenting: nurturance and advocacy. In addition to providing for a child's physical needs, the nurturing functions of parenting include affection, continuous care, dosing of frustration and gratification, and providing an adult model for identification. The advocacy functions of parenting are those of planning and making decisions that mediate the child's involvement in society. They include arranging for the child's education, health care, day care, religion, and mode of social and political expression through decisions about the child's social life, contact with relatives, and exposure to political beliefs and activities. Parental advocacy also includes protecting children and assuring that their rights and priorities are safeguarded and supported (Solnit, 1976).

Advocacy by persons other than a child's parent is required when a child's caretaking unit is vulnerable. Such a child requires more than professional diagnosis, treatment, legal representation, teaching, or casework. Someone, or some process, or both, are required to ensure that the child's developmental needs are met. That added ingredient is advocacy.

Confusion has arisen because child advocacy has been described both as a movement to benefit children generally and as a technique for intervening on behalf of individuals (Bolman, 1973). References are made to both a "child advocacy system" and a "child advocate." In essence, child advocacy is assuming in varying degrees and ways responsibility for promoting and protecting the developmental needs of both an individual child and children in general. The former can be seen as individual case advocacy and the latter as class advocacy. Although legal and political rights are central features (Adams, 1971; Farson, 1974; Gerzon, 1973; Steiner, 1976), child advocacy involves much more (Berlin, 1975).

The general aims of child advocacy at the community level are (1) to know every child, (2) to know what each child needs, and (3) to make sure that needed services are available. Both individual and collective advocacy for children are required to meet these objectives (Lourie, 1972). One appeal of the child advocacy concept is that it brings the consumers of services, that is, children, into the planning process by representation, either through their parents or through adults with competence and knowledge to speak for them. Child advocacy is not simply representing children apart and separate from their parents. It is a complex task that requires the capacity to promote both a child's interests and the congruent interests of those who are essential to the child's welfare, whether they be in the child's home, school, or other parts of the community.

Although the focus of child advocacy is on children, its relationship to parents is crucial. As previously pointed out, children's material, emotional, and psychological dependency upon their parents is such that the child–parent dyad is the basic developmental unit, not a freestanding child. The welfare of parents, then, is inseparable from the welfare of children, and at least theoretically that which promotes the parents' welfare also promotes the child's. Beyond a parent's succorance of a child is the psychological dependency of the child upon the parent as a model for identification. Consequently, the ability of the parent to provide a suitable and adequate model is essential for a child's personality development. Hence, it is apparent that family advocacy is a vital component of child advocacy (Manser, 1973).

The Community Origins of Child Advocacy

The basis for child advocacy rests both upon the responsibility parents have for their own children and society's general responsibility for the welfare of its citizens. Historically, our society's responsibility for the dependent and less fortunate arises from the *parens patriae* doctrine, in which the English king was seen as the father of the country and as ultimately responsible for the welfare of his people. In this sense, the state has a supportive role in relationship to its citizenry. Furthermore, the *in loco parentis* function of government has been a part of the evolution of the American commonwealth, which has assumed general responsibility for the protection and nurturance of children. The basis for child advocacy, then, is either from the delegated authority of parents or of the state when it supplements or replaces parental responsibility in a guardianship role.

The nature of child advocacy is further clarified by a vital semantic distinction between the legal concepts of acting *on behalf* of and *in behalf* of a child. The first phrase portrays advocacy as an extension of a child, and the second phrase portrays advocacy as acting in place of the child. In a legal sense, those who act *in behalf* of children are under no obligation to consult with their beneficiaries or to abide by their wishes. They do what they think is best in the light of their trust obligations. They are free from being ruled by the wishes or opinions of those whom they nominally represent. Such a role differs from acting *on behalf* of, which connotes that the advocate is acting on the part of or in the name of another, or as the one represented might act. Adults are generally accustomed to acting *upon* or *for* or *in* behalf of children and find it difficult to shift to the posture of acting *on* behalf of children. Advocacy in the sense of this book is acting *on* behalf of children, and implies the participation of children in decision-making processes that affect them.

Advocacy is a tool that became popular in the civil rights movement in the 1960s as a means of mobilizing and registering the needs of minority groups. In that usage, as a minority group became able to fend for itself, advocacy of its cause by others disappeared and even became cumbersome. The application of advocacy to children differs, however, because children are unable to exercise influence in their communities and depend upon others to do this for them. This means that advocacy for children is a permanent need, necessitating that advocacy mechanisms be enduring parts of our social system. Since our democratic system is based upon the principle of one person–one vote, our political process is ultimately responsive to pressures felt from people who are represented through elected officials. There must be visible advocacy of a position from those with a stake in its outcome. Because children do not have a vote, it is essential that some means be found of achieving proportionate visibility for them within the political system.

The major impetus for child advocacy came in 1969 in the report of the Joint Commission on the Mental Health of Children with the support of the 1970 White House Conference of Children. A sequence of currents were then operating. First were the persistent efforts of child mental health workers to focus public attention on the critical shortage of adequate children's services. Second was the experience of the 1960s, in which self-help groups and professional advocates demonstrated that advocacy techniques could achieve recognition for minority group rights and improve services to them. Third was the determination of the state governors' committees on children and youth to become more active in developing programs. Fourth were the campaigns undertaken by community action groups to highlight children's needs as they worked to improve living conditions generally. Finally, there was growing interest in efforts to prevent mental illness (Westman, 1973).

The Joint Commission on the Mental Health of Children concluded that promoting the mental health of children was a complicated matter extending beyond the boundaries of health care, penetrating the very fabric of society and involving a wide range of ecological, sociological, cultural, psychological, and biological factors. One of its principal recommendations was that a child advocacy system be established to represent each child in need and children in general at all government levels. The White House Conference on Children further saw child advocacy as a service for individual children and families at risk, both in the form of an ombudsman channel through which individuals could seek redress and through pressing government agencies to become more responsive to the needs of children (Joint Commission on the Mental Health of Children, 1969).

There was a time when the existence of a Children's Bureau or of a state division of children and youth was felt to be sufficient to represent children. In practice, these mechanisms have not proved effective, serving to deflect attention from the more important issue that children should be the concern of everyone. The existence of a Children's Bureau or of a state division of children and youth has advantages; however, it has also permitted the public to assume that someone else is attending to the problems of children, thereby exempting the rest of us from concern about them. The limitations of government structures, such as the proposed child advocacy system, have been amply demonstrated since the institution of the Children's Bureau in 1912. This is discussed further in Chapter 6.

General experience at the state level with the child advocacy concept was gained in Wisconsin over the last decade (Westman, 1976). A general lack of awareness, misunderstanding, and neglect of children's problems, in addition to a very limited application of existing knowledge, was found. In spite of these barriers, the child advocacy concept had fundamental appeal when it was not connected with special interest groups or specific levels of government. The Wisconsin experience suggested that there is a general receptivity to an increasing awareness of the problems of the young.

The Characteristics of Child Advocacy

Whether for an individual child or for all children, there are several characteristics that identify an activity as advocacy in nature. Fundamentally, the child advocacy approach exposes the world as children or a specific child experience it. Rather than looking at a child from an adult's point of view, which contains inherent biases, lacks essential facts, and is of limited scope, the approach is that of looking at the world through a child's eyes and identifying the factors that facilitate and impede that child's development. Advocacy, then, leads to asking questions that are important to children.

The central characteristics of child advocacy are (1) bridging system levels, (2) developmental orientation, (3) conflict resolution, (4) fact-finding techniques, (5) interdisciplinary teamwork, and (6) protecting and promoting the legal rights of children.

SYSTEM BRIDGING

Children are involved in the institutions of their culture not simply as individuals, but as parts of an initial parent–child and later community-centered series of child caretaking systems. The key people are the child, parents, teachers, peer group, and other adult representatives of society. This means that at least three points of view blend in child advocacy: that of the child, that of the parents, and that of society through its peer and adult representatives. The work of advocacy, then, is to build bridges between children and other systems in their worlds. That which goes on within a child's mind must be related to that which takes place at the interpersonal and societal levels. Advocacy reflects, then, a transactional approach that precludes thinking of any part of a child's life as separate and independent of the others.

Identifying the key advocacy issues at a given point in a child's life depends upon awareness of the importance of time, space, and interpersonal context for each child. The nature of a child's life is determined by time, as expressed both in the age of the child and the moment in which a particular event is occurring. This means, for example, that separation from a parent can be tolerated better by older than by younger children. Consequently, rapid decision making by the legal system may be facilitated by the intervention of a health worker.

A child's reactions and needs are also determined by the place in which events under consideration take place, because the nature of the setting determines the attitudes and behavior of a child. Thus, a pediatrician may require information from a child's school in order to assess the child's activity level.

A third element is the interpersonal context in which a child exists at a given point in time, since children are strongly influenced by the people surrounding them. As an illustration, a school teacher profits from information that a social worker can provide about a child's family. An advocate must understand all of these aspects of a child's life in order to draw knowledgeably upon the contributions of relevant systems. Bringing key people together to share information and plan for a child is a central feature of case advocacy. Setting the expectation that this will be done and providing the means to ensure that it happens are important parts of class advocacy.

DEVELOPMENTAL ORIENTATION

Because a child continuously changes in the process of development, it is essential that adults take into account the age of a child, and also that they promote individuation with advancing age. Advocacy recognizes a child's dependency and anticipates the time when a child will not be dependent on the advocate, as is true with parents.

The aim of child advocacy is to facilitate children's development and adaptation. It is based, therefore, upon an acceptance of childhood as a series of stages of life in itself, not simply as preparation for adult life. When childhood is seen as a preamble to life, the natural tendency of adults to dominate children obliterates the coequal nature of human relationships between people regardless of age. As Montessori (1974) pointed out early in this century, adult society has "a subconscious collective agreement to remove and suppress the child under the guise of acting for his good."

An illustration of the ways in which adults unwittingly demean children can be drawn from the language we use in relating to them. Each of the following pairs contrasts a typical biased adult attitude toward a child that does not take into account the child's coequal position with one that does:

directive vs. guiding
authoritarian vs. authoritative
dominating vs. respecting
conditioning vs. educating
knowing best vs. experienced
controlling vs. limit setting
demanding vs. requesting
excellence vs. competence
exploiting vs. nurturing
worry vs. concern

No adult likes to be treated in an authoritarian, dominating, conditioning, omniscient way. Yet adults automatically find themselves behaving in those modes with children. If one adopts the child's point of view, one can see how guidance, authority, respecting, educating, and wisdom-sharing modes are acceptable ways of experiencing adult influence. Simply asking whether or not an adult would like to be the recipient of an attitude or approach taken toward a child is a useful guideline for overcoming dominance of children.

Dealing with ignorance of and indifference toward the unique developmental needs of children is the core of both class and individual advocacy. In the process, "agism" reflected in adult biases must be handled.

CONFLICT RESOLUTION

Advocacy has a general conflict resolution flavor because there are certain inevitable as well as certain optional conflicts that occur whenever an advocacy position is assumed. An inevitable conflict arises between adults and children because the younger generation will ultimately replace the older generation, and this fact inherently contains a threat. Additional inevitable conflicts are based on competition between children and adults for financial, time, energy, and space resources.

The optional conflicts between adults and children are based upon envy, rivalry, and the burdens of child rearing. They have significant irrational components, reflecting the ambivalence that adults feel toward children, deriving from a number of sources (Rexford, 1969). Beyond the fact that they ultimately replace adults, children pose the threat that they may lose control of their impulses and be more immediately threatening to adults. The adult fear of losing control over children is more extreme than justified by the fact that children left to their own devices can run wild. Adults also fear the loss of involvement in their children's lives. Adults have much invested in their children and wish to protect that investment. Moreover, differences in wishes and interests between people of different age groups pose a myriad of potential optional conflicts.

Counterbalancing these inevitable and optional conflicts is the likelihood that, theoretically, what is good for children should also be good for parents, and vice versa. This has led some to suggest that as a general policy the "privacy of the family" should be accorded more respect (Levy, 1976a). Because children depend upon adults as models for identification and as providers of their dependency needs, the successful living and the integrity of their parents is important to children. In fact, one can state the converse, namely, that an unhappy, ineffective, and overwhelmed parent has impaired capacities to help children. Following the same line of reasoning, the rights and needs of the parental aspect of an adult are congruent with those of a child. Under ideal circumstances, then, the interests of children and adults are not in conflict. When adults and children are in conflict, it may be because the adults are not behaving as adults, but as children, and one then sees child-like rivalries, envies, and competition between parents and their children. Strong families allow children appropriate freedom with minimum conflict, but shaky families split open because lines of authority are blurred and conflict abounds. It is likely, then, that more emphasis on the developmental needs of children should help to clarify parental authority, in the long run strenghthening troubled families and reducing intrafamily conflict.

Another important source of conflict lies within each child. That is between a child's wishes and a child's needs. Because of their immaturity, children are often not in a position to make decisions for themselves and to make judgments regarding what is ultimately in their best interests. Frequently, children's immediate wishes may be in conflict with their ultimate interests. It is this aspect of childhood that permits the advocate to assume an authoritative, limit-setting role for young people when they need to be protected from themselves or when their internal conflicts require external resolution.

Whether conflicts lie between children and parents, schools, neighbors, or institutions, their resolution comprises much of the work of individual advocacy.

FACT-FINDING TECHNIQUES

The methods of child advocacy are investigative and factfinding, based upon the study of an individual child or groups of children and drawing upon the application of factual knowledge. Child advocacy cannot be based upon superficial assumptions regarding the lives of children, or upon a lack of knowledge of the personal circumstances of each child. Advocacy draws upon the procedures of the health and legal systems for decision making regarding an individual child more than the procedures of the educational and welfare systems, which must operate administratively upon general assumptions about groups of children. For example, the question of a child's custody cannot be resolved by ideas about what is generally good for children. It must be resolved through knowledge of individual children and their life circumstances. Well constructed generalizations can be useful in establishing public policy through class advocacy, but they cannot provide more than guidelines for individual case advocacy.

INTERDISCIPLINARY TEAMWORK

The operational style of advocacy for children is multidisciplinary. Most problems of significance in a child's life require more than one professional discipline to contribute to their solution. This means that professional disciplines are called upon to operate beyond their own boundaries and to interdigitate with other disciplines. In order to ensure interdisciplinary coordination, an individual who acts as a child's advocate is responsible for both integrating and coordinating the various professional activities.

When interdisciplinary teamwork takes place, each discipline operates with its own unique processes. The health disciplines operate within an investigative model which starts with a diagnostic problem that is solved through the discovery of the origin of the problem and the prescription of a remedy. The legal profession operates within an adversary model which is based upon the assumption that, when opposing views are strongly represented, the ultimate decision of the judicial process will produce an equitable result. The health and legal systems conflict to the extent that the health model tends to assume that there is one ultimate truth, and the legal model tends to assume that there is no ultimate truth, only an equitable resolution of conflict.

In contrast with both the health and legal systems, which deal with individuals, the educator operates in a totally different arena which processes masses of children for specific educational purposes. The educator's mission is to produce change in knowledge and skills in groups of children in the most efficient and effective way possible, and at the least cost. In a similar way, the welfare system shares education's responsibility for masses of people and a low-cost ceiling. Unlike the educator, however, their objectives, established by idealistic legislation, are rarely achievable in practice. The welfare system does well if it simply resolves crises and administers laws. The system contains inherent conflicts between that which the welfare worker would like to do for individual clients and that which can be done for large numbers of clients.

Child advocacy is particularly facilitated when the health and legal professions work in the areas of welfare and education, bringing an orientation toward individual children to areas basically dealing with large groups of people. As an illustration, the child psychiatric consultant has played a cross-fertilizing role in developing the concept of child advocacy. The Joint Commission on the Mental Health of Children was inspired by child psychiatrists with keen awareness of the problems of children. The interdisciplinary training of child psychiatrists brings them into all aspects of children's lives and makes them acutely aware of the overlap, fragmentation, omissions, and lack of continuity in children's services. Through their experience, child psychiatrists clearly see the need for integration, coordination, and continuity of care of any effort to help children (Hetznecker and Forman, 1974). The child psychiatric consultant to educational and welfare systems has provided a bridging role and often functions as a child advocate (Lawrence, 1971).

The last section of this book will treat the various professional systems that serve children in greater detail.

PROTECTION AND PROMOTION OF THE LEGAL RIGHTS OF CHILDREN

At this point we should note that many of the things done for children may not constitute advocacy for them. Industries which are less devoted to helping children and more to their own interests have developed around children. Most people currently working with children, however, are well intentioned. Still, the power of people who control other people's lives should operate under safeguards, even when the intentions of the controllers are benign. From the legal standpoint, these powers require regulation. Child advocacy, accordingly, sets up a useful tension between the rights of children and the rights of people who influence their lives. Important ingredients of child advocacy for protecting and promoting the legal rights of children are (Polier, 1976): (1) the right to counsel and due process, (2) the right to an education, (3) the right to appropriate care and treatment, and (4) the right to equal protection. Each of these matters will be discussed in further detail in Part IV.

The Ethics of Child Advocacy

The role of an advocate involves assuming a degree of responsibility for a child, ensuring that interventions do not harm, and avoiding inappropriately fostering the dependency of the child. One can draw on the background of medical and legal practice for guidance in establishing the ethics of advocacy. Thus, an important issue is the role of confidentiality when a child advocate is involved with the child, siblings, the family, and other members of the child caretaking system. There are times, particularly with adolescents, when a child's welfare depends upon an advocate's ability to respect and maintain confidentiality in relationships to the child. This topic will be discussed later in chapters 11 and 12.

An example of an ethical plight in advocacy is that of psychiatrists who are in effect enjoined from action—and, hence, responsibility—when patients or families refuse treatment. The result is that many adolescents, in particular, are administratively discharged from hospitals, only to find themselves at large in their communities, disavowing treatment and becoming involved in life-threatening and personally disadvantageous actions. In another vein, courts intervene when the physical safety of a child is at risk, but they are reluctant to act when psychological abuse is at stake. A juggling act results in attempting to balance the serious consequences for society of inaction for the individual against the dangers of too ready interference with the rights of parents and youngsters. The ethical dilemmas in outpatient clinics for children and their families pale in comparison with society's challenge in responding to the destructive behavior of youth who refuse treatment and can ultimately be handled only through correctional channels (Eisenberg, 1975).

The most enduring motivation for child advocacy is the enjoyment and satisfaction adults derive from the stimulation, challenge, and emotional rewards children offer to adults. The other side of this coin, however, is that adults need to have their own satisfactions, which do not depend primarily upon children. Advocacy can become exploitative when adults, who depend largely upon children for their primary satisfactions, cannot permit the individuation and growth toward self-fulfillment needed by children. Furthermore, "child rescuing" fantasies that lead to unrealistic intrusions on the lives of children can ignore such things as the right of a family to privacy and the rights of parents. Respect for family autonomy and limited government intrusion on family decision making are vital. Many judges are not in a position to take over parental functions and tend to intervene excessively or insufficiently in family matters, as indicated by frequent reversals of their judgments by appellate courts (Levy, 1976b).

A final ethical aspect of child advocacy is the fact that children identify with and respect adult personalities and behavior, mirroring the strengths and weaknesses of adults and highlighting and exploiting the weaknesses of society. Child advocates, therefore, are in the position of modeling adult behavior for the children they serve. The very process of advocacy itself involves ethical issues that influence children and model behavior.

Conclusion

A decade of experience has revealed that child advocacy is not a simple concept and has differing connotations for different interest groups, ranging from emphasis on liberating children from oppression to one of the roles of parenthood. Common themes are characteristic of professional advocacy. They are system bridging, a developmental orientation, conflict resolution, fact-finding techniques, interdisciplinary teamwork, and the protection and promotion of the legal rights of children. All of these ingredients are necessary if one is to assume a degree of responsibility for acting on behalf of a child or children—the essence of advocacy.

The most important accomplishment of child advocacy activity to this time has been sensitizing the public and child–family professionals to the special needs of troubled children. Viewed in this sense, child advocacy is a movement rather than a service system. It has provided a framework for pooling knowledge, exercising political influence, planning services, and reorganizing professional roles.

The concept of child advocacy offers the public relief from problems arising from inadequate planning for children and youth, increased visibility of efforts to promote the welfare of the young, improved additional services in child caretaking systems, public schools, social agencies, and clinical treatment facilities, and the ultimate preparation of a more competent contributing citizenry. As a result, problems arising in adult life from troubled childhoods should be significantly decreased.

Child advocacy really is a state of mind that guides action. If professionals who work with children develop advocacy skills and social policy makers bear in mind the needs of children, new people designated as "child advocates" are not needed. We do not require many new people to find children in need; this could be done by sensitizing people already on the scene. We do not require new people to know what children need; our present knowledge could be more broadly disseminated and skilled people more effectively trained and deployed in sufficient quantities to meet the population's needs. We do not require new people to make sure that services are available; those responsible for planning and developing services could be sensitized to the needs of children. In other words, consciousness raising so that more people "think child" offers the potential of adding advocacy to the professional roles of people who work with children.

The challenge for class advocates for children is to find leverage points for shifting social attitudes toward awareness and promotion of the developmental needs of children. The following chapters will be devoted to the methods of class and individual advocacy for children. Although difficult to assess at the present time, one of the long-range sources of support for child advocacy may well be adults themselves, who may discover that turning their interests downward in years to the young is a realistic way to preserve their own youthfulness. It is possible that our society has pursued the elusive "fountain of youth" long enough so that it can now move beyond a competitive toward a more generative relationship with the young.

References

ADAMS, P. ET AL. (1971) *Children's Rights: Toward the Liberation of the Child.* New York: Praeger.

BERLIN, I. N. (1975) *Advocacy for Child Mental Health.* New York: Brunner/Mazel.

BOLMAN, W. M., McDERMOTT, J. F., JR., AND ARENSDORF, A. M. (1973) "A New Concept in Social Psychiatry: Child Advocacy." *Social Psychiatry*, 8:26–31.

EISENBERG, L. (1975) "The Ethics of Intervention: Acting Amidst Ambiguity." *Journal of Child Psychology and Psychiatry*, 16:93–104.

FARSON, R. (1974) *Birthrights: A Bill of Rights for Children*. New York: Macmillan.

GERZON, M. (1973) *A Childhood for Every Child: The Politics of Childhood*. New York: Dutton.

HETZNECKER, W., AND FORMAN, M. A. (1974) *On Behalf of Children*. New York: Grune and Stratton.

JOINT COMMISSION ON THE MENTAL HEALTH OF CHILDREN (1969) *Crisis in Child Mental Health: Challenge for the 1970's*. New York: Harper and Row.

LANE, HARLAN (1975) *The Wild Boy of Averyon*. Cambridge, Mass.: Harvard University Press.

LAWRENCE, M. M. (1971) *The Mental Health Team in the Schools*. New York: Behavioral Publications.

LEVY, R. J. (1976a) "Rights of Parents." Chapter in Westman, J. C. (Ed.), *Proceedings of the University of Wisconsin Conference on Child Advocacy*. Madison: University of Wisconsin–Extension, Health Sciences Unit.

LEVY, R. J. (1976b) "The Rights of Parents." *Brigham Young University Law Review*, 1976 (3):693–707.

LOURIE, R. S., AND LOURIE, N. V. (1972) "The New Faces of Advocacy." *Journal of Child Psychiatry*, 11:401–414.

MANSER, E. (1973) *Family Advocacy: A Manual for Action*. New York: Family Service Association of America.

MONTESSORI, M. (1974) *Childhood Education*. Chicago: Regnery.

POLIER, J. (1976) "The Rights of Children." Chapter in Westman, J. C. (Ed.), *Proceedings of the University of Wisconsin Conference on Child Advocacy*. Madison: University of Wisconsin–Extension, Health Sciences Unit.

REXFORD, E. N. (1969) "Children, Child Psychiatry and Our Brave New World." *Archives of General Psychiatry*, 30:25–37.

SOLNIT, A. J. (1976) "Child-Rearing and Child Advocacy." *Brigham Young University Law Review*, 1976 (3):727–733.

STEINER, G. Y. AND MILIUS, P. H. (1976) *The Children's Cause*. Washington: The Brookings Institution.

WESTMAN, J. C. (1973) "Child Advocacy: A Progress Report." *Child Psychiatry and Human Development*, 3:211–215, Summer.

WESTMAN, J. C., AND STILES, C. L. (1976) "A Field Trial of Child Advocacy in Wisconsin." Chapter in Westman, J. C. (Ed.), *Proceedings of the University of Wisconsin Conference on Child Advocacy*. Madison: University of Wisconsin–Extension, Health Sciences Unit.

WHITE HOUSE CONFERENCE ON CHILDREN (1970) 1970 Report. Washington, D.C.: U.S. Government Printing Office.

Part II
The Basic Needs of Children

The loving mother teaches her child to walk alone. She is far enough from him so that she cannot actually support him, but she holds out her arms to him. She imitates his movements, and if he totters, she swiftly bends as if to seize him, so that the child might believe that he is not walking alone. . . . And yet, she does more. Her face beckons like a reward, an encouragement. Thus, the child walks alone with his eyes fixed on his mother's face, not on the difficulties in his way. He supports himself by the arms that do not hold him and constantly strives toward the refuge in his mother's embrace, little suspecting that in the very same moment that he is emphasizing his need of her, he is proving that he can do without her, because he is walking alone.

Sören Kierkegaard

This section is devoted to basic knowledge about what children need in order to progress in their development, a fundamental ingredient of the advocacy role. Without this knowledge, advocacy of the interests of children rests solely on adult opinions regarding what is "good for children" and lacks objectivity. Although there are some generalizations that can form the basis for social policies, it will be evident that generalizations cannot be applied to individual cases.

Chapter 4 develops the thesis that science alone cannot set the objectives and define the methods of child rearing. Those guidelines lie in our culture. The qualities essential for children growing up in American society are outlined: social skills, self-control, learning ability, self-identity, self-esteem, values, and decision-making ability. The development of each of these capacities is then traced throughout the stages of childhood.

57

Chapter 5 describes the family as the basic child rearing unit in our society. An exposition follows of the environmental characteristics known to facilitate development during infancy, early childhood, middle childhood, late childhood, and youth. The chapter concludes that children are remarkably adaptable, and that their very plasticity makes it possible to do many things *to* children without consideration of what ought to be done *for* them.

Chapter 4

The Developmental Needs of Children

"We use foster homes frequently—especially the good ones," said a social worker. "We don't have trouble with toddlers. Most of them are quiet on our ward," said a nurse. "Our divorce didn't affect our children. They haven't said a word about it," explained a mother. "My children are doing well without a father," reported a single parent. These adults believed what they said—and assumed that, as adults, they could speak for children from their own perceptions.

Another expression of a related viewpoint is the position that, unless proved by rigorous research, we know nothing about the needs of children: "There is no research that shows an infant needs a continuous relationship with a mother, or that breast is better than bottle feeding or that two parents in a family are better than one." Both those who say these things from personal experience and those who wish to wait for the results of research overlook the fact that much is known today about the developmental needs of children.

59

Even our knowledge of child development, however, has been influenced by political, economic, and ideological factors (Senn, 1975). Research findings frequently have been interpreted in the light of the prevailing climate of American life. One needs only to recall the popular waves of distortion of the ideas of Montessori, Watson, Gesell, and Spock to confirm the fact that prevailing philosophies convert child rearing ideas into fads, with ultimate scapegoating of the authors when inevitably they fail. As a result, Kagan (Senn, 1975) concluded that the only way to protect data from misinterpretation was not to report it. He was reacting specifically to the misreporting of his Guatemalan study, in which he found infants to be cognitively resilient to changes in their early environment, leading some to infer that we need not be concerned about how infants get started in life. For this reason caution should be exercised in the direct application of child development research to practical problems, as is the case with research in the biological sciences. There is an unfortunate tendency for social science research to receive premature publicity, because of public eagerness for easy solutions to complicated problems.

Furthermore, there is public misunderstanding of the limited capacity of child development research to adhere to the scientific principles of controlled experimentation with precise manipulation of variables and measurement of outcomes (Sears, 1975). Although progress has been made in the prediction of outcome of detailed aspects of children's behavior, experimental research has not and can never totally encompass the entire life of a child, any more than it can be used to guide the life of an adult. The impossibility of using contrived control groups in child rearing practices in itself disqualifies child development research as a source of major influence on social policy and child rearing.

Child development research, however, can contribute to the evolution of our society in an aggregate of small, but significant, ways. For example, Terman's work changed the status of the gifted child from that of an anomaly to that of a valued person. Education has profited from an understanding of positive and negative reinforcements in influencing behavior. In fact, a large body of knowledge of child development now exists that can be drawn upon for answers to specific problems, as summarized by Segal (1978), but it cannot directly guide child rearing. We cannot look to child development research for leadership in rearing children. Neither child psychology nor other branches of developmental study have produced awesome breakthroughs with high social usefulness (Lomax, 1978). And this is not likely to happen. The ways in which we raise our children are in a state of continuous evolution, as defined by society. Child rearing is an expression of culture, not science.

Cast in a broader context, the roles of science and technology in our society are changing, with defrocking of experts as a current side effect. In the past, most human concerns were in response to the challenges and limitations of the natural environment. The future concerns lie much more in dealing with the consequences of technology (Bellow, 1977). The pressing problems facing our society are not simply ones that require scientific objectivity, but ones that entail value and political judgments as well—for example, poverty, entitlement to benefits, ecological hazards, excessive dependence on automation, and our increasing search for individual and social goals (National Science Foundation, 1976). Within this framework, this chapter assembles current knowledge drawn from cultural values, research, and clinical experience about the essential things that children need for robust mental, emotional, and social health.

We will deal first with the cultural context of childhood. We know that primitive societies vary widely in their child rearing practices, and that cultural values are the primary determinants of child rearing. We will examine particularly the differences between child rearing in the Western world and in the People's Republic of China, where the only large-scale implementation of contrasting views exists. The comparison illustrates the plasticity of children, who can be molded to extreme degrees to fit the aims of their societies.

Each society defines its own way of life which determines child rearing styles. Because of the remarkable plasticity of homo sapiens, people of many kinds can be produced. Although the substrates of intelligence, cognition, and temperament are constitutionally determined, the coloring and form of personality are products of life experience. Children do not simply grow "like Topsy" and through their own momentum produce a better society; their internal growth mechanisms depend upon learning from others. Accordingly, we will examine the objectives of child rearing, addressing the question of goals for children in America in the form of competencies that are required for social functioning in our society. We will examine the concept of normality, and whether or not it is useful. Then we will propose a series of target qualities that appear to be the ultimate outcome of successful child rearing. A clearer idea of goals for our children can suggest ways of achieving them.

We will then look at our current understanding of growing up in America (Talbot, 1976). Although the topics cannot be treated in isolation from the others, we will examine innate individual differences in children, the maturation of the brain, and the stages of emotional and cognitive development. Just as the developmental stages reflect cross-sectional understanding of children, the longitudinal child development process offers a conceptual understanding of the ways in which children grow to adulthood.

This chapter will close on the central theme that children cannot develop without adults who are committed to them. At the very least each child needs a caretaking unit, ordinarily within families and always within broader child rearing systems (Kagan, 1977). Although each child is an individual for purposes of discussion, children can be understood only within their caretaking units and communities.

The Cultural Context of Childhood

The wide variation in child rearing practices in primitive societies is well known. Mead, the Kluckhohns, and Spiegel have delineated the ways in which culture influences child rearing (Spiegel, 1971). In a broad sense, Caldwell calls attention to a way of ranking societies in terms of their concerns for children as related to the autonomy provided for adults (1976). A society with a high concern for children and a low concern for adult autonomy, such as exists in the People's Republic of China, makes overriding interventions for children possible in that society. The same was true in Nazi Germany, where the importance of individual adult autonomy was subservient to developing children with a strong commitment to the state. In contrast, the United States is a country with a high concern for children and also high concern for adult autonomy. This creates a conflict between the two, making interventions for children difficult because of the need to consider the rights, privacy, and autonomy of adults. Our society's concern about individuals of all ages creates conflict between individuals of different ages. As a result, the fact that power is in the hands of the adult segment of our society leads their needs to prevail over the young—and over the old, for that matter.

Another social value that has direct implications for the development of children is the way in which success is measured. In the United States success tends to be measured by materialistic achievement. This means that externally visible signs of success are those responded to most readily. As an illustration, the long-range goal of becoming a physician is easily understood; however, the intermediate goals of developing the personality capacities that make it possible to become a humanistic physician are difficult to understand. The lack of attention to the qualities desired of a physician—diligence, humanism, and compassion—has made it possible for people to become physicians without possessing the qualities society expects from that social role. In the same way, the objectives of child development, although necessary stepping stones to adult success, seem nebulous and receive little attention.

Whether a social system's emphasis is upon individuals or groups also strongly colors child rearing. In the United States, the emphasis is on the development of the individual toward self-fulfillment and free exercise of capabilities. The social revolution of the People's Republic of China gave rise to a contrasting social order, in which group values were placed above individual values. American society stresses individuality, privacy, diversity, and support for individual action. Chinese society recognizes the importance of the individual, but places greater emphasis on functioning within the context of larger groups. Theoretically, in America, individual differences are honored, while in China they are minimized. In both the United States and China, however, differences between people are negatively perceived by young children. More specifically, young American and Chinese children seem to perceive all differences negatively. In America the later result is divergency among people—in China, surface conformity.

Kessen (1976) reports observations made in China that might seem attractive to many American parents and schoolteachers. Chinese children show a high level of ability to concentrate and orderliness. He was impressed by the sight of 50 children in a primary classroom sitting quietly until addressed and, when called upon, chanting their lessons in enthusiastic unison. He was even more impressed by the apparent absence of disruptive children. The docility did not appear to be based upon surrender and apathy, because the children were emotionally expressive and socially gracious.

Kessen tried to account for this conspicuously prosocial behavior. Prominent on the list of characteristics of teaching tactics that might play a role were the high ratio of approval by teachers to disapproval, reliance on teaching by repetition, the repeated use of models from the past and the present, the use of persuasion and moralistic reasoning, a close connection between words and practice, and perhaps, above all, the almost serene certainty of the teachers that the children would do as they were taught. In turn, the children learned to expect that they could acquire the skills and personality traits that the teachers expected of them.

On the other hand, Cohen (1977) suggests from his observations in China that creativity and curiosity may be casualties resulting from the strict containment of drives in Chinese children. He also calls attention to the ultimate contradiction: although individualism in the populace is harshly criticized in China, the leaders are revered as powerful, revolutionary individuals.

In spite of the turbulence in China from 1949 to the cultural revolution of the late 1960s, Chinese children have grown up in the presence of remarkable stability. Most Chinese, urban and rural, live their lives in continuous and enduring neighborhoods, knowing both the space and the people of the environment. Chinese adults, whether parents or teachers, appear to share almost without exception a conception of what a properly raised child should be like, in contrast with Americans, who are attuned to fads, experts, and advice columns in newspapers. American child rearing fads are epitomized by this poster in a toy store window (Senn, 1977):

Advice on Child Rearing

1910—Spank them
1920—Deprive them
1930—Ignore them
1940—Reason with them
1950—Love them
1960—Spank them lovingly
1970—To hell with them?

Child development in China is a process in which both adults and children participate with relatively little doubt about, and no analysis of, the goals to be reached. The adults know what children should be like and are certain that children should behave in the expected way. For their part, children join a social structure in which definitions of their behavior are without ambiguity and without conflict. Apparently, under these circumstances, the ideology of expectations becomes the fact of child behavior.

In America the evolution of our basic attitudes toward children has evolved from a puritanical view which recognized the importance of early life training of children. Although the religious aim of saving the child's soul was predominant, the more important underlying motivation was to produce children who would be responsive to the wishes of adults. Although true of other Western civilizations, the United States has had a unique problem in expecting children to conform to that which is "preached" rather than "practiced." The flaw in the American view of children has been the failure to recognize that children pattern themselves after adults, regardless of what adults say. In America adults have said that we wanted our children to be better than ourselves. We have said that we wanted our children to be spared the problems and privations we experienced during our own early years. We have said that we wanted our children to have better childhoods and more opportunities than we had. There has been a resulting discrepancy between the realization of what we say we want for our children and what children actually obtain. As pointedly put by one young adult, "I always wished that my dad would care for me rather than what he wanted for me."

In contrast with China, where the overall child rearing goals appear to aim toward nationally shared objectives, and the family is seen as a facilitating vehicle, American society has spawned open displays of conflict, whether between people or within people, and the family has much more autonomy in determining the direction of children. These parallel, but contrasting, factors of increased openness and increased parental responsibility for children are likely explanations of the more open ambivalence that exists toward children in the United States. A range of other factors contribute to this ambivalence in any society. Basically, it appears to be related to the fact that adults expect to be replaced by their children who, on the one hand, are perceived as threats but, on the other hand, are valued extensions of their parents' lives.

Brief reference to several other societies will further illustrate the influence of social and cultural goals on child rearing. The Soviet Union's system of collective living was seen in purest form in the 1920s when Makarenko, the John Dewey of Russia, worked with orphans of the Revolution and World War I in the Gorky Colony (Bowen, 1965). The objective was to transform vagrant children into that society's image by teaching cooperation, useful work habits, and healthful recreation through submerging individuality, which had been expressed in destructive ways by the children, to group interests by utilizing rewards of group acceptance within a militaristic format. Values were imposed, criticism of adults was denied, and symbolic thought was not cultivated. The effort was successful in bringing most of the children into functioning roles in that society, and the philosophy and practices strongly influenced Soviet education. Of interest, however, is Makarenko's later observation that "no writers or artists came from the Gorkyites—not because there was not enough talent, but because life and its practical daily problems engulfed them."

Although public efforts were made to alter family life to become consistent with Marxist doctrines during the decade following the Soviet revolution, there was no concerted drive to replace the family. The Soviet experience, then, has not actually tested whether or not a better child rearing system exists than the family. Nonetheless, Soviet policy appears to be based upon the assumptions that constant and relatively invariant parental care is required in rearing children and that society is unable to provide adequate substitutes for parents (Bronfenbrenner, 1973; Geiger, 1968).

Another example of a planned approach to child rearing designed to implement social objectives is the kibbutz system in Israel (Neubauer, 1965). The kibbutz objectives were initially to build an agricultural foundation for the Jewish national home in Israel; to create and manage a classless society, with equality between manual and intellectual workers; and to safeguard the needs of the individual, in accordance with the community's tasks and economic capacity.

In the kibbutz, child rearing was part of a planned system of education based on the democratic Jewish educational tradition for boys. The aim was to raise a kibbutz type of person—fit for kibbutz life derived from socialistic principles through linking study with productive labor. Founded upon faith in equality and cooperation, the first aspect of education was the "children's home," which was intended to provide rich activities and contents away from the parents' domicile. The second was integration of organized education, school, and society. The third aspect was multiple mothering, with sharing of child rearing between the family and child care workers, metapelets, in the segregated children's home. The kibbutz form of child rearing has achieved its aims with most children and represents the most carefully implemented and studied system of collective child rearing, but significantly has preserved a strong family focus.

Another example of socially determined child rearing—on a broader scale and with less successful results—is the experience of post–World War II Czechoslovakia (Langmeier, 1975). During a period of radical social, political, and economic reorganization, an increased work force was demanded by rapid industrialization and agricultural collectivization, necessitating employment of women approaching 100 percent in some areas. As a result, a highly integrated network of child care facilities offering permanent or part-time care was developed.

The Czechoslovakian child rearing system had both social and ideological goals, claiming to provide the most suitable environment for rearing children. Not only was the uniform system of progressive and efficiently organized professional care considered superior to average family care from the developmental point of view, but it was seen as a much more appropriate vehicle for imbuing children with a sense of collective responsibility. As family values retreated in the face of extrafamilial demands, and as the numbers of children under permanent or part-time institutional care increased, the old problem of the orphan was replaced by a new problem of social orphans: the children of uninterested parents and broken families. The model of child deprivation became the "collectivized" child, the child who was denied full and direct relationships with the mother in the family, who was inundated with some stimuli and refused others during a long stay in an institution for which the child was developmentally unprepared. Increasing evidence of illness in nurseries, problems around daily separation from parents, difficulties in emotional adaptation and establishment of primary emotional attachments, and serious personality disorders were direct outcomes of this type of care. These untoward results led ultimately to national efforts to rehabilitate the family as the most natural and convenient context in which to rear children in the 1960s.

Illustrating the influence of culture and social conditions on mental development are the observations made by Luria of an "experiment in nature" carried out in the early 1930s (1976). He demonstrated that the thinking of a populace shifted from a concrete to an abstract level when an ancient Islamic cotton-growing culture in Uzbekistan was dramatically transformed from a feudal to a modern collective life style. He found that perception, generalization, deduction, reasoning, imagination, and analysis of one's own inner life changed from the immediate, situational sensory level to an abstract, categorical rational level. Human consciousness was raised from immediate circumstances to awareness of a vastly broader world in that society.

Running through all of these socialistic experiments in child rearing was an impulse to create a social system based upon equal opportunity and interpersonal cooperation within an economically viable framework. Stated in this way, these objectives resemble the goals of American society, which also began as a planned and pioneering social system—actually, the oldest and most enduring of all. Western civilization with its Judeo–Christian roots held the promise of freedom for each citizen, ultimately expressed in the Constitution of the United States. With the ringing phrases that "all men are created equal" and entitled to "the pursuit of life, liberty and happiness," American children were exposed to the dream of self-fulfillment and of a future holding rich and rewarding potential. Because of the relative freedom for individual development, America has become a milieu in which differences between people have gained unprecedented visibility.

In America, "created equal" originally meant equal in the eyes of God. More recently, equality has been construed to mean equal opportunities. For a time the civil rights movement of the 1960s stressed the similarities between races. This was followed, however, by an emphasis upon differences, such as in the "black power" movement. There is now recognition of the differences that exist between people—not only in skin color, socioeconomic class, and degree of physical capabilities, but also in cultural backgrounds. It is noteworthy, however, that the most significant difference between people—namely, intellectual capacity—is still ambivalently recognized and even denied. As we become more appreciative of individual differences, the reality of differences in intelligence is unmasked.

We can no longer distinguish two classes of citizens in America: an intelligentsia and an illiterate, uninformed proletariat. The fruits of the world's most highly developed public educational system are thoughtful, critically oriented citizens. Members of the dominant middle class in America have sufficient intelligence, education, and information, when they can get it, to permit realization of the democratic process through the expression of public sentiment.

At the same time there is a palpable distinction between values associated with the images of "common people" and "intellectuals." Prevalent among "common people" are values that stress self-satisfaction, the importance of a job well done, honesty in relation to others, pride in country, locality, and family, acceptance and respect of leadership, and willingness to delegate responsibility to others. There is a desire to attain the power associated with money and the enjoyment of recreational events, vacations, and leisure. There is a strong emphasis on current living, with a basic faith that life will continue and that basic needs will be sustained. There is a sense of comfort in one's past heritage and in the integrity of values.

In contrast with the foregoing image of self-satisfaction of the common person, the image of the "intellectual" is one of unrest, involving the search for new knowledge, skepticism, and self-criticism. Rather than satisfaction with a job well done, the emphasis is on excellence and on surpassing others. There is a preoccupation with comparisons of intellectual prowess, knowledge of the arts, achievement, brilliance, creativity, and impatience with those who are less highly endowed intellectually. This strong orientation toward the new and the different, with skepticism toward the old and the known, has led to technological, scientific, and intellectual achievements.

The creativity resulting from the interplay of the values of common people and intellectuals has been the unrecognized boon of America. In fact, our democratic system with its legislative representation of the people and its judicial protection of the individual recognizes that the "will of the people" is more powerful in political matters than the intellectual, resolving powers of the mind.

The awesome prospects of creating life, alterning life span, shaping mental development, and exploring outer space raise vital questions about the desirability of pushing the limits of human creativity. A valueless, hedonistic society inspired by brain power "running loose" could lead to the ultimate paradox of maximum technological development in the hands of a disillusioned and rootless race intoxicated by the power of machines without coherent meaning in life.

The pursuit of how long and in how many places can we live is being supplanted by attention to how and why we live. Saul Bellow (1977) commented on what currently engages the central energies of man. For him, it is certainly not art or the rational inquiries of pure science. He calls attention to a yearning for more basic things, "an immense, painful longing for a broader, more flexible, fuller, more coherent, more comprehensive account of what we human beings are, who we are and what this life is for." He suggests a shift from a desire to be "well off" to a yearning for "well being."

In the final analysis, for establishing our society's priorities and objectives, we probably cannot look to universities or to government institutions but, rather, to the will of the people. America has added to the objective of equal opportunity for self-fulfillment the priority of meaning in life—the achievement of a rewarding and unique self-identity for each individual. As can be seen, we have more to learn about child rearing from our own culture than from other social systems. We can also learn about the objectives of our society by clarifying our cultural values. Ultimately, we are concerned with the quality of American life, which only people can define. Although a pluralistic society—more a "mixing bowl" than a "melting pot"—there are uniquely American cultural values that can be identified and used to explicate our child rearing objectives. Perhaps the most simply stated aim is the balanced development of the individual within society without submergence of either by the other.

Child Development in America

THE OBJECTIVES OF CHILD REARING

There are several approaches to elucidating the objectives of child rearing in America. One is in terms of achieving a state of "normality," or freedom from "abnormal" developmental consequences. Another is to identify pragmatically the characteristics of adults who function competently in society.

Before proceeding further the elusive concept of normality deserves examination. Four perspectives can be used (1) normality is health; (2) normality is utopia; (3) normality is average; and (4) normality is process (Offer and Sabshin, 1966).

The concept of normality as health is based upon the traditional medical-psychiatric approach which views health as the state that exists when no manifest pathology is present and one is reasonably free of pain, discomfort, and disability. The normality as health perspective remains popular and is considered to have research and conceptual advantages, because disease is easier to measure than positive states of health.

Normality as utopia conceives of normality as optimal functioning or "self-actualization." This position is increasingly attractive in preventive medicine, which has enlarged the horizons of illness to include its earliest, subtle manifestations. As gross pathology steadily decreases, the issue of a model of normal health becomes more appealing. Unfortunately, the normality-as-utopia perspective makes the normal not only a person to be admired, but also one who is seldom, if ever, seen in flesh and blood.

Normality as average is based on the mathematical principle of a bell-shaped curve of distribution of qualities, and radically departs from the first two, which visualize normality and abnormality at opposite ends of a straight line continuum. This line of thinking has appeal in psychological and sociological research, which is based upon the averaging of scores, with deviancy judged at each end of a continuum.

In contrast to the other three perspectives, normality as process sees normal behavior as the product of interacting systems that change over time. For example, the Eriksonian concept of epigenesis defines normality in terms of the successful mastery of each of seven stages in personality development. This view permits maladaptive behavior to be regarded as transient and even necessary at certain stages in the development of an individual. It also implies that the concept of normality changes from time to time. This perspective has the advantage of closer correspondence to actual experience than the other models. (Erikson, 1963).

Following the process view of normality, Vaillant (1977) seeks tangible evidence of success in the areas of working and loving, based essentially on concepts of social competence. He feels that characterological adaptive styles determine whether environmental stress produces defeat or heroism. His work and that of Cox (1970) suggest that much of the increased stress observed in the lives of the emotionally ill is a result, not the cause, of poor adaptation. They believe that neurosis occurs in healthy individuals, and that symptoms are less valuable clues to mental health than success in the areas of working and loving. Their emphasis is upon personality strengths rather than weaknesses.

In contrast with the approach of setting child rearing objectives simply in terms of normality and abnormality, the process conception of normality leads to the possibility of pragmatically identifying the essential qualities possessed by people who function competently in our society. In the final analysis, our society's concern is that individuals realize their potentials within the context of becoming contributing or nonburdensome citizens. The pragmatic approach has the value of casting society's objectives for children in terms of that which society expects in adult life. Because there is no consensus about the external trappings of a fulfilled life in childhood or adulthood, this approach defines adults who function competently in society as those who are capable of contributing productively to the common welfare.

If we accept the premise that our society expects child rearing to produce individuals who can both pursue their own interests and contribute to group living within an economically viable social system, the following qualities can be identified in competent adults in our society:

1. Social Skills
   a. Ability to communicate
   b. Ability to relate to others
   c. Ability to be useful to others
   d. Ability to initiate self-expressive activity
2. Self-control
   a. Ability to delay gratification
   b. Ability to tolerate frustration
   c. Ability to work
3. Ability to Learn
   a. About one's self
   b. About other people

       c. About the world
4. Values
       a. Commitment to adopt and adhere to social values
       b. Commitment to accommodating self-interests to social realities
5. Responsibility for Decision Making
       a. By accurately observing
       b. By objectively evaluating
       c. By expressing judgments
6. Self-identity and Self-esteem
       a. As a unique person
       b. As a unique gender
       c. As a unique personality

With the development of the above characteristics, it is likely that an individual will be prepared to fulfill one's potential and will be capable of experiencing satisfaction in life.

For the basic social skills of living, one can rely upon the unfolding of the brain's function through the appearance of walking, talking, and making sensory contact with world. The child's brain must be stimulated, however, in order to develop fully. In our complex Western civilization, it is impossible for children to become functioning adults solely through the emergence of their own neurological potentials. The acquisition of social skills depends upon learning language in order to make wants known and to relate to other people. The ability to relate to people is the necessary foundation for being valued and needed by others. The individual child is an inextricable part of a social matrix. The irreducible unit in early human relationships is the dyad, not the solitary child.

Next, the personality skills of tolerating frustration and postponing gratification are required so that one can relate to the world without being distracted by inner impulses that interfere with performing tasks and cooperating with other people. Furthermore, a range of learning skills are required to gain information about oneself, other people, and the world. Moral values are necessary to guide dealings with other people and to achieve meaning in life through setting ideals. The ability to make decisions, or choose between options, is essential for assuming responsibility for one's life.

Once social functioning has been achieved, however, it becomes apparent that recreational, creative, and humor-stimulating skills are necessary in order to achieve meaning and enjoyment in life. One needs to learn how to take advantage of outlets for physical activity and share pleasures with others. All of these cannot be imposed upon the individual from the outside, but are the result of an individual's integration with other people and the aims of society, marked by awareness and acceptance of one's identity as a unique person. Recent experience with people moving rapidly upward in economic status shows that whether one is wealthy or poor, black or white, the most critical issue is one's acceptance of oneself—one's self-esteem.

Our past child rearing practices have tended to socialize children for economic utility as adults rather than fulfilling their potentials. Simply preparing one for usefulness to others, however, overlooks individuals' usefulness to themselves. We have tended to view competition, for example, as excelling over others for the satisfaction of besting other persons. Competition, can also be used to test one's own capacities with satisfaction derived from achieving one's maximum as measured against the maximum efforts of others. In this sense, competition with another person facilitates the fulfillment of one's own capacities—the competitor is an ally rather than an enemy.

Several tendencies in Western civilization have thwarted, and highlight the importance of emphasizing, the development of self-identity. They are an emphasis on conformity which overshadows individuality; an emphasis on behavior modification which overlooks motivation; the denial of dependency on others; the replacement of hope, faith, and shared pleasures by destructive competition; and a contentment with "fitting in" rather than creatively stimulating mutual individual and group satisfactions. The result is a range of identity problems leading people today to ask, "Who am I? What am I? What is the meaning of life?" An important goal of child rearing, then, is to facilitate meaning in life. Existence is frustrating without meaning, even for the well fed, well housed human being, as our experience in combating poverty and racism has demonstrated.

INDIVIDUAL DIFFERENCES IN CHILDREN

Understanding child development is understanding the development of a zestful, emotionally expressive child who moves toward experiences as well as understanding a child who retreats from emotional contact with the environment (Sroufe, 1978). An important explanation of such extremes can be derived from an understanding of individual differences in children (Westman, 1973).

Individual differences influenced by genetic and biological factors appear in children on such dimensions as intelligence, sex, temperament, cognitive styles, personality, mental and physical disabilities, skin color, physical attractiveness, and bodily maturational rates. Another range of individual differences are related to life style and home circumstances, such as being adopted, a foster child, or a stepchild, and differences in religion and nationality. Specific individual differences are described further in Chapter 8.

A single model of development does not do justice to the individual differences in children; nor does a model derived for the male adequately account for the developmental progression of females. Individual patterns vary greatly between children in the developmental process, especially in rate, evenness, flexibility, smoothness, and coherence (Flapan and Neubauer, 1975).

When considering individual differences on dimensions, as mentioned above, it is important to ask the question, Different from what? The answer is relatively straightforward—namely, differing from other people—although it is also possible to perceive differences within an individual when compared with a previous time in life. Actually, an averaging standard is not needed in order to talk in terms of differences, if we accept the fact that each person naturally differs from others. A more accurate definition of difference does not entail statistical deviation from most on a bell-shaped curve, but simply the fact that each organism by its nature differs from others.

The concept of individual differences in endowment which lead to the unfolding of various kinds of cognitive, emotional, and behavioral styles makes it possible to conceive of each child as having a template of capacities at conception that are facilitated by subsequent environmental experience. The child has a definite influence on the environment. Children stimulate their environments and react to their environments so that development is truly a transactional experience in which both sides of the equation are impinging upon and influencing each other. During early life individual variations are centrally related to parent–child relationships and later on to sibling, peer, and other significant adult relationships.

As an example of the individual difference concept, Bell (1971) found that a high tactile threshold, meaning a low sensitivity to skin stimulation, in infants was correlated with sustained goal orientation and vigorous efforts to solve frustrating situations in nursery school. In contrast, infants with a low tactile threshold, or a high sensitivity to skin stimulation, showed at nursery school age briefly sustained goal-directed behavior and were seen as inactive, clumsy, and uncoordinated. Neither of these characteristics were clinically significant, but they did contribute to variations in personality. In a similar vein, Murphy found that children with low sensory sensitivity, low autonomic reactivity, low drive, and good developmental balance functioned more smoothly and naturally in environmental encounters than children with the opposite temperamental characteristics. Individual differences on a variety of dimensions, then, can explain variances in children and adults and, in some instances, psychopathology (Murphy, 1962).

Various aspects of a child develop in different ways and at different rates (Freud, 1965; Nagera, 1963). The influences of maturational rate, independent of chronological age, are as crucial for our understanding of psychological development as are the influences of differential experiences (Wolff, 1977). Thus, a child's ability to relate to people is a developmental line that shows unique aspects for each child. Another example of a developmental line which proceeds differently for children and at a different rates is the ability to think in terms of symbols, so that some children are able to learn how to read at the age of three and others do not develop this capacity until the age of eight. An individual child's personality is made up of many components, and each of these components develops as a part of the whole, but with its own inner rhythm and rate. The developmental line time schedule varies from one child to another, making it difficult to generalize even across age groups regarding children. In order to understand an individual child's behavior, that child's position on a given developmental dimension must be regarded in the light of a particular stage of life.

Striking individual differences in children are ordinarily perceived as "bad," in part because of "foreigner anxiety," which is an innate negative response to any living thing perceived as different and potentially threatening (West, 1967). Of much greater importance is the learned aspect of differences, based upon jealousy, rivalry, cruelty, competitiveness, scapegoating, and anything else related to getting ahead at the expense of others. Because young children are self-assertive, self-centered, and potentially cruel, they can focus all of these things on an individual who differs significantly from the others. As a result, children respond to a "pecking order" strongly influenced by physical size, attractiveness, and mental ability. It is of interest to note, further, that children aspire, not really to be the same as all the others, but to be the same as children of high status. The desire to be like others, then, is not aimed at the middle ground, but at the highest status level.

Running through the following discussions of developmental lines and stages, then, should be an awareness that variations between children in endowment and developmental rates transact with life experience to produce the personality and behavior of a specific child.

THE PROCESS OF CHILD DEVELOPMENT

Understanding the world of children depends upon an appreciation of the complex process of child development. Child development has been approached from a variety of points of view: behavioral, interpersonal, mental, cognitive, and emotional (Lichtenberg, 1971). An integration of all of these approaches is necessary in order to understand a real, living child. Furthermore, individual genetic endowment, maturational unfolding, critical stages, interpersonal relationships, and social adaptation are all involved. The successful negotiation by each child of phase-specific developmental tasks depends upon previous developmental phase solutions, and it is carried on and worked out further in subsequent stages. Deficiencies, defects, or delays in relation to a given developmental phase distort and are continued in subsequent stages. At the same time the child has an innate urge to grow, explore, investigate, manipulate, and master the environment.

An inescapable problem in studying the development of young children is the fact that the long-range repercussions of either what seem to be normal or abnormal manifestations cannot be fully known. Internalized residuals of infantile experience may manifest themselves much later in life. For example, Schiller (1957) found that chimpanzees could only put together interlocking sticks to form a rake to obtain food if they had achieved the appropriate level of neurological development and if they had the experience of playing with the sticks during their earlier life.

Childhood is the beginning of the life cycle and it is comprised of several stages: infancy, early childhood, middle childhood, late childhood, and youth. It is this fact that has led many people to feel uncertain as to what children need, an uncertainty that can be remedied if one recognizes the particular age period of a child. Children need different things at different ages, making it difficult to generalize about all children and adolescents. A grounding in the developmental stages of children is essential for anyone attempting to understand or plan for them.

As do all aspects of the body, the brain grows and changes throughout the life cycle, most spectacularly during the early years. In fact, it is the rapid development of the brain during the first several years of life that produces the most dramatic changes of the life cycle, transforming a relatively inert organism into a human being. The physical development of brain tissue follows an evolving course, with progressive increase in brain size and weight throughout childhood to approximately the age of 18. Although the number of brain cells forming the biological substrate of the mind is basically established before birth, connecting cells appear during the first year of life, and there is a considerable increase in brain connective tissue and in the size of the brain cells themselves into the fifth year of life. Some fiber tracts continue to show growth (myelinization) beyond the years of puberty to the end of the third decade of life. There is anatomical evidence, then, that the brain assumes adult characteristics by the age of 18 in most individuals.

Another source of information on brain development is from electrical studies. Immaturity of the electrical activity of the brain is apparent prior to the age of 18, with specific accelerations in change around the ages of nine and 14, developmental stages that show critical changes in cognitive ability. It is no coincidence that there is a correspondence between the state of brain tissue, brain electrical activity, and political rights at the age of 18.

We will now examine each of the previously mentioned target qualities necessary for competent functioning in our society and trace its development. As will be seen, each of these qualities constitutes a definable line of personality development. Although actually inseparable in their emergence, we can conceptualize developmental lines for (1) social skills, (2) self-control, (3) ability to learn, (4) acquiring values, (5) responsibility for decision making, and (6) self-identity.

DEVELOPMENT OF SOCIAL SKILLS

Of all the qualities needed for successful living in our society, the most fundamental is the ability to relate to other people. A distinction should be made between simply relating to people, the impairment of which is seen in the autistic child, and forming affectionate ties with people, the impairment of which is seen in the socially adept but emotionally unattached psychopath. Both kinds of relating depend upon the unfolding of innate capacities shaped by human stimulation. They differ, however, because the ability to relate instrumentally to other people does not in itself include commitment to or caring about other people. Ordinarily, the ability to relate and the ability to form emotional ties with people are not separated when children are raised by devoted parents with mutual dependency, trust, and affection. Under institutional circumstances, however, when children are raised by multiple adults without reciprocal trust, dependency, and affection the development of social relating skills takes place without emotional attachments. In fact, for vulnerable infants, even social skills and physical growth do not develop without devoted, intimate parenting (Langmeier, 1975).

The development of the capacity for human relationships is a gradual and delicate process (Malone, 1967). Actually, it is not critically connected with entering the world through birth. The biological birth of the human infant and the psychological birth of the individual are not coincident. The former is a dramatic, observable, and well circumscribed event; the latter, a slowly unfolding intrapsychic process (Mahler, 1975). The human infant is born "prematurely" physically and psychologically because the large head size created by the phylogenetically advanced human brain exceeds at a certain point the limited size of the female pelvis. As a result, the first two months of life are really an extension of intrauterine existence (Montagu, 1961).

The baby's introduction to people begins prior to birth through parts of its body having contact with parts of its mother's body, at first through the cushion of warm amniotic fluid in the uterus. The shock of entering the relatively cold outside world at the time of birth is compensated for by full sensory contact with a cuddling, feeding mother recapturing for the infant a "fluid, unbounded twilight sort of world" (Escalona, 1953). In this state, objects seem to swim into view and recede from the infant's point of view. Although babies do not "know" their mothers in the first weeks, they receive a myriad of sensory-motor impressions of their mothers around feeding care, gradually leading to the formation of a mental image of the mother. Feeding is emphasized because it is essential for physical survival but also includes soothing, cuddling, and rocking. The whole range of parenting care, such as diapering and bathing, creates pleasurable, tension-reducing experiences for the baby as the foundation for human relationships are laid down. Infants vary in patterns of sucking, sleep, wakefulness, and elimination, calling upon their mothers to adapt to the particular needs and patterns of each baby. There is also variability in infants' abilities to communicate their needs and in their responses to comforting efforts. Similarly, mothers vary in their attitudes, sensitivity, and responsiveness to their babies' cues.

Although physically separated by birth, the child needs to be psychologically united with the mother during most of the first year of life in the form of a "nursing couple" deriving mutual satisfaction from each other. Parenting during the first year is not simply feeding, diapering, and providing child care. More important, it is forming an affectionate attachment bond through the emotional and psychological nurturance of the child. The baby's need for stimulation and relatedness is so intense and time consuming that the parenting person must feel a personal commitment to "my baby" in order to foster a sense of importance, worthiness, and trust in the child. In order to meet this consuming need, the mother is motivated by her attachment to her baby and rewarded by the growing signs of the baby's attachment to her. For example, at around two months, the smiling response is the first significant milestone indicating attachment to the parenting person: the baby's first sign of love for another person. If psychological union does not take place, or is weak, between parent and child during the first five months, the child may not develop a sense of trust in others and the capacity to love. Having been loved is the prerequisite for the ability to love. Even worse, some children are more vulnerable to deficient mothering than others, and physical and developmental retardation can result.

In the second half of the first year there is a rapid increase in infants' motor development, permitting crawling, standing, and ultimately walking. Infants begin to initiate social interchanges with their parents, to show preferences and desires, and to attempt to interact with the stimulations reaching them. Some time in the second half of the first year, usually around eight or nine months of age, as the infants' love for their gratifying parents becomes established, "stranger anxiety" appears as they distinguish their parents from strangers. An infant focuses emotional attachment on the mother especially through relating to her face, the vehicle for emotional, verbal, and nonverbal communication. Once having learned the face and body of the parenting person the baby begins to distinguish and to show curiosity, colored with apprehension, toward strangers, a landmark in relationship capacity that signals that children can distinguish their own bodies from their parents', and their parents' from others. As reciprocal adjustment and familiarity occur, a parent can say with conviction, "I know my baby."

Initially, attachment behavior is mediated by responses on these simple lines. From the end of the first year it becomes mediated by increasingly sophisticated feedback systems that incorporate images of the environment and the self. These systems are activated by certain conditions and terminated by others. Among activating conditions are strangeness, hunger, fatigue, and anything frightening. Terminating conditions include the sight or sound of a parent and, especially, happy interaction with the parent. When attachment behavior is strongly aroused, termination may require touching, clinging to, or being cuddled by the parent. Conversely, when the parent is present or nearby, a child ceases to show attachment behavior and instead explores the environment (Bowlby, 1977).

Parallel with the transition from infant to toddler through becoming upright and walking is the child's growing ability to communicate through the development of language, adding the capability of expressing nuances of wants and feelings (Lewis, 1977). With increasing individuation from the parent during the second year of life, the toddler practices physically being with and leaving her. Concomitantly, "separation anxiety" occurs when the child senses the parent is not immediately available. During this phase, the emotional availability and acceptance of the parent is necessary to cushion the ambivalence felt by the child. During the last half of the second year a child alternates between pushing mother away and clinging to her, and the beginning use of "I" signifies further psychological differentiation from the parent.

Until the middle of the third year of life most children do not have completely internalized images of the parents, permitting them to "remember" that their parents exist even when not physically nearby. During the third year children develop the capacity to be away from their parents for periods of time, and they respond to reassurance that their mothers will return. Children are then capable of branching out to other adults, siblings, and peers. The increased waking hours permit a child to move beyond the fundamental primary attachment to the parent to an ever widening interpersonal and social world, the content of which continues to be shaped by subsequent family relationships.

Children approach the fourth year as increasingly complex and resourceful personalities capable of a considerable amount of self-reliance and initiative. They are ready to meet new situations and actively explore new experiences. Among the new worlds they may enter is a nursery school or day care. Against the continuing background of their supportive, guiding home life, many children at age three are ready to broaden their base of operation and learning and to negotiate their separation concerns through relationships with peers and teachers. They can learn the vital social skills of cooperation and compromise, and the important experience of friendship with peers.

Toddlers show interest in other children initially through looking, parallel play, and fleeting contact. Cooperative interchanges among children do not suddenly emerge but, rather, are the result of a series of steps in a complex interplay of many developmental factors, taking place slowly over time (Whiteside, 1976). By the age of four most children enjoy associative play, in which two children play together with general agreement about theme but with each following one's own ideas, wishes, and rules. Out of associative play emerge quasi-friendships. Truly cooperative play begins as children approach the age of five. Mastering this developmental task is critical if children are to use peer contacts in a gratifying and growth producing way during later school years.

Relationships with peers are important to children after the third year of life, both to provide for increased models for identification and the development of cooperative group living skills, epitomized by learning to share and to take turns gracefully to promote pleasurable social interactions. In the long range, the peer affectional system is the most prevading and important of all human relationships. Beginning through transient interactions among infants, crystallizing in social relationships with agemates, and expanding through childhood and adolescence, peer relations are ultimately expressed in marriage, parenting, and working relationships.

In sum, a baby becomes a human being through intimate relationships with other human beings, beginning through psychological birth from one's mother over a period of three years and continuing to develop throughout life. The critical period for acquiring the capacity to love is through being loved totally, from the baby's point of view, during the first year of life, and gradually entering an ever widening circle of shared love relationships. Essential to this process is a parent who knows "my baby" and a child who knows "my parent."

DEVELOPMENT OF SELF-CONTROL

Both for the sake of social living and personal comfort, children must come to terms with their own bodily feelings, wishes, and urges. Older children who are at the mercy of their impulses and sensations are essentially unsocialized, and they are frustrations both to themselves and others. The ability to control oneself through delaying gratification and tolerating frustration, accordingly, is an essential personality quality not only to carry on relationships with people but to manage one's own life as well.

Children vary widely in the patterns of regularity of their biological rhythms and the intensity of their urges. Temperamental qualities, such as activity level and threshold of responsiveness, also influence the ease with which a child can master inner impulses. Some, therefore, have an easier task than others in developing self-control. The basic foundation for self-regulation is established early in life when the baby learns to establish pleasurable sleep, feeding, and elimination patterns. A "good start" in life is signified by a dominant sense that good feelings predominate within and outside one's own body. This is achieved through the comfortable acceptance and cherishing of the infant's body by the parent, a precondition to comfort and acceptance of the child's own body and its functions. Thus, feeding, whether breast or bottle, that occurs in an atmosphere of tension and strain imparts displeasure to a potentially pleasurable body function, creating an inner discomfort associated with feeding.

Furthermore, the baby emerges from an omnipotent view of a totally responsive and controllable world to progressive encounters with the unpleasant reality that one must learn to submit to the influence of others and accept personal limitations. As children's motor, language, and expressive skills increase they can explore interpersonal and material fields, making discoveries which assist in orienting themselves to their own bodies, people, and things. While toddlers explore and learn about the world, assert emerging independence, and try to affect their environment, they also need to learn to curb their wants, gain control over their bodies, and cope with their parents' attitudes and wishes. Children need to learn that their parents can firmly place limits, but that they can transgress prohibitions and incur parental disapproval without losing parental love. Accordingly, an oppositional phase, when the assertiveness of the toddler runs counter to parental wishes, is an important learning experience for the child. It is a declaration of independence with no intent to unseat the government (Fraiberg, 1977).

The matter of mutual regulation between adult and child faces a test in toilet training. If outer control is too rigid or too early, training robs the child of gradually learning to control elimination and other functions willingly and by free choice. Young children relinquish free elimination out of love for and the wish to please their parents, in addition to their own satisfaction in accomplishment.

Another important part of socialization involves learning to control aggressive feelings. Since the frustrating parent, toward whom the child expresses aggressive feelings, is also the loved parent, a state of ambivalence exists. Gradually, through repeated experiences and the parents' patient guidance, the child learns to bring aggressive feelings under control.

If children learn self-control during their early years, the foundation is laid for a later life of greater comfort than if the child does not learn the limits of personal influence early. Not only does the child who lacks self-discipline require continued limit setting in school and the community in later life, but the child experiences the world as frustrating and unfair and clings to earlier fantasies of omnipotence. Not only does the child need the application of firm and fair limits from adults, but also the modeling of adults who can cope with frustrating situations and accept limits themselves.

As can be seen, an important ingredient of early relationships is helping a child to relinquish an egocentric view of the world. This begins with establishing comfortable biological rhythms accommodating gradually to adult schedules, and hinges on the critical second and third years of individuation, during which a child knows the love of one's parents through their willingness to take the time and effort required to set limits. Thereafter, experience with other children provides the opportunity to learn how to share and take turns, further strengthening a child's ability to control impulses.

The road to developing mature self-discipline runs the entire course of childhood, in part because of the growing list of expectations from others, and also because of the emergence of strong urges and feelings, especially with the onset of puberty. Preadolescents and adolescents, accordingly, depend upon external controls, both as reassurance to themselves and as foils for their challenges and testing of limits as they forge their own ability to control themselves. The young need adults who can be loved and hated, defied and depended upon to set limits, not just mechanical controls administered by disinterested adults. A living relationship between persons around control issues gives the elbow room necessary for true growth (Winnicott, 1965). Social support of the value of self-discipline is also needed. Since self-indulgence is frequently modeled and implicitly encouraged by public influences, adults significant to a child may be the only dependable sources of modeling self-discipline.

DEVELOPMENT OF LEARNING ABILITY

Interwoven with growing awareness of and control of oneself is an awareness and control of animate and inanimate objects in the world as well. As babies emerge from their totally egocentric, omnipotent shells, they make contact with parts of their own and their parents' bodies, both perceived as parts of a foreign "out there." Through such things as discovering they can control their own hands, slowly and painstakingly, infants build pictures of their own whole bodies and whole bodies of other adults. In the process, the repeated clashes between the infant's wants and reality lead to the ability to distinguish inner fantasy and wishes from external reality. A growing fund of knowledge is accumulated through experience, first of the existence of things, both animate and inanimate, and then of the ability to manipulate things. Each child learns to sort out those things that can be manipulated from those that cannot.

A child's curiosity leads to contact with the widening world and is the wellspring of learning. Basically open to exploring all aspects of the world, a child finds that certain areas give rise to displeasure in the form of parental disapproval, both direct and sensed, and curiosity in those areas is inhibited. For example, parental reaction to young children's exploration of their bodies and their products influences the children's degree of comfort with and knowledge about their bodies. To the extent that secrets and mysteries remain regarding their own bodies, children are burdened with unrequited curiosity and illusions about themselves. When facts are known, mastery is possible. When fantasies abound, unchallenged by reality, illusion does not yield to the satisfaction of mastery. The optimal expression of curiosity, then, is through the sensation of gaining knowledge, resolving ambiguity, or mastering a problem. The result is a satisfying sense of competence, as illustrated by the prototypical beaming exhilaration of a toddler on taking the first steps alone. When this kind of learning is exciting for both the child and the parents, a solid foundation for later learning develops. When curiosity is not predominantly followed by discovery and mastery, a child becomes wary of learning.

All learning builds upon existing ideas and abilities. It is not putting information and skills into an empty receptacle. The learning process is the vehicle for a child's gradual modification of fantasies about self, others, and the world, all of which are brought toward reality by the "hard data" of the world. The result of learning is mastery and a sense of competence. Essential, however, is the capability of the child's cognitive equipment and thought processes. Depending upon age, a child's perception of reality is more or less accurate and always influenced by existing mental set, waking state, or fantasies. Thus, an eight-month-old can learn to say "Mama," but not "mother," a two-year-old can learn the meaning of "I," but not "we," and a three-year-old can learn to say the word "adoption," but not comprehend its meaning.

Unless a child's attention and mind are fully engaged, learned "facts" are sterile and lack personalization. Play is a child's means of learning about and mastering the world. In fact, the nature of a child's play is a cue to the level at which useful learning can take place. During the third year, children are able to learn about the nature of things they can personally manipulate. Two years later cooperative play permits children to digest real life situations through "pretending." In both instances a child's interest is in discovering facts about the personally experienced and enlarging world of things and people.

Play is a natural product of the processes of physical and cognitive growth. The emergence of play depends in part upon the very young child's experience of play with adults. Although subject to individual differences, infants raised with exposure only to purposeful behavior by adults may not fully learn to play. As the voluntarily controlled activity of childhood, play is intricately related to the child's mastery and integration of experiences (Garvey, 1977).

It is to the child's advantage to expose fantasies to reality through play, and gradually to season infantile notions with assimilated facts. The result is smooth progression with continual adaptation of fantasy to reality. Curiosity is the motive for adjusting inner beliefs to the realities of the external world. Children then gradually relinquish play as the modality for learning and adopt more realistic games and, ultimately, academic work. As the young child's work, play needs to flower as a precondition for later academic learning in school (Omwake, 1963).

From a baby's rattle, through a toddler's "teddy bear," to a young child's tricycle, the methods and objects employed in a child's learning should be appropriate to the child's motor, cognitive, and social level of development. Of greatest importance is a child's interest and curiosity as a guide to education during these years. One can impose other forms of learning, such as academic skills; however, they are not useful to the child if curiosity about them does not exist. The danger of imposing adult learning patterns on young children is that the motivation for learning—curiosity—and the means of learning—play—may be sidetracked or squelched, depriving the child of progression through the necessary developmental sequences that precede academic learning. A child then may prematurely adopt adult rationality, leaving a core of unmodified infantile fantasies covered by a "pseudoadult" facade.

Premature imposition of adult expectations, such as learning to read, without an expression of interest, means that children's fantasies are not engaged, and the learning task creates an unintegrated "pseudoadult" skill which is seen by children as an accommodation to the adult world but not as a part of themselves. In some cases resistance to that foreign part of oneself is expressed through blocks to later academic learning. Conversely, when the child's fantasy and interest are captured and the cognitive capacities are acquired, academic learning, such as learning to read, occurs with ease.

During the early school years, a child becomes capable of rational, cause–effect thinking. Children then possess sufficient self-control and maturity to engage in academic learning "for learning's sake alone." Ultimately, at the end of preadolescence, they assume the capacity for complex abstract thinking. Coping skills and increasing knowledge of the world can then be acquired.

ACQUISITION OF VALUES

Kessen offers a commentary on current American society. He notes a shift away from personal responsibility, as expressed in the attitude "I don't have an opinion on anything, you go solve the problem." In his view, the tendency over the last fifty years in America has been to shift responsibility from persons to institutions, not only for technical services but also for moral and ethical decisions. He attributes this decline in the importance of personal responsibility to the absence of strong moral imperatives in child rearing from both parents and society (Kessen, 1976).

On the other hand, studies of primate and human societies suggest that innate values are built into our species. These include a desire for dominance, a desire for approval, gregariousness, a desire to work with others for common goals, a desire to make or build something, and a desire to contribute or do something meaningful for society. These values have been the underpinnings of the social evolution of homo sapiens; they arise from drives that motivate and color human behavior in the context of attachment to parenting adults (Pugh, 1977).

From our knowledge of child development, we know that it is not necessary to teach a child to distinguish simply between "bad" and "good." From the earliest weeks a baby can express pleasure and displeasure, discriminating between "good" and "bad" parenting during the first year. Babies know what is "right" and what is "wrong" in relation to their wishes. This fact highlights the true nature of values— they reflect what is "right" and "wrong," at first for oneself and later for other people as well. The development of values, then, expands upon the momentary awareness of what is good or bad for the individual to include awareness of long-range consequences of actions for both the individual and society.

Values are essential ingredients of any culture and its socialization process. It is not surprising, then, that the values children develop are of profound importance to society. We find that adults are especially concerned about the propriety of children's behavior, their respect for authority, and their conformity to cultural expectations. The things that children "should" and "should not" do are legion—as they are for parents.

The early existence of a child's capacity for good and bad discrimination also exposes as fallacious the belief that, unless concerted efforts are made to provide formalized moral education, children will not grow up with a sense of right and wrong. This view is appropriate only if one takes the opposite position—that children should not be exposed to values at all and will develop their own *de novo*. If raised with this expectation, children would become adults who consider largely what is bad or good for themselves without strong concern for social values. The experience of most children, however, is exposure to the values of their parents and social institutions through both modeling and interpretations by the adults. Parental traits and values are absorbed through identification. Although the process of identification may be disguised and even superficially rejected by the young, the modeling influence of parents is the most powerful influence on personality development.

The essential intervening mechanism, then, for moving from a "right" for me to a "right" for me in accommodation to a world of others value system, is the experience a child has with parents and other adults. If a toddler discovers that pleasing Mother is advantageous so that Mother's approval begets personal pleasure, or that Mother's disapproval begets displeasure, the initial step toward a social value system has been taken. In this climate, children associate the reactions and welfare of their parents and significant adults with their own actions and wishes. Conversely, children need to experience adults who value their welfare and model sympathy, empathy, and respect for others. The fundamental motivations to adopt values are pleasure from pleasing others and discomfort from disapproval by others. Both depend upon the presence of attachments to adults that lead each party to care about the pleasure or displeasure of the other. Without that attachment, a child's value system toward others is based simply upon avoiding the discomfort of the disapproval of adults. The element of caring about pleasing and obtaining the approval of adults is missing. In later life, this person may be aware of social values but have little commitment to them.

Another critical step in acquiring values is a child's internalization of the parents' image during the third year of life, so that the child carries an awareness of parents when they are not immediately available. Built upon this internalized image are the attitudes and prohibitions of the parents, providing the basis for a conscience that can increasingly govern behavior in the parents' absence, a phenomenon that reaches full expression between the ages of five and eight.

Thus far, the most important influence is what parents do, both directly in mediating approval and disapproval with their children and indirectly through the example they set in their lives by giving priority to the interests of their children. As a child begins to use language, more abstract expectations can be set so that direct experience can be supplemented by verbal explanations of values. Language makes it possible for children to take in their parents' prohibitions as their own. Words can substitute for acts. For example, a toddler can be helped to understand that a flame is "hot" and will hurt if touched. Although still at a personal level of bad or good, the introduction of verbal symbols sets the stage for the later verbal expressions of values. Although no substitute for directly experiencing another child's anger at one's refusal to share a toy, the effect of a child's behavior on others should also be explained in words so that an interalized guideline can be formed.

Bettelheim (1976) points out that values are necessary for an understanding of the meaning of life and are not suddenly acquired at the age of chronological maturity, or at any particular age. This achievement is the result of a long developmental course; wisdom is built up, step by step, from most irrational beginnings. Unfortunately, too many parents want their children's minds to function as their own do—as if children's understanding of themselves and the world did not develop as slowly as their bodies do. To find meaning in life, children must become able to transcend the confines of a self-centered existence and believe that they will make a significant contribution—if not right now, then at some future time. This belief is necessary if they are to be satisfied with themselves and with what they are doing; only hope for the future can sustain us during the adversities that we inevitably encounter.

As mentioned, of first importance in providing such experiences is the impact of parents and others who take care of the child; however, cultural heritage also plays a vital role. When children are young, this heritage reaches them best through literature. Much of the current literature intended to develop the minds and personalities of children, however, fails to stimulate and nurture those resources needed most in order to cope with difficult inner problems. Bettelheim feels that the majority of children's books currently available attempt to entertain or inform, or both, but are so shallow that little of significance can be gained from them. The idea that by learning to read one may later be able to enrich one's life is experienced as an empty promise when the stories that children listen to or read are vacuous. For a story to truly hold a child's attention, it must entertain and arouse curiosity. But for a story to enrich life it must stimulate imagination, help to develop intellect and to clarify emotions, be attuned to anxieties and aspirations, give full recognition to difficulties, suggest solutions to the problems that perturb, and promote confidence in the future.

In order to master the psychological problems of growing up, a child must be able to cope with what goes on in the unconscious mind. This ability is achieved not by attaining rational comprehension of the nature and content of the unconscious, but by becoming familiar and comfortable with it through spinning out daydreams—ruminating on, rearranging, and fantasizing about suitable story elements in response to unconscious pressures. By doing this, children fit fantasies from their unconscious into conscious ideas and play.

For this purpose fairy tales have an unequaled value because they offer new dimensions to the child's imagination, suggesting images with which to structure daydreams. A fairy tale helps children to understand themselves, guiding them to find solutions to the problems that beset them metaphorically. The purpose in telling a fairy tale to a child ought to be a shared experience of enjoying the story, even though what makes for this enjoyment may be quite different for child and adult. While the child enjoys the fantasy, the adult may derive pleasure from the child's enjoyment. Telling a fairy tale with a purpose other than that of enriching the child's experience turns it into a cautionary tale or a didactic experience. Children do not need to have the meanings of fairy tales explained to them. If parents tell their children fairy tales with a feeling for the meaning that the story had for them when they were young and with sensitivity to the fact that children derive personal meaning from hearing the tale, then children feel understood in their most tender longings, in their most ardent wishes, in their most severe anxieties, and in their feelings of misery. Children feel that they are not alone in their fantasy lives—that they are shared by the persons whom they need and love most. Under such favorable conditions, fairy tales communicate to children an intuitive understanding of their own nature and of what their future may hold. They sense that to be a human being means accepting difficult challenges, but that it also means encountering wondrous adventures.

The most comprehensive study of the development of values in children has been carried out by Kohlberg (1977). His interest is in the process of reasoning, not simply in moral judgments. His work is based upon the presentation to children of stories that contain conflicts between rules and a child's wants. He describes six stages in the development of moral reasoning, each dependent on cognitive development and exposure to the modeling of values.

Stage 1. Punishment–obedience orientation: The physical consequences of an action determine its goodness or badness regardless of motivation, need, or extenuating circumstances.

Stage 2. Instrumental–relativist orientation: The right action is determined by its utilitarian value to oneself and occasionally to others. Cooperation is a matter of "you scratch my back, and I'll scratch yours," not of loyalty, gratitude or justice. Nevertheless, society is seen as a group of individuals like oneself, no longer solely controlled by authorities and relying upon pragmatic reciprocity.

Stage 3. Interpersonal concordance or desire for approval orientation: A person's motives and desire to please are important in evaluating behavior at this stage. How one fits into one's role from the other's point of view is most important. The concern is for the approval of family, teachers and friends. Conformity is high to stereotypical images of what is majority behavior. Self sacrifice is seen as necessary. Group loyalty is high.

Stage 4. Law and order orientation: An abstract concept of moral law is reached that considers the rights of all and adjudicates conflicting group interests which might have been experienced in Stage 3. Right behavior consists of doing one's duty, showing respect for authority and maintaining the given social order for its own sake.

Stage 5. Social contract–legalistic orientation: The Stage 5 person rejects the fixity of the law and distinguishes between areas of personal freedom and those which concern the general good. Moral judgments are seen as a matter of personal opinion. Law is seen as a creation of man designed to resolve conflicts. Laws can be examined and reformed. One is "free" of the law until one is subjected to it because of self interest or the overriding interests of society. This stage is the level of the "official" morality of the United States Constitution.

Stage 6. Universal ethical principle orientation: This is the stage of moral heroes such as Gandhi or Martin Luther King, Jr., who had abstract and ethical principles about justice and the dignity of human beings which enabled them to see beyond social utility. The guiding principles, such as the Golden Rule, are universal rather than subject to one society's welfare and are logically comprehensive and consistent.

Progress from one of Kohlberg's stages to the next depends upon emotional, social, intellectual, and cognitive development.

It is important to assess the stage at which a child is functioning and neither to underestimate nor to exceed the child's capacity. There is also a wide range of levels at which adults function in terms of these stages. Moreover, individuals function at different levels under differing circumstances. Kohlberg found that a person could understand or be appealed to one stage of reasoning higher than that on which the person was currently operating.

By applying Kohlberg's stages to the lives of adults, we see that some adults do what they are told to do because of fear of authority (Stage 1), or because conformity will bring them pleasure (Stage 2), or because they are expected to conform by their subgroups (Stage 3), or because conformity is the law (Stage 4). These levels could well be the stages at which the majority of adults function. In Kohlberg's sequence, however, the two higher levels of moral reasoning, based on principles rather than perceptions of the social system, are influential in our society. It is during late adolescence that youngsters both examine and develop their own principles of judgment and come to realize that our social order is not the only one. The fact that other societies have other systems leads to questioning of standards and traditions which have been handed down. Being able to look at alternative social orders "from the outside" is a necessary, but temporarily disorienting, step toward reaching the highest levels of moral reasoning.

In essence, to acquire a useful set of values, children need to have experienced high priority in the lives of parenting adults and to have learned to respond to the approval and disapproval of others. Children assimilate the values modeled by their parents and other significant adults through identification. With situationally related explanations of the usefulness of values, children acquire guidelines to facilitate social living. In order for this process to unfold, children need adults who are not only committed to their welfare but who are available at times of social confrontations to provide verbal explanations. Unless committed to helping a child understand social interactions, which in practice takes time to talk with the child often at busy moments, adults tend to deal only with the child's behavior. Under these circumstances a child learns "right" and "wrong" out of fear of punishment, not because of awareness of the personal utility of values. The value, then, is perceived as effective only when punishment is an available consequence. The result may be the attitude that "it's wrong only if I get caught."

Children need values and cannot develop socially rewarding lives without them. Only adults with interest and time, however, can help children acquire personalized values of enduring significance. After being internalized during the years of middle childhood, values are reappraised, refined, and even temporarily rejected during the preadolescent and adolescent years. Of greatest importance is not an intellectual awareness of social values, but incorporation of them in the daily decisions of living.

DEVELOPMENT OF RESPONSIBILITY FOR DECISION MAKING

Values are the personalized guidelines by which children and adults conduct their lives. In themselves, however, they have little significance except as they influence actions. Many people have extensive intellectual value systems, but their behavior does not reflect them. Children frequently point out that they are expected to do as their parents say rather than as their parents do. The growing child's capacity to make decisions, then, is the vehicle through which value judgments are expressed. Our interest here is in a child's emerging ability to assume responsibility for personal decision making in specific areas at an adult level of judgment.

The developmental line of responsibility for decision making deserves particular consideration because its substantial achievement marks the end of childhood. The essence of childhood is the dependency of children upon adults to make important decisions in their lives. Consequently, an important aspect of childhood is being protected from the responsibility of having to make decisions prematurely. Children gradually develop the ability to exercise adult-level judgment and make decisions at uniquely individualized times and rates so that generalizations must take into account a wide range of variations. There are at least three factors involved in a child's ability to make responsible decisions: first, the child's capacity to observe situations accurately; second, the capacity to evaluate these observations objectively; and third, the capacity to express evaluative judgments to others coherently.

THE ABILITY TO OBSERVE ACCURATELY

The first capacity, to observe accurately, is related to a child's ability to perceive reality. The accurate perception of reality may be questionable enough for adults, but the innate egocentricity of children heavily flavors their perceptions of reality from infancy through early adolescence. As described by Piaget, childhood egocentrism signifies the absence of both self-perception and objectivity (Shantz, 1975). Certainly, during the first two years of life, a child is in a state of simply discovering the rudimentary aspects of home and community which constitute the child's entire world.

From the ages of two to six, children learn symbolic labels for people and things, with limited awareness of their circumstances and without an accurate sense of time and space. A four-year-old knows a sibling only as "Tommy," not as a brother; a five-year-old can walk to school, but not make a drawing of the route. Young children can identify certain simple emotions in others from facial cues or from knowing the other person's situation if that situation is familiar to them. They are not able to anticipate other people's thoughts, however. They probably characterize other people in terms of physical appearance and their interactions with the person (e.g., "he plays with me"), using strong positive and negative value judgments.

Important achievements in social understanding usually appear between five and seven years of age. There is recognition that others see physical objects differently and that others can have different thoughts than they do. Children this age are able to discriminate accidental from intended actions of others. There is also some ability to distinguish "good" from "bad" intentions in allocating blame. People are still characterized by appearance and possessions with simple evaluative traits (e.g., "nice," "mean").

Middle childhood, from six to 11, is the time of dramatic advances in social understanding. Social inferences progress to the level of the child's understanding that personal thoughts, feelings, and intentions can be the object of another's thinking. Children can view simple social episodes from the position of each participant and maintain a consistency among viewpoints in each episode. When judging others' blameworthiness, they can weight the intentions of others more than the damage done. At this age, children also show the ability to infer the feelings of others when they are in situations largely familiar to them. They also describe others less in terms of surface characteristics and more in terms of their covert attributes—attitudes, abilities, and interests. A child now attends less to the movements and statements of people and more to inferred inner experiences and social relations between people.

Even the perceptions of children during middle childhood are determined by what they know and how they feel about things or situations. Evidence that contradicts their beliefs is rationalized to fit their own preconceptions. More fundamentally, performance on tests of simple perceptions do not achieve adult levels of accuracy until about the age of 11 (Kohen-Raz, 1971). The ability to observe accurately non–emotionally laden events, then, is not seen until after the age of 11, when the ability to construct an overall realistic and rational picture of the universe is acquired. Prior to that time, perceptions are strongly influenced by preexisting sets and by emotional reactions and attitudes. This means that, prior to preadolescence, children literally live in their own perceptual worlds and do not experience events in the same way as do adults. It is not surprising, then, that adult recollections of childhood differ so markedly from actual physical and historical realities.

Even during adolescence there is a distortion of perception in interpersonal and personal areas based upon the self-conscious sense that "the whole world is watching me"—an adolescent remnant of egocentrism. In early and middle adolescence the young person's perspective extends further to include oneself, the other person, the inner experience of each, and the relation between oneself and the other person as a third-party observer might understand it. There is also a spontaneous tendency to try to explain the thoughts, feelings, and intentions of other people. The adolescent can recognize contradictory tendencies in others and relate situational factors to another's behavior (Shantz, 1975).

THE ABILITY TO EVALUATE OBSERVATIONS OBJECTIVELY

The second capacity involved in responsible decision making is to evaluate situations objectively once they are perceived and, even under optimal circumstances, this does not mature until preadolescence. The capacity to understand events develops gradually from the discovery that objects exist even when they are not seen, near the end of the first year, to an understanding of the meaning of abstractions, such as the "future" and the "past," during the preadolescent years. In between, children are oriented to the "here and now" and evaluate things and events in terms of personal significance to themselves. Unlike a four-year-old, a seven-year-old can understand that "Tommy" is a brother and that "Daddy" is one of a class of fathers. Also, unlike a four-year-old, a seven-year-old can recognize that the quantity of clay does not change when made into a different shape. Unlike the seven-year-old, an 11-year-old can fully comprehend that the volume of water does not change when poured into containers of different shapes (Piaget, 1969). During middle childhood, however, children tend to attribute life to inanimate objects and do not comprehend the biological finality of death. They can think about ideas that pertain to their own personal lives but cannot put themselves in the shoes of others, even though they are able to assume acting roles in school plays.

It is after the age of 10 or 11 that children begin to think of themselves, their roles in life, their plans, their beliefs, and the finality of death. Thus, a 13-year-old said, "I find myself thinking about my future and then thinking about why I was thinking about my future." They become able to detect "phoniness" in the expressed ideals and behavior of others. Their thinking achieves independence from egocentric, personal experience, making it possible to compare, combine, and match ideas without specific pertinence to their own lives. They can understand concepts such as freedom, nature, government, force, and beauty. They become increasingly able to talk to a second person while taking into consideration the point of view of a third person not present. The growing ability to exercise critical judgment makes it possible to evaluate intentions behind acts (Shantz, 1975).

Between the ages of 13 and 16, adult levels of abstract thinking appear, with improved ability to systematize and verbalize formal reasoning. There is growing awareness of the arbitrariness of personal viewpoints; however, egocentrism persists in the form of the personal conviction that they are the first ones to experience the new sensations, feelings, and thoughts that are appearing in their lives. This sense of uniqueness also tends to have the flavor of invulnerability and immortality. Also characteristic of this age is self-consciousness, so that each adolescent is simultaneously an actor and the audience. These factors account for the fluctuations between logic and irrationality and the inaccurate judgments made about oneself and others (Elkind, 1971).

By the age of 15 or 16, the capacity for adult-level logical and abstract thinking becomes firmly established. Adolescent egocentrism is overcome gradually by the process of interacting with others of the same age, which permits both differentiating between and integrating one's own preoccupations and those of others. Building upon the maturing central nervous system, older adolescents add the essential ingredient of experience as they expand their base of knowledge and learn means of applying their newly found reasoning capacities to the realities of the world. The more complex the society, the longer the experiential aspect of judgment and evaluative capacity takes to mature. Although continuing to be refined throughout life, that capacity seems to crystallize during the mid-twenties in our society.

A specific example of the development of the capacity to evaluate observations can be seen in the evolution of children's views of loyalty. Children from three to five appear to equate trust in friendship with peers with physical capabilities ("If I give him my toy he won't break it—he isn't strong enough"). Loyalty is equated with physical proximity and strength. From five to 11, trust is based upon intentions and not just physical abilities. But trust is a one-way street; children equate trust with getting a friend to do one's bidding ("I trust a friend if he does what I tell him"). Loyalty is now equated with unilateral obedience to oneself or a leader. From the age of 11 to 14, trust is seen as equal reciprocity ("If you do something for him, he will do something for you"). Loyalty is equated with exchanging favors or mutual liking. From 14 to 16, trust embodies a belief in consistency of friendship through "thick and thin"—not only exchange by sharing, but also by supporting each other. Loyalty is equated with "all for one and one for all." Finally, among older adolescents and adults, friendship is viewed as an ongoing process in which trust means an openness to change and growth as well as stability. Loyalty is equated with willingness to sacrifice for others (Selman, 1977).

THE ABILITY TO EXPRESS JUDGMENTS COHERENTLY

The third capacity, the ability to express one's evaluations coherently, depends not only upon the levels of language development and articulation but, more important, on a child's sense of the consequences of doing so. Whether through withholding or exploitatively manipulating, children, as do adults, handle their opinions and judgments for self-serving purposes. Fears of being mistaken, of being disloyal, of provoking punishment, or of hurting others may lead to silence or avoidance of venturing opinions. On the other hand, resentment, anger, or jealousy may lead to vengeful displays of judgments of others. To complicate the matter even further, adolescents may lack words or ideas to fully express their views.

Of great importance also is the fact that the disposition to share opinions differs immensely between peers and adults. Disclosures to peers are less likely to be influenced by children's accommodation to what they think is expected of them than are disclosures to adults. Especially with children prior to the adolescent years, reporting is heavily influenced by immediate circumstances. A child may feel one way at one time and in one circumstance and another way in another situation, even minutes before or after. The expressions of opinion by children are strongly influenced by their emotional and physical states.

All of these factors point to the complex nature of interviewing and communicating with children, particularly if their viewpoints are desired in matters of importance in their lives. Unfortunately, the tendency is either to ignore children in matters affecting them or to involve them inappropriately. Another problem is that children tend to appear to be more mature and informed than they are in reality. This is particularly the case with older adolescents who, because of their ability to formulate and express opinions as do adults, are also assumed to have sufficient experience to assume responsibility for their own lives. To make matters even more complicated, the least mature children and adolescents are the most likely to insist upon assuming responsibility for themselves and tend to be the most skilled in manipulating adults. Thus, a teenager who demands freedom to engage in self-destructive activities because "it's my life" may make logical sense but is not reflecting a realistic, mature understanding of the responsibilities that all adults have to themselves and to others.

The most critical fact of adolescent development is that there are wide differences in individuals of the same age in physical growth, emotional maturity, and social judgment. Some teenagers possess maturity in all of these areas at the age of 15, others have not developed these capacities at the age of 25. It is clear that one of the developmental hazards for adolescents is their ability to act in ways that not only create immediate frustrations for them, but that also pose long-range deleterious effects. An impulsive, uncontrolled act can lead an adolescent to a pathway that will ultimately be self-destructive. Furthermore, parents can both knowingly and unwittingly harm an adolescent's present and future life. The stakes are too high to ignore the fact that an adolescent's judgment and wishes can lead to self-defeating decisions and actions. This wide range in maturity points up the folly of arbitrarily selecting a chronological age at which adult responsibilities are awarded. For general matters, such as voting age, responsibility is arbitrarily established. However, past experience in universal screening of 18-year-olds through the Selective Service disclosed that a significant number of youth did not attain sufficient maturity to function in military life, leading to a surprisingly high rejection rate. Still, ages are established for these rights or responsibilities because of the argument that all young people are affected, and the immense numbers preclude individual screening. On the other hand, this argument is contradicted by the fact that all states have established individual screening for the right to obtain a driver's license.

To draw several generalizations from the state of our knowledge of child development, we can presume that, prior to the age of about 11, children are not able to observe accurately events and situations in their lives. Although they may be able to offer useful pieces of evidence in the apprehension of a criminal, for example, they are not able to provide objective information about themselves, their families, or other people, particularly in emotionally laden situations. Prior to the age of about seven, children are not able to understand the meaning of words such as "divorce," "adoption," and "death." Until the age of about 11, such abstract concepts are interpreted in highly personalized, self-centered ways. Youngsters over the age of 11 can be astute observers of people, things, and events. Older adolescents also can make objective judgments about aspects of their lives in which an adequate experiential base exists. They are not prepared, however, to make holistic judgments affecting their present or future lives in our complex society.

As can be seen, the capacity of young people to form, evaluate, and report their opinions has a developmental course and is related both to the interaction of the maturing central nervous system and life experience. The growth of the brain determines the sequence in which new functions appear, and individual differences, in addition to life experience, influence the age at which they appear. Some children mature more rapidly and more comprehensively than others. The disrupting influences of physical or emotional illness, family problems, poverty, and social conditions also play critical roles in determining how children perceive, judge, and express their viewpoints. Unfortunately, too many children are either forced into or demand inordinate responsibility for decision making in their lives.

The most fundamental characteristic of childhood is dependency upon adults. Although most people move through their dependent years smoothly, some have tortuous journeys. Those who are the most eager to assume adult responsibilities and shuck off childhood are often those who have not fully absorbed the developmental lessons of childhood and are the least prepared to assume adult responsibilities. It is evident that special skills and knowledge are required to obtain valid information and judgments from young people when important decisions are made in matters affecting their lives. Talking with a child is not a simple matter.

DEVELOPMENT OF SELF-IDENTITY AND SELF-ESTEEM

How persons regard themselves is critical to the operation of all societies. In societies emphasizing conformity, a person's self-esteem tends to depend upon the esteem of others, fostering "other-directed" persons. In America the emphasis has been more upon self-esteem that does not depend upon continuous reinforcement from others, fostering "inner-directed" persons. The groundwork for either state is laid during the early years of life.

The first step toward developing an awareness of oneself is signaled by infants' discovery that their hands, initially perceived as separate things, can be controlled and are parts of their bodies. During the last third of the first year, infants become aware of their whole bodies as separate from the world of things, especially from the bodies of their mothers. As a toddler, a child adds the dimension of personhood when the pronoun "I" becomes a way of expressing one's will. This development also signifies psychological birth.

During this time the esteem held for a child's body and its functions by the parenting figures lays the foundation for the child's self-esteem. If a child's eating, elimination, and sleeping functions have been tenderly ministered to, these basic life functions are positively valued. Mechanical attendance to these functions, on the other hand, does not draw out pleasurable emotions, and in some instances the gruff or disgusted handling of the child stimulates unpleasant feelings in the child about bodily functions. The yield of "tender, loving care" is children's basically positive regard and pleasure from their bodily functions. Without this foundation, the child is left with a basically indifferent or negative sense of body functions.

The child's sense of identity, then, is based upon the synthesis of an infant's picture of self and the world gained through a continuous process of being stimulated by the environment. The sounds heard and the things seen, touched, smelled, and tasted—in addition to the sensations arising from being held and cuddled—all form a coherent picture of the self and world when they occur in meaningful patterns that emanate from adults who care about and direct their communications to the child.

Conversely, if sensory stimulation is infrequent, excessive, or unpatterned, a child responds to each sound, vision, touch, odor, taste, or movement without experiencing meaning, and with apprehension because there is no coherent pattern. For such children, sounds are noise rather than messages; visual stimulation of the coming and going of people who are not relating to the child is bewildering; touch, taste, and smell may be separately associated with doing forbidden things; and body movement is frightening because it is not accompanied by soothing, comforting intentions. The result of this unpatterned, meaningless stimulation is a lack of integration of stimuli that through their synthesis should become a coherent picture in which sounds, sights, smells, touches, tastes, and body sense are related to each other in a way that connotes "I am all right, I am safe." When care is delivered in pieces by different people in distracting, overstimulating environments, the child lacks the coherent sense that "I am cared for," which is the synthesized message that comes from caretakers who are committed to the child's welfare.

Children who receive fragmented care, whether in the hands of a single or many parent figures, have a fundamental deficiency in their sense of identity and lack the underlying sense that "I am a person who has been valued by others." Of great importance also are individual differences in children's channels of information processing and in synthesizing capacity. This means that some children are more vulnerable to identity problems than others.

The toddler's development of psychological personhood depends upon the acceptance and understanding of adults, since the experience of one's individuality is frequently expressed through "I want" and "I won't." An atmosphere of delight and pleasure in children's growing autonomy reinforces their pleasure in their own abilities and actions. The pleasure of adults in their first words, sentences, and ideas adds an additional dimension of self-esteem for functions of the mind in addition to those of the body. Conversely, the absence of shared delight in performance, or the discouragement or penalization thereof, leaves children with little sense of pleasure in their mental functioning or with the clear message that their minds and wishes are bad. Although each child possesses an internal thrust toward a positive image of self, the degree of positive self-esteem, and certainly low self-esteem, depends upon the reflected appraisals of others. According to Erikson (1963), "from a sense of self control, without loss of self-esteem, comes a lasting sense of autonomy and pride."

The appearance of an internalized mother image in the third year makes it possible for children to separate from their mothers (Mahler, 1975). As the concept of "I" emerges, children often go through a period of concern about bruises or scratches, even imperceptible ones. It is as though the child's sense of integrity and completeness as a personality is intimately bound up in a sense of bodily intactness and wholeness. The separation and individuation process culminates in the third year in a sense of identity, in which the various differentiated aspects of the self are united. At this time, children can sense themselves as active, competent, and desirable. Indeed, the whole range of self-awareness during the fourth and fifth years of life centers around individual differences in body size, strength, skin color, dexterity, facial appearance, and distinguishing physical characteristics. Each child senses these differences and reacts to them to the extent that they are differentially treated by other children and adults. The sense of being a boy or girl occurs in the setting of discovering fundamental physical attributes, as well. To this point, a child's identity grows from awareness of body, personhood, gender, and physical appearance.

As a child develops an increasingly differentiated sense of self, the cultural assignment of gender identity elaborates upon biologically determined sex differences (Stoller, 1968). Strongly influenced by parental attitudes toward masculinity and femininity, but also shaped by the interests and behavior of peers and broader social contexts, the child develops a sense of gender identity, with positive and negative valuations depending upon life experience. Parallel with the specific matter of gender identity is a growing repertoire of experience and activities regarded as the child's "own" and contributing to an integrated sense of self.

As the aspect of personality that continues to mature and change throughout life in response to the critical issues of each stage of the life cycle, self-identity becomes more finely tuned and harmonious, with an increasing variety of social roles throughout childhood and early adulthood (Erikson, 1963). As the child enters the broadening world of school, the acquisition of academic, recreational, athletic, and social skills permits further differentiation in knowledge of oneself and a myriad of dimensions open upon which the child can value—or devalue—oneself. If the child has built in a solid, positive sense of personal value during the years of early childhood, the tendency is to accept successes and failures without basically altering self-esteem. On the other hand, if that basic sense does not exist, or underlying self-esteem is low, the child's successes or failures influence self-esteem inordinately. A child with basic self-confidence is not only prepared to achieve self-realization, but also to accept failures and disappointments without loss of self-esteem.

The teenage years bring the maturing person into articulated relationships with other people and the social system, permitting a more sophisticated awareness of who, what, and where the individual person is. In our complex society the postadolescent years are further devoted to matching of abilities, ideals, and aspirations with the realities of society's career, interpersonal, and cultural opportunities. The hoped-for outcome is a sense of meaning, purpose, and significance in one's life. All of these hinge upon the degree to which childhood has prepared the individual to become a contributing member of society—not a burdensome one. The ultimate *need* of the child become adult is to *be needed* by others and by society.

Conclusion

We cannot look to scientists and research for more than guidance on specific child rearing techniques. The objectives of child rearing are not susceptible to controlled experimentation, deliberate manipulation of variables, and specification of definable outcomes. Rather, child rearing flows from the overall aims of culture and society. Clarifying the values and aims of our society is the route to the directions and styles of child rearing.

In America there is great concern for both the autonomy of adults and children, in contrast with other social systems, which weight one more than the other. More fundamentally, our society values individualism and, at least theoretically, it prizes individual differences. These underlying themes permeate our approaches to children.

The overall objective of child rearing in America is the balanced development of an individual's potential to permit competent functioning within our social structure and economic system. The salient, specific qualities that are needed in order to function competently in American society are social skills which include the ability to communicate, relate, and be useful to others and the ability to initiate self-expressive activity. In order to function socially, the individual must also develop the ability to delay gratification, tolerate frustration, and carry out work. Further needed is the ability to learn about oneself, other people, and the world. A value system is necessary with the commitment to adapt and adhere to social values and to accommodate self-interests to social realities. Important to achieving independence is the ability to assume responsibility for decision making through formulating judgments and expressing one's opinions. Finally, each individual should establish a self-identity as a unique person in order to achieve meaning in life, hopefully with high self-esteem. Each of these target qualities has a developmental course expressed in progressively more complex ways as a child moves from one developmental stage to the next, each building on the foregoing states. The development of these qualities depends upon the modeling of adults committed to the welfare of each child.

Child rearing practices are the means through which a society socializes children within caretaking units, which in turn are influenced by broader child caring systems and the total political, economic, and cultural context. In this chapter we have offered an approach to clarifying American child rearing objectives within that framework. In the next chapter we will examine the articulation of these developmental needs with the environments that impinge upon children.

References

BELL, R. Q., WELLER, G. M., AND WALDROP., M. R. (1971) "Newborn and Preschoolers: Organization of Behavior and Relations Between Periods." *Monograph of the Society for Research in Child Development*, Serial No. 142, Vol. 36, Nos. 1–2.

BELLOW, S. (1977) "The Nobel Lecture." *The American Scholar*, Summer, 1977: 316–325.

BETTELHEIM, B. (1976) "Reflections." *New Yorker*, 52: 31–36, August 2.

BOWEN, J. (1965) *Soviet Education: Anton Makarenko and the Years of Experiment*. Madison: University of Wisconsin Press.

BOWLBY, J. (1977) "The Making and Breaking of Affectional Bonds. I. Aetiology and Psychopathology in the Light of Attachment Theory." *British Journal of Psychiatry*, 130:201–210.

BRONFENBRENNER, U. (1973) *Two Worlds of Childhood: U.S. and U.S.S.R.* New York: Pocket Books.

CALDWELL, B. (1976) "Optimal Child Rearing Environments." Chapter in Westman, J. C. (Ed.), *Proceedings of the University of Wisconsin Conference on Child Advocacy*. Madison: University of Wisconsin–Extension, Health Sciences Unit.

COHEN, T. B. (1977) "Observations on School Children in the People's Republic of China." *Journal of Child Psychiatry*, 16:165–173.

COX, RACHEL (1970) *Youth into Maturity*. New York: Mental Health Materials Center.

ELKIND, D. (1971) "Egocentrism in Adolescence." Chapter in Thornburg, H. D. (Ed.), *Contemporary Adolescence: Reading*. Belmont, Calif.: Brooks/Cole, pp. 50–56.

ERIKSON, E. H. (1963) *Childhood and Society*. New York: Norton.

ESCALONA, S. (1953) "Emotional Development in the First Years of Life." Chapter in Senn, M. E. (Ed.), *Transactions of the Sixth Conference*. New York: Josiah Massey, Jr. Foundation Series.

FLAPAN, D., AND NEUBAUER, P. (1975) *Assessment of Early Child Development*. New York: Aronson.

FRAIBERG, S. (1959) *The Magic Years*. New York: Scribner.

FRAIBERG, S. (1977) *Every Child's Birthright: In Defense of Mothering*. New York: Basic Books.

FREUD, A. (1965) *Normality and Pathology in Childhood*. New York: International Universities Press.

GARVEY, C. (1977) *Play*. Cambridge, Mass.: Harvard University Press.

GEIGER, H. K. (1968) *The Family in Soviet Russia*. Cambridge, Mass.: Harvard University Press.

KAGAN, J. (1977) "The Child in the Family." *Daedalus*, 106:33–56, Spring.

KESSEN, W. (1976) *Childhood in China*. New Haven: Yale University Press.

KESSEN, W. (1977) Quoted in Senn, M. J. E., *Speaking Out for America's Children*. New Haven: Yale University Press.

KOHEN-RAZ, R. (1971) *The Child from 9 to 13: Psychology and Psychopathology*. Chicago: Aldine-Atherton.

KOHLBERG, L. (1977) *Assessing Moral Judgment Stages: A Manual*. New York: Humanities Press.

LANGMEIER, J., AND MATEJCEK, Z. (1975) *Psychological Deprivation in Childhood*. New York: Wiley.

LEWIS, M. (1977) "Language, Cognitive Development and Personality." *Journal of Child Psychiatry*, 16:646–660, Autumn.

LICHTENBERG, P., AND NORTON, D. G. (1971) *Cognitive and Mental Development in the First Five Years of Life: A Review of Recent Research*. Public Health Service Publication No. 2057. Washington, D.C.: Superintendent of Documents.

LOMAX, E. M. R. (1978) *Science and Patterns of Child Care*. San Francisco: Freeman.

LURIA, A. R. (1976) *Cognitive Development: Its Cultural and Social Foundations*. Cambridge, Mass.: Harvard University Press.

MAHLER, M., PINE, F., AND BERGMAN, A. (1975) *The Psychological Birth of the Human Infant*. New York: Basic Books.

MALONE, CHARLES A. (1967) "Guideposts Derived from Normal Development." Chapter in Pavenstadt, E. (Ed.), *The Drifters*. Boston: Little, Brown.

MEAD, M., AND WOLFENSTEIN, M. (1955) *Childhood in Contemporary Cultures.* Chicago: University of Chicago Press.

MONTAGU, A. (1961) "Neonatal and Infant Immaturity in Man." *Journal of the American Medical Association,* 178:156–157.

MURPHY, L. B. (1962) *The Widening World of Childhood.* New York: Basic Books.

NAGERA, H. (1963) "The Developmental Profile." *Psychoanalytic Study of the Child,* 18:511–540.

NATIONAL SCIENCE FOUNDATION (1976) *Research on Effects of Television Advertising on Children.* Washington, D.C.: National Science Foundation.

NEUBAUER, P. B. (Ed.) (1965) *Children in Collectives: Child-rearing Aims and Practices in the Kibbutz.* Springfield, Ill.: Thomas.

OFFER, D., AND SABSHIN, M. (1966) *Normality: Theoretical and Clinical Concepts of Mental Health.* New York: Basic Books.

OMWAKE, E. B. (1963) "The Child's Estate." Chapter in Solnit, A. J., and Provence, S. A. (Eds.), *Modern Perspectives in Child Development.* New York: International Universities Press.

PIAGET, J., AND INHELDER, B. (1969) *The Psychology of the Child.* New York: Basic Books.

PUGH, G. E. (1977) *The Biological Origin of Human Values.* New York: Basic Books.

SCHILLER, P. H. (1957) "Innate Motor Action as a Basis of Learning." Chapter in Schiller, C. H. (Ed.), *Instinctive Behavior.* New York: International Universities Press, pp. 264–287.

SEARS, R. R. (1975) "Your Ancients Revisited: A History of Child Development." Chapter in Heatherington, E. M. (Ed.) *Review of Child Development Research,* Vol. 5. Chicago: University of Chicago Press.

SEGAL, J. (1978) *A Child's Journey: Forces That Shape the Lives of Our Young.* New York: McGraw-Hill.

SELMAN, R. L., JAQUETTE, D., AND LAVIN, D. R. (1977) "Interpersonal Awareness in Children: Toward an Integration of Developmental and Clinical Child Psychology." *American Journal of Orthopsychiatry,* 47:264–274, April.

SENN, M. J. E. (1975) "Insights on the Child Development Movement in the United States." *Monograph of the Society for Research in Child Development,* Serial No. 161, Vol. 40, Nos. 3–4.

SENN, M. J. E. (1977) *Speaking Out for America's Children.* New Haven: Yale University Press.

SHANTZ, C. U. (1975) "The Development of Social Cognition." Chapter in Heatherington, E. M. (Ed.), *Review of Child Development Research,* Vol. 5. Chicago: University of Chicago Press.

SPIEGEL, J. (1971) *Transactions: The Interplay Between Individual, Family and Society.* New York: Science House.

SROUFE, L. A., AND MITCHELL, P. (1978) "Emotional Development in Infancy." Chapter in Osofsky, J. (Ed.), *Handbook of Infancy Research.* New York: Wiley.

STOLLER, R. J. (1968) *Sex and Gender.* New York: Science House.

TALBOT, B. (1976) *Raising Children in Modern America: What Parents and Society Should Be Doing for Their Children*. Boston: Little, Brown.

VAILLANT, G. E. (1977) *Adaptation to Life*. Boston: Little, Brown.

WEST, J. (1967) "The Psychobiology of Racial Violence." *Archives of General Psychiatry*, 16:645–651.

WESTMAN, J. C. (1973) *Individual Differences in Children*. New York: Wiley.

WESTMAN, J. C. (1975) "Guidelines for Determining the Psychological Best Interests of Children." Chapter in Allen, R. C. (Ed.), *Readings in Law and Psychiatry*. Baltimore: Johns Hopkins University Press.

WHITESIDE, M. F., BUSCH, F., AND HORNER, T. (1976) "From Egocentric to Cooperative Play in Young Children." *Journal of Child Psychiatry*, 15:294–313, Spring.

WINNICOTT, D. W. (1965) *The Family and Individual Development*. London: Tavistock.

WOLFF, P. H. (1977) "Maturational Factors in Behavioral Development." Chapter in McMillan, M. F., and Henao, S. (Eds.), *Child Psychiatry Treatment and Research*. New York: Brunner/Mazel.

Chapter 5
Child Rearing Environments

Although varying considerably in styles, families are found as child rearing units in all human societies, and in nonhuman primates studied thus far as well (Eaton, 1976; Murdock, 1960; Schneider, 1961). Social experiments in the Soviet Union, the People's Republic of China, and Israel that initially deemphasized the family have found parent–child relationships to be essential components of social group living. As Reiss points out, the family has evolved in all societies from an internalized set of norms that defines the obligations of kin to their newborn children elaborated upon genetically determined urges to nurture. The failure of any one generation to provide nurturance would severely limit the ability of its children to become functional adults and threaten a society's survival (Reiss, 1971).

An awareness of the fundamental characteristics of a family is necessary for an objective view of family life in the midst of popular, roman-

103

ticized images of this institution (Clarke-Stewart, 1977). In essence, a family is one or more adults, related or not, by choice or circumstance, who have come to take primary and sustained responsibility for the care of one or more dependent people, usually children, and usually all domiciled together (Hobbs, 1975). The dyad comprised of an adult committed to the care of a dependent person is the critical element of a family. According to this view, then, two adults living together, married or not, do not comprise a family.

One currently popular view is that the family in the Western world has undergone drastic changes over the last century so that it is now threatened by extinction. Actually, the pre–Industrial Revolution Western European family was not as imagined—namely, a family type characterized by early marriage, a complex co-resident group, and close ties among kin. In fact, the "traditional" Western European family was unique among other traditional societies because, probably since the fourteenth century, it was as is the "modern family," typified by late marriage for women, a large proportion of unmarried childbearing age women, a separate household at marriage, and small households comprising only a single conjugal unit. In the intervening centuries there has been a waxing and waning of kin living patterns, depending upon changing economic conditions and migration, just as is true today in America (Hunt, 1970; Wrigley, 1977).

It is likely that the flexibility of the Western European family and the reliance upon the small conjugal household made it well suited to survive major economic and social changes. Although the immediate impact of the Industrial Revolution on family structure may have diluted family strength, its concomitant durability was essential to the Industrial Revolution itself. The apparent weakness of the small family unit, in fact, has been the family's long-range strength through its mobility and capacity to adapt to social conditions.

Misconceptions abound regarding the American family. The popular belief is that there are two discrete kinds of families: the "nuclear family" with two parents and children, and the "single-parent family" with one parent and children. The fact is that most single-parent families are in a transitional state between having had two to having one parent in the home, with the other in the background. With increasing frequency, children move from one family format to another, entering the single-parent form when a divorce occurs and later moving into a remarried form, gaining stepparents and step or half siblings, and possibly, through adoption new legal parents.

More important, however, some children in single-parent families have more interaction during visits with fathers than those in nuclear families in which psychological distance exists between parents and children. To complicate the matter further, children in single-parent homes may have more contact with their mothers than children in two-parent families in which both parents are working.

The option of American adults to choose from increasing variations in life styles has led to experimentation with a variety of living arrangements, ranging from unmarried couples to communes. An earlier expectation was that this trend would decrease the popularity of the family and another belief was that adults would elect to have no children, both of these points of view stressing the unpleasant burden of family life. It appears, however, that the opposite is occurring, with the choice of family living resulting from greater forethought. With the availability of abortion and contraception, children who are currently born tend to be more planned and wanted than in the past. The trend seems to be shifting from a time in which marriage and child rearing occurred as a matter of tradition toward a time in which more deliberate choice is being exercised in forming families. Some women are childless by choice. Clinical studies of women who have been sterilized or use contraception for that purpose suggest that a rational approach for certain women who see themselves as unable or unwilling to raise children is to seek ways of effectively avoiding pregnancy (Kaltreider, 1977).

There is evidence that modern life styles are making family responsibilities more onerous for many. Studies of dual-career families find that the mothers in particular experience difficulties in respect to the proliferation of role demands in both home and job situations. There has been a tenfold increase in the number of working mothers between 1940 and 1977 when 50 % of all mothers with children under eighteen were working outside of the home (U.S. Department of Labor, 1978). The greatest strain in the maternal role is related to guilt and anxiety. Child rearing among middle-class Americans is time consuming, particularly because of the emphasis on indirect and verbal discipline techniques. The career mother is particularly vulnerable because the demands on her time and absence from home preclude attention to these diffuse needs (Johnson, 1977).

All of the foregoing point to the need for a realistic appraisal of American families. First of all, the U.S. Bureau of Census Statistics for 1977 can be used to dispose of several misconceptions (U.S. Bureau of the Census, 1979). The nuclear family is not rapidly disappearing from the American scene, as evidenced by the fact that 79 percent of the families with children included two parents. Single-parent families comprised 18 percent and living situations in which there was no parent, 3 percent. The composition of nuclear families is noteworthy, however. In 1977, 66 percent of the children under 18 were living in families with both natural parents present and in their first marriage (for black children, 45 percent, and for white, 73 percent). This means, then, that more than one-half of black and one-fourth of white schoolchildren are living in an atypical home, in the sense that they are living with one or both parents who are stepparents; or are living with a separated, divorced, widowed, or unmarried parent; or are living apart from either parent (Carter, 1976).

Another misconception is that single-parent families consist exclusively of mothers with large numbers of children. Of the 18 percent single-parent families, one in 10 are living with the father, and the average number of children in a single-parent family is 2.2. Another commonly held belief is that most single parents are unwed mothers. Actually, 29 percent of the single-parent families were created by divorce, 28 percent by separation, 26 percent through widowing, and 9 percent outside of wedlock. The last popular misconception is that all single-parent families are indigent. The fact is that 35 percent of the single-parent families are on welfare, constituting an inordinately high percentage, but not the majority.

As this data reveals, approximately 10 million children presently live with one parent. As indicated in Chapter 1, according to one estimate, by the time they reach 18, 35 percent of all American children will have spent an average of five years in a single-parent home. Thus, the single-parent experience is not confined to the 18 percent currently living that way. As indicated previously, these patterns are probably not unfamiliar ones in the waxing and waning of family life styles in Western Anglo-Saxon civilization.

Bane also points out that the percentage of women remarrying after divorce has risen along with the divorce rate so that the percentage of children living with a single parent has not increased as rapidly as the rising divorce rate would indicate. Moreover, as the divorce rate has been rising, the death rate among parents has been decreasing, so that a statistical exchange has taken place between death and divorce as causes of family breakup (Bane, 1977).

Functions of the Family

Families are typically viewed as benefiting children. Overlooked is the fact that, although adults have ambivalent feelings toward children, many adult satisfactions and investments in children are vital to the welfare of adults as well.

The biological continuation of one's own protoplasm through one's offspring has deep unconscious, primordial significance. Consequently, the birth of a child and early child rearing is a biologically, emotionally, and psychologically fulfilling experience for adults. The biological drive toward procreation is resisted with great difficulty and, if resisted totally, may be a source of problems in itself.

The fact is that children are not unilaterally dependent upon parents. Family units are really reciprocating exchanges of care, contact, communication, and control between parents and children. Thus, for the young child and parent, one can think in terms of reciprocity of the nursing couple, the talking couple, the learning couple, and the playing couple (Anthony, 1974).

It may be helpful to look at the things that society expects parents and children to do with, for, and to each other and also to bear in mind that society's expectations may conflict with the expectations of parents and of children. It is evident that parents have the right of guardianship by the fact that the child was born or legally awarded to them. Parents determine the life style and the standards of everyday conduct which influence the child's religion and affect basic religious identifications and ethical values. They may influence the kind and extent of education, the decision of vocation, and level of later adult achievement. The quality of health care the child receives depends not only on the availability of health services in the particular community, but also upon the extent that the parents utilize it when needed. Even when guardianship is removed from parents, unless parental rights have been fully terminated by court action, the right of parents to notice of judicial proceedings involving their children and the right to give or withhold consent to the child's adoption are preserved.

Whenever discussions of the functions of the family take place, whether in political, legal, or clinical areas, the underlying expectations of families in our society must be taken into account. Kadushin summarizes these expectations as follows (1974):

1. To provide an income that will meet the needs of the child for food, clothing, shelter, education, health care, and social and recreational activities.
2. To provide love, security, affection, and the emotional support necessary for the healthy emotional development of the child.
3. To provide the necessary stimulation for intellectual, social, and moral development.
4. To help socialize the child through teaching behavior that is customary and acceptable to the social group and through disciplining the child.
5. To protect the child from physical, emotional or social harm.
6. To maintain family interaction on a stable, satisfying basis so that an effort is made to meet the significant needs of all members of the family and to resolve discomforts, frictions and dissatisfactions, and to meet emotional needs through accepting, affectionate responses.

7. To provide a fixed place of abode, so as to legitimize the child's membership in the larger social group and provide a clearly defined identity for the child in the community.

On the other hand, our society also has expectations of children, largely reciprocal to those of parents:

1. If the parent role requires that the parent teach the child the appropriate attitudes and values of the society, the responsibility of the child is to learn these attitudes and values and to act in accordance with them.

2. If the parent's role is to discipline the child, the child's role is to accept such discipline, to obey the parent, and to make necessary changes in behavior. The child is expected to display behavior that is acceptable to the family and to the community.

3. The child is expected to meet some of the emotional needs of parents by responding affectionately to them, confiding in them, and respecting them. Children are expected to act in a manner that will be a credit to their parents and community.

4. Children are expected to cooperate with their parents in protecting themselves from danger and harm, and in meeting their physical, emotional and educational needs. Children are expected to eat the food offered, to go to the school provided, and to refrain from activity likely to be physically, socially or emotionally damaging.

5. Children have some responsibility for maintaining family unity and reducing family tensions by cooperating and sharing with other members of the family, and by showing loyalty to the members of the family group.

6. Children are expected to perform whatever appropriate chores are asked of them, and to care for whatever clothes, toys, furniture, etc., the parents provide.

There is increasing awareness of the heavy demands placed on parents in today's rapidly changing world, with recognition of the frequent limitations of parental strength in an industrial, urban society. To be a parent, indeed, is a demanding task. A level of competence and skill above that needed for one's personal functioning in society is obviously required to be a parent. The question of how to determine a parent's ability to discharge these functions and how to ensure that adults are capable of being parents is of great importance in America today.

Single-Parent Families

Because of the growing number of children who will spend time in single-parent families, we will devote special attention to them. The most fundamental difference between a single- and two-parent family is that marriage is distinctly separated from parenting. The two-parent family life style includes the responsibilities and pleasures of both marriage and child rearing, whereas the single-parent family focuses solely on child rearing. The ramifications of this fact are complex. They include the absence of readily available support from another adult for the single parent, as expressed through the loneliness reported by many single parents. Another consequence is that children are involved in family roles ordinarily occupied by an adult—for example, the boy who becomes the "man of the house."

It is useful to distinguish between a single-parent *family* and a single-parent *home*, because the actual life style of a single-parent family depends upon a variety of extrafamilial circumstances. The extremes range from a mother and children living with her parents in an extended family home, as commonly encountered in black Mississippi families, to an isolated parent and child living without social supports in a one-room urban ghetto apartment. In between are a variety of possibilities that include the virtual functioning of a two-parent family in which the separated parent, usually the father, maintains financial, emotional, and social responsibility for the children through an elaborate visitation arrangement. As can be seen, the single-parent family has a larger variety of forms than the two-parent family.

Assuming the single-parent home to be one in which a parent and children live independently, the family life is most commonly arranged around the parent's employment, and delegation of child care occurs, particularly for young children. This means that family interactions and stresses are early in the morning and in the evening. More homemaking tasks are delegated to children and the single parent bears a greater burden of evening and weekend routine household and shopping tasks than in two-parent homes. Even though day care centers assist in some communities, the logistics of transportation, attending meetings, and keeping informed of child activities may strain the resources of the single parent in arranging these activities for the children. Without an assisting adult, which can occur in two-parent families also, the single parent must expend additional effort to keep up with the school and community lives of the children. For example, conferences with teachers are difficult to schedule during working day hours.

Although little reliable information is available on this point, the emotional tone of the single-parent home deserves special attention. The image of harassed, fatigued, irritable single parents attempting to fill their own social needs in the face of continued demands from their children is probably inaccurate. The time demands of an adult social life and child rearing do necessitate compromises between the two, however. The social life of a single parent does not automatically flow as it does for a married couple. It is likely that many, if not most, single-parent homes have a positive emotional tone, particularly for the two-thirds with separation and divorce in the background, for which the single-parent state might be less tension-ridden than the previous two-parent family.

Indirect evidence on satisfaction with family life of single parents can be drawn from the Quality of American Life Survey, which found that married women were satisfied with family life four times more than neutral or dissatisfied; whereas divorced or separated women were equally as likely to be satisfied or neutral or dissatisfied with family life (Campbell, 1976).

For single parents who work, arranging child care is a major task. The best out-of-home care for young children is usually offered by nursery schools which have limited hours. Partly because of the more convenient hours for working parents, day care staffs work long hours in poor facilities with little equipment. The working conditions and low wages lead to a high turnover, so that most workers are inexperienced. If parents were charged the full cost of quality care the price would be prohibitive, so that public support is needed. As a result, single parents either spend large amounts of time and energy selecting and working for the day care center of their choice or they ignore the matter.

A relaxation in job requirements, both from the point of view of hours and opportunities, has made it possible to accommodate more to child rearing than was possible in the past. Thus, infants of working mothers may find themselves with their mothers at work for various proportions of time. The current realities, however, tend to place children in day care from eight to ten hours on a five-day-a-week basis and permit little flexibility for child rearing leaves of absence, part-time work, and other than day shift working schedules. Part-time employment, however, is not economically feasible for most single parents. The two common child rearing situations in single-parent homes, then, are those of a welfare supported mother at home with her children or a working mother delegating child care.

Under optimal cicumstances, single-parent families have contact with separated parents, friends, relatives, and neighbors who relate to their children. There tend to be multiple adults in the children's lives, and this may include a significant relationship outside the family, such as with a Big Brother or Big Sister. Although some single-parent families lack identification models other than the single parent, many provide multiple models for their children.

One of the special concerns in single-parent homes is the development of impulse control and self-discipline in children. Because of the multiple adults involved in their lives, and sometimes because of parental overprotection or neglect, children tend to lack the limit setting provided in a home with two adults who are able to support each other in setting limits. The result is that children growing up in single-parent families may lack self-discipline.

Another factor in the single-parent family is the relationship of the children to friends of the single parent. At one extreme is the transient involvement with adult friends of the single parent, posing repeated painful separation experiences for them and contributing to a chaotic situation at home. At the other extreme are enduring stable relationships with the single parent's friends who become surrogate parents for the children. In either case the situation is more complicated than with the two-parent family.

From the point of view of the children's perceptions and attitudes toward adults, it is likely that children in single-parent families are thrown more upon their own resources to develop adult relationships, and thereby may gain greater skill in social relations. One of the points made by single parents who chose that life style is that their children grow up with broadened social horizons. It is also likely that those children are exposed to attitudes and values that do not reflect traditional thinking. The buffeting, disappointment, and disillusionment experienced by some single-parent families, on the other hand, undoubtedly lead these children to develop resentment and distrust for adults.

Extensive research has been carried out on the role of the father in child development and the effects of the father's absence. In experimental situations, a child's response to either father or mother during the first two years is more a function of the nature of the parent-child interaction than of a biological predisposition (Kotelchuck, 1976). The father is the primary role model for the young boy, but only when the father–son relationship has been affectionate. Fathers also play a role in the cognitive and moral development of competence in their offspring, particularly sons (Lamb, 1976). In boys the effects of the father's absence may appear as feminized behavior during the preschool years, but with increasing age these effects often disappear or are transformed into compensatory masculinity. In girls the effects of the father's absence are minimally evident during the early years; however, during adolescence, problems in responding appropriately in heterosexual relationships may become apparent.

The effects of the father's absence, both direct and indirect, are most evident if the father leaves during the preschool years, but they can be modified by positive factors, such as a mother who fosters appropriate gender role behavior and the presence of male siblings.

It is evident that the single-parent family is a complex phenomenon that requires an understanding of social expectations, specific family traditions, and previous experiences, practical economic and physical conveniences of living, social and interpersonal challenges and opportunities, and intrapsychic experiences. For single parents who elect this life style, one fact becomes salient: they do not feel a strong need for intimacy in relationships with people of the same age or have had experiences which lead them to believe it is not possible. Whether or not this represents a deficiency in the capacity for intimacy and therefore constitutes a problem or whether it is simply a variation is a matter of judgment. It is evident, however, that intimacy in single-parent families exists between the parents and children. The risk is that the parent-child relationship may be given exaggerated importance and used to fill emotional needs in the adult to the detriment of the child. At the very least, the child does not have the opportunity to experience a bond between two adults in intimate family living. From the developmental point of view, this is probably the greatest influence of the single-parent family on children. Even when an adequate visitation program has been worked out with the absent parent, the child is not exposed to a model of a mutually rewarding marriage bond.

Optimal Parenting

In the preceding chapter we summarized current knowledge about the needs of children along specific lines of development. We will now place the general needs of children in the perspective of each stage of life. Before doing so, however, several considerations about parenting deserve attention.

Wealthy mothers have not, in the past, brought up their own children, for reasons of status; in this century working mothers are ceasing to bring up their children, for reasons of need; and professional mothers for reasons of competing intellectual and cultural interests and responsibilities. This leaves the hard core of middle-class women, who, despite all temptations, stubbornly insist on doing their own mothering. In another vein, Israeli kibbutz mothers turn over rearing of their children to metapelets on both ideological and practical grounds, so that men and women share equally in running a kibbutz. All of this has stimulated questions about parenting roles for both women and men.

Most important, our society has discarded the security of the old world order based upon the image of a powerful father that permeated the family, church, and state. The American revolutionary age of throwing off the authority of a British king has been reflected in a subsequent trend toward the rejection of parental authority, as sons take their fathers' places, even showing lack of respect rather than rivalry. This attitude permeates current society so that experience and tradition tend to be suspect rather than respected. Without a new model, there is a diffusion of responsibility and anonymity which may account for a general loss of concern about meeting expectations and a lack of interest in ideas that call for active, constructive participation—the tendency is to "let things slide" (Mitscherlich, 1963). Nowhere is this more apparent than in the recent trend toward "anything goes" in child rearing practices.

Further compounding uncertainty about what is expected of them is the progressive shift from the peasant tradition, in which the lives of their parents took place before children's eyes, through industrial family life, in which the parents' work ceased to be visible to the children but could still be talked about and comprehended, to the most recent state of office workers, whose working lives cannot be comprehended even when efforts are made to explain them to children.

It is no wonder, then, that the current child rearing ethos is characterized by confusion and lack of direction. A fundamental shift toward clarifying child rearing objectives, the developmental needs of children, and child rearing styles is necessary to avoid the consequences of ignoring the dependency of children upon adults for nurturance, protection, regulation, modeling, guidance, and encouragement to become independent persons. As we do so, however, it is important to recognize that an individual child does not exist as a solitary unit. A child is dependent on dyadic subunits and larger child rearing systems within society. Because it is used for socialization purposes by society, childhood is also a focus of conflicts between the interests of children, families, schools, and broader society. A number of influences compete for expression through children.

From the outset, children are dependent on others for survival. All of their physical needs must be met consistently if they are to thrive. Sustained parental apathy or hostility will almost certainly prejudice development, as seen with infants who "fail to thrive" (Rutter, 1974). Consequently, from infancy, children must be capable of expressing their tensions and attracting help from others. Generally, even the least observant of parents can learn to recognize a child's physical needs. More difficult to interpret are a child's emotional needs. Not only is a child far less able to express them, but they are infinitely more complex and subtle. A child's attempts to communicate them may be overlooked or misunderstood. The child's total dependence makes the development of a sense of separate existence essential from the outset. Without it, children would be straws blown in the wind. So many complex skills must be mastered in our society, and so many internal and external obstacles overcome, that without encouragement from others and a sense of self-confidence, there is little likelihood that any real maturity can be reached.

It is essential that from the beginning children must receive from those around them encouragement and assistance in their development. Such assistance makes it possible for them to correct inappropriate responses, and to pattern their behavior in ways which are suitable for later adult life in the community. Indeed, just as there are innate, genetically determined factors prompting children to seek out the bodily satisfactions essential for general development, so there is also an equal need to be taught how best to communicate and thereby to discharge tensions most efficiently. Where consistent parenting has made it obvious that their needs will be met and that they are capable of communicating their needs effectively, children will absorb sufficient self-assurance to develop further. However, when parental inadequacy has failed to give them either the certainty that essential satisfactions will be forthcoming or the knowledge that they are communicating effectively, they will continue searching ineffectively for ways of relieving their tensions.

Even more dramatically, Heber and Garber's controlled studies offer evidence that maternal inadequacy is associated with progressive decline in the IQ of children. The longer the exposure to such lack of "maternal supplies," the greater the decrement in IQ. They also found that such deprivation effects can be reversed by intensive intervention in early life (Heber, 1968; Garber, 1975).

Parenting required for healthy personality development seems to consist largely of a willingness to assist and enjoy the normal maturation of a child (Group for the Advancement of Psychiatry, 1973). Where a parent views any situation from a child's standpoint, and understands what is needed, no serious personality distortion follows, regardless of the child rearing techniques employed. Where, however, child rearing situations are battlegrounds for parental hostility, an exaggeration of a child's personality development may take place. The most critical factor is that an affectionate bond exists between parent and child. No child rearing techniques will succeed in a hostile interaction.

Some parents have extraordinary difficulty in relating satisfactorily to their children. Usually, such parents suffered frustration in their own childhoods and were not given adequate approval or opportunities for self-assertion as children. These parents did not obtain sufficient personality integration to give unquestioningly to their own children. They, therefore, tend to see parenthood primarily as a means of satisfying their own needs rather than as means of assisting an infant to maturity. Furthermore, many young adults are preoccupied with concerns about their own potential adequacy as parents rather than finding themselves drawn to the intrigue and excitement of nurturing a child.

Our task now is to review knowledge about optimal child rearing environments that can facilitate an unobstructed movement of children through the various developmental stages of their lives within society's child caring systems. Before doing so, a comment should be made about the unfortunate tendency to talk in terms of "training" children, casting adults in the role of patterning, teaching, or training children—and dogs. As adults, we do not like to think of ourselves as being "trained." Winnicott cogently points out that substituting "facilitating" child development for "training" is more accurate and humane (1965).

We will view the panorama of early development, emphasizing the first four years of life because of their critical importance in establishing the foundations of human existence. It is during these early years that an individual's abilities to relate to other people, to master self and environment, and to commit oneself to social values sink their roots. As can be surmised, the stakes for society of less than adequate formation of these capacities during these early years are high indeed.

INFANCY

Each infant requires an adult who is unconditionally committed to that child's welfare, and one who will respond to distress signals, give comfort when needed, relieve tension, and be an interactive social partner (Fraiberg, 1977). As a part of the "nursing couple," the primary caretaker mediates between the baby and the environment and regulates the intensity of stimulation, being the source of both gratification and frustration. To the extent that the parent's responses are predictable, the child's environment—and life—acquire continuity. If a child is exposed regularly to several parenting figures, there should be discriminably different levels of relationships with them. Such a relationship increases the likelihood that one caretaker will develop particular sensitivity to the individual characteristics and needs of the infant. In this way, the infant will experience different levels of relationships and will be able to form a clear primary attachment. With dispersion of mothering functions among several caretakers, the likelihood of each one developing feelings of attachment to an individual child is diminished (Yarrow, 1968).

The importance of the primary infant-parent attachment has been pragmatically recognized in societies that employ communal child rearing—for example, in the Soviet Union every working mother is entitled to full pay for four months after her baby is born and may remain home with her child for up to one year and retain the right to her job (Meers, 1968). In an Israeli kibbutz, the mother does not work at all for six weeks and does not return to a full working day for nine months, coming to the baby mornings and afternoons during the first year of life (Neubauer, 1965).

During infancy, the parent is an initiator of stimulation through smell, taste, touch, sight, hearing, and movement sensations resulting from the baby's physical contact with the parent's body. This physical contact gratifies the child's need for tension reduction and raises the infant's general awareness and responsiveness to the environment. This includes bringing the baby into contact with things to be manipulated to encourage the child to solve problems. During the first months, smell, taste, and tactile-kinesthetic sensations are the most important, gradually being supplemented by visual and auditory perceptions.

Consistency and repetition in an infant's experience help create a physical and psychic state conducive to learning. A baby needs significant periods of time free from major discomfort and tension to give attention to people and things in the environment. Within that atmosphere, variety and contrast created by playing, talking to, and handling the baby sharpen the baby's perception and responsiveness through the process of imitation.

Stated in another way, the primary caretaker's activities help an infant establish smooth vegetative functioning through providing food in the right quantity, timing, and rhythm. She cares for the infant's body, keeping it not too cool, not too hot, dry and free from skin irritations. She provides protection from overwhelming stimulation which is too exciting or interferes with sleep, soothing also the upset baby. At the same time she sees that adequate sensory stimulation is available—for example, holding the baby during feeding while both gaze at each other. Babies also need responses from familiar voices to reinforce their own vocalizations. During the crawling phase they need space and places to explore, being allowed to discover things for themselves rather than being exposed to new places and opportunities too rapidly or too slowly.

The earliest exchanges between mother and baby influence a baby's developing powers of understanding so that the mother–child relationship is the crucible not only of emotional, but of intellectual development. Unfortunately, the age-old soothing techniques of swaddling, rocking, and suckling so effective in calming babies are rarely discussed with mothers of first babies today.

Extensive research has been carried out on what has been called "maternal deprivation," best summarized in Bowlby's work on attachment and separation and Langmeier's survey of the field (Bowlby, 1969, 1973; Langmeier, 1975). We now take for granted that many children admitted to hospitals or residential nurseries show an immediate reaction of acute distress; that many infants show developmental retardation following admission to poor-quality institutions and may exhibit intellectual impairment if they remain there for a long time; that there is an association between delinquency and broken homes; that psychopathic character disorders may result from multiple separation experiences and institutional care in early childhood; and that some children from rejecting and affectionless homes fail to develop physically. The issue now is not whether, but why and how, children are adversely affected by the failure to develop, distortion, or the disruption of bonds of attachment (Rutter, 1974).

Whether or not the primary or maternal bond innately differs from those developed with other people, the primary bond is especially important because of its greater strength. Although most commonly with the mother in our society, the primary bond need not be with a biological parent, the daily caretaker, or a female. Furthermore, the person with whom there is a primary bond is important for some things and not for others. For some aspects of development the same-sex parent has a special role, for other aspects the person who plays and talks most with the child, and for other aspects the person who feeds the child. The father, mother, brothers and sisters, friends, teachers, and others all have an impact on development but their influence and importance varies for different facets of development (Rutter, 1974).

The concept of "maternal deprivation" has been useful in focusing attention on the possible grave consequences of deficient or disturbed care in early life. The problems are too complex and individually variable, however, to be understood by limiting attention to the mother–child relationship. Past research on the early stages of child development has involved too exclusive a focus on the bond with the mother, with insufficient attention to the influence of others who play important roles, even in infancy: fathers, siblings, relatives, and sitters (Clarke, 1977). We know that blood relationship, the provision of physical needs, and constant availability are less important in child–parent bond formation than the quality of the love relationship. The attachment grows through reciprocal interaction in the comfortable play and exchange between parent and child rather than through the simple relief of bodily needs.

THE TODDLER STAGE

The toddler stage brings the rapid development of new functions such as walking, talking, self-feeding, and playing with toys. Toddlers need protected, selective exposure to the widening world in which they are intensely interested. The environment, then, should be "childproof" so that dangerous or fragile objects and places do not create an overly restrictive atmosphere. Toddlers need supervised freedom so that they can gradually learn to cope with environmental hazards. A child's curiosity about words, names, and the nature of things and phases can be met through picture books and excursions with trusted persons. Without support, a child is easily panicked by too much stimulation. This is a period of rapid passive learning during which children take in more than they can respond to verbally.

The socialization process that takes place during the second year does not proceed easily unless an adult to whom the child has developed a strong tie is available at least during parts of each day and is responsive to the child as an individual. The feeling of trust and deepening affection, the gradual fusing of ambivalent emotions, the establishment of controls, the growing awareness of the self, and the distinction between the self and the outside world fail to become stable, integrated parts of the personality unless this condition is fulfilled (Pavenstedt, 1967). Delegation of child care should be to other familiar adults, not to a group.

Control of bowels and urine and the acceptance of cleanliness in toilet habits flow from the example and approval of cherished adults. The process is facilitated by the discomfort of cold, wet diapers. In a literal sense, children become members of a community when they accept the necessity for cleanliness. Children's willingness to accede to the wishes of others—at a time when they can make decisions and choose between alternatives—is an important model for the entire process of socialization. All of this is enhanced by a child's use of a transitional object, such as a "security" blanket or toy, which permits a gradual and manageable shift from the earlier exclusive possession of the primary attachment figure.

Often overlooked are the many separations that the mother goes through in permitting the individuation of her child. The interdependence between the mother and child during the toddler phase poses many individuation opportunities which are difficult for both child and mother, both of whom are naturally ambivalent about separating from each other.

While the toddler explores a widening world, the early and comfortably firm introduction of limits helps in the discovery of dangers and the interests and needs of other people. The supervision of an adult is not only to provide support and reassurance, but also to provide reasonable frustrations through firm limit setting, so that the child becomes familiar with the constraints of both physical reality and group living. The overall American emphasis on individual freedom does not mean total freedom during the years of childhood. In fact, without accommodating to social realities early in life, a person may be continually frustrated during later years when the protection and indulgence of parenting is withdrawn.

Knowledge about the effects of day care prior to the third year of life is gradually accumulating. A recent study compared two groups of middle-class children who had entered day care at age two and at age three with well matched control groups (Blehar, 1974). The children's reactions to separation from their mothers and reunion and to proximity to a stranger were carefully measured in a standardized situation. Compared to controls, both groups of day care children showed less favorable reactions to their mothers and more avoidance of strangers. Results appeared more emphatic for the three-year-olds who, in contrast with children cared for in their homes, cried more upon separation, searched more for the absent mother, and touched, yet resisted, her more; they also engaged in markedly less exploratory behavior. The younger day care children also showed more avoidance behavior, possibly indicating a detachment process; the older ones manifested more anxious, ambivalent detachment. If these results are confirmed by others in this country, concern about the developmental effects of early day care, as reported in Czechoslovakia, are justified (Langmeier, 1975).

In the late 1920s and 1930s in the United States, two-year-olds were enrolled in nursery schools. But the results were unfavorable because the highly competitive two-year-olds' aggressive attacks outran the capacity of one teacher with a group of children to maintain peace. Children in such groups often were not happy and were anxious when separated from their mothers. As a result, by the mid-1940s many private nursery schools limited enrollment to children three years and older, and then beginning with half day attendance. More recently, smaller groups with lower adult-to-child ratios and more gradual separation of children from their parents suggest that the needs of two-year-olds can be met in highly specialized group care (Murphy, 1968).

Early Childhood

There is a point, varying widely in onset, at which each individual becomes a "person" and is no longer a "baby." Shedding diapers, tolerating separation from parents, and using adult language all signify that one has reached the threshold of entering society. During the middle of the third year, the transition from the toddler stage to becoming a young child is marked by a child's capacity to carry an internal mental image of mother, permitting longer periods of separation, if necessary, for a full day toward the end of the third year.

During this age separation should occur not by taking the child away from the primary attachment figure, but with her continuous assistance in leaving the child in a reassuring environment. Separation is a step toward independence and a higher form of self-awareness. Through separation from her, a child begins to observe mother on a new level of differentiation which will lead to sex differentiation. She is seen not only as mother, but also as a woman; the father then also becomes a man and the child a boy or a girl. The observance of anatomical differences between the sexes raises questions about them. It is important for children of this age to be in contact with adults and other children of both sexes in an atmosphere conducive to the free expression of curiosity and the answering of questions. Suppression of curiosity or denial of sex differences is confusing for the child and obstructs a comfortable development of a sense of self-identity. Imitation of and identification with an adult of the same sex primarily and the opposite sex secondarily facilitates adopting a comfortable gender identity.

The intensity of pleasure in bodily functioning is unique for this period and never reaches the same height again. This pleasure seems to give boundless energy for the repetition of physical activities so that running, jumping, and rolling may be repeated to exhaustion. Thus, open space for freedom of movement is a requirement for this age. Small rooms which inhibit exploration and motor activity may interfere with these important developmental experiences. Space limitation may force the child into "wild" activities which continually lead to more restrictions from adults. Under undue restrictions, some children tie themselves to adults with increasing dependency or negativism; others may be led to precocious verbal or fantasy substitution for action. With overrestriction, joyfulness gives way to caution and self-confidence to overcontrol. The explorer may become prematurely harnessed with impairment of self-image.

Special attention to the magical thinking characteristic of the young child is warranted because of the need to help children of four and five distinguish between frightening fantasies and actions (Fraiberg, 1959). Most important, children need adults who can accept and absorb violent, patently ridiculous fantasies without squelching or humiliating them. These fantasies are particularly pleasurable and frightening when they involve romantic wishes toward the parent of the opposite sex and hostile wishes toward the parent of the same sex. Particular problems are posed for a child when real life events reflect the fulfillment of wishes—for example, when the separation of parents fulfills a boy's fantasied wish to marry his mother and elminate his father.

A child's curiosity expands from "What's that?" to "Who's that?" questions, including an awareness of self as expressed through the use of "I" and "my." Even collective child rearing systems have found that the possession of things and a personal space are necessary ingredients of an individual's development of a sense of self, perhaps reflecting an innate need for personal territory. The basic possessions of children are less an expression of materialism and more a developmental need to individuate and experience separation from attachment figures through possession of something that belongs to no one else. By possessing some things exclusively, the child can learn the significance of sharing as well.

When together, children of this age are more accurately viewed as being in a group rather than as members of a group. At this age it is not the group that decides what will be played, it is the individual child. The group, therefore, should be small and should permit the continuity of a one-to-one relationship between an adult and each child. Rivalry for the exclusive attention of adults leads to confrontations which contribute to learning how to share attention. Other children become important as beginning friends or as objects of fear and anger, necessitating adult mediation to prevent overwhelming experiences. The more the group is seen as consisting of individuals in their own right, the more a child is able to find a comfortable place.

The routines of group living prepare a child to anticipate events and bring about a sense of regularity. Aiding a child to shift from free play to story time to resting is one of the essential functions of the adult. Activities should be set up in such a way that interruptions are possible at certain expected times, but still allow for finishing tasks. Encouragement to shift from one activity to another should recognize a child's wish for completion and achievement.

The rest time should be free from group stimulation so that children can enjoy activities from their own personal initiative and interests. Wide individual differences exist so that some children sleep and others engage in quiet solitary activities. For some, this is a period of regression into autoerotic activities, such as masturbation and thumbsucking. For others, it is a shift from motor activity to reverie. Still others seek close physical contact with adults.

The ability to "make a friend" signifies an important step in a child's development—the first independent act outside of the familiar child rearing system. Prior to that time a child has related to other people, usually older, who have been caretakers fulfilling the child's dependency needs. At some point a child begins to interact with other children in a cooperative way, most taking the initiative in seeking companionship. Although such unilateral friendships are temporary and susceptible to quarrels and disenchantment, the acquisition of a "pal" gives the child unique social and emotional experience not found in sibling relationships. During the fourth and fifth years of life, when a child is three and four, development is facilitated by group experiences with peers. For children raised in families there is a need for nursery school, while those in day care need opportunities for dyadic activities between children. Too many children miss the opportunity for these critical early friendships, both because of isolation from peers in homes and "drowning" in exposure to too many peers in group care. The opportunity to play with a peer either at home or in quiet, undisrupted corners in day care settings are vital to achieve the intimate opportunity for discovery and identification with someone else of the same developmental stage. This need persists throughout life.

Establishing a foothold in a peer group is a developmental task for the older young child. A child gains an appreciation of status and social identity among a group of developmental equals, expanding self-concept and differentiation from family members. By achieving acceptance in the group through subordinating self-interest and becoming sensitive to group approval, the child gains a measure of self-esteem from a "we-feeling" gained through belonging to the group.

Of great importance to a child's later approaches to work and recreation is the opportunity to assimilate the widening world of experience through play. At all ages the play of children is primarily concerned with portrayal and participation in real life situations. Except in pathological situations, young children use their imaginations less to create an unreal world and more to enact real roles, to simulate reality, and to fill in gaps for objects and capacities they lack. Play further permits learning vicariously about real life situations unavailable to the child because of limitations in status, ability, and opportunity.

One of the primary functions of peer play is the discovery and utilization of social and cultural patterns. Play acquaints a child with the existence of social rules and regulations and their positive, as well as negative,

consequences. Earlier the child discovered personal reality through interaction with adults, now social reality is discovered through interaction
with peers.

The most natural for children, and the most disturbing for adults, are
the various forms of free play, as seen in other primates: running, romp-
ing, catching, and rough-and-tumble. Free play is the creative expression
of both affectionate and aggressive feelings and sets the stage for formal
play through establishing the ability to "give and take" and the mutual exploration of strength and agility (Harlow, 1974). Young children need the
unfettered opportunity for free play with adult supervision but not domination. Creative play with raw materials, such as blocks and paints, also
provides for a sense of self-actualization and mastery.

The matter of toys and play materials deserves special attention, less
because of what they are and more because of attitudes toward them on
the part of both adults and children. On the one hand, toys can be seen as
a way of showing affection to children, and the quantity and quality as a
measurement of adult regard for the child. More commonly, in our affluent society, giving into a child's material request is the "easy way out" for
parents who feel guilty about shortchanging the child in other ways, or
who do not recognize the importance of learning to control urges to acquire during the early years.

When filling a developmentally appropriate need, toys are appreciated and used, but the young child is not served well in the long range if
a wish to have something is equated with receiving it. On the other hand,
toys and play materials can be distorted in the other direction. Some
adults hold the view that each play object should develop a skill: "the
child should have cubes and cups to practice eye–hand coordination."
Toy stores are filled with "educational toys," each one offering the hope
of providing a child with an advantageous edge in developmental progress. In balance, young children have a need for the judicious acquisition
of toys that truly are needed for play and that do not connote the adult's
regard for the child or the child's exploitation of the adult. This is the
arena in which both self-discipline and values about material things are
developed.

All of these considerations emphasize the social, emotional, and developmental nature of group care for young children. These are not years for
academic education. In fact, the imposition of passively experienced education either through nursery school or television during this period of life
is premature and runs the risk of depriving children of needed free play,
creative expression, and peer experiences. Early childhood is such a critical period of life that it deserves the most understanding and quality of attention. Unfortunately, it has received the least of each.

Of great importance, also, is the fact that there is wide variation between children, making generalizations by chronological age most diffi-

cult and accounting for significant fluctuations in the same child from one time to the next.

Caldwell has made a significant breakthrough in summarizing optimal child rearing environmental experiences as related to outcome in later life. Through the use of the Home Observation for Measurement of the Environment instrument, her group found 15 optimal child rearing environmental qualities that apply generally to the early years of life (Bradley, 1977):

1. Gratification of physical needs and providing for the health and safety of the child.
2. A high frequency of adult contact, preferably with both sexes and with a small number of adults.
3. A positive emotional climate permeated with trust and with assurance to the child that the parents will be there when the child needs them.
4. Recognition and acceptance of individual differences in children by significant adults.
5. An optimal level and pattern of need gratification which is not too much, nor too little, not too immediate, nor too late. This includes opportunities for joy, group contact, quiet and solitary reflection.
6. Variation within patterned sensory and informational inputs that are not too strong nor too weak.
7. People who love and support a child and provide cues regarding appropriate behavior and their adult values.
8. Limited restrictions on a child's exploratory behavior to avoid snuffing out curiosity.
9. A rich and varied cultural experience based upon family background and each individual's heritage.
10. Careful organization of physical and temporal environment so that a child can develop expectancies and predictability in order to provide a cognitive map through which children can interpret space and time.
11. Simple play materials to facilitate the development and coordination of sensory-motor processes. Someone also needs to invest the toys with value, for example, a boy who says "I don't have anything to play with" may pick up a toy that his mother has handled and indirectly suggested he use.
12. Gradual exposure to and participation in the world of work not as a passive recipient but as an active contributor.
13. Opportunities to share talents and skills without destructive criticism. Adults must control destructive peer criticism, for example, laughing at mistakes and teasing each other.

14. Overlap between different environments in which the child is expected to function, for example, between home and day care center by interaction between parents and staff.
15. Adults who find children to be satisfying and rewarding.

MIDDLE CHILDHOOD

The time comes when children can assume responsibility for personal safety in familiar neighborhoods without major safety hazards. Ordinarily, this is around the age of five and reflects the development of cognitive, judgmental, and motor functions that permit circumscribed times of self-responsibility. The acquisition of these skills heralds the "stable" years of middle childhood, from five through eight.

As children move out into their neighborhoods, they also are prepared to enter the intellectual and cultural aspects of society as well. At the ages of five, six, and seven, children embrace the exciting world of school and neighborhood play. In a formal sense they learn to read and cipher, and informally they discover the lore and folkways of children, orally transmitted in the form of age-old games, tales, and customs. The peer group performs a largely unrecognised socializing function through passing on these traditions.

Although adults from outside the family have related previously in caretaking and supportive ways to young children, it is during the early school years that children look for and assimilate adult models for identification. Teachers, public heroes, and older children are adulated just as children glorify their own exploits through daydreaming. Acceptance by these idealized figures then is needed; rejection or indifference by them can negatively influence the child's attitude toward school and society. If the child's initial enthusiasm is generally welcomed, the child's academic career is off to a good start. If not, the entire academic road may be rough. For this reason, an understanding of individual differences in capacities and developmental rates is essential at the outset of formalized schooling.

The ages of five through eight represent the period during which children are capable of establishing their places in their homes, schools, and communities. "My family, my home, my school, and my friends" become important factors in establishing a solid foundation for "my life." Because of the child's need for this solid foundation, changes in location of home and school have a more disruptive effect than before or after these years. Children need to "settle in" to their newly found "working" and social lives.

Like home and school, the peer group is an important socializing institution. With peers, children learn much of their poise in dealing with persons outside the intimate family circle, acquire techniques of sociability, self-assertion, competition, and cooperation, and develop sensitivity to group expectations, censure, and approval. The peer group provides a new source of values and standards, also providing children with support in shifting emotional anchorage from their parents.

During the years of middle childhood, children become capable of rational thinking and enthusiastically engage in the acquisition of reading, writing, and arithmetic skills. Although some children can be taught these skills at earlier ages, the natural maturation of the brain brings these capacities at individually determined rates with several years variation, necessitating careful handling of those who are maturing at slower rates. Through the acquired use of symbols, academic skills enable integration into society.

From a child's point of view, all developmental factors open the child to acculturation by society—"all systems are go." The plasticity and educability of these years permits the absorption of culture. If society, largely through schooling, does not respond to this opportunity, a child may be lost to it. Middle childhood, then, constitutes society's chance to influence its young who have been prepared by their caretakers of earlier years. From myths and realistic social roles are drawn the content of play, as well as values that guide the child in becoming a member of society. Familiarity with one's culture is the product of the middle years. If it is not achieved, the child may become alienated not only from school and peer group but from society as well (Sarnoff, 1976).

LATE CHILDHOOD

The years between nine and thirteen have been largely ignored in the past. They are ambiguously referred to as preadolescence or the subteens. Even though schools have not known how to relate to this group effectively, the fact that this period involves unique developmental issues has not been fully appreciated. These years are the peak of childhood, bringing childhood dreams and fantasies to their fullest development within the context of reality, as through creating a personal world of adventure through "science fiction." The preadolescent years do not constitute a separate stage, but are the culmination of childhood.

The most important factor fostering development in late childhood is the peer group, not the intellectual stimulation of the school curriculum. This is a paradox when the remarkable cognitive and mental development of this age is considered. As children gain considerable skill in coming to grips with reality, they go through intense emotional experiences based upon the realization that the world beyond their families is no longer mysterious or dangerous. They discover that the world is subject to rules and laws that can be mastered. As a consequence, children gain confidence and become ready to loosen emotional ties with their families in order to strengthen their social relationships with the broader world. This readiness is decisively reinforced by the peer group, which helps children to translate the cognitive knowledge they are gaining into new social and emotional experiences. The central tendency for older children is striving toward freedom from parental and adult control in an attempt to gain status and emotional security among peers. A developmental revolt of varying intensity against adult authority leads to daring to disobey parents and teachers at the same time that there is willing acceptance of orders from peer group leaders. Paradoxically, the superficial antagonism between the sexes is actually an expression of a striving to strengthen gender activity.

In the socialization of older children the adult plays at least three different roles: (1) the restricting and protecting adult, (2) the educating, demanding adult, and (3) the grownup friend or "near adult" (Kohen-Raz, 1971). Intimate knowledge about the "real world" and its values cannot be adequately transmitted by the peer group. Only adults can be trusted to perform this task. Without a "near adult" influence to balance the influence of the peer group, older children are vulnerable to an antisocial direction, as currently illustrated by the pleasure-oriented cults of drug usage, skipping classes, and "partying," a direction that begins during the late childhood years.

It is no wonder that adults encounter great difficulties in establishing contact with older children, who often seem dull-witted, difficult, strange, stubborn, and unreliable. Actually, children of this age test adults to find out which of the three previously mentioned roles the adults intend to play. Consequently, it is natural that they provoke, play tricks on, deceive, and nag adults to force them to reveal their attitudes. Adults are damned if they try to keep everything under control and break up the peer group. They also fail if they pretend to be "one of the kids" and betray their true potential as grownup friends. Because our society does not institutionalize the "near adult," except through people such as scout leaders and coaches, many children experience a developmental lack in their need for a grownup friend. Adults, or more conveniently, teachers, neighbors, and youth workers who cultivate that role are needed.

The intellectual level of older children is close to that of the average adult and would theoretically satisfy the requirements of many semiskilled and skilled occupations. Thus, in primitive cultures where social and economic factors permit, older children leave the family. In previous generations of our own society children of these years entered vocations.

Since school is the major occupation of older children in America it is important to recognize that the hormonal, physical, mental, and emotional changes of this period tend to loosen moorings to their families and teachers, and to their own childhoods. An important aid in solidifying their own achievements is the opportunity to experience leadership and status with younger children. The practice of segregating children of this age in junior high schools or middle schools has deprived young people of their need to place a capstone on childhood. Daily contact with younger children helps older children to recognize and integrate their achievements and to achieve more advanced maturation. Although quite capable of victimizing the younger, older children are also rewarded by opportunities to teach and help younger children. They are also not ready to be placed in competition with teenagers. Their developmental needs are for adult recognition of their seniority in childhood, integration in a peer group, and individual, intimate contact with an adult friend.

YOUTH

Unfortunately, the image of adolescence is one of storm and stress based more upon superficial signs of nonconformity, particularly adolescent faddish behavior, and moments of childish regression than the fact that teenagers are generally rebellious and irresponsible. This exaggerated view of teenagers is of complex origins and obscures the fact that adolescence is an important, lawful, and describable stage of development through which the vast majority smoothly progress as people do through any other stage of the life cycle (Bandura, 1971; Offer, 1969). Because a small minority of teenagers are involved in visible community problems and because of the occasional indiscretion of most, adolescents have not been realistically viewed as the beginning adults they are.

The more complex the society, the longer adolescence lasts. In a primitive society adolescence may correspond to physical puberty. In our society it probably extends from the onset of puberty to the mid-twenties, an arbitrary age period based upon the assumption that no one can be classified as an adult prior to 14 and no one can be classified as a dependent child after the twenty-fifth birthday. Furthermore, sex differences with an average of two-year earlier onset of puberty for girls than for boys and individual variations in physical, emotional, and social maturity make generalizations about age most difficult. Indeed, the central question for each adolescent is, "When am I old enough to. . .?"

Our society has passed through two phases in its treatment of youth. In the first, the "work phase," youth were brought as quickly as physical maturity would allow into adult jobs. In the second phase, the "schooling phase," youth are being kept as long as possible in school and out of the labor force. Schools are oriented toward cognitive achievement, imposing dependency on and withholding authority from young persons who are kept in the role of students. We are faced, however, with the task of creating opportunities for all youth to become adults in all ways, not just intellectual ones. A third phase, accordingly, has been proposed, including, but not limited to, school and adding alternative environments to prepare youths more fully for adult social roles (Coleman, 1974).

Under favorable conditions of freedom from social demands or family responsibilities and exposure to an educational environment designed to promote and direct intellectual growth, adolescents can devote full time and energy to perfecting physical, social, and intellectual skills. They are able to explore ideas, ideals, roles, beliefs, theories, commitments, and all sorts of possibilities at the level of thought. Adolescents can create mentally more desirable alternatives for themselves and for society. There is more than a little egocentrism in this high-flown thought, but the adolescent perforce achieves a "decentering" through interaction with peers and elders, and, increasingly, with the assumption of adult roles and responsibilities. The focal point of the decentering process is entrance into the occupational world or the beginning of serious professional training. Adolescents become adults when they enter their vocations (Neimark, 1974).

Environments for youth should be addressed to expand the personal skills and resources of each individual in preparation for assuming responsibilities that affect other persons. Of the desirable personal resources, the following stand out: skills necessary for obtaining a job, capability to manage one's own affairs, and the capability to become a consumer not only of material goods but of cultural offerings. Of the activities involving other persons, the following are important: experience with persons differing in social class, subculture, and age, the experience of having others dependent on one's actions, and involvement in interdependent activities directed toward collective goals as leaders and followers. All of these skills and experiences serve to refine one's sense of identity and self-esteem.

The segregation of youth from other age groups—in particular, working adults—was in part responsible for the development of the "youth culture" in the last decade. That alienated and detached separate world of youth persists today in a variety of forms ranging from detached social groups in high school to distinct movements that change in form but focus upon counterculture charismatic leadership (Kett, 1977). Without attachments to adult models, youths naturally turn to the peer group, which in turn can be manipulated by leaders who both fill dependency needs and offer an attractive life style, which parenthetically can be either hedonistic or ascetic in orientation.

Modifications in school structure should be made to correct the imbalance that now exists in which young persons can only be in student roles. Increasing and emphasizing the nonacademic content, alternating school and work, making school facilities available for recreational, social, and athletic activities after school hours, bringing adolescents into the management of school discipline and most critically reducing educational unit size so that face-to-face socialization is possible especially within the context of a large school—all of these are being and can be implemented in school systems.

Beyond the schools, however, is the need for communities to legitimize the social and recreational needs of adolescents through providing more than homes and street corners for the social lives of teenagers. The availability of youth organizations, social centers, entertainment and community service volunteer jobs can do much to provide for the nonschool aspect of teenagers' lives. For youth after high school, we should not overlook the benefits of public service jobs, such as in the armed forces and Peace Corps, in filling the need for youth to live through their "psychosocial moratorium" (Erikson, 1963).

In brief, teenagers need both education in the "schooling" sense and opportunities to assume and develop their capacities for responsibility. The latter are deficient in the lives of most teenagers, leaving them without knowledge of their capabilities and without full awareness of the importance of assuming responsibility not only for themselves, but for others as well. More important, we should shift from linking responsibility to chronological age and base it on demonstrated capability. Adolescents can aspire to adult privileges and responsibilities and be relatively unaware of their limitations. They require life experience beyond the maturation of their mental equipment to provide the basis for decision making and developing judgment.

Although it is evident that anyone requires orientation, training, and experience to become capable of decision making in a new job, it is often difficult for an adolescent to recognize that assuming specific adult responsibilities is of the same order. But herein lies a possible answer to the question of what rights and responsibilities are within the grasp of an adolescent at a particular age. Individual variations could be accounted for by offering graduated steps toward each responsibility, with demonstration of a skill or decision-making capacity as the point at which a responsibility can be assumed. The principle is simple enough: in questionable instances, a trial of responsibility can determine an individual's readiness to assume it. For many parents, reluctance to permit adolescents to try something themselves only delays maturation and breeds rebellion. The essential point is that adolescents need graduated early pathways to responsibility so that they are not confronted with wrenching sudden shifts into responsibilities that prove overwhelming.

The adolescent generation has always reflected, and will undoubtedly continue to reflect, both the strengths and weaknesses of contemporary society. As such, youth holds a mirror up to the adult world, which is generally not pleased by what it sees. We are both afraid of and threatened by young people. It is not pleasant for adults to be reminded of their weaknesses and to face the criticisms of the young who see our faults so clearly. It is not pleasant for parents to witness the progressive growth of their children away from them. It is discouraging for many adults to accept the fact that our young people will no longer need adults, and one day may care for us. But the obvious fact is that one day the young will take the place of the older. It should be no surprise, then, that adults hold ambivalent feelings toward youth and that the potential for misunderstanding and mistrust abounds between generations.

Ecology and Children

The phenomena of urbanization and modern technology have been generally unfriendly to children. Any barriers between children and the rhythms and resources of nature must be critically examined to determine whether or not they have destructive implications for the socialization of children. More involvement of architecture, engineering, environmental design, natural resource management, and regional and urban design in planning for children is needed (Gump, 1975; Canter, 1976).

A specific example of improving housing design to benefit children is through acoustical conditioning to reduce the role of noise as a contributing factor to family strife (Westman, 1971). Accumulated research on the effects of the ecological environment on children demonstrates, however, that the improvement of interior dwelling arrangements and facilities will not solve the problem of secure and active living in communities for children. We must ask to what extent are the places, persons, things, and events which suggest interesting activity and sociality available to children. Space that is easily monitored is necessary for young children. Outdoor play space and commercial settings frequented by school age children are needed. Access to other children of comparable play age are important as well. Danger that prevents the use of informal outdoor space for socialization should be minimized.

The "neighborhood" is really a child-oriented concept. For most adults living in a neighborhood offers conveniences, but for children neighborhoods provide essential developmental experiences because they represent the arenas in which children learn about the world beyond their homes. Of greatest importance is the ability of children to gain mastery over the experiences encountered in their early neighborhoods. The templates for later interactions with people and places are formed in the neighborhoods of early life.

Relative safety and comfort in their early environments permit children to concentrate upon adapting their ever expanding and changing abilities to a relatively constant, predictable, and dependable world. Because they themselves are rapidly changing, children do not need changes in neighborhoods to provide stimulation and challenges. Most children are enriched by exposure to a few new supportive adults and places during the third year of life and to stimulating and educational environments during the fifth year. From eight to nine they seek out an expanding peer group and are ready for more organized schooling. Friendships, athletics and social activities gain priority in high school. From the developmental point of view, then, even when living in the same home children experience at least four different neighborhoods reflecting their expanding worlds. By implication, if moves are to take place, these junctures in a child's life would be less disruptive than other times for the child.

If the neighborhood is experienced in a positive, engaging way, a child develops a sense of belonging to a community with inherent responsibility to others and a sense of involvement in and influence upon the world. If the neighborhood is experienced as threatening or indifferent, a child may not achieve that sense of involvement and participation in a community. As can be seen, the neighborhood in which a child grows up has significant implications for the society in which that child is to live.

Particular emphasis should be placed upon a child's neighborhood during the early school years. It is at this time that a child's development has proceeded to the point where an active exploration of new people and places can take place independently. The child can walk to school and discover a myriad of "I can do it myself" experiences. The independent, face-to-face contact with the school, stores, neighborhood streets and houses, playmates, flora and fauna build a picture of the world which becomes an indelible part of that child's later memories and attitudes. The inevitable accidents, injuries, and transgressions become opportunities for a child to learn how to handle responsibility, obtain help when needed, and help others. When these events take place among people who care enough to respond, a child's sense of belonging to a place and people has positive connotations. When other children and adults do not respond or are indifferent, a sense of alienation or hostility toward others develops, with all-too-familiar implications for antisocial behavior.

These points are particularly important in our currently mobile society, which includes transporting children to schools outside of their neighborhoods. Busing in itself does not disrupt the neighborhoods of rural children, for whom it permits the creation of a more complete neighborhood when distances between people are great. In urban areas, however, the separation of a child's educational experience from the child's home neighborhood and peer group can discourage the sense of community that is important in that child's social development. It is no wonder that urbanization and overcrowding over the years have created large numbers of people who have grown into their adult years without a sense of community responsibility and "roots."

Another important influence on child development must be taken into account since the technological advent of television (Liebert, 1973). Because of its auditory and visual attractiveness to young and school age children, its powerful effects on the attitudes, values, and behavior of children are only beginning to be appreciated. American children between the ages of two and 11 average 26 hours a week of TV viewing. For all children most viewing is done throughout the day, every day, with a peak at 8:00 P.M. The single most powerful effect is the passive, nonparticipatory absorption of time, reducing spontaneity, conversational opportunities, free play, and reading. Television has broadened children's knowledge of the world, but it has potent effects on attitudes and on the modeling of social, sexual, and aggressive behavior as well. Television is the modern world's added socializer, motivated in part by public interest but more importantly by the promotion of materialistic consumption. As such, its positive and negative roles in child development must be recognized (NIMH, 1977; Stein, 1975; Howe, 1977).

Conclusion

Because they are remarkably adaptable and resilient, children can find nutriment even under arid and unrewarding parental conditions. In extremes, they do not complain about physically abusive parents nor do they realize that indulging their immediate pleasures leads to long-range frustrations. They can be left to fend for themselves, as in the case of the wild boy of Averyon, or they can be taught to perform adult labor by the age of four. Thus, the fate of children is in the hands of their families and society. They cannot be asked to set goals for their own rearing. The gratitude or remorse of children will be known only when they, themselves, become adults.

Even more, the rearing styles of children should not be simply a matter of adult preference. In extremes, parents either would pursue their own pleasures and ignore their children or tyrannize their children with unwarranted domination and oppression. Just as there are certain essential elements in physical growth—vitamins, minerals, and proteins—there are essential experiential elements for personality growth. These are simple and straightforward. The child requires a predictable environment in early life with a few continuous, dependable adult models who can be incorporated as identification figures by the child. Also essential is a well defined environment, so that the child can learn to separate fantasy from reality. When reality is obfuscated, the child becomes confused and cannot learn adaptive coping skills.

The family has endured through centuries of drastic changes because it has been comprised of a marital couple with adaptable numbers of children reflecting the times. All the evidence we have suggests that child rearing is most enjoyable, enriching, and successful when performed jointly by a mother and a father in the context of a secure marital relationship. On balance, the traditional family arrangements work fairly well. Despite the age-old challenges of radicals on both the left and the right, there is no better way to raise children than the family. As Winston Churchill said of democracy, it is the worst way—except for all the others (Glazer, 1978).

Methods of child rearing are part and parcel of the culture in which they are formulated and, accordingly, cannot be treated in isolation from society's priorities for children. These priorities are expressed through direct influence on child rearing systems and indirect influence on parents. If both parents must work on a full-time basis to earn a living wage, the indirect impact is to place their participation in child rearing at a secondary level of priority. If mothers are not able to recess from working responsibilities after childbirth and both they and fathers are unable to divert time to their children during the early years, child rearing again is given low priority. If the cost of raising children is prohibitive for parents, adults may choose not to have children or a greater cost is incurred through public payment for child care and the long-range cost to society of less-than-adequately raised children.

In sum, the priorities given to child rearing, and its consequent styles, are a product of the priorities set by culture and society. Our evolving society must place a high priority on child rearing or face extinguishing itself. There are few limits to what can be done *to* children. The question is what needs to be done *for* them.

References

ANTHONY, E. J., AND KOUPERNICK, C. (Eds.) (1974) *The Child and His Family: Children at Risk.* New York: Wiley.

BANDURA, A. (1971) "The Stormy Decade: Fact or Fiction." Chapter in Thornburg, H. D. (Ed.), *Contemporary Adolescence: Readings.* Belmont, Calif.: Brooks/Cole.

BANE, M. J. (1977) *Here to Stay: American Families in the Twentieth Century.* New York: Basic Books.

BERGER, N. (1967) *The Rights of Children and Young Persons.* London: Cobden Trust, pp. 1–2.

BLEHAR, M. C. (1974) "Anxious Attachment and Defensive Reactions Associated with Day Care." *Child Development,* 450:683–692.

BOWLBY, J. (1969) *Attachment and Loss*, Vol. 1, *Attachment*. New York: Basic Books.

BOWLBY, J. (1973) *Attachment and Loss*, Vol. 2, *Separation: Anxiety and Anger*. New York: Basic Books.

BRADLEY, R. H., AND CALDWELL, B. M. (1977) "Home Observation for Measurement of the Environment: A Validation Study of Screening Efficiency." *American Journal of Mental Deficiency*, 81:417–420.

CAMPBELL, A., CONVERSE, P. E., AND RODGERS, W. C. (1976) *The Quality of American Life: Perceptions, Evaluation and Satisfaction*. New York: Russell Sage Foundation.

CANTER, D. (1976) *Environmental Interaction*. New York: International Universities Press.

CARTER, H., AND GLICK, P. C. (1976) *Marriage and Divorce: A Social and Economic Study*. Cambridge, Mass.: Harvard University Press.

CLARKE, A. M., AND CLARKE, A. D. B. (1977) *Early Experience: Myth and Evidence*. New York: Free Press.

CLARKE-STEWART, A. (1977) *Child Care in the Family: A Review of Research and Some Propositions for Policy*. New York: Academic Press.

COLEMAN, J. (1974) *Youth: Transition to Adulthood*. Chicago: University of Chicago Press.

EATON, G. G. (1976) "The Social Order of Japanese Macaques." *Scientific American*, 237:97–106.

ERIKSON, E. H. (1963) *Childhood and Society*. New York: Norton.

FRAIBERG, S. (1959) *The Magic Years*. New York: Scribner.

FRAIBERG, S. (1977) *Every Child's Birthright: In Defense of Mothering*. New York: Basic Books.

FREEDMAN, L. Z. AND ROE, A. E. (1958) "Evolution and Human Behavior." Chapter in Roe, A., and Simpson, G. (Eds.), *Behavior and Evolution*. New Haven: Yale University Press, p. 461.

GARBER, H. L. (1975) "Intervention in Infancy: A Developmental Approach." Chapter in *The Mentally Retarded and Society*. Baltimore: University Park Press.

GLAZER, N. (1978) "The Rediscovery of the Family." *Commentary*, March, pp. 49–56.

Group for the Advancement of Psychiatry (1973) *The Joys and Sorrows of Parenthood*, Report No. 84. New York: Group for the Advancement of Psychiatry.

GUMP, P. V. (1975) "Ecological Psychology and Children." Chapter in Heatherington, E. M. (Ed.), *Review of Child Development Research*, Vol. 5. Chicago: University of Chicago Press.

HARLOW, H. F. (1974) *Learning to Love*. New York: Aronson.

HEBER, R., DEVER, R., AND CONRY, J. (1968) "The Influence of Environmental and Genetic Variables on Intellectual Development." Chapter in Prehm, H. J., Hamerlyrick, L. A., and Crosson, J. E. (Ed.), *Behavioral Research in Mental Retardation*. Eugene: University of Oregon Press.

HOBBS, N. (1975) *The Futures of Children*. San Francisco: Jossey-Bass.

HOWE, M. (1977) *Television and Children*. Hampton, Connecticut: Shoestring Press.

HUNT, D. (1970) *Parents and Children in History: The Psychology of Family Life in Early Modern France*. New York: Basic Books.

JOHNSON, C. C., AND JOHNSON, F. A. (1977) "Attitudes Toward Parenting in Dual-Career Families." *American Journal of Psychiatry*, 134:391–395, April.

KADUSHIN, ALFRED (1974) *Child Welfare Services*. New York: Macmillan.

KALTREIDER, N. B., AND MARGOLIS, A. G. (1977) "Childless by Choice: A Clinical Study." *American Journal of Psychiatry*, 134:179–182, February.

KETT, J. (1977) *Rites of Passage: Adolescence in America 1790 to the Present*. New York: Basic Books.

KOHEN-RAZ, R. (1971) *The Child from 9 to 13: Psychology and Psychopathology*. Chicago: Aldine-Atherton.

KOTELCHUCK, M. (1976) "The Infant's Relationship to the Father: Experimental Evidence." Chapter in Lamb, M. E. (Ed.), *The Role of the Father in Child Development*. New York: Wiley.

LAMB, M. E. (1976) "The Role of the Father: An Overview." Chapter in Lamb, M. E. (Ed.), *The Role of the Father in Child Development*. New York: Wiley.

LANGMEIER, J., AND MATEJCEK, Z. (1975) *Psychological Deprivation in Childhood*. New York: Wiley.

LIEBERT, R. M. (1973) *The Early Window: Effects of Television on Children and Youth*. New York: Pergamon Press.

MEERS, D. R., AND MARANS, A. E. (1968) "Group Care of Infants in Other Countries." Chapter in Chandler, C. A., Lourie, R. S., and Peters, A. D. (Eds.) *Early Child Care: The New Perspectives*. New York: Atherton Press.

MITSCHERLICH, A. (1963) *Society Without the Father*. New York: Harcourt, Brace and World.

MURDOCK, G. P. (1960) "The Universality of the Nuclear Family." Chapter in Bell, N. W., and Vogel, E. F. (Eds.), *The Family*. Glencoe, Ill.: Free Press.

MURPHY, L. B. (1968) "Individualization of Child Care and Its Relation to Environment." Chapter in Chandler, C. A., Lourie, R. S., and Peters, A. D. (Eds.), *Early Child Care: The New Perspectives*. New York: Atherton Press.

NATIONAL INSTITUTE OF MENTAL HEALTH (1977) *Television and Social Behavior*, Vols. 1–5. Washington, D.C.: Superintendent of Documents.

NEIMARK, E. D. (1974) "Intellectual Development During Adolescence." Chapter in Horowitz, F. D. (Ed.), *Review of Child Development Research*, Vol. 4. Chicago: University of Chicago Press.

NEUBAUER, P. B. (ED.) (1965) *Children in Collectives: Child-rearing Aims and Practices in the Kibbutz*. Springfield, Illinois: Charles T. Thomas.

NEUBAUER, P. B., AND FLAPAN, D. (1976) "Developmental Groupings in Latency Children." *Journal of Child Psychiatry*, 15:646–664.

OFFER, D. (1969) *The Psychological World of the Teen-ager: A Study of Normal Adolescent Boys*. New York: Basic Books.

PAVENSTEDT, E. (Ed.) (1967) *The Drifters: Children of Disorganized Lower-Class Families*. Boston: Little Brown.

REISS, J. L. (1971) *The Family System in America*. New York: Holt, Rinehart and Winston.

RUTTER, M. (1974) *The Qualities of Mothering: Maternal Deprivation Reassessed*. New York: Aronson.

SARNOFF, C. (1976) *Latency*. New York: Aronson.

SCHAFFER, R. (1977) *Mothering*. Cambridge, Mass. Harvard University Press.

SCHNEIDER, P. M., AND GOUGH, K. (1961) *Matrilinear Kinship*. Berkeley, California: University of California Press.

STEIN, H. H., AND FREIDRICH, L. K. (1975) *Impact of Television on Children and Youth*, Chicago: University of Chicago Press.

U.S. BUREAU OF THE CENSUS (1979) *Current Population Reports*, Series P-20, No. 333, "Marital Status and Living Arrangements: March 1978" Washington, D.C.: U.S. Government Printing Office.

U.S. DEPARTMENT OF LABOR (1979), *Working Mothers and their Children*. Washington, D.C.: Women's Bureau, Employment Standards Administration.

WESTMAN, J. C. (1971) "The Need for Sound Control in the Home." *Public Hearings on Noise Abatement and Control*, 7:324–330. Washington, D.C.: Environmental Protection Agency.

WINNICOTT, D. W. (1965) *The Family and Individual Development*. London: Tavistock.

WRIGLEY, E. A. (1977) "Reflections on the History of the Family." *Daedalus*, 106:71–85, Spring.

YARROW, L. J. (1968) "Conceptualizing the Early Environment." Chapter in Chandler, C. A., Lourie, R. S., and Peters, A. D. (Eds.), *Early Child Care: The New Perspectives*. New York: Atherton Press.

Part III
Strategies of Child Advocacy

Children are potentially free and their life directly embodies nothing save potential freedom. Consequently, they are not things and cannot be the property either of their parents or others.

George W. F. Hegel

This section describes how advocacy for children can take place. Class advocacy for children provides the social matrix within which individual advocacy becomes possible. Both are interdependent.

Chapter 6 deals with class advocacy as a means of influencing social policies. When individual advocacy fails, or for many children who suffer from global social problems, the only redress is through changing child caring systems. This chapter defines social policy, how it is determined, how it can be influenced, and obstacles to influencing it. A proposal is endorsed for a fundamental social policy committed to the conservation of this nation's developmental potential through supporting child development and family life. Specific means for carrying out such a policy are through improving child caring systems, ensuring access to specialized child supportive services, and cultivating individual differences in children. Various legislative, judicial, and educational methods of class advo-

137

cacy are then outlined. Rather than a separate child advocacy system, sensitizing existing systems to the needs of children and the education of professionals are proposed as more realistic vehicles for child advocacy.

In Chapter 7, the techniques of individual child advocacy are defined. Because advocacy techniques vary with the times and places in which professionals encounter children, the concepts of primary, secondary, and tertiary care are employed to explicate the nature of advocacy. At the first point of contact at the primary care level, advocacy techniques include sensitization to children's views of their lives, case finding at successive developmental milestones, and system-bridging methods of intervention. At the secondary care level, advocacy takes place through the integration of diagnostic studies and coordination of treatment by a designated case manager who can formulate a life plan for each child and follow that child to ensure continuity of care. At the tertiary care level, more complicated cases can be managed through planned temporary or permanent alterations in a child's life situation and guardianship. Although occasionally leading to a new life for the child through termination of parental rights, case advocacy generally means supporting and strengthening a child's family in its parenting functions.

Chapter 6
Class Child Advocacy

This chapter will deal with class child advocacy, the essential background for individual case advocacy. Without a context favoring the healthy development of children generally, it is difficult to meet the needs of an individual child. Surprisingly to some, promoting the general interests of children has not been an easy task. Such a simple thing as a kindergarten was seen in 1851 as a threat to the Prussian government. At that time military police closed Froebel's "garden for children," because it was regarded as a step toward collectivism. A similar rationale was evoked more than a century later in 1971 when a federal day care bill was vetoed because it might threaten the integrity of the American family and constitute a step in the direction of communism.

These dramatic examples illustrate the fact that actions taken for children stimulate reactions because of their long-range implications for society beyond whatever benefit they may provide for children. Overshadowing legitimate efforts to promote the interests of children, then, are fears of menace to society at one extreme, and appropriate caution about their long-range implications at the other extreme. Because class child advocacy cannot be based upon simplistic, quick solutions to immediate problems, knowledge of the process through which social policy is formed is essential for class advocacy. It is clear that, short of a major revolutionary cataclysm, the most dramatic form of policy change which America has fully experienced only once at its inception, deliberate changes in social policy have taken place as a result of planfully and patiently pursued long-range strategies.

First of all, we will define social policy; then we will examine how social policy is determined. This will be followed by ideas about how social policy can be influenced and obstacles to its change.

What Is Social Policy?

Although the organizing core of human societies from the tribal level on, social policies have only recently been seen as subjects for thoughtful study. The development of planning for the future as a scholarly pursuit through the discipline of futurism has focused attention on translating present and past experiences into guidelines for the future. Although intellectuals from the time of Plato have written about ideal societies, the injection of the future into general public awareness is distinctly a twentieth-century phenomenon. Past popular thinking about the future was largely about life after death, rather than about those who will be living on the earth after the death of its present inhabitants. This awareness that the current generation has an obligation to future generations is the climate in which the idea of planning for the future has grown.

Fundamentally, social policy is the crystallization of popular sentiment in a society arising through evolutionary or revolutionary means. Social policy is the articulation of a society's wishes for itself. Social policy, then, guides government in formulating public policies politically and society in formulating traditions and customs culturally. Because of the elaborate checks and balances of our democratic system, American social policy varies with the times and is formed slowly through an elaborate feedback system comprised of the interaction of our culture as expressed through popular sentiment with the legislative, executive, and judicial arms of government. An example of a social policy is support of an image of American military strength in the world. A resulting public policy is the commitment of funds to the defense budget. An example of a social policy that could evolve would be a commitment to support strong family units as social institutions. This might then lead to legislated public policy for the benefit of families.

A social policy does not become public policy unless its theme is implemented at national, state, or community levels—or all three. The theme of maintaining America's strength in the world would not constitute public policy unless it affected the actual support of military forces. Public policy is often expressed through the expenditure of government funds. In that sense, high spending means high priority and low spending means low priority. It is the monetary aspect of public policy that attracts attention. This leads to the impression that national problems are solved through the expenditure of funds. For example, some social critics made the point that the high dollar commitment to national defense and the low dollar commitment to social welfare in the 1960s meant that if more money had been spent, poverty might have been eradicated. This view of public policy stresses the role of government as the source of monetary resources for solving social problems. An outgrowth of this view is that social ills, specifically those affecting children, can be resolved through spending more money on them.

Beyond monetary impact, however, important aspects of public policy are expressed through policies that guide the legal, welfare, educational, and health systems. Profound changes in society can occur through legislative and judicial case laws that influence the behavior of people without the expenditure of public funds. Although late in showing its effect, the Fourteenth Amendment of the Constitution led to the U.S. Supreme Court decision in *Brown v. The Board of Education* which has affected the education of black children throughout the country. Without the direct expenditure of money, the lives of many people were altered by the public policy that black children deserve equal educational opportunities that could not be attained through separate schooling. In another vein, the legal policy of favoring mothers dominated past court decisions in child custody contests. On the other hand, public policy that concentrates largely on determining eligibility for the distribution of welfare funds has not solved the problem of poverty and has inadvertently undermined the integrity of welfare families.

Social policy actually determines priorities throughout society. An example is the public expectation of quality performance of service, which has resulted in a variety of forms of standard setting. Government standard setting by federal, state, and local agencies plays an important role, but providers of services and insurance carriers also make significant contributions in setting standards for services. The influence of consumers sets the social policy that one is entitled to value received for goods and services. Although there is tension between the profit motive and quality, whether in the professional or business world, there is little question that, when mobilized to public view, quality performance is expected. In the health field, examples of standard setting carried out by nongovernment agencies and reflecting the social policy of expecting quality performance are the Joint Commission on the Accreditation of Hospitals, which sets

standards for both facilities and professional conduct in hospitals, specialty practice certification boards, which certify professional competence,
and professional standard review organizations, which review the case
practice of physicians.

How Is Social Policy Determined?

In our pluralistic American society social policy is determined by the
interaction of many forces. The most obvious is the political process. The
purpose of our political process is to plumb sentiment to find out what the
direction of social policy should be. Based upon the direct translation of
individual sentiments from the "town hall meeting" model, our political
system involves the complex emergence of leaders who gain support
through specific issues in competitive races for positions within the range
of government levels. These leaders, in turn, translate the social policies
they represent into public policies through their actions. The political
system has its own methods and momentum apart from the issues it confronts, influencing social policy itself. This is often in the form of compromise between conflicting viewpoints. Because children do not participate in the political process, which depends upon the representation of
interest groups, issues related to children do not readily gain visibility in
politics.

Once formulated, public policy is further influenced by the executive
and administrative systems that operate at all government levels and set
administrative guidelines for administrators. Although supposedly sensitive to popular influence through elected officials within the various
levels of government, administrative systems have an autonomy of their
own. This leads to tension between administrative and legislative bodies
at all government levels. Although primarily established to carry out
legislated policies, the executive and administrative systems can lend
their power to setting public policy and influencing broader social
policies.

An example is the effort by the President to crystallize a social policy
to conserve energy through informing and educating the public. Essential
to this was adoption of energy-conserving measures by the citizenry in
response to the popular conviction that energy conservation is worthwhile. Within the broad context of a social policy to conserve energy were
a variety of more specific forms of public policy expressed through legislation to reduce energy consumption, find new energy sources, and expand
energy production.

There is another mechanism for determining social policy, at times
incisively, as in *Brown v. The Board of Education*. This is by the devel-

opment of case law through the interpretation of legislation and the Constitution in litigation in the courts. The evolution of case law has strongly affected the behavior of judges in carrying out what they feel represents social policy in individual cases. In essence, the judicial system is the arm of society that brings social policy to bear in controversial matters.

Another important determinant of social policy is the influence of social critics, usually journalists and professional writers, who inject ideas that contribute to the thematic content of social policy through the mass media. Ordinarily not publicly visible, but even more important in many ways, are religious groups and leaders. Strong opposing views on social policy regarding abortion are examples of sentiments mobilized through religious groups. Less obvious are the religious values that influence social policies regarding such issues as promoting the interests of minority groups.

How Is Social Policy Influenced?

We have identified important means through which social policy is determined; we will now consider ways in which it can be influenced. One of the most important points is that a specific issue must be within the domain of social policy in order to have a chance of influencing it. Many issues are injected into the public arena, some temporarily influencing public policy, only to fall on barren soil without influencing social policy. A perennial example is the censorship of pornographic materials. Such an issue, although capable of generating widespread attention, is not important enough to most people to generate consensus on social policy unless it involves children directly. The voluntary rating of motion pictures and public outrage when children are pornographic subjects illustrate the point that consensus in popular sentiment can lead to a social policy on pornography. That social policy is also an example of one that has affected theaters through rating films for viewing by children without the need for legislated public policy.

In the human services area, many proposed projects have not been implemented because they were too specific to be expressed in social policy. Thus, street workers were proposed as a solution to juvenile delinquency by converting delinquent gangs to constructive purposes through the influence of an empathic social worker. Experiments in this vein failed, and the idea of changing delinquents through individual interventions did not become social policy because it addressed only one facet of the broad problem of delinquency.

Another point in influencing social policy is whether or not an issue is significant. Something is of importance because it affects a large number of people or because it is severe and should not happen to any single individual. The issue must also be capable of resolution. It is not sufficient simply to call attention to a problem and deplore it; feasible alternatives must be offered for resolving the problem.

Some issues do fall readily within the area of social policy. First are those related to government spending and taxation. A second area relates to public safety, both in the form of national defense and crime control. Another area of current importance is providing opportunities for self-realization for minority groups. Other issues are related to catastrophes, health care, conservation of natural resources, and recreation.

Generally speaking, social policy can be influenced if issues focus on the process rather than on the content of a particular area. It is difficult to obtain agreement on content—for example, on what things children should know at a given educational level, such as how much American history a child should know by the third grade. One can obtain agreement, however, on what children should be able to do at a given developmental level. Thus, all children should learn how to read during their early school years. One reason why little social policy has been generated about children is that our society has entrusted children to the educational system, which is content rather than process oriented.

Actually, the health system has a better chance of influencing social policy on child development than does the educational system. The health system is process oriented, looking at development from the point of view of milestones and a child's performance at a given point, as measured by a developmental quotient. In contrast, the educational system is relatively content oriented, concerned about what children know, as reflected in its reliance upon the intelligence quotient. The health system, then, is developmentally oriented, the educational system is behaviorally oriented. Although individual teachers are concerned about the process of education, the educational system is more concerned about what is being taught. When the health system is involved in education, it is more concerned about how learning takes place than what is learned.

The health system encompasses the family, community, school, and other aspects of the child's life. The educational system must relate largely to children apart from the other child caring systems. Educators are drawn into, but cannot manage, family problems. Another difference is that the health system is based upon the diagnosis and treatment of individuals. In contrast, the educational system is oriented to groups of children. In essence, the health system asks *how* is a child doing and employs developmental review or assessment (process). The educational system asks *what* is a child doing and employs tests of achievement (content).

In order to influence social policy, an issue must be clearly defined. The health system, with its reliance on the biological and social sciences, can identify a problem with sufficient clarity and strength so that there can be agreement that it exists. A frequently cited example is the discovery of phenylketonuria. Once this disorder was identified and could be seen as a public risk, social policy was established to prevent it. The health system is a potentially powerful source of social policy because an issue that is a threat to health commands attention. The gradual emergence of a social policy that limits the infringement of smokers on nonsmokers is an example. Public policy on smoking has also been legislatively expressed. In regard to children, concern about the impact of television on children originated in the health system.

A specific example of a way in which a child psychiatrist influenced social policy was when Leo Kanner, in the 1930s, carried out a study of mentally retarded people who were released from institutions on writs of habeus corpus and placed as servants or reclaimed by their families. Kanner followed them and found that few were able to function socially. At the same time they had produced many children, but were unable to cope with child rearing. His findings were reported in the *Baltimore Sun* in 1938, and the ensuing publicity led to a cessation of the releases, based simply upon legalities by the court system. This is an illustration of how a clinical study dramatically affected social policy. It is also a timely reminder that interventions with handicapped people based simply upon a single legal point can lead to unfortunate social consequences. In Kanner's instance, the health system made a significant contribution to a social policy, which then influenced legal practice (Eisenberg, 1977).

As can be seen, influencing social policy involves much more than contacting one's legislator. It takes place through the education of the public, professionals, and politicians through the mass media, through participation in the political process and formal educational programs in ways that clearly identify problems of social relevance and offer feasible solutions.

Obstacles to Influencing Social Policy

Because of the chasm between the accepted knowledge of child development and its application, it is important to examine carefully the obstacles to influencing social policy affecting children. Many people are frustrated when they find that proposals based upon logic and scientific evidence do not penetrate social policy.

Although there are instances in which parents have sacrificed themselves for their children, one of the most obvious factors is that children are not considered until the needs of adults are met. As long as adults are preoccupied with their own basic or survival needs, it is unlikely that they can focus and sustain attention on their children.

Another factor is that, because life includes many calculated risks, a particular hazard must be recognized as more than should be expected in life in order to focus attention on it. For example, many children are unhappy, but so are many adults. The argument must be faced that the unhappiness of children is not a cause for concern because certain bruises in development are part of living, and even character building. Some people construe attention to children as a form of permissiveness that overlooks their need for learning to cope with stress and frustration.

Some say Americans do not like children. Actually, as individuals, American parents do care for their children and do their best for them. It is not that we as a nation have a dislike or hatred of children. The explanation may lie in the way that we differentially regard our own children and other people's children. The competitive individualism of American society and the fear of economic dependency justifies and even encourages us not to be concerned with other people's children. If we believe that we are all on our own, we are absolved from responsibility for others' children. The attitude that people are responsible for themselves, coupled with the feeling that the family is a private castle, adds to the feeling that to assist parents and children is to make them dependent and weak. All of these feelings conspire against the concern and generosity needed for public policies favoring children (Keniston, 1977; Senn, 1977).

Another obstacle is that the political process is based upon compromises and must reconcile discrepancies between the ideal and the practical because the benefits of the ideal may not justify the cost. Since most social policies affecting children have long-range benefits, it is difficult to assess and justify the short-range costs of children's programs.

Another factor is the timing of an issue, and whether or not it fits into a popular ambience that might be pro- or anti-science, pro- or anti-intervention, or pro- or anti-self-determination. A particular epoch that emphasizes self-determination, feels disillusioned with science, and stresses avoiding intervention in personal lives will be a difficult time for advocating interventions for children. Another example is a time in which planning for parenthood is caught between the emotionalism of "right to life" or "right to be a wanted child" movements. At the other extreme, the Joint Commission on the Mental Health of Children was formed in a climate favoring attention to childhood, following President Kennedy's assassination by a man who had been identified, but not treated, as an emotionally disturbed child.

One of the most important obstacles is essentially a systems problem. Typically, all programs for children are ranked at the same categorical level with specific programs for adults. For example, alcoholism, drug abuse, rape prevention, suicide prevention, and other similar categorical programs are thought of at the same level with all programs for children. Overlooked is the fact that children's services exist in similar categories.

The only appropriate categorical level for all children's services is at the same level as all adult services. Furthermore, different kinds of services are required for different ages of children—for example, therapeutic nursery schools for young children and adolescent clinics for teenagers.

Another obstacle lies within the field of child development itself. Some have taken the position that, until we know that what is recommended will produce all of the desired effects, experts should not try to make recommendations. Since decision makers look to people who have professional competence to make judgments about matters that they must decide, for people who are most knowledgeable to avoid making recommendations for children is inappropriate (Richmond, 1977).

Comprising almost one-third of the population, children constitute the largest minority group in America. The typical obstacles to influencing social policy exist for children as for other minority groups: (1) minority in numbers; (2) lack of ability to articulate needs; (3) traditional system barriers to change; (4) disparity in values from the majority; and (5) lack of knowledge of need. Children have different interests and priorities than do adults and even have their own cultural characteristics. Furthermore, children are minorities within minority groups. All of these things add the problems of minority groups to advocacy for children.

A Social Policy for Children: The Conservation of Developmental Potential

A seminal idea is needed around which social policies for children can be formed. The most fundamental fact is that children are the next generation and hold its potential. Noshpitz proposes that social policies for children be based upon the Principle of Conservation of Developmental Potential (1977). According to this principle, a society succeeds or fails in direct proportion to the way that it enhances or impedes the development of its children. In other words, a society that encourages, protects, and furthers child development will do better than one that does not. A society can conserve its developmental potential, or waste it. If it does conserve it, the society will be more productive and innovative, achieve higher artistic levels, provide better parents for its children, offer more justice to its citizens, have more solidarity as a people, and offer more satisfaction for individuals. The general policy that emerges from this principle is that our society should endeavor by every means at its command to conserve the developmental potential of its children.

At no time in the life cycle is the rate of growth, and vulnerability to insult, as great as in childhood. Societal concern, protection, and help are required to ensure that those delicate, intangible, fragile, web-like developmental processes unfurl with all their richness and complexity preserved, and that each developmental stage builds securely on the health and integrity of what has gone before.

The potential of our children is an immense wellspring of uniquely precious quality, a realizable asset that is peculiarly humane in character, that is not primarily economic although it has extraordinary economic implications, that is all too easily and quite typically wasted, exploited, or destroyed, that is given much lip service and insufficient support, and that will reap an abundant harvest if nourished, preserved, and protected. We know that there are critical intellectual capacities that are failing to unfold, capacities to grow both physically and emotionally that are not being realized, levels of psychosexual maturity that are not being attained, and capacities to love and work that are stifled with resultant withering of some portion of our children's potential humanity. All this because of our failure to throw the full weight of society's efforts and energies into the kind of work necessary to protect and preserve our children's developmental potential.

Behind any conservation program there must be a good deal of genuine caring for what is preserved. If not, there should be at least an enlightened self-interest in terms of the benefits to society that justify the immediate cost and effort. It is self-evident that children who are better able to learn, remember, and work will make for a more productive society; children who are better able to control their impulses and keep their emotions in check are the long-range answer to a safer society; and children who are able to develop tenderness, compassion, and feelings for other people will make for a happier society.

Noshpitz proposes ways of conserving development. To conserve it, we must consider its vagaries, its vicissitudes, and its multiple potentialities in the face of inherent difficulties. We must do preventive things to avoid trouble, growth-enhancing things to maximize potential, and therapeutic and rehabilitative things to cope with such troubles as may appear. There are two inseparable levels at which the work of conservation must go on. One is the conservation of child caretaking systems, primarily the family and schools, and the other is the conservation of individual capacities through supportive services and fostering individual differences in children.

CONSERVING CHILD CARETAKING SYSTEMS

Child caretaking system conservation implies a host of action programs: housing, income protection, legal services, community organization, disease prevention, nutrition maintenance, population control, city planning, coping with racism, fostering the dignity of parenting and a range of adult educational and counseling services that protect family function, enhance family feeling, and prevent family disruption. It implies that we teach parents parenting, that we cope with child abuse, that we teach corporations to consider the effect on children of moving families, that we teach hospitals how to maintain dignity in waiting rooms, that we teach police how to approach family difficulties, and that we teach politicians what they lose when they vote against family support legislation.

Important lessons have already been learned from the experience of child advocates in the realm of social policy. One is that existing child caretaking systems must be emphasized rather than focusing attention solely on an individual child or on shifting child rearing functions away from parents. Ordinarily, no one has the degree of commitment to children as do their parents. That kind of parental commitment does not exist in institutions, foster homes, or hired adults. A grave fallacy exists in the notion that children can be helped best through public programs that work directly with a child. A glaring illustration is the way in which cash payments for each individual child through the Aid to the Families of Dependent Children program has resulted in financial advantages that induce a single woman to avoid public acknowledgment of a child's father and to have a large number of children in order to increase her income. Another devastating illustration is the welfare policy of removing children from their homes as the first intervention rather than the last when families founder.

Where adequate child caretaking systems do not exist, they should be created. If a child does not have parents, they should be provided permanently. If a school system does not have specialized educational services, they should be added. If day care is not available, it should be provided.

Of equal importance is concern about the competence of child caretaking systems. This means that we serve children through concern about what helps their parents meet their children's needs. We serve children through concern about employment for their parents, housing, and other community aspects of family living. From the school's standpoint, children should be served by promoting the welfare of their teachers. What enhances teacher morale and professionalism should be good for children. Similarly, in day care, there should be concern about promoting the welfare of the day care staff and their working conditions. What is good for the day care system should be good for children, too. As can be seen, the most effective social policies for children are not a range of separate programs with the child as the recipient, but those that support child caretaking systems.

A clear statement of the task for child advocates in social affairs is made by Bower (1972). He draws upon Kardiner's description of *Key In-*

tegrative Social Systems (KISS), which are the primary institutions that give pattern and meaning to the basic personality of individuals and to the society in which they live. The Key Integrative Social Systems are (1) families; (2) health services, especially to prospective mothers and young children; (3) peer-play arrangements—both formal and informal; and (4) schools. He then describes *Ailing-in-Difficulty* (AID) institutions for children who are unable to function adequately in KISS. The interplay between the KISS and AID institutions is critical in determining whether or not the AID institution will be a temporary haven or a stepping stone toward the third system level, the *Illness-Correctional Environments* (ICE). The ICE institutions, such as prisons and mental hospitals, paradoxically offer the fewest options for growth and healthy change for those who need these opportunities the most. Bower points out that the AID and ICE system levels should be weighted in the direction of preserving and strengthening the KISS institutions. This model provides useful guidelines for determining priorities for expending limited funds.

All of these considerations point to the central objective of conserving the developmental potential of children through support of the economic, emotional, social, and psychological welfare of their families. Because of the current vulnerability of the family, parents should have greater rewards for investing in family life, their own career development, and the development of their children.

There is a prevailing myth of family "self-sufficiency" that implies that families are freestanding, independent, and autonomous units relatively free from social pressures. If a family proves less than independent, if it is visibly needy, or if its members ask for help, then it is by definition not an "adequate" family.

In a sense parents have had to take on more of an executive rather than a direct function in regard to their children, choosing communities, schools, doctors, and special programs that will place their children in the best possible hands. The lives that parents are leading, and the lives for which they are preparing their children, are so demanding and complex that parents cannot have—and often do not want—traditional kinds of supervision of their children. Although most of this change has come about because of shifts in the nature of our society, not because of selfishness or immorality or negligence of the individual parents, the myth of the "self-sufficient" family persists.

Unfortunately, as executives, parents have little authority over those others with whom they share the task of raising their children. On the contrary, most parents deal with those others from a position of inferiority or helplessness. As a result, parents today are often coordinators without significant voice or authority. Although they have the responsibility for their children's lives, they too frequently do not have the voice, authority, or power to make others listen to them.

Parents make mistakes, but they make fewer mistakes than government or business would in raising children. The government is a clumsy parent. Our goal, therefore, should be to enable parents to pay for the help they need in raising children, keeping subsidization of the operating costs of public services as limited as possible. Families should have the financial and political power to select and control the services they receive.

As an economically productive unit, the family relieves society of the cost of child rearing and contains taxpaying adults. Social policy should be oriented toward relieving parents of financial pressures resulting from the state of the economy and competing adult concerns. For example, the income tax structure should support the family rather than undermine it. Income tax deductions should reflect the realistic cost of raising children in families in the same way that business and charitable expenses are recognized in terms of actual cost within reasonably averaged guidelines. As shown in Chapter 1, the typical costs of child rearing can be calculated accurately as a basis for tax deductions.

Beyond economics is the greater value to society of the socializing role of the family in creating future responsible citizens. Optimal social and environmental circumstances can strongly support the development of a sense of responsibility in children. At a general level, this is promoted through reducing the destructive effects of poverty, physical illness, and emotional disturbance in society. More specifically, however, a sense of responsibility in children is inspired by parental models of responsibility. If society is to produce responsible citizens, then, it must support responsibility in parents.

The stakes for society when families are not supported were revealed by an in-depth study of disadvantaged families by the North Point Project in Boston (Pavenstedt, 1967), which showed that striking retardation and deviancy in the development of children resulted from disorganized family lives. Located in the heart of a low-income neighborhood, the Project was a multiservice center providing comprehensive social work, health, mental health, nursing, and day care services for families and children. One aspect of the Project was an income maintenance program; however, it was demonstrated that, although this did reduce the stress in the families, it was not sufficient to salvage the children. Because these children did not receive playful interaction with their mothers, they did not build up internalized experiences and information essential to later learning, contributing to a characteristic drifting quality so strikingly seen in those children as they unsuccessfully tried to adapt to the world by imitating more competent children and adults. If sufficient general improvement in quality of life could be reached so that the children, as recipients of their mothers' love, could counteract the self-devaluation so pervasive in the family and neighborhood, they would build the internal stability of personality needed for later social and academic learning. The point is that not only does the family produce a sense of responsibility in the child, it is also the first agent for developing the learning capacity of the child.

The North Point Project illustrates the need to develop a graded approach to parents who show evidence of being unable to manage their children adequately. Idealistically, Caldwell has suggested a way of approaching this through a social policy that each child is entitled to a competent family (1976). According to her view, the first service for a family in difficulty would be parent education and counseling. The next step would be to devise incentives that would provide practical gains for the parents if they assume their parenting roles more adequately. The third level would be to mandate direct clinical treatment, and if this was not successful, to impose court-ordered sanctions that would alter the custody of the child through termination of parental rights.

PROVIDING SUPPORTIVE SERVICES FOR CHILDREN AND FAMILIES

Since services for individual children and their families vary in complexity, scope, distribution, and quantity, it is helpful to think of a continuum ranging from those services required by all children at all times to those required by a few children at certain times. Although not needed to specify the nature of services, social policy is needed to ensure that services are available, and that they are of high quality. Many existing public services for children are of inferior quality, tending to undermine families without benefiting children (Lasch, 1977).

One model for the delivery of these services, described in detail in the next chapter, is to distinguish levels of primary, secondary, and tertiary care. Simply stated, *primary care* refers to the initially encountered services at the point of entry to the delivery system. For example, primary care for physical health problems is provided by a family physician or a family clinic. *Secondary care* refers to the next level of referral from the primary system for the understanding and management of more complicated problems that cannot be as effectively handled at the primary care level. An example is the child who requires surgery and leaves the primary care clinic level to enter a hospital and receive the care of a surgical team. *Tertiary care* is the next level of referral for more specialized care requiring an order of personnel and facilities not practical at the secondary level because of cost and complexity justified only by a large population base. Examples of tertiary care in the health area are heart and kidney surgery facilities.

Supportive services for children should be available to all children at the primary, secondary, and tertiary levels. Primary care is delivered in the schools, mental health, health, and social services. In Kardiner's terms, these are KISS institutions. The secondary care level corresponds to AID institutions. Families should have help in coping with crises through counseling, homemaker services to support parenting, and brief voluntary separations, particularly with teenagers. All families should have the same resources as prosperous parents who are able to employ others at times of crisis or vacation. At the secondary care level coordination and collaboration between health, education, mental health, legal, and welfare services is important.

An important secondary care level function with implications for class advocacy is identifying the nature of children's dysfunctions, so that society's priorities can be applied for the allocation of as-yet-scarce treatment resources and the development of new services. Thus, children with major dysfunctions that have significant impact on society through violent behavior should receive the highest priority for preventive and therapeutic services in addition to research. Of second priority would be children who have dysfunctions now, but with the social impact becoming manifest later, such as those with learning disabilities. Of third priority would be children with dysfunctions that exercise a less broad and long-range impact on society, such as children with psychoses. Of last priority would be children with dysfunctions that have or will have little impact upon society, such as those with neuroses and adjustment reactions.

As this ranking suggests, our current priorities are in the reverse order. In order to rearrange and carry out more socially realistic priorities, a social policy mandating the availability of the following secondary care level services is needed: (1) clinical diagnostic facilities, (2) direct outpatient treatment, (3) temporary alternative living facilities, (4) psychiatric consultation to primary care workers, and (5) innovative model treatment programs.

At the tertiary care level, the optimal level of quality care for children is largely undeveloped, except in the health care subspecialties. At the present time the tertiary care level is often represented only by ICE institutions, such as state hospital children's units, state schools for the retarded, and state correctional facilities for the delinquent. In some areas residential treatment programs exist, and interdisciplinary diagnostic programs are beginning to appear. It is at the tertiary care level, however, that the most critical review is needed to ensure that programs are truly beneficial to children.

Another vital function of tertiary care is its role in training professionals for the supportive systems. Although teaching and training must take place at all levels in the system, the coordinating base most logically lies at the tertiary level. Unless adequate provision is made for the training, consultative, and planning functions of the tertiary care level, the primary and secondary care levels' need for renewal and quality control are overlooked. Furthermore, it is not possible to attract the kind of professional staffing required to maintain quality tertiary level care without training and research capacities.

Two important ingredients of this delivery system model deserve special emphasis. First, the system should operate with free interchange between the various levels of care. Although it is apparent that an individual using the system passes from the primary through the secondary to the tertiary levels of care, generally, it is also true that the tertiary level should work in close harmony with the secondary and primary levels. The channels between the levels are two-way.

The second characteristic of this model is that responsibility for coordinating a specific case should be fixed at the most effective point in working with families in the system. Although responsibility may be temporarily transferred from one level to another, there should always be a point at which case responsibility is fixed. The effort involved in coordination may vary from time to time, but it is always needed. This is particularly important for children's services, because children cannot maneuver their way through the system and coordinate services as can adults. For most children, parents perform this function; however, many children do not have access to this kind of personalized advocacy.

As can be seen from the array of loosely affiliated or disconnected services at the primary, secondary, and tertiary levels, responsibility for obtaining and coordinating services for a particular child cannot be expected to "just happen." For youngsters who do not have parents who can assume this role, and for those who do but their parents cannot find services, advocacy functions from outside the family are required. Social policy that mandates the availability of services for children and families is important if the resources and channels are to exist for the pursuit of individual case advocacy.

A specific example of class advocacy in the mental health area is through coordinating groups of people with similar needs. From the point of view of children, it is useful to stimulate the development in communities of Big Brother programs and of foster grandparent programs, in order to match children with special needs with adults who have special offerings which could be utilized through work with children. The parents of emotionally disturbed children can be organized to become politically active in obtaining needed services and legislative changes for their children in the same way as have the parents of the mentally retarded.

SUPPORTING INDIVIDUAL DIFFERENCES IN CHILDREN

Another important ingredient of social policy to conserve the developmental potential of children is the recognition and honoring of individual differences in children. This is an example of a policy-shaping attitude more than of programs. Individual differences in temperament, cognition, and intelligence exist from earliest infancy, originating in both constitutional factors and in the unique features of each child's environmental experiences. Vital to each child's development are the attitudes encountered toward emerging individual differences. Just as the devoted mother perceives and is responsive to the special characteristics of each of her children, treating them differentially, so the optimal school program should aim at enhancing, not minimizing, the differences among its students. A society undergoing rapid change, one in which survival is an issue, upheaval a way of life, and the future roles and functions of its members unpredictable, can best safeguard its continuance by promoting the greatest possible diversity among its population (Westman, 1973).

The current tug-of-war between individualism and conformity to the requirements of social living reflects society's present inability to distinguish acceptance of individuality from license to express individuality. Our social actions tend toward the extremes of either generalization of permission for total self-expression or the requirement of total conformity. Perhaps one explanation for this rather primitive, alternating attitude of extremes is that, in fact, the social sciences have not yet themselves defined the basic ingredients of individuality. Underlying society's reticence to accept individuality lurks the fear that individual recognition may not have social utility, and that individual expression might be unacceptable and destructive to society's regulating functions.

Certainly, a basic shift from an expectation of uniformity to an expectation of variability follows an acceptance of individual differences in children. The shift to an acceptance of differences rather than consternation because of them, or the older view of expecting and hoping for homogeneity, could be followed by child rearing and educational goals that would sharpen adaptive differences rather than minimize them in children. The result could be a shift from an emotionally laden "deviance" attitude toward differences between people, with resulting rejection and isolation of those who differ, to a more objective "variance" attitude, with resulting acceptance and tolerance of those who differ. De Tocqueville graphically described the situation that exists when a society denies individual differences in people:

> There is in fact a manly and lawful passion for equality which incites all men to wish to be powerful and honored. This passion tends to raise the humble to the ranks of the great; but there exists also in the human heart a depraved taste for equality which impels the weak to attempt to lower the powerful to their own level.

STATE OF THE ECONOMY AND CHILDREN

This exposition would not be complete without reference to the impact of the general state of the economy—currently, one of inflation—on children. Although enemies of all ages, inflation and recession are particularly harsh on children because they force preoccupation with adult economic survival, detracting attention and deflecting resources from children. The direct effect of inflation on children is through the curtailment of spending so that new programs cannot start. Furthermore, because they are usually the most recently developed, children's services are the first cut in an economic crunch. The poor are especially affected, forcing children to resort to stealing. Inflation also increases the costs of school systems and erodes the quality of education.

In a more subtle manner, the factors contributing to inflation are often based upon lack of self-discipline, modeling increased spending rather than restraint. Inflation feeds on the attitude that increased money is the answer to solving problems rather than conserving resources and living within a budget. Most important, inflation erodes family life, necessitating two full-time working parents, in many instances. The cost of raising children increases, becoming formidable, leading to a decrease in the number of children. The erosion of financial security increases family problems over money, in addition to stirring up national unrest over the dwindling value of money. Because of the increased cost of family-oriented homes, families tend to live in smaller quarters, increasing discomfort and personal strain. Inflation also robs parents and families of leisure time, forcing an emphasis upon making more money, detracting from the pleasures and satisfactions of family life. Because inflation subtly affects the quality of life, it inevitably affects the quality of child development. Much more than the economic security of the future generation depends upon the control of inflation.

The Methods of Class Child Advocacy

A decade of experience with the concept of child advocacy, proposed by the Joint Commission on the Mental Health of Children, has tested a number of ideas and spawned more. The critical issues exposed through advocacy efforts relate to poverty, inflation, inadequate services, legal rights of children, devaluation and lack of support of parenting, inadequate training of professionals, lack of community planning for children, insufficient emphasis on the social and moral development of children, and a propensity for reactions to crises rather than long-range planning (Knitzer, 1976).

The last point merits special attention. Scientists frequently charge that legislation is too slow in responding to scientific advances, overlooking the occasions on which the law has responded swiftly but inappropriately (Ferster 1975). Two examples can be cited. First, when knowledge about genetics was still in its infancy, laws authorizing compulsory sterilization of the mentally ill and mentally retarded were passed, on the assumption that these conditions were hereditary. Years later, after thousands of persons had been sterilized, scientists reported that the inheritability of these conditions was still, and always had been, in doubt. A second, more recent example was the legislative response to child abuse. In less than five years after the initial description of the "battered child" syndrome, almost every state enacted a child abuse law. Most legislation, however, failed to specify what was to happen after child abuse was reported, and failed to provide for funds to carry out the law-reporting provisions, much less for treatment or prevention. Yet many states were under the impression that they had solved the problem because they had passed child abuse legislation.

Careful thought should be given to how rapidly legislation should follow scientific advances, and the effect of contemplated action upon the persons involved. The following questions should be raised: (1) How certain is the scientific knowledge on which a proposed law is based? (2) What action should legislation take because of it? (3) Who would be affected by the law? (4) How will the law affect the rights of involved persons? (5) What will be the benefits or detriments of the law to society? and (6) What will happen if the interests of the affected person and the law conflict?

With these considerations in mind, we can understand the fate of earlier recommendations that a national child advocacy system be created and our experience with specific child advocacy projects. The proposal of the Joint Commission on the Mental Health of Children in 1969 of a national system of child advocacy extending from the community level, through regions, states, and the federal government, was not implemented, but it did stimulate activity at both federal and state levels. Because the most effective routes to children are through their support systems, focusing attention on children outside of existing systems, such as through newly created advocacy programs, perpetuates the errors of the past.

The New York State plan illustrates the degree to which child advocacy was suggested as a newly structured part of government. The New York proposal was that a permanent child advocacy commission have the power to hold hearings, take testimony, subpoena witnesses, require state agencies to provide necessary material, act as *amicus curiae* in cases involving New York State children, and review the programs and budgets of agencies with responsibilities for children.

At the national level in 1973, Senator Ribicoff introduced an amendment to the Social Security Act providing for local and governors' councils of child advocacy. This amendment was not enacted, however, on the grounds that advocacy was too controversial. As this federal legislative effort for child advocacy was in progress, a number of state committees were convened. In 1971 North Carolina established a governor's advocacy commission on children and youth. At the same time a governor's committee for children and youth in the state of Wisconsin was transformed into a governor's advocacy committee for children and youth, and a New York State committee published a report on child advocacy. When the New York committee withered away three years later, it had given birth only to an interagency council on children, composed of the heads of all the state divisions serving children. In Wisconsin, the governor's advocacy commission for children and youth was abolished in 1975 when funds for its renewal were not appropriated.

The passage of time, then, has not borne out the feasibility of a national child advocacy system. One of the problems with any formalized child advocacy system is that it would simply become a reporting mechanism through which data would be collected and funneled upward, without assurance that this information would have impact on legislation. It also had the disadvantage of establishing a new bureaucracy.

Further evidence of the lack of feasibility for a child advocacy system has emerged from the "grass roots" level. A number of specific programmatic efforts in child advocacy during the early 1970s were evaluated (Kahn, 1973). These projects stressed case, but included class, advocacy. Some projects concentrated on one system, such as the schools. Others focused on several target systems sharing a common issue. The projects were sponsored by a variety of groups, government bodies, existing private organizations, and specially funded private organizations. The general impact of these projects was to influence local practices and then to phase out as separate programs, not to grow into advocacy systems.

The problem remains that the political process and government itself do not have mechanisms for representing the interests of children. Edward Zigler, the first director of the Office of Child Development, graphically described the problems involved in maintaining a focus on the needs of children and their families within the context of administrative reorganization (Zigler, 1977). One of the fundamental problems is related to the tendency to assume that the educational system is responsible for children, overlooking the fact, as this book signifies, that many systems affect children and that coordination of them depends upon working through families, not through systems responsible for a part of the lives of children. Of the greatest importance is gaining interdisciplinary support for and participation in organized efforts for children. This is especially true if state offices of child development are formed (Early Child Development Project, 1975).

Effective mechanisms for representing children within the federal government are still to be found. One proposal is a child and family impact statement similar to the environmental impact statement that is required for construction and manufacture in areas that have ecological repercussions. It is not unreasonable to require that any activity affecting children and their families should be examined from the point of view of its undesirable impact on children. Such a plan could require the addition of a child and family impact statement to the environmental impact statement now required for new activities, with similar reporting and monitoring mechanisms. This proposal has appeal as a mechanism with authority that places the interests of children at a monitoring rather than at an advisory level. The preparation of an impact statement is the responsibility of the contractor for a specific project, the cost of which would be built into the overall cost of the project rather than as an expense for the government.

Of particular interest is representing the interests of children in the growing federal programs that will regulate the demand for and supply of health services. The demand for services will be regulated through Professional Standard Review Organizations that set standards for the nature and duration of hospital and outpatient treatment. The distribution and supply of health care resources will be regulated through Health Systems Agencies, which will plan and monitor health facilities, equipment, personnel, and services. At the state level, the implementation of the Community Human Service Concept provides an opportunity to participate in the coordination and integration of services for children (Curtis, 1974). Special effort will be required to ensure the participation of child advocates in the activities of these programs.

In another vein, the legal recourse of children against technological hazards would be created and enhanced by children's compensation laws that bypass cumbersome mechanisms for establishing connections between industrial activity and damage inflicted. Since children do not participate in political decisions about community or personal risk, they should not be prevented from suing for damage that they suffer from manufacturers, vendors, or employers. Moreover, manufacturers of products aimed at the children's market should be required to conform to the same standards that a reasonable parent would hold toward a child (Keniston, 1977).

A number of enduring expressions of class child advocacy have emerged, varying in sponsorship and aims. Children's lobbies have been established in several states to influence legislation. Professional organizations, such as the American Orthopsychiatric Association, have addressed social issues that affect children. The Mental Health Law Project and the Children's Defense Fund are examples of organizations operating within the legal sphere and participating in class action suits for children. At the national level, consortia have been formed to bring together the numerous organizations concerned about children on specific issues. Handbooks have been prepared by these organizations to aid child advocates. The Coalition for Children and Youth publishes an annual *Directory for Child Advocates of Congress and Federal Agencies*. Others are *The Children's Political Checklist*, published by the Education Commission of the States, and *A Child Advocate's Handbook for Action*, by the Children's Defense Fund. Within federal agencies, greater administrative recognition of children should take place to ensure the visibility of children's interests.

A relatively untapped source of power to influence social policy are the parents of children with special needs. Not only can they initiate legal action in specific cases, but through organizations they can increase their impact. There are key points especially sensitive to such influence. These are during the formulation of legislation, during the annual preparation of public budgets, and at times of program evaluations.

Professionals who are aware of the unmet needs of children have the particular opportunity and obligation to contribute information to aid legislative bodies and judges in understanding situations in which they lack experience or expertise. It is important to keep legislative leaders informed and to help them to view children's interests as promoted less through cash benefits, benevolences, or charities and more through long-range programs that improve their lives. Professionals must be prepared not only to document the savings in human resources but the cost, efficiency, and future impact of legislation that affects children in the community and nation. The patient and persistent educational efforts of knowledgeable professionals have been and remain the backbone of class child advocacy (Lourie, 1975; Werkman, 1972).

Special study groups, university centers, and institutes are needed to address the problems of children. The Carnegie Council on Children, created in 1972, is an example of the kind of contribution that can be made by a private foundation. Its work emphasized the impact of society on children through evaluating the relationship between contemporary American society and child development. Similar projects utilizing the "brain trust" approach are needed to stimulate thought about children. The work of the Child Development Association has stimulated recognition of the need for a National Child Development Profile.

The professional training of journalists and political scientists should include awareness of the needs and problems of children as a categorical group. Furthermore, undergraduate, graduate, and continuing education in child advocacy should be a part of the educational experience of all professionals who work with children.

The President's Commission on Mental Health (1978) has stressed prevention of mental illness and recommended comprehensive prenatal care, adequate nutrition, early childhood intervention, developmental day care, preschool programs, such as Operation Head Start, and teaching children how to strengthen coping and problem-solving abilities. The needs of children and programming for them are of such magnitude that a commission is needed devoted primarily to them.

Perhaps the most feasible method of child advocacy is through the infiltration of social systems with people personally experienced or trained in children's fields. In addition to visible, formally commissioned advisory groups, such as a Presidential Commission on the Mental Health of Children, the election and appointment of child advocates to positions influencing children at all levels would be helpful. The logical result of such a trend would be the expectation that anyone responsible for programs that affect children should have knowledge and experience in working with children.

Conclusion

As the nation's largest permanent minority group, children encounter special problems in achieving recognition and representation in social policy. For their advocates, familiarity with the means of determining and influencing the cultural and political climate is vital. Advocacy for individual children is difficult, if not impossible, without the enabling support of social policies that highlight the general needs of all children.

As America devotes more attention to planning for the future and recognizes that the current generation of children *is* the future, there is growing interest in promoting the healthy development of children and preventing disability during childhood. Devising methods to enhance the development of children and surmounting the obstacles to influencing social policies that affect children are the tasks of class advocacy for children.

A commitment by our society to conserving the developmental potential of our citizenry is one means of realistically concentrating social and government energies on policies that will identify and foster methods for realizing competent maturity for our children. The key to future planning is recognition of the dependency of children upon those who rear them and upon their environments. The errors of the past have resulted both from the relative neglect of children and focusing programs on children rather than on child caretaking systems, particularly families. When child caretaking systems founder, supportive services must be available for them as well as for individual children.

Because they are especially susceptible to harm from existing national problems such as inflation, poverty, poor housing, overcrowding, racial discrimination, and ecological pollution, children require special consideration in the formulation of most social policies.

One of the most productive areas for social research would be to establish the high cost of neglecting children. We can no longer rely solely on good will and acts of charity to provide for children—we need factual economic points that will impress social planners. We know that large sums of public monies are squandered on some children who eventually become adult drains on the economy, either through criminal or welfare careers. The redeployment of public funds at critical points that will benefit children would result in no more, and eventually less, cost. We could meet the needs of *all* children for less than we are now spending on a *few* through new social policies that protect and promote child development.

A social policy to conserve our society's developmental potential would build checks and balances into a system that now almost routinely fails to recognize and meet the needs of children and their families. It would be a vehicle for focusing energies and for generating new ideas about how children should be served by public and private institutions. One child out of six is now actively harmed by a "stacked deck" created by the failings of our society. To try to change those children who are born unequal is to avoid the more important task of changing the structural forces that keep them this way. Schools, the institutions traditionally called upon to correct social inequality, are unsuited to the task; without economic opportunity to follow educational opportunity, the equality of opportunity can never be realized. Class child advocacy requires a social policy which provides adequate income and jobs for parents and adequate educational, health, and mental health care for all children.

Class child advocacy can be a significant force in ensuring that mandated services exist, that children have access to those services without regard to race, income, or handicapping conditions, and that the services do what they are supposed to do. Furthermore, there will be a need for sustained evaluation of the way that child caretaking systems and services function and malfunction and, in turn, affect children (Knitzer, 1976).

A decade of experience with the concept of child advocacy has demonstrated that new and separate advocacy systems are probably not required. In fact, they tend to deflect attention and energies from taking into account the needs of children in all social policies. Preferable to a newly created child advocacy system is sensitizing existing systems by stimulating awareness of the ways that each program or action affects children and by formal and informal education of parents, professionals, and politicians in the needs of children and their families. Our aim should be to create social policies that recognize children as our "most precious natural resource" and families as "the building blocks of our society" (Keniston, 1977).

References

BOWER, E. M. (1972) "KISS and Kids: A Mandate for Prevention." *American Journal of Orthopsychiatry*, 24:556–565, July.

Brown v. The Board of Education, 347 U.S. 483 (1954).

CALDWELL, B. (1976) "Optimal Child Rearing Environments." Chapter in Westman, J. C. (Ed.), *Proceedings of the University of Wisconsin Conference on Child Advocacy*. Madison: University of Wisconsin–Extension, Health Sciences Unit.

CHILDREN'S DEFENSE FUND (1976) *Title XX: Social Services in Your State, A Child Advocate's Handbook for Action*. Washington, D.C.: Children's Defense Fund, April.

COALITION FOR CHILDREN AND YOUTH, *Directory for Child Advocates, Congress and Federal Agencies*, 1910 K St., N.W., Washington, D.C., 20006.

CURTIS, W. R., AND NEUHAUSER, D. (1974) "Providing Specialized, Coordinated Human Services to Communities: The Organizational Problem and a Potential Solution." Ford Foundation Seminar Position Paper No. 4, Harvard School of Public Health.

EARLY CHILD DEVELOPMENT PROJECT (1975) State Offices of Child Development, Report No. 8. Denver, Colo.: Education Commission of the States.

EDUCATION COMMISSION OF THE STATES (1977) *The Children's Political Checklist*, Denver, Colo., 80295.

EISENBERG, L. (1977) "Child Psychiatry Perspectives: The Cultivation of Children." *American Journal of Child Psychiatry*, 16:529–539.

FERSTER, E. Z. (1975) "The Excess Y Chromosome—How Should the Law Respond?" Chapter in Allen, R. C. (Ed.), *Readings in Law and Psychiatry*. Baltimore, Md.: Johns Hopkins University Press.

JOINT COMMISSION ON ACCREDITATION OF HOSPITALS (1974) *Psychiatric Facilities Serving Children and Adolescents*. Chicago: Joint Commission on Accreditation of Hospitals.

JOINT COMMISSION ON THE MENTAL HEALTH OF CHILDREN (1970) *Crisis in the Mental Health of Children*. New York: Harper and Row.

KAHN, A. J., KAMMERMAN, S. B., AND McGOWAN, B. G. (1973) *Child Advocacy: Report of a National Baseline Study*. New York: Columbia University School of Social Work.

KANNER, L. (1942) "Exoneration of the Feebleminded." *American Journal of Psychiatry*, 99:17–22.

KENISTON, K. (1977) *All Our Children: The American Family Under Pressure*. New York: Harcourt, Brace, Jovanovich.

KNITZER, J. E. (1976) "Child Advocacy: A Perspective." *American Journal of Orthopsychiatry*, 46:200–216, April.

LASCH, C. (1977) *Haven in a Heartless World: The Family Besieged.* New York: Basic Books.

LOURIE, N. V., AND BERLIN, I. N. (1975) "Child Advocacy: Political and Legislative Implications." Chapter in Berlin, I. N. (Ed.), *Advocacy for Child Mental Health.* New York: Brunner/Mazel.

NOSHPITZ, J. D. (1974) "Toward a National Policy for Children." *American Journal of Child Psychiatry*, 13:385–401, Summer.

PAVENSTEDT, E. (Ed.) (1967) *The Drifters: Children of Disorganized Lower-Class Families.* Boston: Little, Brown.

PRESIDENT'S COMMISSION ON MENTAL HEALTH (1978) *Report to the President,* Vol. 1. Washington, D.C.: Superintendent of Documents, No. 040-000-00390-8.

RICHMOND, J. (1977) Quoted in Senn, M. J. E., *Speaking Out for America's Children.* New Haven: Yale University Press.

SENN, M. J. E. (1977) *Speaking Out for America's Children.* New Haven: Yale University Press.

WERKMAN, S. (1972) "Child Psychiatry and the Legislative Process." *Journal of Child Psychiatry*, 11:30–51, January.

WESTMAN, J. C. (Ed.) (1973) *Individual Differences in Children.* New York: Wiley.

ZIGLER, E. (1977) "Who Will Speak for Children and Families? A Case for Strengthening OCD." *American Journal of Orthopsychiatry*, 47:564–567, October.

Chapter 7

Individual Child Advocacy

All children require advocates, and most have them in the form of their parents. The large number who do not, however, must rely upon other adults, especially professionals who work with children.

For most professionals, an advocacy role in relationship to children does not come naturally, largely because professional practice with children has been influenced strongly by adult approaches. Except under circumstances of mental incompetence, professionals do not ordinarily assume responsibility for what happens to adults. They limit themselves to diagnostic, treatment, and consultative functions, with the assumption that adults are responsible for following through. Inappropriately, the same stance has been transferred to children. Many professionals, consequently, regard intervening on behalf of a child as intrusive, as it would be for an adult. Overlooked is the inevitable dependency of children upon adults in all or parts of their lives. The challenge for professionals, then, is

165

to know when and how to assume responsibility for aspects of a child's life appropriately.

In a broad sense, all adults are responsible for children in areas of safety. Adults naturally step in when children are in physical danger. Advocacy extends this to include psychological and developmental danger as well. Adult citizens also generally recognize their responsibility to support child caring systems, such as schools. Beyond that, certain adults, because of their professions, have responsibility for children in special areas. Teachers, physicians, lawyers, and social workers hold responsibilities inherent in their work with children. These responsibilities for an aspect of a child's life are entrusted to them by those who are legally responsible for the child: parents, guardians, or the state.

Advocacy for a child, then, means assuming responsibility for all or a part of a child's life. Full advocacy responsibilities for children are ordinarily limited to parents, legal guardians, or agencies. Lesser degrees of advocacy are built into the roles of professionals who work with children, as detailed in Chapter 3. In this sense a professional's responsibility is not limited to performing diagnostic functions without assuming some degree of responsibility for ensuring that the information gained is used to benefit the child. Thus, in an advocacy role, a school psychologist would consider psychological testing incomplete if the results were not shared with a child and with responsible caretakers for the child's benefit.

A deeper appreciation of advocacy functions, which can be assumed by professionals in varying degrees and ways, is conveyed by the following illustrative roles through which advocacy can take place: ally, collaborator, promoter, protector, provider, spokesperson, defender, ombudsman, advisor, facilitator, integrator, coordinator, agent, helper, intervener, negotiator, interpreter, intermediary, decision maker, educator, and stabilizer.

Because advocacy links professionals to furthering the interests of the consumer of their services, it is important to take notice of the decline in the automatic respect accorded professionals. The images conveyed by the foregoing roles also reflect the expectations that people hold for professionals. As a mere technician, the future professional will not be accorded the respect that now goes with professional status unless individuals are satisfied with their services. If individuals become interchangeable in the eyes of professionals, then individual professionals will become interchangeable in the eyes of clients. There is an increasing tension between the obligation of professionals to the intellectual tradition of which they are a part and their responsibility to serve the interests of their clients. As a result, professionals must work more effectively in teams of other professionals and learn to listen more attentively and explain their diagnoses and their strategies more fully to their colleagues, clients, and the general public (Yarmolinsky, 1978).

One way of conceptualizing specific advocacy functions is to analyze them within a systems framework of primary, secondary, and tertiary child caring services (Bolman, 1967; Bolman and Westman, 1967; Hansen, 1970; Perlmutter, 1976, Rafferty, 1969). In this conception, as illustrated in Figure 1, primary care refers to the work of professionals who are the first point of contact for a child with a problem and includes the most general and broad knowledge of normal and abnormal child development. Advocacy responsibility relates to reaching out to find children in need of help and ensuring that their special requirements are understood. Secondary care functions are assumed by professionals whose expertise is specialized and who provide diagnostic, treatment, and consultative services. At this level, advocacy responsibility relates to understanding a child and securing indicated services. Tertiary care functions are assumed by professionals who provide diagnostic and treatment services for the most complicated cases that require altering the course of a child's life on a temporary or permanent basis, as through residential placement and permanent custody changes. The tertiary care level is also the hub of teaching and research functions. At this level, advocacy responsibilities relate to ensuring that children receive services for as long as required with continued follow-up.

Primary Care Advocacy Functions

The point of entry into the primary care system for children and adolescents is the first professional contact capable of identifying the nature of a problem and, in appropriate instances, handling the problem without the involvement of secondary and tertiary levels. This view of primary care includes family physicians, pediatricians, public health nurses, school psychologists, social workers, family and social agency workers, the clergy, marriage counselors, court workers, and community workers. Professionals working in primary care roles provide consultation to each other and can draw upon consultative support in their work, as do professionals at the secondary and tertiary levels.

Although crisis intervention is a function of the primary care levels, in some instances the actual management of a crisis includes secondary and perhaps tertiary levels of care. In contrast with medical emergencies, mental health and social crises of children tend to involve the breakdown of families and community resources leading to the need for more complicated interventions. Such crises are seldom resolved by intervention solely with the child or at the primary care level.

Many professionals who work in primary care have not had the opportunity to become sensitized to the ways in which children experience their

PRIMARY CARE (Entry to Professional Services)

HEALTH	MENTAL HEALTH	EDUCATION	SOCIAL SERVICES	LEGAL SYSTEM
Health Care Providers	Community Mental Health Centers	School Counselors, Social Workers, Psychologists	Family Counselors, Social Agencies, Youth Services, Child Care Facilities, Clergy	Law Enforcement, Juvenile Courts, Attorneys

SECONDARY CARE (Specialized diagnosis and treatment)

Medical Specialties	Psychiatric Services	Specialized Educational Services	Foster Care, Child Caring Institutions	Correctional Institutions

TERTIARY CARE (Interdisciplinary diagnosis, treatment, consultation, teaching, and research)

Health Science Centers	Psychiatric Hospitals		Residential Treatment Centers	

FIGURE 1.   Levels of Child Advocacy

lives. Their training and background has been to act upon children. For this reason, knowing when and how to assume an advocacy role requires sensitivity to issues which are important to children, knowledge of ways of reviewing the developmental progress of children in order to identify those in need of help, and skillful application of intervention techniques. The advocacy responsibility at the primary care level is to reach out to children with psychological and developmental problems.

SENSITIZATION TO CHILDREN'S LIVES

The foundation for assuming advocacy roles with children is sensitivity to issues that are important to children. At the most basic level, three questions are important to each child at all stages of life. The first is "What am I?" Children are concerned about their intelligence, personalities, and physical appearance. They are also concerned about what they can do and can't do related to their skills, abilities, talents, and developmental level. Second, each child is concerned about "Who am I?" Children want to know about their identities, including their biological, familial, and cultural origins. Third, each child is concerned about "Where am I?" Children want to know about the opportunities and resources available to them. They want to know about the places in which they live and their positions in society.

Beyond these basic questions children have about themselves, a second area of sensitivity to the special nature of time, place, and interpersonal context in children's lives is useful. Time is of basic importance in that it identifies longitudinally the age of the child and in present time the moment in which a particular event is occurring. Children change drastically with age and also with brief shifts in time of day. Place is important since the setting in which an event takes place alters the attitude and behavior of a child. Children react differently in familiar and unfamiliar surroundings. The next element is the interpersonal context in which an event takes place. The coinciding and conflicting expectations that adults and children hold for each other strongly influence the behavior of children. Children are much more sensitive to time, space, and context than are adults who have developed greater stability through more extensive life experience.

A third area for sensitization is to the developmental needs of children. Some knowledge of developmental norms and what children need at various stages in their lives is useful, as outlined in Chapter 4.

A fourth area for sensitization relates to an ability to accept children's natural emotions and interests. A variety of children's impulses may be distasteful to adults who are not able to fully accept and understand the primitive emotions and fantasies of children. This is particularly true for aggressive and sexual urges. Some adults are unable to work effectively with children because they are consciously and unconsciously threatened by children's impulses.

A fifth area for sensitization is to an awareness of determinants of behavior. Knowledge of only the ways children conduct themselves is not a sufficient basis for advocacy. One must be oriented to the causes of behavior in order to understand behavior, which may conceal rather than convey its meaning. The younger the child, the less one can depend upon words as reflections of a child's intent. Such meaning may be expressed through behavior that cannot be understood in adult ways. For example, a child's superficial expression of anger may mean dependency, and a child's superficial expression of affection may mean a lack of attachment and an inability to form appropriate dependent relationships.

A sixth area for sensitization relates to the uniqueness of each child's personality and family background. One should be acquainted with individual differences in temperament and cognition and with the importance of a variety of family structures and events in children's lives, especially the experiences of adoption, bereavement, divorce, and foster placement.

All of these aspects of sensitization can help professionals to understand a child's point of view and needs. Adults should be aware of the tendency for their own experience, values, and emotions to color their reactions to children. For example, a "rescue fantasy," frequently expressed through personal involvement in a child's life, may lead an adult to take unrealistic or premature actions to save a child from adversity. The simple technique of asking how one would feel and respond if in the child's position is a beginning step. Then the adult can adapt that point of view to the circumstances and age of the child. Beyond that, however, communication with children is a complicated matter requiring more skill than is ordinarily available at the primary care level. The younger the child, the more reliance must be placed on indirect communication, as through play interviews.

DEVELOPMENTAL REVIEW

With a background of sensitivity to the life situations of children, case finding can take place. This is done through identifying the signs that indicate a significant problem exists. In crises the existence of a problem is evident; under most circumstances, however, it is necessary to reach out and find children in need of help. When that takes place, it is essential for the child to have access to needed diagnostic and treatment resources (American Orthopsychiatric Association, 1978; Stringer, 1978).

The most effective approach to case finding is not through cross-sectional screening of children but, rather, through periodic review via existing child caring services to ensure that development is proceeding adequately. The detection-of-disease model is less useful than a model of longitudinally reviewing the progress of a child's development along the dimensions detailed in Chapter 4. Since development takes place along a number of lines, developmental review consists of the assessment of a profile of a child's assets and liabilities, and of the transactions between a child and significant people in the context of a particular setting in which the child is found at a particular time in life. Developmental review is concerned with what goes on between child and environment at the biological, psychological, social, and cultural levels (DHEW, 1977; Henderson, 1978; Hersh, 1978).

Because of the critical importance of a child's age in determining the existence of a problem and because children rarely directly signal their need for help, there is a need for a conceptual model for the developmental review of children, comparable to periodic physical examinations. For this purpose, a series of critical developmental checkpoints for growing children can be identified (Group for the Advancement of Psychiatry, 1972). These key points of transition—or *milestones*—correspond to the emotional, psychological, and cognitive stages of development. Each milestone marks a change in social roles, significant maturational shifts, critical psychological experiences, and pivotal skill acquisitions. A milestone, then, is a nodal point in development that can be observed, measured, or inferred at critical times in each child's life.

In addition to the milestone approach, accommodation should be made to the fact that children bring unique sets of attributes into families and environments that comprise "their worlds." Each child matures at a different rate in skeletal, motor, language, cognitive, social, and emotional development. Each child enters school with a different set of expectations and capacities for learning and social behavior. Each child progresses through unique academic, social, and personality development through the school years. Each child faces a different set of possibilities and choices at the end of schooling.

The milestone checkpoints maximize the likelihood that physical, mental, emotional, and social disorders will be detected early. Noshpitz has proposed the following classification of children at each milestone checkpoint: the gifted, the competent, the vulnerable, the stressed, the troubled, the disturbed, and the severely disabled (1974). As an illustration, when this typology is applied to school age children, the *gifted* child might profit from resource counseling. The *competent* child would require no service other than identification of his unique qualities for himself and his school. The *vulnerable* child might receive primary care level attention because of illness or family problems. The *stressed* child might receive primary level care in the form of remedial tutoring, Big Brother referral, or guidance counseling. The *troubled* child might receive secondary care level psychiatric care. The *disturbed* child might need tertiary care level intensive residential treatment. The *severely disabled* child might require lifelong specialized care.

The milestone evaluation of children is a complicated process, involving not only individual children, but also their parents, siblings, living situations, and communities. Gaining a total picture of each child is necessary in order to make appropriate judgments. It should be emphasized that developmental assessment does not consist of tests and procedures that can be simply carried out and scored. The complete assessment of development requires the mature, seasoned judgment of professionals trained in the area. The need for this evaluation, however, could be determined through a three-stage process of review (Department of Health, Education, and Welfare, 1977).

Stage 1 would consist of review of the biological dimensions of development within the framework of the pediatric physical examination, which would also include an opportunity for the child and family to discuss any stresses or problems with which they would like help, or to identify strengths and support systems that could be engaged to further the child's development. An assessment of the child's functioning would be based upon the parents' reports on the child's developmental skills and emotional and behavioral status.

Stage 2 would involve the direct observation of the child's functioning, utilizing a broader range of techniques that can be applied in the child's home, day care or school, and the clinic (Wahler, 1976).

Stage 3 would include a detailed review of the biological, psychological, family, environmental, social, and cultural domains. The psychological domain particularly would include evaluating a wide variety of functions: cognitive, coping, emotional, language, and special sense development. This kind of evaluation would probably draw upon secondary and tertiary care level skills.

From the standpoint of priority, all stages of life do not warrant equal attention. The periods of greatest sensitivity and lack of adequate attention today are early childhood, a silent period, and adolescence, a time when problems are both seen and heard, but little is done to resolve them. Attention to developmental checkpoints, therefore, should stress the first five years and the teenage years. Of the two, early childhood offers the greatest potential for high yield from the investment of services on both humanistic and economic grounds. One model for implementing the milestone approach places priority upon seven checkpoints: (1) the unborn child, (2) birth, (3) early childhood, (4) school entry, (5) the third

MILESTONE	TIME
I	The unborn child
II	Childbirth
III	2½ to 3½ years
IV	4½ to 5½ years
V	7½ to 8½ years
VI	10½ to 11½ years (girls) 11½ to 12½ years (boys)
VII	15½ to 16½ years

FIGURE 2.   Developmental Milestones

grade, (6) the sixth and seventh grades, and (7) the eleventh grade. Figure 2 outlines this model, and a series of more detailed descriptions of each milestone follows. The variables that influence the availability and quality of care indicated at each milestone are less those of knowledge than of place of residence and economic factors, such as urban or rural residence, and poverty.

MILESTONE I

Time:
    The prenatal period.

Objectives:
    To assure that each child is born a wanted child with access to a competent child rearing system through evaluating the following factors:

1. Maternal health and nutrition.
2. Preparation of mother for childbirth.
3. Education of mother and family members in child care and development.
4. Screening for detection of genetic anomalies in unborn infants.
5. Programs for unwed mothers.
6. Infant placement and adoption services.
7. Competent obstetrical care.

Location:
    Clinics, hospitals, neighborhood centers.

Personnel:

Physicians, nurses, nutritionists, social workers, community workers. For this milestone and the others in some locations, paraprofessionals are essential to provide the communication links between services and population where there are significant differences in language, custom, and life style (Group for the Advancement of Psychiatry, 1972).

Rationale:

The foundation for adequate child rearing is laid prior to a child's birth. The rights of unborn children include assurance that receptive and competent environments for their dependent years exist. The future of the child is too important to be left simply to the vagaries of parental wishes and hopes. Young parents in particular need special attention to ensure that the needs of their children are adequately recognized and met. At this time the stage is set for success or failure in child rearing, and it is a key point for aiding individuals and couples to recognize the forthcoming responsibilities and problems of family living. This milestone overlaps with Milestone VII, which includes education for family living for prospective parents.

MILESTONE II

Time

The neonatal period.

Objectives:

To assure that an adequate child caring environment is available for each child through evaluation of the following factors:

1. The physical, mental, and temperamental characteristics of the infant (Brazelton, 1973; Eagle, 1977).
2. The adequacy of infant nutrition.
3. The quality of the initial emotional and feeding relationship between mother and infant.
4. The need for family life and infant care education for the parents.
5. The ability of the family unit to handle family or social stress.
6. The need for social services and aid for the family to make use of them.

Location:

Hospitals, clinics, and neighborhood centers.

Personnel:

Physicians, nurses, social workers, nutritionists, and community workers.

Rationale:

The aim of this milestone is to provide planned and systematic support for the family as it receives the child. It is the beginning of a process in which the needs of children can be made known, and appropriate services mobilized for them. Although barriers related to language and custom have led professionals to regard populations who fail to use available services as "hard to reach," it is more accurate to say that these groups are "hard to serve." They are reachable, but their multiple needs are difficult to meet. For this reason, outreach approaches using paraprofessional personnel can make significant contributions at this time when parental attitudes toward developmental review can be positively influenced.

MILESTONE III

Time:

Early childhood, age 2½ to 3½.

Objectives:

Prevention, early identification, and treatment of obstacles to development through evaluation of:

1. The quality of the family environment.
2. Emotional development.
3. Neuromuscular development.
4. Language development.
5. The child's readiness for a day care or nursery school program.

Location:

Homes, clinics, child care centers.

Personnel:

Physicians, nurses, social workers, child care workers, community workers.

Rationale:

The third milestone does not correspond to an easily recognized event such as birth or school entry but it does relate to the time at which children usually have matured sufficiently to engage in social relationships. The third year of life is recommended because it is the earliest time that a complete biopsychosocial assessment is practical. It also is a point at which the effectiveness of parenting can be practically evaluated (Rafferty, 1969). The monitoring of this period ordinarily is carried out by families with the support of a family physician. The family and health workers can identify and correct a variety of potential developmental obstacles ranging from impaired vision or hearing to orthopedic conditions, and disorders in speech and sphincter control. When development goes well the process does not attract social, political, or legal attention. However, when it does not, the later consequences for the child's development can be devastating.

MILESTONE IV

Time:
School entry, age 4½ to 5½.

Objectives:
To assure that each child enters the school system with identified and understood capacities and adequate family supports and to facilitate the child's transition from home to school, from siblings to peer group, and from parents to teachers. Specifically to assure that:

1. Children who already have been identified as having special needs have received adequate treatment.
2. Children who either have individual developmental differences or children whose birth date makes them significantly older or younger than most are programmed so as to minimize the possibility of their variation becoming the source of an educational or behavioral deviation.
3. High-risk children are reassessed to determine continued needs.
4. Sensory defects, especially in vision and hearing, language problems, and maturational lags that interfere with the learning process are identified.
5. Children with identified problems are offered needed services.
6. Families have adequate support systems.

Location:
Schools, clinics, neighborhood centers, child care centers.

Personnel:
Physicians, nurses, speech diagnosticians, educational psychologists, child care workers, social workers, community workers, child psychiatrists.

Rationale:
Public education should tailor educational programs to the abilities and liabilities of individual children and move beyond large-scale processing of masses of children through uniform schedules and curricula. An understanding of the unique requirements of each child at the point of school entry permits individualized planning and increases the likelihood of the child's successful engagement with the academic learning process.

The availability of an objective evaluation of each child's capacities and needs, accordingly, would provide reassurance to parents and the schools regarding the appropriateness of school planning.

MILESTONE V

Time:
Third grade, age 7½ to 8½.

Objectives:
To assure that each child has developed the basic learning skills and possesses sufficient personality maturity to function effectively in the role of student. The specific points for evaluation are:

1. Reading and arithmetical levels.
2. Communication skills.
3. Vision and hearing.
4. Interpersonal interests and skills, particularly with peers.
5. Gender identification.
6. Existence of emotional and behavioral symptoms.
7. Existence of family or community stress.

Location:
Schools, clinics, professional practice.

Personnel:
Schoolteachers, administrators, psychologists, physicians, social workers, language and reading diagnosticians, nurses, child psychiatrists, mental health clinics, and community workers.

Rationale:
The third grade is a pivotal year for the school age child. By this time the basic foundations for learning should be acquired. If deficiencies exist, the child's academic career is jeopardized. Learning and behavior problems become compounded after this time by repetitive failures. Children of this age are in a phase of relative behavioral stability during which emotional and mental problems can be identified. Future expectations held by parents and school for each child can also be brought in line with demonstrated capacities at this point.

MILESTONE VI

Time:
Sixth grade for girls (age 10½ to 11½).
Seventh grade for boys (age 11½ to 12½).

Objectives:

To assure that each child is making a satisfactory transition into the physiological, emotional, and social aspects of adolescence with sufficient personality maturity and independence to permit satisfying peer relations, the management of choices in school curriculum, and a comfortable acceptance of self. The specific points for evaluation are:

1. Physiological growth.
2. Emotional maturity.
3. Academic achievement in the light of capacities.
4. Existence of emotional and behavioral symptoms.
5. Existence of family or community stresses.
6. Peer, recreational, and extracurricular satisfactions.
7. Opportunities for the discussion of self-concept, sexuality, and personal objectives.

Location:

Schools, clinics, professional practice.

Personnel:

School psychologists, social workers, counselors, physicians, nurses, child psychiatrists, mental health clinics, and community workers.

Rationale:

The onset of puberty requires a personal adaptation to physical and sexual growth for each girl and boy, the former engaging with this before the latter. Providing an evaluation at this point offers the possibility of enhancing the formation of self-identity through personalized self-reflection for each child and by helping those with low self-esteem. The incidence of behavior problems tends to peak during the eighth grade, indicating the desirability of a prior checkpoint.

This period also is characterized by a wider range of individual choice in curriculum planning and marks the beginning of increased contacts with a larger number of teachers and more varied course content than previously experienced.

MILESTONE VII

Time:

Eleventh grade (age 15½ to 16½).

Objectives:

To assure that each youth has adequately achieved the aims of education and is prepared to engage with issues of career choice, family living, and social responsibilities. The specific points for evaluation are:

1. Readiness to assume social responsibilities.
2. Academic achievement in light of capacities.
3. Social and recreational opportunities.
4. Opportunities for discussion of self-concept and career planning.
5. Opportunities for counseling as a capstone to sex and family education.
6. Existence of emotional and behavioral symptoms.
7. Existence of drug abuse and venereal disease.
8. Existence of family and community stresses.

Location:
Schools, clinics, professional practice.

Personnel:
School and vocational counselors, psychologists, physicians, social workers, nurses, child psychiatrists, mental health clinics, and community workers.

Rationale:
The later years of high school are a crucial period for the development of an individual's personal identity and the integration of the physical and sexual aspects of puberty. Preparation for this culturally structured transition from adolescence to adulthood through an opportunity for self-examination during the eleventh grade would enhance each youth's self-identity. Attention focused on the importance of living this period fully also should aid in the resolution of frequently postponed adolescent issues.

Intervention Techniques

Interventions with children are particularly delicate because the actions and personalities of adult professionals make lasting impressions on the attitudes and identifications of children. Accordingly, adults bear the responsibility of carefully considering the impact of their actions, or failures to act, on children. It is readily apparent that the manner in which doctors and nurses approach a child determines whether or not a minor pain will be experienced traumatically by the child. It is less obvious and more important, however, to know the impact of presumably routine actions that affect children. Thus, a social worker who placed a child in a foster home became the focus of nightmares because of that child's misconception that she might come and take him away if he misbehaved.

When the existence of a problem is suspected, the need for assuming responsibility as an advocate for the child should be weighed. A child may be identified as needing further attention; however, diagnostic and treatment services may not be sought at that particular time for a variety of reasons related to the accessibility of services and the motivation of those responsible for the child. A primary care advocacy technique under those circumstances is to find a point of entry into the child's life through a key person, or gatekeeper, who can influence the responsible adults. This may be a relative, community or religious leader, or ultimately a judge. When the appropriate gatekeeper has been found, skill is required to orient the gatekeeper to the need for action. This is a delicate operation that may require a number of points of leverage in order to convince the gatekeeper that action is indicated. Special skill in bridging systems involves informing as many people who have responsibility for the child as possible about the child's needs. The aim is to obtain cooperation between systems through helping responsible adults become aware of each other's interests and aims. Frequently, this means sensitizing the parents, schools, and courts to the existence of a child's problem (Gatti, 1976).

> A case example illustrates the steps involved in establishing the role of advocate. In this case, a lack of direction between the various systems dealing with a hospitalized woman's foundering children was detected by her psychiatrist. Child psychiatric consultation was obtained, and it became evident that a variety of people including a family court commissioner, another adult psychiatrist, a clergyman, a family clinic, three social workers, a school psychologist and two community workers were not coordinated in their efforts to help this mother and her children. A conference was held involving all of these professionals in the mother's adult psychiatric unit. The mother had custody of the oldest two of her five children and her former husband wished to assume custody of all five children in his new family created through his remarriage. At the conference a plan was devised for the father, who actually was caring for all five children while the mother was hospitalized, to obtain legal custody of the oldest two rather than return them to his former wife. The psychiatric team treating the mother had assumed that the oldest two of her children were important to the mother's mental health because she needed the challenge of rearing them. When they recognized the adverse effect of such an arrangement on the children and that the children could not be utilized as a treatment resource for the mother without taking their interests into account, they acceded to the plan. When the father assumed custody, the mother's dramatic clinical improvement revealed that the stress of child rearing and the mother's ambivalence toward the children were precipitating factors in her acute psychotic state. In this case the psychiatric team treating the mother was the gatekeeper with influence that made it possible to implement a life plan for her foundering children.

Three strategies can be used at the primary care level of advocacy (McGowan, 1973). The first is collaborative, in which the advocate attempts to elicit the interest or support of other adults through posing the child's problem as a joint responsibility on which they must work together. A second strategy is mediatory, in which the advocate acts as an intermediary in the hope of negotiating a relationship between the child's agents and a helping system. A third strategy is adversarial, in which the advocate envisions a child caring system as an opponent and proceeds accordingly through pressure or coercion. McGowan found in a survey of advocacy by social workers that the adversarial strategy was used in only one in four cases, the remainder responding to collaborative and mediatory strategies. Actual practice substantiates that child advocates are usually not antagonistic to existing systems and adversarial in their approach.

All professionals at all levels require consultation services. Consequently, an important primary care skill is knowing when and how to seek consultation. At the primary care level this may be seeking help in determining whether or not to intervene, how to intervene, what to do in direct treatment, and where to make referrals.

The primary care skill of referral for evaluation and treatment entails knowledge of resources, how to use them, and how to ensure that the child and family are oriented toward the service in such a way that it is used successfully. Not only do parents need orientation, but the child should understand what is going to happen as well. Very frequently, the simple step of informing a child of a planned diagnostic procedure is overlooked, and misunderstanding occurs with loss of potential benefit through impaired cooperation of the child. With sensitivity to the child's viewpoint, explanations can be couched in concrete terms that respond to that child's questions. The advocacy aspect of referral is assuming responsibility for following through on referrals, ensuring that a child receives service and evaluating the progress of services. This is particularly important when a child moves through the secondary and tertiary care levels because of the tendency toward extrusion of the child from the mainstream of life as child caring systems and peers "close ranks" behind the child. For example, encouraging the school to "hold a desk" and to maintain contact with the family of a child placed away from home is a helpful antidote to the strong tendency for schools and communities to assume that such children no longer exist.

A case illustration of primary care level advocacy is a community worker's activity with a 16 year old eleventh grader who had been suspended from school four times for truancy. He was on probation and had already spent six months in the county school for delinquents. His mother worked as a waitress, and his father was in a state hospital alcoholic program.

The community worker recognized that the boy's home and school were not meeting his needs and convinced a probation officer that psychiatric study was needed to develop a plan for his future. The worker also recognized that the boy needed a fresh start away from the drugs and alcohol that permeated his peer group. An outpatient evaluation was arranged two times, but the boy failed to keep the appointments. He also failed to keep several job interviews.

Several months later the boy was arrested for vandalism. In court he promised to attend school and stay out of trouble. The first day in school he missed five out of six classes and was suspended. Shortly thereafter, he took money from his mother's purse, and she told him to leave home. When he returned to court for violating probation, the community worker recommended admission to a state residential treatment center rather than return to the county school. This was accomplished and six months later the boy was placed in an adolescent group home with special education appropriate to his low reading level and continued outpatient psychotherapy. The community worker maintained a continued relationship with the boy, visiting him periodically to check on his progress.

Although this chapter is devoted to individual advocacy, an illustration of the way in which a particular professional might function as an advocate can be gained from the levels of advocacy in the professional life of a primary care physician, as described by Schmitt (1978):

1. Informing parents about obtaining services from community agencies.
2. Intervening personally or through correspondence in assisting parents to obtain services.
3. Attending staff meetings in other child caring systems regarding a patient.
4. Participating in community adult or child education lectures and panels.
5. Participating in a multidisciplinary team.
6. Joining a class advocacy group as board member or medical advisor.
7. Joining national committees or organizations devoted to the special needs of children.
8. Catalyzing the formation of a new class advocacy group addressing an unmet need the physician personally considers important.

Secondary Care Advocacy Functions

Secondary care encompasses health, mental health, specialized education, correctional facilities, and child caring welfare services, representing the five predominating streams of supportive services for children (Figure 1). They cover the range and variety of public and private sector services required to handle child–adolescent problems. It is at the level of secondary care that much disagreement and misunderstanding exists regarding categories of disability and services. At this level questions are raised about defining whether or not a problem is mental illness, emotional disturbance, mental retardation, dependency, neglect, or delinquency. It is also at this level that socioeconomic status and cultural background influence the category into which a given child falls. Agencies, professionals, and institutions tend to respond to the people they process in the nature of "what they do" and the kind of service each one is designed to provide. An advocate is needed to focus attention less on what an agency ordinarily does and more on what a specific child requires.

Although the labels applied by each of these service categories vary considerably, the human problems they deal with are remarkably similar. A youngster founders because of a combination of mental, emotional, intellective, cognitive, behavioral, family, and social problems. The children differ only in the degree to which each of these factors is involved. Not only are the children similar, but each of the existing separate service channels aim to do similar and complementary things under optimal circumstances. The problem, then, is that categorization of children leads to fractional management of a part of a child's problem by professionals who have almost identical goals, methods, and backgrounds but work in physically separate and disconnected programs. At the secondary level, then, the most important need for advocacy is in coordinating and maintaining continuity of evaluative and treatment services for each child.

Under optimal circumstances, the mental health system, as an illustration of one part of the child caring system, includes the following components: crisis intervention, outpatient evaluation and treatment, consultation to primary and secondary care professionals, brief hospitalization for children and adolescents, day treatment service, family treatment, and community service programs (Glasscote et al., 1972). These programs should be linked to the other child supportive systems through a collaborative network. This range of mental health services illustrates the complexity of child–adolescent mental health services and the importance of coordination, collaboration, and consultation at the secondary care level (Hetznecker, 1974).

Advocacy at the secondary level is needed during evaluation of the child's life circumstances in the form of ensuring that information from primary care professionals reaches the secondary care level. The evaluation involves the synthesis of psychological, social work, medical, legal, educational, and psychiatric information. This can be carried out by an interdisciplinary team or by an individual practitioner with access to the full range of information. In either case it is essential at this point that someone, if not the parents, be identified as the child's pro tem advocate. At this point the formulation of the child's special needs takes place, and it is imperative that the diagnostic studies be integrated. The pro tem advocate should be a professional capable of such integration.

The next secondary care level advocacy skill is formulating a life plan based upon the alternatives available to a child. This means looking beyond the immediate problem to the child's long-range interests. A life plan begins with an evaluation of where a child should live and with whom when there is more than one option. It includes a treatment plan that identifies the resources needed to promote and remedy deficiencies in the child's development. It anticipates the child's special needs at subsequent developmental stages. When applicable, it also includes a tentative evaluation of future living arrangements in the light of the child's interests.

The ingredients needed to formulate a life plan are as follows: (1) developmental history, (2) family history keyed to the child, (3) diagnostic interviews with the child, (4) psychological testing, (5) educational achievement testing, (6) family dynamic assessment, (7) medical evaluation, including indicated laboratory procedures, (8) longitudinal and current school observations, (9) home and community field study, and (10) legal evaluation of fulfilling the rights of the child and parents. Determining the interventions that are feasible in a child's life involves weighing the available alternatives and assigning them priorities based upon their detrimental and beneficial effects on the child.

The next advocacy skill is interpreting the interventions that are recommended. Beyond helping adults responsible for the child recognize that a problem exists is the process of aiding them to seek help. More than a surface view of the child's problem must be developed since a common misperception of a child's problem is reflected in the statement "everything is all right now." Frequently parents are unaware of, or for various reasons are unable to accept, the existence of a problem.

Another secondary care level advocacy skill is protecting the privacy and confidentiality of the child and the family. This involves general concepts of confidentiality and specific knowledge of confidentiality within the family system with sensitivity to generational differences in needs and interests. This area is discussed in more detail in Chapter 12.

The last and most important secondary care level advocacy function is selecting a case manager to replace and continue the role of the pro tem advocate. This means coordinating treatment, counseling parents, and consulting with specialized educational services for the child, among other things. At times it means obtaining legal support for alterations in the custody of the child. Most important, it means ensuring that there is a professional advocate for the child who has general responsibility for coordination, although other members of a therapeutic team might have specific advocacy functions. The essential point is that services for the child must not be fragmented and must be continuous over time. At this point most programs for children break down. One professional must be designated as the person to whom the parents and child can turn in times of need and who will keep a watchful eye on the implementation and continuous revision of the child's life plan. This person may have more or less direct involvement at a given time, but the presence of that individual is essential for a successful outcome for the child.

An illustrative case is a five year old boy who was involved in a child custody dispute. His attorney, a *guardian ad litem*, in conjunction with an adult psychiatrist, arranged for a child psychiatric evaluation which included a study of both disputing parents and the child and resulted in awarding custody to the father. The following ingredients were coordinated by the child psychiatrist over the next two years: counseling of each divorced parent, attorney conferences, child psychotherapy, social agency collaboration, counseling with the mother, followup counseling with both parents, agency-family collaboration, court testimony, and counseling of both parents about the child's interests on their remarriages.

The location of the case manager coordination can lie in a hospital, clinic, mental health center, private practitioner, child caring institution, placement agency, or other clinical service. The nature of the educational system itself precludes the assignment of the case manager role to school personnel. At this point the distinction between clinical and educational services becomes apparent. Schools are responsible for providing for those aspects of the child's life that fall within the province of education. Educational personnel can function at the primary care level and support case management at the secondary and tertiary care levels. Their primary responsibility is to the school system, however, and they do not have a client or patient relationship to the individual child and family to form the basis for case management. By their nature, then, school systems are not designed to assume responsibility for guiding and monitoring a child's treatment plan.

A case example is a child with the hyperkinetic syndrome who was referred to a child psychiatrist by a parent and an adult psychiatrist for evaluation. As a part of the evaluation, a collaborative study was carried out with the public schools, child neurological consultation was obtained and interviews were carried out with the parents and the child. The recommendation was that the child return to a regular class rather than continue in a special education class in which he had been inappropriately placed. A school conference was held to develop a management plan with the principal and teacher. Parent counseling, child psychotherapy, family therapy, chemotherapy for the child and follow-up consultations with the teachers and principal were carried out to ensure coordination and continuity of the treatment plan.

Since a child's life plan spans years and changes occur in child caring agencies and personnel, the case manager function must be the responsibility of a relatively permanent person or capable of smooth transfer between persons. The functions of the case manager are coordinating, integrating, monitoring, and evaluating progress of the services that a child receives. Such advocacy may also involve stimulating communities to develop needed services when they do not exist (Adams, 1976).

A case illustration is a child with early infantile autism who was referred to a child psychiatrist by a pediatrician during the third year of life. An evaluation was carried out, and the child psychiatrist coordinated the following elements of care which took place in sequence over eight years: parent counseling, mother–child therapy, language therapy, nursery school consultation, consultation to specialized educational services in the public school and child psychotherapy. Included in the management of this child was the class advocacy activity of the parents who organized a mental health association committee to stimulate the development of services in their community for emotionally disturbed children.

Another case example is a child with symbiotic psychosis who was referred to a child psychiatrist by a pediatrician at the age of five. After a child psychiatric evaluation, the following forms of treatment were coordinated by the child psychiatrist over the following six years: parent counseling, chemotherapy for the child, family therapy, child psychotherapy and consulting to specialized educational services in the public schools. A critical element was helping the parents to seek the development of statutorily mandated specialized educational services in their school system.

Tertiary Care Advocacy Functions

At the present time, only a small segment of the population has access to a complete range of the most highly specialized services for children. Moreover, most correctional and residential facilities for children operate without essential interdisciplinary components. The situation is more favorable for specialized pediatric care; however, even physical health care is unavailable for many who live in poverty and lack competent primary care as well. Even for high-income groups with access to the finest pediatric and child psychiatric attention, all components of comprehensive care are often not conveniently accessible.

An illustration of the complexity of tertiary level advocacy is a two year old child referred by a social agency to a child psychiatrist because of parental neglect, maternal deprivation and mental retardation. After the child psychiatric evaluation, the following sequential steps took place over the next two years: periodic developmental assessments, support of foster placement through agency consultation, evaluation of the biological parents, determination of the need to terminate parental rights, arranging for agency custody to support a permanent foster placement after termination of parental rights, consultation with the district attorney and defense attorneys, special educational consultation, language therapy, therapeutic nursery placement of the child and foster parent–child therapy.

The essential ingredients of tertiary care are comprehensive interdisciplinary evaluation, residential treatment, outpatient treatment, consultation service, professional education, and research programs. A distinction between the care of physically ill children and the mentally and emotionally handicapped is necessary because the latter are ambulatory and may require longer term treatment. A single tertiary care service can handle the problems arising from regional primary and secondary levels in the mental health, educational, and social service systems. As is evident from its functions, tertiary care is often affiliated with a university health center.

The geographical location of tertiary care is critical since treatment for troubled children and adolescents is most effective when provided in the mainstream of the child's life. The most effective methods of treatment involve an interdisciplinary team working in a family–community network. For these reasons, beyond convenience to the consumer, tertiary care should be easily accessible to the youngster's home and should include free working relationships with primary and secondary levels of care.

The staffing of a tertiary care center should include a comprehensive range of evaluative capacities, including the following: psychomotor maturation, physical growth, intellectual capacity, language development, coping skills, learning skills, temperament, emotional development, personality development, parental child rearing practices, family living experiences, hearing and visual acuity, and knowledge of community resources. The disciplines needed to provide these services and to utilize the center for training include: pediatrics, child psychiatry, child neurology, social work, nursing, special education, clinical developmental psychology, communicative disorders, medical genetics, occupational therapy, nutrition, physical therapy, and vocational rehabilitation.

At the tertiary care level, there is a need for a number of programs related to specific age groups. Depending upon the region, they include therapeutic nursery schools for young children, residential treatment for school age children, and outpatient and inpatient services for adolescents. Furthermore, the need to maintain a direct linkage with the primary care level necessitates community consultation capability.

A specific function of the tertiary care level is to back up milestone review at the primary care level. It is possible in rural areas to provide primary care through a mobile unit sponsored by a tertiary care service, particularly through the use of trainees. Teams based at the tertiary level can be deployed to carry out developmental reviews. For example, a three-person team comprised of a public health nurse, a clinical psychologist, and a social worker can constitute a traveling developmental review team based at the tertiary care level. The public health nurse relates to pediatrics, communicative disorders, and nutrition for consultative support; the clinical psychologist to child psychiatry, child neurology, and education; and the social worker to community agencies.

In order to provide professionals for the primary and secondary care levels, teaching and training functions at the tertiary care level are needed for undergraduate, graduate, and postgraduate education. Trainees from the range of disciplines can be oriented to interdisciplinary teamwork and the capabilities of practicing professionals can be renewed and upgraded through in-service training. There is a great demand for comprehensively trained professionals in most children's services.

Another tertiary care level function is altering a child's environment through hospitalization or residential placement in order to obtain specialized treatment services. This is indicated when a family and a community are unable to meet the treatment needs of a child. The advocacy function at this level is ensuring that the therapeutic placement is in the child's interests and that it does not result simply from default on the part of the family and community.

> A case illustration is a fourteen year old boy admitted to the adolescent ward of a state psychiatric hospital. He had a long history of placement in several child care institutions and although his mother had retained custody after divorcing his father, he had not lived with her for six years. Visitation with the mother continued in spite of its destructive influence on him. In fact he was discharged from a child care institution because of thefts which occurred while he was visiting his mother. Unsuccessful efforts were made by the state hospital to engage the mother in counseling, and she continued to sabotage the treatment program. During his hospitalization, an attorney was retained by the boy and his mother to obtain release from the hospital because he was there on a voluntary basis, initially with his mother's approval. Therapeutic intervention with the boy induced him to remain in the hospital for the duration of his six month course of treatment. Because home visits were retarding treatment, court custody was sought and obtained. With temporary agency custody it was possible to make treatment decisions without the mother's approval; although she continued to play a role in his problem. Court ordered outpatient therapy was carried out while he was placed in a group home and his psychiatrist provided consultation to the group home staff. Backed by the court, the treatment program ultimately successfully shifted the youngster into a vocational program in high school. In this case the active intervention of a child psychiatrist was required in order to establish a community structure within which outpatient therapy for the boy could be effective. The child psychiatrist functioned as therapist, consultant and advocate. He was not able to carry out a counseling role with the boy's mother. The key intervention was psychotherapy with the boy, however, it could not have succeeded without the court's support and community recognition of the pathogenic role of his mother in his life.

A related advocacy function is either temporarily or permanently altering the nature of the relationship between a child and the parents through legal means. A large number of children are in tertiary level care because courts are reluctant to act in situations in which parental rights should obviously be terminated. Lacking is a professional person with sufficient knowledge and background to put together the facts about a child's life experience, bridge the legal and mental health systems, and make a convincing argument for the termination of parental rights in court. Within the health system a forensic child advocacy team, similar to the team approach in renal, cardiological, and other medical specialty areas (Evans, 1975), with legal participation, is one means of effectively influencing court action.

Experience has shown that when termination of parental rights is carried out appropriately, the parents are relieved of the guilt that previously made it impossible for them to relinquish legal responsibility for their child. It is most difficult for some parents to face their inability to raise their child and to voluntarily surrender their parental rights. Furthermore, although it is possible to work therapeutically with parents for whom termination of parental rights is to occur, sometimes it cannot be done until after a court has actually terminated their rights to the child. It may be unthinkable for a parent to "give up a child" voluntarily, but it is face saving to be able to say that the judge "took my child away from me." More frequently, temporarily assuming guardianship for a child by a court or agency facilitates planning and obtaining needed treatment for a child. This provides children with the kind of legal guardianship and support needed when their own parents are unable to function in that capacity. The current emphasis on the right of children to refuse treatment highlights the importance of using more convincing legal processes to ensure that children receive treatment.

A case illustration is a ten year old boy referred to a psychiatric consultant by a family agency. He had spoken of wishes to kill children placed with his mother who was earning money through day care. The consultant recommended a child psychiatric evaluation, which was carried out. The history disclosed that the mother had four previous children removed from her home because of her inability to care for them. Although she was now engaged in family day care, she had been declined a license for group day care in the past and had circumvented the statutory license requirement by having less than four children in her home. It was determined that the child was potentially violent and further information from the school indicated deteriorating performance and episodes of bizarre behavior. A counseling effort was carried out with the parents unsuccessfully, and it was ascertained that the mother had a severe personality disorder and the father alcoholism. The boy was admitted to a child psychiatric facility for further study after court custody was obtained as a result of the child psychiatrist's recommendation resulting from a joint conference involving the family agency, previous community social workers who had been involved with the mother and the school social worker. The mother retained an attorney to counter this move, however, expert testimony was introduced by a *guardian ad litem* appointed for the child indicating that agency custody was in the child's interests. Consultation was further provided to the court in order to obtain a treatment oriented foster home which would be accessible to outpatient therapy. The county social service agency also was alerted to the fact that the mother was caring for other children on a family day care basis, however, they were unable to take action because she was outside the current law. After a period of a year it became evident that the mother was not accessible to various offers of treatment services in the community, and the father's alcoholism deteriorated so that he was placed in a state hospital because of his organic brain syndrome. At that point, permanent subsidized foster care was ordered and custody of the child was transferred to the state division of family services. In this case the child psychiatrist acted as a therapist, counselor, consultant, coordinator and initiator of legal action. It was the child psychiatrist's knowledge of the law in this matter that ultimately led to an appropriate outcome through handling legal interventions that would have sabotaged the child's treatment course. This case also illustrates the impotence of communities in dealing with gross psychopathology in parents and in intervening for children, even when they are obviously deleteriously affected.

Conclusion

For most children, parental advocacy is generally sufficient. A large number of children, however, depend upon professionals to play an advocacy role in their lives. This chapter has been devoted to advocacy skills that aid professionals in appropriately assuming responsibility for finding children in need of help, understanding their special requirements, and ensuring that those requirements are met.

A barrier to child advocacy is the professional tradition to rely upon the cooperation of the individual to be helped. This is a generally viable approach with adults and is an expression of a value that stresses individual freedom, both to prosper and to fail. Because children are unable to articulate and meet their needs, however, professional work with children inherently includes a responsibility to promote and protect each child's interests. Beyond offering diagnosis and treatment, then, professionals have an obligation to ensure that children receive and profit from required services.

At the level of primary care the thrust of advocacy is through case finding, developmental review, and intervention. At the secondary care level the emphasis is on formulating a life plan and ensuring coordination and continuity of care through designation of a case manager. At the tertiary care level the emphasis is upon comprehensive teamwork and stabilizing a child's life.

Although the responsibility and the means for substantially intervening in the lives of children falls within the legal system, understanding and formulating the needs of children is the province of the clinical professions. Courts have a basis for definitive action when the helping professions can convincingly demonstrate a rationale for changing a child's life situation. Without advocacy skills, professionals lack the ability to perceive and implement the kinds of actions required to ensure the viability of a life plan necessary to a child's healthy development.

In most cases the ability of professionals to practice effective advocacy makes it possible for children to remain with their parents in their homes through realistic, even though sometimes initially resisted, interventions with their families. Advocacy for children need not be intrusive or adversarial if based upon the natural dependency of children upon adults to make wise decisions for them. In most cases, when reason can be brought to bear on a child's problem, a solution satisfying to all can be found. Ordinarily, the lack can be found in the resolve of adults to do what they know is best for children. When courage, patience, and persistence undergird reasonable knowledge, successful advocacy usually follows.

The hope for child advocacy is based less upon the altruistic desire of adults to help children and more upon the satisfaction that comes from participating in significant change and progress in the development of children. Every child with a significant developmental problem is served most effectively by professionals with an interest in ensuring that the child's special needs are met. This can be achieved most effectively through the designation of a case manager with the responsibility of coordinating and monitoring services provided for the child. The lack of coordination and continuity of care is the cause of our failure to help many children and is the most compelling reason for ensuring that advocacy skills are included in the training of all professionals who deal with them.

References

ADAMS, P. (1976) "Local Community Change for Service to Children." *Child Psychiatry and Human Development*, 7:22–30, Fall.

AMERICAN ORTHOPSYCHIATRIC ASSOCIATION (1978) "Developmental Assessment in EPSDT." *American Journal of Orthopsychiatry*, 48:7–21, January.

BOLMAN, W. M. (1967) "An Outline of Preventive Psychiatric Programs for Children." *Archives of General Psychiatry*, 17:5–8, July.

BOLMAN, W. M., AND WESTMAN, J. C. (1967) "Prevention of Mental Disorder: An Overview of Current Programs." *American Journal of Psychiatry*, 123:1058–1068, March.

BRAZELTON, T. B. (1973) "Neonatal Behavioral Assessment Scale." *Clinics in Developmental Medicine*, No. 50. London: Spastic International Medical Monographs. Philadelphia: Lippincott.

DEPARTMENT OF HEALTH, EDUCATION AND WELFARE (1977) *Developmental Review in the EPSDT Program.* Washington, D.C.: U.S. Government Printing Office.

EAGLE, D. B., AND BRAZELTON, T. B. (1977) "The Infant at Risk—Assessment and Implications for Intervention." Chapter in McMillan, M. F., and Henao, S. (Eds.), *Child Psychiatry Treatment and Research*. New York: Brunner/Mazel.

EVANS, S. L., FISHER, G. D., AND REINHART, J. B. (1975) "Experience with a SCAN Program in a Children's Hospital." Presented at the 1975 Annual Meeting of the American Association of Psychiatric Services for Children.

GATTI, F., AND COLEMAN, C. (1976) "Community Network Therapy: An Approach to Aiding Families with Troubled Children." *American Journal of Orthopsychiatry*, 46:608–617, October.

GLASSCOTE, R., FISHMAN, M., AND SORIS, M. (1972) *Children and Mental Health Centers*. Washington, D.C.: American Psychiatric Association.

GROUP FOR THE ADVANCEMENT OF PSYCHIATRY (1972) *Crisis in Child Mental Health: A Critical Assessment*, Vol. 8, Report No. 82. New York: Mental Health Materials Center, February.

HANSEN, M. F. (1970) "An Educational Program for Primary Care: Definitions and Hypotheses." *Journal of Medical Education*, 45:1001–1006, December.

HENDERSON, P. B. (1978) "A Developmental–Adaptive Model for Use in Service—Matrix Planning for Youth." *Child Psychiatry and Human Development*, 8:162–174.

HERSH, S. P. (1978) "Sweden's Approach to Health Screening for Preschool Children." *American Journal of Orthopsychiatry*, 48:33–39.

HETZNECKER, W., AND FORMAN, M. A. (1974) *On Behalf of Children*. New York: Grune and Stratton.

MCGOWAN, B. G. (1973) *Case Advocacy: A Study of the Intervention Process in Child Advocacy*. New York: Child Advocacy Research Project, Columbia University School of Social Work.

NOSHPITZ, J. D. (1974) "Toward a National Policy for Children." *Journal of Child Psychiatry*, 13:385–401, Summer.

PERLMUTTER, F. D. ET AL. (1976) "An Instrument for Differentiating Programs in Prevention—Primary, Secondary and Tertiary." *American Journal of Orthopsychiatry*, 46:533–541, July.

RAFFERTY, F. T. (1969) "Systems Model for the Child Care Industry." Joint Commission on the Mental Health of Children, Working Paper, Task Force V.

SCHMITT, B. D. (1978) "Editors' Introduction." *Child Advocacy and Pediatrics, Report of the Eighth Ross Roundtable*. Columbus, Ohio: Ross Laboratories.

STRINGER, L. A. (1978) "Mental Health Work in Children's Health Centers: Learning from Five Years' Experience." *American Journal of Orthopsychiatry*, 48:40–55, January.

WAHLER, G., HOUSE, A. E., AND STEINBAUGH, E. E. (1976) *Ecological Assessment of Child Problem Behavior: A Clinical Package for Home, School and Institutional Settings*. London: Pergamon Press.

YARMOLINSKY, A. (1978) "What Future for the Professional in American Society?" *Daedalus*, 107:159–174, Winter.

Part IV
Advocacy Issues in Child Caring Systems

In the green years of childhood the young begin their irreversible march into the future with the resolution and sweet calmness of innocence. The march of childhood goes on as long as the human race endures, an affirmation of new hope and the freshness of life that comes with every generation. The message proclaims another chance for mankind.

United Nations Children's Fund

This section illustrates the importance of a broad conception of child advocacy. Although each child caring system poses unique issues related to furthering the interests of children, advocacy is an interdisciplinary enterprise and cannot be complete without taking into account all facets of a child's life. Fragmented advocacy limited to one system perpetuates our past errors of devising only short-range, partial solutions without taking into account the complex long-range needs of children. Knowledge of systems serving children other than one's own is vital to effective advocacy.

Chapter 8 is devoted to the largest institutional child caring system—the schools. As much or more than families, schools socialize children and convey American culture. Although the history of education in the United States is studded with innovations, the basic problems of schooling relate to old issues: teacher–pupil ratios, classroom discipline, and relevance of curricula. As is true of any massive system, schools have developed their own momentum, and the consumers, the children, are frequently not considered in their operations. The roles of the states, school administrators, teachers, students, and parents are discussed in the context of the rights of children to an education. Specific issues for advocacy in education are then highlighted: individual differences in children, classification, record keeping, teaching social values, and behavioral control.

The history of the law's view of children is sketched in Chapter 9. In modern law the uniqueness of children is slowly being recognized through age grading, the psychological best interests of the child standard, and awareness of the urgency of speed in litigation affecting children. The legal rights of children are then addressed in the form of a composite Bill of Rights for Children. The problems of the juvenile court system are also highlighted, with particular attention to the dilemmas created by its legal and social service roles. The variegated facets of family law are then described, especially the inherent incompatibility of dealing with family problems in an adversary format, particularly child custody and guardianship. Finally, the need for more formalized teamwork between the legal and mental health systems is pointed out.

In Chapter 10 the problems of social services for children are addressed. The origins of social welfare are traced, shedding light on the chronic ambivalence harbored by society in devising and implementing welfare programs. The current state of the welfare system is described, emphasizing its fragmented, crisis-oriented response to parts of social problems without coherent long-range planning. The range of public and private social services for children, including foster care, adoption, and group care, are then outlined and viewed from the point of view of affected children. The need for greater professionalism in providing social services is essential to shift the welfare system from mechanically to humanistically relating to children who lack parents fully able to meet their needs.

The aspects of health care for children raising advocacy issues are discussed in Chapter 11. The responsibility of health care workers to educate children in promoting health and preventing disease is addressed. The right of children to health care is then viewed in the light of the large numbers of children who do not receive adequate care. As a corollary, the long-range impact of health nonintervention or intervention, such as hospitalization, on children is considered. The issues of informed consent and confidentiality are treated from the point of view of children. The complicated matter of child abuse, including reporting systems, is then discussed as an example of a clinical area in which varying degrees of advocacy are required. Finally, the current concern about child abuse is used as an example of how increased collaboration between the health and social service systems can help families that are foundering.

Chapter 12 deals with children in the mental health system, the youngest of the child caring systems, but in many ways the most appropriate base for carrying out advocacy for children. It was the Joint Commission on the Mental Health of Children that identified child advocacy as a needed and practical concept. The specific advocacy issues in mental health areas relate to the right to treatment, the right to refuse treatment, informed consent, confidentiality, the misuse of classification, and the risks of treatment. The contributions of child psychiatry to community mental health and child caring systems are cited, and the interdisciplinary nature of child mental health practice is proposed as a model for general approaches to the problems of children. Because the mental health of children encompasses their physical, intellectual, emotional, and social well-being, child mental health principles form the foundation of both individual and class child advocacy.

Chapter 8
Children and the Schools

School buildings are society's bricks-and-mortar recognition of childhood. They absorb the lion's share of local taxes, with a total national cost of over $120 billion (Boyer, 1977). More than any other public institution, they reflect the character of their immediate surroundings because they are under the control of local citizens.

That our schools are in serious trouble is evident from such social indicators as increasing rates of juvenile delinquency, the large numbers of graduates who fail to read with proficiency, and a decline in SAT test scores among college applicants, the most privileged of our youth. Even more disquieting is the violence in large city high schools which have adopted jail-like security measures. Although less than the 37 percent rate in 1950, 25 percent of high school students drop out before graduation. Moreover, 2 million school age children in the United States are not attending school (Children's Defense Fund, 1974).

Schooling is a huge growth industry, only now showing the first signs of tapering off because of the recent period of decline in birth rates. There are now 60.1 million students in grade schools, high schools, and colleges. In 1984, 57 million are estimated, with 33 million in grade schools in contrast with 34.3 million now, 13 million in high schools in contrast with 15.8 million now, and 11 million in college in contrast with 10 million now. These forecasts indicate that there may be 6 percent less children in public schools in 1984 (U.S. Census Bureau, 1977).

A synopsis of the history of education will help to place our current situation in perspective (Atkinson, 1962). According to Philippe Aries, schools came into being when childhood was recognized as a special age period by middle-class families in eighteenth-century Western Europe. As middle-class children began to receive consideration and respect within their families, the educational system began to reflect bourgeois conceptions of childhood. Subsequently, schools became mechanisms for diffusing this ethos among other social classes.

In America schools have been at the core of a swiftly changing society. For the most part, they have worked reasonably well in the transition from a frontier and rural society to a society primarily urban, highly complex, and based increasingly on technological and scientific developments. Indeed, it may be said that education made that change possible.

As early as the 1750s, an enduring dualism in American education was established in the form of a striving for a balance between what Benjamin Franklin referred to as the "useful" and the "ornamental." It involved, on the one hand, teaching skills of a specific kind and, on the other hand, teaching general understanding to enable one to deal better with the affairs of life (Bruner, 1961). The first outpouring of reform spirit upon urban schools, however, was in the mid–nineteen hundreds when educators, like Horace Mann, were stirred to action by the "social dynamite" they saw in the slums. Stimulated by concern about the preservation of an ordered, cohesive society and anxious about the status of their children, middle-class parents sought better schools. The goals were utilitarian and mounted through ideological campaigns to sell education to an often skeptical, sometimes hostile, and usually uncomprehending working class. The reformers were determined to impose their innovations on the community and ultimately did so through compulsory school laws, as in Massachusetts in 1852 (Katz, 1968).

The American public educational system, as we now know it, was established in the early part of this century to prepare children for meeting the social and economic demands of adult life. It was based upon the expectation of the late nineteenth-century reformers that education would be a vehicle for social reform (Lazerson, 1971). Schools were expected to preserve the moral and social traditions; however, educators were not simply to be leaders of chilren but, more important, to be makers of society. In 1911 Lewis Terman of Stanford University said, "The future belongs to the educators. The war lords no longer exist, and clergymen and lawyers are waning in influence."

During the nineteenth century the prevalent educational theory was based upon developing mental discipline (Kolesnik, 1962) in which the purpose of education was to expand the powers of the mind, like developing muscles, and storing it with knowledge, like furniture. Specifically, the student was "taught the art of fixing attention and directing train of thought; analyzing a subject; following the course of an argument; awakening, elevating and controlling the imagination; arranging with skill the treasures which memory gathers; and rousing and guiding the powers of genius." In sum, one educator said, "Don't take the backbone out of education by making it interesting—it doesn't matter what they study as long as they don't like it!"

At the turn of the century, the concept of "social efficiency" dominated educational thinking. In 1909, Call reflected the social efficiency theme when he said, "The aim of public schools is not to promote academic training, but to enable pupils . . . to become socially and serviceably efficient." As a result, practical studies in the industrial arts, physical education, and home economics were introduced into high school curricula. The emphasis upon manual training was to teach values of honest labor, industriousness, thrift, and pride in self.

The schools were also seen as important agents of the American "melting pot." To this end, kindergartens were to reshape urban family life and teach immigrant parents the mores and behavior patterns of the traditional home through their young children. Evening schools and community centers were established to inculcate citizenship and bring cohesion to the heterogeneous urban populations, anticipating by half a century the tools of the War on Poverty of the 1960s.

Time was to bring disappointment for the social reformers, and by 1915 mass education was not found to be an effective means of producing broad social change. Frustrated by attempts at urban reform and community building, the city schools turned toward isolation from urban life, and educational administrators developed schools like well run industries. The schools became separate from the community and grew on a centralized, integrated, standardized model. Business principles superceded social reform aims. Still, the ideals of educators reflected the earlier faith that schooling would allay the disorganization of the city, the plight of the impoverished, the assimilation of the newcomer, and the adjustments to a technological, industrialized economy (Lazerson, 1971).

A third movement next supplanted mental discipline and social efficiency as a rallying theme. Educators were influenced by John Dewey's protests against the harsh discipline and meaningless drills of the nineteenth century. The Child Study Movement, exemplified by the work of G.

Stanley Hall, provided a counterpoint for the social efficiency theme by stressing the needs of children and the desirability of freedom, spontaneity, and interest in learning.

In this vein John Dewey and Francis Parker were exponents of an educational philosophy which became known as Progressive Education, based upon principles such as these:

1. Individual differences among children must be recognized.
2. Children learn best by doing and having a vital interest in what they are doing.
3. A child must be taught to think critically rather than to accept blindly.
4. Education is a continuous reconstruction of living experience that goes beyond the four walls of the classroom.
5. The classroom should be a laboratory for democracy.
6. Social goals, as well as intellectual goals, are important.

In 1919, the Association for the Advancement of Progressive Education was founded and became the arena for discussions of educational innovations, calling attention to the fact that education persistently ignored the needs of children and adolescents and the social problems confronting them. The collapse of the AAPE in the 1950s left a void in pedagogy which still has not been adequately filled.

Between 1880 and 1920 the high school became a definite place for one-third of the nation's youth to go for five or six hours a day, five days a week, nine months a year to see and talk with friends; it was a setting with assigned and not unduly burdensome tasks and a home away from home. It was a promising route for getting ahead in a competitive world (Krug, 1969).

The first compulsory education law was passed in 1852 in Massachusetts, with similar laws following in all other states concluding with Mississippi in 1918. By 1930, the question in education was whether secondary education or New Deal programs should assume custodianship for all American youth (Krug, 1972). During the early thirties the Great Depression reduced the labor force, and mandatory education to the age of 18 was seen as a cure for unemployment by decreasing the numbers of workers. The tug-of-war between educators and New Deal reformers was ultimately resolved by the onset of World War II, which forced the elimination of federal programs for youth, such as the Civilian Conservation Corps and the National Youth Administration. World War II also brought greater emphasis upon authority and quieted the progressive educational influences, also bringing vocational education back into respectability after a decade of denigration.

In essence, our educational system has been influenced by two at times polarized themes: one to prepare children to become contributing, productive citizens and the other to promote individual self-fulfillment. The former leads to stress on technical skills and the latter to acquiring knowledge and wisdom, continuing Franklin's "useful" versus "ornamental" dualism.

As a part of the socialization process, sharing responsibility with the family, the media, and other aspects of the community, the educational system now aims to prepare people to enter the work force of a materialistic, vocationally oriented society. The aim is really to prepare people for citizenship in such a way that they will not create burdens for the system, but will be contributing members. These long-range aims, however, are ambiguous and have little meaning to children in the day-to-day work of school. The children are concerned about conforming to the system and participate in its activities without obvious awareness of the ultimate aims of citizenship and self-fulfillment. Furthermore, these long-range objectives are difficult to measure. It is extremely difficult to monitor a system whose aims are preparing people for later circumstances. Thus, none of the long-range goals seem to have immediate relevance to the short-range objectives of day-to-day schooling.

The second educational purpose of self-fulfillment is reflected in recent statements such as that of the Harvard Committee (Kolesnik, 1962): the aim of education is "the development of intelligence able to operate well in all fields and to deal with new problems as they arise." The specific objectives to achieve this are fostering:

1. the ability to think effectively;
2. to communicate thought;
3. to make relevant judgments;
4. to discriminate among values.

The emphasis is upon developing the powers of the student's mind through "orderly habits of thought in well-informed disciplined minds."

Another aspect of self-fulfillment is the use of leisure, which is gaining increasing attention (Maritain, 1943). Presumably, liberal education provides a background for enjoying the fruits of knowledge and beauty. The education of tomorrow, therefore, will probably be oriented not only to career development and citizenship, but also to the use of leisure time.

In assessing these trends in education, we find ourselves alternating between eras in which academics in the form of reading, writing and arithmetic, and the acquisition of information are stressed, and eras during which the socialization and vocational purposes of education are stressed (Crow, 1964). These cycles do not seem to affect the brighter and more motivated children, whether catered to or ignored. Inside or outside the classroom, they find a way to learn. But on the less talented and interested, cycles do have an impact. As pointed out by the late Margaret Mead, at the present time many young Americans cannot write simple, grammatically correct, and well organized prose. Too often, what the students know floats unanchored and awash; they cannot organize their thoughts. All of this is happening in a world in which so much depends on the basic skills of paying attention, organizing facts, and communicating ideas. She concluded, "Young people must learn to read and write or they will turn into old people who wish they had."

In contrast with other societies, American education seems to be moving more and more toward an interactional philosophy in which not only are the children acted upon by the teachers, but the children influence the teachers and the educational objectives and procedures. It is this participant aspect that characterizes the educational system of a democracy such as the United States. Our educational system is the embodiment of what a democratic society expects its children to be, and, in turn, is the prime shaper of the nature of society through the next adult generation.

The most significant current influence on our educational system is based upon the profound implications of accepting childhood as a legitimate stage of living itself rather than simply as preparation for adulthood. When childhood was seen only as preparation for later life, the school curriculum and schedule were oriented toward changing children rather than accepting and relating to their current state. The past viewpoint has played down and ignored the activities of children, which are not seen as work in the adult sense. The play experience has not been appreciated as an essential developmental antecedent of work in the young child.

Even during the pre–World War II years educators were exposed to the student's point of view as illustrated by a famed letter from a pupil, "John Jones," published in the November 1938 issue of *Progressive Education:*

> Why not have a course in personality in High School? This should be a course in which boys and girls are taught to dance, talk interestingly, dress with good taste and get along with each other. I want to know why you teachers did not tell and teach about life and the hard, critically-practical world. . . . I wish I had been taught more about family relations, child care, getting along with people, interpreting the news, paying off a mortgage . . . how to budget and live within the budget, the value of insurance, how to figure interest.

All of this calls attention to the school's role in social development. The environment of the school contrasts sharply with that of the workplace. It focuses on learning rather than doing; it provides opportunities for self-development at the expense of contributing to others. Its thrust is comparative rather than cooperative. Safe passage through the schools depends simply upon academic grades.

No educational task is more critical than cultivating youth's idealism and concern for the general welfare by providing experiences to permit their fullest flowering. Work will remain work, but its significance will be greater if work is seen as contributing to the social enterprise. "Do your own thing," even with the proviso that your "own thing" is simply not to injure others, is grossly insufficient as a precept for social living.

There will be a serious failure in the process of socialization if our citizens come to maturity without a sense of obligation to others. Social groups as different in their political structure as the Israeli kibbutz movement and the collectives in China have succeeded in evoking responsible performance in their youth and, at least to some extent, in instilling a sense of social obligation and of personal worth, but all this appears to be exacted at the heavy price of the loss of individual choice. On the other hand, we have stressed individuality at a considerable cost to social connectedness. Actually, these values are not antithetical. Our social context exists to foster personal freedom; and self-fulfillment enables the individual to contribute most effectively to society (Eisenberg, 1976).

It is evident that the role of schools is compounded by our society's drastic reworking of goals and priorities. In the past productivity has been measured in economic terms. A realignment is taking place through the appearance of interest in what might be called a quality-of-life index (Morse, 1975). Americans want material things, but increasingly they want attention paid to the quality of life. Is one's life satisfying, enjoyable, pleasant, meaningful, and worthwhile? Does it result in a feeling of well-being and self-esteem? This trend charges schools with the additional responsibility of helping children to learn how to obtain satisfaction in both social and personal living.

A means of placing the educational system in perspective is offered by Bower, who points out that schools are one of three basic institutions vital to children (1972). The first is the family, which is the mediating bridge between the child and the outside world and helps the child develop the ability to relate to people, to trust adults, and to know basic concepts. The second basic institution is the peer system, of greatest importance during the play period and through the adolescent years when youngsters form social relationships. The third institution is the school, which is largely a symbol learning institution. Bower calls attention to the need for greater integration of these systems, which he euphemistically calls KISS—Key Integrated Social Systems. The essential point is to recognize schools as one part of children's lives, inseparable from the others.

In Bower's view, the school system is a prescribed and unique society in itself. As KISS institutions, the schools provide opportunities to learn impulse control—for the use of the imagination, for working alone, and for working with others. Bower would like to see the school as a place that develops symbolic competence in children as a basic commodity, along with food, shelter, and clothing.

In spite of all its limitations, our existing educational system does engage many children impressively and generally does respond to the needs and capacities of the young. About 45 percent of those who graduate now go on to college, up from 33 percent in 1960. Fortunately, the presence of talented and dedicated teachers overrides the problems of the system and translates education into viable and engaging learning experiences for many children.

Whatever we do to improve education, we cannot rely upon a vision of a once vital and meaningful schooling to which we must return. We must face the painful fact that this country, on any large scale, has never known vital urban schools, ones which embrace and are embraced by the community, which formulate their goals in terms of the fulfillment of the individual instead of the fear of "social dynamite" or the imperatives of economic growth (Katz, 1968). Contrary to earlier hopes that they could be the instruments of social reform, public schools have tended to follow society rather than to lead it. There is a wide gap between the rhetorical goals of schools to help the disadvantaged and the fact that they have selected individuals for opportunities according to a hierarchical scheme which closely parallels existing social class patterns. Although the potential still exists, public schools have not realized the hopes of social reformers through the years (Greer, 1972).

In the final analysis, all public expenditures should be justified by their benefits to society. The cost of educating children cannot be treated as an individual expenditure yielding an individual benefit, because children are an inextricable part of society and the present embodiment of future society. As the economist Vaizey pointed out, the social purpose of education is the pursuit of knowledge and is justified by the continuous rise in our society's standard of living to which it has undoubtedly contributed (1962).

Characteristics of the Educational System

The educational system, with its public and private components, has unique characteristics that distinguish it from the health and legal systems. As an instrument of socialization, the educational system processes groups, not individuals, and operates with a cost ceiling. Like the family, the system has built-in generational differences because it is managed by adults and the consumers are young people. It requires an extensive physical plant which occupies most of the day hours of children. Although the system is generally unresponsive to short-range influences, other than innovations in teaching methods, it is affected by local communities on long-range policy issues through elected school boards and less formally structured community ties. Ultimate local control is exercised through budgets which are linked to taxation levels (Kinder, 1978).

At this point, the educational system should be contrasted with the health system, which is oriented toward individuals rather than groups and has no cost ceiling. The health system also permeates the mainstream of life, but it can interrupt all other social systems in order to protect public health or treat the disease of an individual. Public health measures can shut down or alter operations of segments of society, and the medical needs of an individual can interrupt the lives of others in the process of obtaining help. The health system has limited socializing aspects related to the promotion of health and is influenced by scientific advances and the needs of patients.

A similar comparison with the legal system is also important. The legal system shares the qualities of the health system in that it is oriented toward individuals, crosses other systems, has no cost limit, and can assume priority over all other systems. Unlike the health system, which resolves problems through the scientific establishment of facts, the legal system resolves problems through an adversarial process and is guided by social policies in the form of legislation.

These differences between the educational system and the health and legal systems are important, because the essence of child advocacy in education is infusing the educational system with elements of the health and legal systems. Because advocacy for a child focuses the resources of the educational system on an individual, it may encounter basic resistances in the system. Paradoxically, a child advocate may be a foreign body in the educational system, because the system is generally equipped to process groups of children rather than treat or represent individuals (Paul, 1977).

When we deal with individual legal rights in the educational system, we must take into account preserving the guiding power and effectiveness of the system. In usual civil matters, a judge who decrees that a fortune belongs to one claimant rather than another need not consider whether Claimant A will be corrupted by the money or Claimant B will put it to good use. In education, however, the determination of individual rights inevitably must also consider the purpose of a system which is not solely concerned with equity or justice (Kirp, 1974). In this sense the rights of individuals in schools are influenced by the supervening right of states to compel school attendance, to regulate educational content, to regulate the lives of children and their teachers, and to regulate socialization or indoctrination of students. Other legal questions relate to the right of school administrators to implement social policy in the schools, the academic freedom of teachers, the right of students to participate in their own governance and educational management, and the rights of parents in educating their children.

THE ROLE OF GOVERNMENT IN EDUCATION

Because education is under the control of states, there is an American school system but no national system of schools. There are autonomous school systems in each state and territory and in the District of Columbia. Their similarities are more significant than their differences, however, because curricula are influenced by nationwide book publishers, the federal Office of Education, and the professionalism of teachers. Because the states have delegated school policy making to local community school boards, there is a tension between national and professional trends and the finances and politics of localities. The aspirations of educators, therefore, must contend with the financial realities of community school budgets.

The basic constitutional framework within which a state can regulate schooling was established by the U.S. Supreme Court decision in *Pierce v. Society of Sisters*, endorsing the power of a state to compel attendance at *a* school but not to specify *which* school. In *Pierce*, the Supreme Court ruled that the state may compel attendance at a school, but that parents have the right to choose between public and private schools. Courts have further specified ways that a state may socialize children in public schools to particular norms that are deemed desirable. The limits on schools have been based upon distinguishing between socialization as a legitimate function of American schools and propagandizing as it might occur in totalitarian countries. Judicial questions raised about curricula have dealt largely with religious content, such as reading the Bible and praying. Other legal issues have been related to patriotism, such as saluting the flag, and mores, such as in the use of obscenely offensive textbook materials. Beyond these matters, courts have been reluctant to become involved in the content and schedules of schools.

THE ROLE OF SCHOOL ADMINISTRATORS IN EDUCATION

Unlike adults who have wide personal liberties, children are compelled to be in school for much of the time until the age of 16 or 18, depending upon state statutes, and their activities in school are controlled by persons over whom they have little influence. The scope of the control exercised by a school over children has extended not only to where they must be, what they must do there, and what they must talk about and when, but also to such intimate matters as how they must dress, how they must wear their hair, whether they may smoke, and even when they may go to the toilet.

School administrators bear the responsibility for providing the physical facilities, instructional materials, personnel, curriculum support, and schedule, presumably within an atmosphere conducive to learning, for the education of children. In order to carry out these responsibilities, administrators should have knowledge of the developmental stages of childhood, the nature of motivation, and the need of the young for physical and recreational activities. It is also important for administrators to recognize that children in school are in contact not only with adults but with their peer groups, and that provisions must be made for their social lives.

The school administrator occupies a strategic position in between the school board, teachers, children, and parents (Sarason, 1971). Although nominally charged with implementing social policy for education, their significant pressures arise from other administrators and teachers. Insulated from hour-to-hour contact with children, administrators still influence the atmosphere of schools through selecting and managing the personnel who work with children. Because of the overwhelming pressures of budgets and operation of the physical plants, the professionalism of administrators involves more business administration than education. The access of administrators to children is ordinarily around problems, significantly behavioral rather than academic. Their training rarely prepares them for this role. It is no wonder, then, that administrators find themselves immersed in resolving crises, whether they be fiscal, personnel, interstudent, or parental in nature. They have little opportunity for thoughtful planning. Accordingly, administrators are evaluated in terms of political rather than educational effectiveness.

Generally speaking, schools have been free from judicial intervention and from direct involvement with the legal system. Courts pleading lack of expertise have been wary of interfering with the discretion of school officials to control and educate their students. When legal issues have been raised with school administrators, they have been largely to protect children from arbitrary and irrational disciplinary actions. The U.S. Supreme Court however, held in 1977 that the 8th Amendment ban on "cruel and unusual punishment" does not apply to physical punishment in the schools (*Ingraham v. Wright*, 1977). Although Massachusetts and New Jersey forbid corporal punishment in public schools, state courts have generally ruled that teachers may use reasonable force to maintain discipline in schools.

Matters related to personal appearance, morality, behavior offensive only to adults, political activity, free speech, and behavioral control have also been raised. Courts have increasingly held that children suspended from school on the grounds of misconduct can be disciplined only under regulations which are precisely written and which do not abridge fundamental constitutional rights, and only then in conformity with the due process clause of the 14th Amendment.

In *Goss v. Lopez*, the Supreme Court for the first time outlined the minimal procedures administrators must follow before they can suspend children from school (Anson, 1975). The Court held that when a state provides mandatory education for its children, that education cannot be taken away for disciplinary reasons, even temporarily, without due process of law. Specifically, it ruled that students must be given oral or written notice of the charges against them and, if the students should deny these charges, an opportunity to hear the evidence against them and to present their own version of the facts. Of greater importance is the likelihood that suspensions are seldom necessary to maintain order in the schools. Many school districts have developed more effective alternatives (Children's Defense Fund, 1975).

Although addressing older youth, one case has relevance to public schools. In *Dixon v. Alabama Board of Education*, the ruling was made that due process requires notice and some opportunity for a hearing before a student at a tax-supported college can be expelled for misconduct. This includes the right to cross-examination, to counsel, to records of the proceedings, to impartiality, and to a hearing prior to suspension. The Court recognized that such a hearing with the attendant publicity and disturbance of college activities might be detrimental to the college's educational atmosphere and impractical to carry out. Nevertheless, the rudiments of an adversary proceeding must be preserved without encroaching upon the interests of the college. In that particular case, the college was required to give the student the names of the witnesses against him and an oral or written report of the facts to which each witness testified. He was also given the right to present to the college board his own defense against the charges and to produce either oral testimony or written affidavits of witnesses on his behalf. The results and findings of the hearings were required to be presented in a report open to the student's inspection. If these rudimentary elements of fair play were followed in the case of misconduct, the Court felt that the requirements of due process of law would be fulfilled.

Another case relates directly to public schools. *Tinker v. Des Moines Independent Community School District* established the fact that behavior must be disruptive in order to bear limitation, and wearing armbands by students was not considered sufficient to produce disruption. In that case in 1969, three teenagers planned to publicize their opposition to the Vietnam War by wearing black armbands in classes. The school administrators learned of the plan and instituted an anti–armband regulation. The students persisted in their symbolic protest and were sent home. In subsequent litigation, the federal district court and the court of appeals upheld the school's right to issue the regulation, holding that it was reasonably related to the school's power to prevent disturbance of classroom discipline. Taking a different view, the U.S. Supreme Court reversed the two lower courts, declaring that the wearing of armbands was closely allied to the expression of "pure speech," a fundamental right, the abridgment of which by government action required the most compelling reasons. The Court could find no such compelling reasons in that case.

In *Papish v. Board of Curators of the University of Missouri*, a graduate journalism student was expelled for distributing a campus newspaper that contained "indecent speech." The U.S. Supreme Court held that the school had legitimate authority to enforce reasonable regulation as to the time, place, and manner of speech and its dissemination. The university in this case, however, disapproved of the content of the newspaper rather than the time, place, or manner of its distribution. Since the 1st Amendment leaves no room for the operation of a dual standard in the academic community with respect to the content of speech, and because a state university's action could not be justified as a nondiscriminatory application of reasonable rules governing conduct, the student's expulsion was reversed.

Another kind of administrative problem is illustrated by *Benskin et al. v. Taft City School District* when eighteen California schoolchildren were allegedly coerced into taking a medication as a condition for attending school. The suit also charged the children were placed in classes for the mentally retarded without the knowledge or consent of their parents. In essence, a physician working with the school board made the recommendation that methylphenidate be prescribed for hyperactive children. Among the issues was the fact that the medication was recommended without an adequate diagnostic study, and without taking into account the manifold approaches to hyperactive children. In the background was the fear of nonconspiratorial coalescing of those in various positions of authority—school administrators, federal government, drug companies, teachers, and physicians—to medicate children. The essence of the problem was that administrators were using a medication in a relatively indiscriminant way rather than adapting the educational process to an adequate diagnostic understanding of each individual child.

In general, school administrators have wide latitude in establishing reasonable rules and regulations to guide the behavior and conduct of students as long as they are not arbitrary, based on controversial values, prejudicial or related to personal appearance and behavior that is not substantially disruptive to the educational process. School administrators, however, must observe the concepts of due process and fair play in dealing with children.

THE ROLE OF TEACHERS IN EDUCATION

Bower (1972) suggests that teachers and students need new role models. In his view the first schools were universities and the paradigm of lecturer and student was one of nutrition—ingestion, digestion, absorption, and regurgitation. In those days the teacher was the source of knowledge. Now the teacher is no longer the only necessary or desirable disseminator of knowledge. Teachers should be mediators in the same sense as parents. Education that is significant to the child requires a sparking, an emotional charge, between learner and idea. It is, as Freud described it, "an incitement to the conquest of the pleasure principle and to its replacement by the reality principle." But Freud went on to say, "The substitution of the reality principle for the pleasure principle denotes no dethronement of the pleasure principle but only a safeguarding of it." The schools of today require a new working paradigm—an integrative rather than a nutritional one—which can relate emotions and interests to cognitive experiences so that each has access to and can enhance the other. Compassion, humanism, understanding, and acceptance can thereby be used to facilitate the development of competence and coping skills.

In a similar way, the decision-making skills of teachers and administrators are untapped models for children in learning how to make decisions. Helping children to learn decision making is one of the most needed additions in the course of their public school education. Teachers and administrators could more routinely and systematically include children in decisions regarding school schedules, class placement, and curricular content—less to make decisions, more to learn *how* to decide.

Teachers are the central carriers of school practices that socialize children, but they operate within constraints, as do the students. They cannot simply interact with children according to their desires and personal styles. They must adapt not only to the children, but to the institution, to the principal's requirements, to other teachers' attitudes, and to the standards by which they are evaluated. There is little allowance in teacher schedules for the reading, discussion, and intellectual development, as essential for effective performance in primary and secondary education as at the college level. Furthermore, the teachers' custodial functions sometimes outweigh their educative function: constant paperwork intrudes upon their teaching time; the requirement of behavioral control in the classroom may be beyond what is desirable for a good learning atmosphere; and conformity to the institution, rather than creative teaching, may be the key to success.

Teachers are neither more nor less able than students to challenge the policy decisions of administrators or elected school officials. Contrary to popular belief, however, teachers can engage in public activities that affect the schools. In *Pickering v. Board of Education*, a teacher was dismissed for writing a letter to a newspaper criticizing the way in which the school board and the superintendent handled proposals to raise new revenue for the schools. The teacher's subsequent dismissal was ruled unconstitutional by the U.S. Supreme Court. The Court held that the interest of the school administration in limiting teachers' opportunities to contribute to public debate is not significantly greater than its interest in limiting a similar contribution by any member of the general public. It concluded that a teacher's exercise of the right to speak on issues of public importance may not furnish ground for dismissal from public employment.

Despite the similarities between teachers and students in their dependency upon the structure of school systems, there are many differences related to the obvious age and maturity of the teachers and their ability to bargain collectively for compensation, working conditions, and employment benefits. A teacher voluntarily seeks and obtains employment, while the student is required to be in school. Teachers are also models for student conduct and attitudes. One of the outgrowths of the "free school" movement of the 1960s has been the awareness that teachers themselves are more effective if they confront their own motivations and feelings toward both students and the educational system. When teachers fail to understand their own anger and aggression, they may become involved in power games with their students, to the detriment of both (Rothman, 1976). This is particularly important in overcrowded urban schools in which teachers face escalating psychological stress and physical assault (Bloch, 1978).

THE ROLE OF STUDENTS IN EDUCATION

Young people naturally look to adults as authorities over them both at home, in school, and in the community. As a part of the development of their own independence, however, young people also tend to test authority as they establish the boundaries of their power and the power of others. This developmental fact must be taken into account because it is not realistic to expect complete and unquestioned conformity on the part of young people to school curriculum, schedule, or procedures. Testing of authority is part of growing up and should be anticipated.

The impact of the school on young people beyond the school hours should also be taken into account—for example, the large number of hours that youth are expected to spend in doing homework. The social development of many children, particularly in peer associations and athletic participation, may be handicapped by excessive academic pressures. Many children devote more after-hours time to their schoolwork than adults do to their jobs. A balanced view of educational expectations within the total life of children is needed.

Most educators agree that students should assume more responsibility for their educations (Minuchin, 1969). The problem is how to do so at the various stages of development. One practical way is through setting personal objectives for self-improvement and self-evaluation. There is still a tendency for the educational system to place the responsibility for the education of children on teachers rather than on youngsters themselves, to the detriment of both. The desirability of student participation in their own governance in school, however, does not mean that students should run schools. There would be no purpose in having an administration and faculty if students knew how to manage their own affairs.

The matter of student participation to the extent of their capacities and interests in shaping their educational lives deserves careful consideration. As children grow older, they can assume more responsibility for this; however, it should not be overlooked that even during the high school years there is a strong need on the part of the student for educational guidance and for help in appreciating overall life goals and career development. There have been many efforts to bring career choice earlier into the educational experience, and it is important to recognize that until the end of the adolescent years, youngsters should not be expected to commit themselves to careers. Adolescents have a developmental need to experiment in different role situations and often wax and wane in their career interests.

Recognition of the student's point of view is embodied in various bills of rights for students, such as the following:

1. The right to a school which cultivates the students' sense of identity, work, and independence by taking their needs, attitudes, and ideas seriously.
2. The right to a school experience which enhances learning competence and self-esteem.
3. The right to interact with sensitive, well trained teachers.
4. The right to develop skills in competent living for coping with life demands.
5. The right to work, play, and learn in a school milieu free from fear and organized to provide for social growth.
6. The right to mingle, cooperate, argue, organize, and relate to their age group as well as across ages.
7. The right to systematic opportunities to study society's problems and the quality of life and personal growth.
8. The right to receive training in democracy with an explicit code of social expectations.
9. The right to a school that evaluates its procedures to ensure continued responsiveness to students' needs.

THE ROLE OF PARENTS IN EDUCATION

In *Pierce v. Society of Sisters*, the U.S. Supreme Court upheld the right of parents to choose between public and private schools. In *Wisconsin v. Yoder*, a more subtle issue was addressed because of the refusal of Amish parents to send their children to either public or private school until the age of 16, as required by the state's compulsory school attendance law. The Supreme Court reaffirmed the right of parents to influence the education of their children and added support of their religious belief that education was completed at the eighth-grade level. The Amish parents were given the right to violate the state compulsory education law and keep their children at home once they completed the eighth grade. This exception was granted by the Court because it was felt necessary to the free exercise of religion and involved the right of a limited class of parents to make decisions concerning family life. Justice Douglas, writing a dissenting opinion, was the only member of the Court to stress the interests of the children: "On this important and vital matter of education, I think the children should be entitled to be heard. While the parents normally speak for the entire family, the education of the child is a matter on which the child will often have decided views. It is the future of the student, not the future of the parents, that is imperiled in today's decision. It is the student's judgment, not his parents', that is essential if we are to give full measure to what we have said about the Bill of Rights and of the students to be the masters of their own destinies."

Although *Yoder* did not adequately address the rights of children, it was based upon a policy of reinforcing the influence of the family, reflecting an awareness that the school system can weaken the family unit through its primary focus on children. Because schools are not oriented toward strengthening the family unit and improving their effectiveness with children, a shift toward collaboration with and supporting parents is needed. At the same time, the power of parents may be subject to limitation if it appears that parental decisions will jeopardize the health or safety of a child or lead to a potential but significant social burden.

Beyond the role of parents as taxpayers in determining educational policy through their school boards, it is reasonable to expect that many parents, if offered an opportunity by the schools, would help in areas where they are needed. A variety of studies have indicated success in involving parents in programs in such a way as to benefit the academic achievement of their children. Although possibly initially threatened, teachers can experience parents as allies in their children's learning and be rewarded through collaborating with parents in helping their children learn to be more effective and competent human beings. Berlin calls for more parent involvement in education, with parents assuming the role of advocates in their children's learning (Berlin, 1975). If a positive role for parents is not found, a recent lawsuit against the Copiague, New York school district might become a trend. In that city, parents sued the school for educational malpractice because their son could not read beyond the fourth-grade level on graduation from high school and was not prepared for employment. His father said, "My son is not a moron. He just never got a proper education."

The Child's Right to an Education

Although it is generally assumed that all children have a right to an education, the matter is not as straightforward as it seems. *Brown v. Board of Education* was a landmark decision in several ways, one of which was the finding that, if denied the opportunity for an education, a child may not succeed in life. Another element was that, when a state has undertaken to provide mandatory public education, it must be available to all children. Later, in 1973, through *San Antonio Independent School District v. Rodrigues*, however, the U.S. Supreme Court held that the U.S. Constitution provides no explicit right to education. The majority opinion was that education is less justified as a basic right than adequate food, clothing, and housing, which are necessary for survival but are not constitutionally guaranteed rights. As it stands now, then, all states have assumed the responsibility for educating their citizens and in so doing have made education a state, but not federally, guaranteed right for children.

When states do provide educations for their children, courts have held in a variety of decisions that equal educational opportunities should be available to all of them. Again, however, the apparently straightforward requirement of equal educational opportunities becomes exceedingly complicated in its implementation. The Harvard Educational Review highlighted the issues involved in this question (Coleman, 1966). The considerations fall into two general categories. The first relates to the availability of equal educational resources, such as per pupil expenditure, curricula, school buildings, libraries, attendance areas, and teacher–pupil ratios. The second category relates to equal educational results, as measured by student achievement, job skills, and readiness to assume employment and citizenship. Which category is used hinges on which is more reliable: equality in resources, the easier to define and measure, or equality in outcome, the more elusive to quantify.

A further complication is the fact that an individual's benefit from education depends upon factors outside of the influence of the schools within the child and the family. Moynihan and Westman, for example, found correlations between school achievement and family structure (Moynihan, 1969; Westman, 1967). This has supported the view that schools can be expected to provide educational resources, but that the responsibility for profitable use of them lies with the child and family. There is a growing trend, however, to hold the schools, not the child, responsible for educational achievement. This has been the inevitable result of measuring the value of public investment in education by its results. There is a shift, accordingly, from evaluating the educational system through the quality of its physical plants, programs, and personnel to evaluating the quality of its product—students' achievement.

The most logical conclusion is that equality of educational opportunity means equality of educational result, given the same individual input. With such a definition, inequality might come about from differences in the school experiences or in individual backgrounds and abilities. A striking example of inequality, then, would exist for children from households in which a language other than English is spoken. Such a definition would imply that educational equality is reached only when the results of schooling for individuals of comparable abilities are the same for racial and religious minorities as for the dominant group. An example of court willingness to specify the content of education in this aspect was the decision in *Lau v. Nichols*, requiring the San Francisco school system to take into account the special instructional needs of Chinese-speaking children.

Because of all of these complicated factors, the Coleman Report of 1966 was prepared for the Department of Health, Education and Welfare. The resulting federal and legal policies illustrate the way in which data can be used to support the current political ethos. The Report was interpreted to mean that integration of schools, subsequently implemented through busing, was the most effective means of ensuring equality of educational opportunity. The Coleman Report did not then, and there are not research findings now that would, justify such a generalized solution to the problem of inequality of educational opportunity (Coleman, 1966 and 1978; Harvard Educational Review, 1969).

The attempts of the 1960s to remedy the school failure of disadvantaged children simply through educational intervention failed because they did not take into account the full poverty–poor maternal health–malnutrition–social deprivation–school failure–unemployment cycle (Birch, 1970). This lesson was learned at the turn of the century, but it was forgotten.

Another difficulty with any generalized legal policy, such as integration of school attendance through school busing, is that one remedy may create another problem. The most serious constitutional issue raised by physical school desegregation is that it challenges one kind of organization that a democratic society may wish to choose for its schools: an organization in which the schools are the expression of a geographically defined community on a small scale, regulated in accordance with the democratically expressed views of that community. Busing and other administrative considerations force a shift away from the neighborhood school concept, which in the long range may be a more compelling response to the interests of the children.

Another kind of general approach to inequality in educational opportunity has been through attacking unequal funding of education. In *McInnis v. Shapiro*, the U.S. Supreme Court concluded that there is no constitutional requirement that public school expenditures be made on the basis of pupils' educational needs without regard to the financial strength of local school districts. Consequently, unequal educational expenditures per student based upon variable property values and tax rates of local school districts do not amount to discrimination in themselves. Furthermore, in *San Antonio Independent School District v. Rodrigues*, the Texas system of financing public education through property tax was challenged because less school money was available in communities with a low property tax base. The U.S. Supreme Court concluded that there is need for reform in tax systems; however, the financial inequities do not violate the Constitution, and the ultimate solution must come through the democratic process of legislation. This area remains controversial and will continue to see litigation, as indicated by the 1977 ruling of the Connecticut Supreme Court that financing education primarily through property tax was unconstitutional because it led to unequal educational opportunity. The New Jersey Supreme Court adopted a similar position in 1973.

There is a trend toward more sophisticated and specific judicial approaches to remedies for educational inequality, as illustrated by the District of Columbia ruling in *Hobson v. Hansen*. Because Washington, D.C., had a student body that was 90 percent black, the remedy of integration did not apply for the poor black and white plaintiffs. The decision required revisions in a number of areas, including improvement of pupil and teacher assignment practices, changes in the school building program, abolishing a tracking system based on tested ability, requiring compensatory specialized education, and undertaking metropolitan planning with neighboring Maryland and Virginia suburbs. *Hobson* is an example of a painstaking examination of significant aspects of a school system and tailoring the remedies to a locality rather than applying a general policy. This approach also corresponds with a growing trend for courts to function at the level of administrative review of objectives, rather than assuming responsibility for devising educational procedures and risking incompetence in an unfamiliar system.

Another important area of court activity has related to equal educational opportunities for the mentally and emotionally handicapped. In *Mills v. Board of Education* in 1972, the conclusion was reached that no child eligible for a publicly supported education in the District of Columbia could be excluded from a regular public school assignment unless such a child was provided adequate alternative educational services with a constitutionally adequate prior hearing, and periodic review of the child's status and progress were carried out. The District of Columbia was enjoined to provide each child of school age a free and suitable publicly supported education regardless of the degree of the child's mental, physical, or emotional disability.

Another similar case was *Pennsylvania Association for Retarded Children v. Commonwealth* in 1972, which specified that a free, public program of education and training appropriate to each child's capacity be available, and that placement in a regular public school class was preferable to placement in a special public school class, and that placement in the special public school class was preferable to any other type of program of education and training. The argument that insufficient funds are available to provide publicly supported education for every kind of exceptional child was struck down. Both *Mills* and *PARC* also provide for elaborate safeguards before children may be assessed and placed in the special programs that take them out of the educational mainstream.

The wisdom of these decisions is reflected in the fact that many states subsequently enacted mandatory education laws. In these laws, not only is education mandated for all children, but procedures are established for ascertaining the needs of each child, for the participation of parents, for an assignment process to an appropriate specialized education program, and for an appeals procedure. Federal Public Law 94-142 now requires that states provide education for all handicapped children in order to qualify for federal educational funding (Ballard).

In summary, courts have entertained general issues on the nature of educational opportunities that an individual can demand from the state. These demands may be affirmative, asserting an entitlement to educational opportunity, equal access to the schooling process, or a specified educational outcome. They may also be framed negatively, such as asserting the right to be free of race, sex, or social class discrimination in the public schools. In a recent "right to education" suit, a Maryland judge held that "education is any plan or structured program administered by competent persons that is designed to help individuals achieve their full potential." In this light, every type of training is a form of education. With the passage of time, then, it is likely that courts will stimulate more attention to educating each child appropriately and approach the growing social expectation that each child should graduate from high school as well.

Specific Child Advocacy Issues in Education

As a means of identifying specific areas in which schools can improve their abilities to meet the needs of children, we will highlight individual differences, classification procedures, record keeping, ability grouping, and education in values.

INDIVIDUAL DIFFERENCES

Behavioral scientists and educators know that teaching is more effective when individual differences in students' prior knowledge and level of development are taken into account (Messick, 1976). What is only beginning to be recognized is that differences in styles of learning, thinking, creative expression, and temperament are also important factors that can facilitate or impede learning in school (Tyler, 1977).

In the past, individual differences in children have been recognized administratively more than in actual teaching. The earliest form was expressed through simply eliminating students who failed at each successive stage of school. At the opposite extreme has been selecting students who are retained at a grade level until requirements are mastered, such as in an ungraded primary level which can be completed in two, three, or four years.

Other common forms of educational accommodation to individual differences have been primarily classificatory. They involve such organizational mechanisms as by school type, such as schools for vocational training or schools for the retarded; differentiation by section within tracks organized by ability or achievement level in particular subjects, such as honors and regular classes or elementary, intermediate, and advanced sections in language instruction; and differentiation within a class, such as ability or remediation grouping.

Beyond these administrative practices, there are many possibilities for individually oriented teaching adaptations through matching instruction to learner weaknesses and learner strengths (Talmadge, 1975). The result of this approach is the individualized prescription of instruction through an initial "diagnostic" process to identify the learner's characteristics and a matched "treatment" instructional course. One of the discoveries of this approach is that, no matter how one tries to make an instructional program better for someone, it may become worse for someone else. For example, a technique devised to promote creative thinking in some students may also interfere with creative thinking in other students.

The cognitive styles related to learning are beginning to be identified. The most intensively studied is cognitive field dependence versus field independence. This quality is a reflection of a person's ability to deal with a part of a perceptual field separately from the field as a whole, or the extent to which one can separate items from an organized context. Those who are field dependent rely upon the whole more in perceiving a part than do those who are field independent. This cognitive style influences gravitation of students toward subject matter areas in school and toward occupations afterward. Field-dependent people tend to be sensitive to peer values and authority and are more likely to enter careers involving interpersonal contact than do field-independent people, who are more likely to favor mathematics or engineering careers. Each style contributes to high achievement in the area to which it is suited. Thus, field-independent student nurses did particularly well in surgery and field-dependent student nurses in psychiatry (Witkin, 1976).

Other distinct cognitive styles have been identified but studied less thoroughly (Messick, 1976). One is conceptualizing style, which tends to be through thinking of things in terms of their functions (relational conceptualizing), thinking of things in terms of their appearances (analytic–descriptive conceptualizing), or thinking of things in terms of their membership in classes (categorical–inferential conceptualizing). These three styles tend to appear developmentally in the sequence of relational thinking as more characteristic of young children, analytic–descriptive thinking of older children, and categorical–inferential thinking of adults, but there are significant individual differences within all age groups.

Sensory modality preferences are also found. Some children favor the kinesthetic sense (physical or motoric thinking), others visual imagery (figural or spatial thinking), and still others auditory imagery (verbal thinking). These three sensory modes of understanding experience— through the mind's hand or the mind's eye or the mind's ear—emerge developmentally in that sequence, as does conceptualizing style, but there are significant differences within age groups as well.

Scanning refers to a child's method of focusing attention. It varies widely in vividness of experience and scope of awareness. A high scanning propensity is associated with meticulousness, concern for detail, and sharp, yet wide ranging, focus of attention. Children with a low scanning propensity are less precise in their behavior and less observant of events taking place around them.

Another style is constricted versus flexible control of attention, which refers to differences in susceptibility to distraction and interference. It varies with the extent to which an individual constricts attention to relevant cues and actively inhibits competing learned responses. Some children have less control of their attention span and are more readily distracted than others by environmental events, to which they habitually respond.

Leveling versus sharpening concerns individual variations in the assimilation of memories. Persons at the leveling extreme tend to blur similar memories and to merge perceived objects or events with similar perceptions from previous experiences. Sharpeners are less prone to confuse similar objects and may even magnify small differences, thereby exaggerating changes and heightening differences between past memories and present perceptions. Levelers are prone to make prejudiced judgments. Sharpeners tend to learn less readily from past experience.

Reflection versus impulsivity involves the speed and adequacy with which ideas are formulated. Reflective persons tend to ponder various possibilities before deciding, while impulsive persons tend to offer the first answer that occurs to them to answer a question.

Compartmentalization is another style of thinking which refers to the degree to which one tends to isolate ideas and objects into discrete, relatively rigid categories. When extreme, compartmentalization leads to inertia in thinking and a limitation in creating ideas, making it difficult to write themes, for example.

Converging versus diverging thinking refers to the degree to which an individual relies on logical conclusions and correct outcomes (convergent) in contrast with favoring variety and high volume of outcomes (divergent). The former is associated with a scientific and the latter with an artistic bent.

Risk taking versus cautiousness refers to consistent differences in persons' willingness to take chances and expose themselves to risky situations. Risk takers are likely to guess on examination questions and to feel confidence in their judgments.

With awareness of these natural variations in the way that children perceive, think, and behave, educators are able to understand children who previously have been seen as frustrating. These qualities can also be appreciated in ourselves as adults and have much to do with life interests and occupational choice.

The preceding individual differences have come from the work of educational researchers who have focused on differences that appear in school activities. A biological basis for individual cognitive differences of as yet unappreciated importance lies in the fact that persons vary in the degree of dominance of the functioning of the right and left sides of the brain. The right cerebral hemisphere is the seat of relating the body and thinking in space. It is the source of holistic or "big picture" thinking. The left cerebral hemisphere is the seat of attention to specifics through analytical thinking and the site of the mechanics of language. There is anatomical evidence that individuals vary in the relative sizes of the right and left cerebral hemispheres (Galaburda, 1978).

A more comprehensive understanding of individual differences in children's temperaments has come from the work of Thomas and Chess (1977). They identified a series of temperamental qualities in young children that influence the ways in which children behave in their homes and schools. They identify differences between children in activity level, rhythmicity of biological functions, approach–withdrawal behavior, adaptability to new or altered situations, intensity of reaction to stimuli, threshold of responsiveness to stimuli, quality of mood, distractibility, attention span, and persistence in activities.

Three personality types emerge from various combinations of these qualities: the "easy child," the "difficult child," and the "slow-to-warmup child." The "easy child" eats and sleeps well, is friendly with strangers, accepts frustration, learns new rules quickly, and poses minimal problems for parents and teachers.

The "difficult child" has irregular biological rhythms, shows withdrawal responses to new stimuli, is slow to adapt to change, has frequent negative moods, becomes frustrated easily, and has temper tantrums. When these children do adapt, however, they function easily, consistently, and even ebulliently. Environmental experience is crucial in determining whether their ultimate behavior becomes predominantly adaptive or maladaptive.

The "slow-to-warm-up child" quietly withdraws from new stimuli, does not exhibit intense reactions, but in early life clings to the parent when introduced to a stranger, an action often regarded as shyness. In school the child may be perceived as slow or uninvolved, and in extreme cases as frankly retarded. When allowed to move at their own speeds, however, these children become deeply involved in activities and may be highly imaginative. If these children's slow adaptability is interpreted as timidity or lack of interest and they are pressured into a fast warmup, their natural withdrawal tendency may be intensified. If their increased holding back in turn stimulates increased impatience and pressure in teachers, the stage is set for further isolation and introversion with disengagement from the educational process.

From the educational standpoint, the most important individual differences are in intelligence. The genetic aspects of intelligence are compounded by the relationship of intelligence test performance to family size and the spacing of children. Zhaonc found that intellectual performance increases with decreasing family size (1976). Children born earlier in a sibship perform better on intelligence tests than later children when intervals between successive births are relatively short. Long intersibling spacing appears to cancel the negative effects of birth order and in extreme to reverse them. Absence of a parent is associated with lower intellectual performance by children. The evidence from this study supports a follow-up of nursery school children, in which it was found that academic achievement was correlated with many factors but most strongly with the structure of the family (Westman, 1967).

Another critical individual difference is in the rate of both physical growth and mental maturation. Not only do children mature at different rates in the onset of puberty, but more subtle variations occur in the rate of maturation of such cognitive abilities as reading and the capacity to manipulate symbols (Tanner, 1961).

The most obvious difference between children is between the sexes (Seiden, 1976). The evidence indicates that there is a tendency for girls to test somewhat higher on general intelligence measures during the early school years and boys during the high school years. Through the preschool and early school years, girls exceed boys in most aspects of verbal performance. Girls learn to read sooner, as reflected in the fact that there are more boys than girls who require remedial reading programs. By the age of 10, however, a number of studies show that boys have caught up in their reading skills. Throughout the school years, girls do better on tests of grammar, spelling, and work fluency. Girls receive higher grades than boys throughout the school years, even in subjects in which boys score higher on standard achievement tests. Boys consistently do better on spatial tasks throughout the school years. On measures of analytic ability, boys of school age score consistently and substantially higher than girls.

According to Maccoby, these major sex differences appear unrelated to adult sex roles, actual or anticipated (1974). It is unlikely that a girl of nine does poorly on an imbedded figures test because she thinks that this kind of skill is not going to be important for her later on in life and well on a spelling test because she thinks that kind of skill is going to be important. Furthermore, it is doubtful whether either children or adults see the ability areas with the greatest sex differences as sex role specific. This is not to say that sex role stereotyping is irrelevant to intellectual development, but it is doubtful whether sex differences in the cognitive styles of spatial ability and analytic style can be understood in terms of their relationship to role expectations of one sex or the other.

One of the most important changes occurring in schools related to the unequal treatment of the sexes is in athletics. All high school interscholastic athletic rules generally prohibiting girls from participating in boys' interscholastic athletic programs were nullified in 1973 by *Brenden v. Independent School District 742.*

Efforts to ablate recognition of sex differences can achieve unrealistic extremes, however, as illustrated by a Department of Health, Education and Welfare regulation holding that schools receiving federal funds must permit both sexes to join a choir unless a specific range of voices is desired. It disallowed federal funding because a sixth-grade boys' choir was ruled to be inconsistent with federal policy since boys and girls sing in similar ranges in the sixth grade.

The time has passed in which being poor in itself signifies a useful way of describing differences in children. The concept of "culture of poverty" has not been shown to have meaning to educators. Thus, attitudes associated in the past with the culture of poverty, such as orientation to the present, passivity, and cynicism are actually realistic responses to the facts of poverty. Differences between the "haves" and the "have nots" are more a matter of responses to different possibilities for achieving generally similar goals than a matter of widely divergent goals. All youth aspire to the "good life." Because of differences in opportunities, the "haves" are more optimistic about, attuned to, and willing to conform to the demands of society. The "have nots" are understandably more disaffected, withdrawn, cynical, angry, and less willing to commit themselves to a striving that stands a poor chance of success (Leacock, 1969). Poor children vary as widely as do middle-class children on the foregoing dimensions of individual differences.

In summary, individual differences occur in a wide range of human qualities influenced both by nature and nurture. Individuals show more differences in qualities between each other than similarities. There are differences in home life, religion, culture, biological or guardianship tie with parent, intelligence, temperament, personality, cognitive ability, and physical qualities, such as skin color, physical attractiveness, and physical handicaps.

The tendency is to evaluate differences in terms of desirability or undesirability. This is an outgrowth of psychometric ability measurement which attaches value judgments to behavior. We are just beginning to break free from the shackles that ability measurement imposed on us and to look at individual differences without imposing value judgments.

Because of the wide range of things that happen to children who are perceived as different, ranging from social isolation through scapegoating, it is important that educators do everything possible to heighten the value of differences, rather than to foster their negative valence. There is a crucial distinction between negative forms of recognizing differences among children in the form of prejudice and positively valuing differences among children so that their individual needs can be taken into account. The challenge for educators is to find ways of adapting the educational experience to individual cognitive, intellectual, temperamental, and physical variations in children to enhance the value of schooling for all (Silverberg, 1974).

THE CLASSIFICATION OF CHILDREN

All children are subject to grading and classifying by schools and, for that matter, peer groups. The premise is simple enough. Children ought to be associated with other children of similar ability and interests. Even Plato in his *Republic* sorted out children to become philosophers, warriors, or artisans according to whether they possessed gold, silver, or lead talents of mind. Today schools have tracks for pupils. There are gifted students, college-bound students, vocationally bound students, learning and visually handicapped students, neurologically and orthopedically handicapped students, and slow learners, in addition to students with speech defects, learning disabilities, mental retardation, and developmental disabilities. The logic for differentiating among students because of intellectual performance or potential is compelling. There is no question that the school system ought to have ways of differentiating among students so that there can be appropriate groupings of abilities and interests. The challenge is how to do it without harming children.

In spite of an array of special program classifications, American education has been severely criticized because it does a fair job of educating the average child, but a poor one for those above or below average. Furthermore, criticisms leveled against classification are based upon the fact that it misidentifies or misclasses significant numbers of students, that it is racially discriminatory, and that it denies some students an equal opportunity for education. The dilemma is graphically portrayed by Hobbs (1975):

> Children who are categorized and labeled as different may be permanently stigmatized, rejected by adults and other children, and excluded from opportunities essential for their full and healthy development. Yet categorization is necessary to open doors to opportunity: to get help for a child, to write legislation, to appropriate funds, to design service programs, to evaluate outcomes, to conduct research, even to communicate about the problems of the exceptional child.
>
> Children may be assigned to inferior educational programs for years, deprived of their liberty through commitment to an institution, or even sterilized, on the basis of inadequate diagnostic procedures, with little or no consideration of due process. Yet we have the knowledge needed to evaluate children with reasonable accuracy, to provide suitable programs for them, and to guarantee them recognized due-process requirements.
>
> Large numbers of minority-group children—Chicanos, Puerto Ricans, blacks, Appalachian whites—have been inaccurately classified as mentally retarded on the basis of inappropriate intelligence tests, placed in special classes or programs where stimulation and learning opportunities are inadequate, and stigmatized. Yet these children often do need special assistance to manifest and sharpen their unappreciated competences. Improved classification procedures could increase their chances of getting needed services.
>
> Classification of a child can lead to commitment to an institution that defines and confirms that child as delinquent, blind, retarded, or emotionally disturbed. The institution may evoke behavior appropriate to a label, thus making the child more inclined to crime, less bright than talents promise, and more disturbed than in a normal setting. Yet families and communities are not equipped to sustain or contain some children; families require relief, and the child may need the protection and specialized services of an institution and the opportunity it presents for instruction and treatment on a twenty-four-hour basis.
>
> We have a multiplicity of categorical legislative programs for all kinds of exceptional children. Yet the child who has multiple handicaps, who does not fit into a neat category, may have the most difficulty in getting special assistance.
>
> Voluntary and professional associations, organized around categories of exceptionality, have effectively pressed for financial appropriations for exceptional children. Funds and services have increased substantially in the past

decade. Federal, state and local bureaus, also organized by categories of exceptionality, are well staffed and busy. *Yet* associations, bureaus, and service agencies compete for scarce resources; there is much duplication of effort; services for children are poorly coordinated; continuity of care is seldom achieved; and children get lost in the system over and over again.

When brought to the courts, the matter of classifying students presses the limits of judicial competence in educational policy. The court is placed in the position of acting as a schoolmaster in an uncomfortably literal sense. Furthermore, classification practices lie at the heart of the school's claim to professional competence. Any challenge of classification may be perceived as a threat to that competence and strenuously resisted.

The greatest legal concern is the damaging effect of misclassification. The magnitude of this risk was illustrated by *Hobson v. Hanson* in 1965, which ordered that henceforth no students were to be assigned to special education classes without first being evaluated by clinical psychologists. As a result, 1,272 students, already in the special academic track or about to be enrolled in it, received an evaluation. The evaluations revealed that 820—almost two-thirds—were improperly thought to require assignment to the special academic curriculum.

Another untoward result of classification was addressed in *Larry P. v. Riles* in 1972, when the California Supreme Court ruled that a school could not place black students in classes for the educable mentally retarded on the basis of criteria which relied primarily on the results of IQ tests because a consequence of following such criteria was racial imbalance in the composition of classes. Expert testimony was utilized to question the validity of tested IQ results with socially disadvantaged children.

At the core of classification are the methods used to make judgments. The reliability and validity of most psychological and social tests are the least impressive with the children in most need of study. For the middle ranges of ability and age, tests of intelligence do have predictive value; however, with young children and foundering children, tests results are misleading and frequently inaccurate. This means that a thorough diagnostic study taking into account developmental, intellectual, temperamental, family, cultural, and ecological factors is required in order to understand a child's educational needs. The Hampstead Profile is an example of a comprehensive descriptive diagnostic system (Bolland, 1965; Flapan, 1975). The study has no value to the child, however, unless resources are available to carry out an educational prescription. Although politically useful in order to determine the need for specialized education, simply identifying a child's special needs does not help the child and adds the risk that nothing will be done for the child because a suitable program does not exist.

A general point about the evaluation of school performance is relevant in this discussion of children with special needs. It is the fact that current standardized testing practices do not disclose *what* students have learned as much as *how* they perform in comparison with other students taking the tests. This is because "norm-referenced" scoring is the most widely used technique. This procedure spreads out student scores in both directions from the average on a scale producing a "bell-shaped" statistical curve. Students are thereby ranked according to their percentile ranking in relationship to other students. But what the student actually does, or ought to know, is not revealed.

A more useful approach is through "criterion-referenced" testing, which measures a student's performance against a previously agreed-upon set of objectives rather than the performance of fellow students. These tests reveal whether or not students have learned what educators, parents, and the community have agreed they should learn. Theoretically, all students could equally meet their established objectives, which might differ substantially from one individual to the next.

The testing issue is of profound importance for the educational process itself. Criterion-referenced testing requires criterion-referenced education, that is, education based not only upon clearly defined learning goals but also on techniques for reaching those goals. If we were more concerned about testing students on exactly what we wanted them to know, we would be more successful in knowing what their education should be. Criterion-referenced testing would not accentuate status discrimination by comparing students with each other, but on the degree to which each child meets the objectives of an educational prescription. This is particularly important for children with special needs because realistic objectives can be set for them. Necessary comparisons between the same objectives could be made, but it would be a secondary rather than a primary purpose.

We know now that many classifications schools impose on students are stigmatizing, as are those of the broader society (Kirp, 1973). These school classifications can reduce both the individual's self-esteem and value in the eyes of others. From the earliest years the appraisals of others mold one's self-concept and self-esteem, but the formal school's classification is particularly painful because it is novel. It is an official revelation that a child is different from others. The school's inclination to cope with a particular learning or social problem by isolating those who share that problem further reinforces the child's sense of stigma. Stigmatized children learn through contact with schools that they have been devalued by both schools and society. Children perceive all too well what the school's label means. In one study those assigned to special education classes were ashamed to be seen entering the special education room because they were often teased by other children and dreaded receiving mail that might bear that compromising identification (Mercer, 1973). Students assigned to the general or slow learner track described similar feelings: "Regular teachers make us feel dumb. Their attitude is nobody has been able to do anything with you, and I can't do better."

Differences among school children are perceived by other children without the school's label, and it would be folly to ignore them. To treat everyone in exactly the same fashion benefits no one. Yet even with that qualification, the consequences of schools' classification systems are awesome. Their psychological ramifications extend beyond the child. They reach the family and the peer group. Moreover, the curriculum offered to the "slow" or "special" child is less demanding than that provided for "normal" children. Even if children assigned to special classes do creditable work, they fall farther behind the school norm. The initial assignment to special education may begin a self-fulfilling prophesy. Children's belief in their inferiority is reinforced by the knowledge that they are increasingly unable to return to the regular school program. In addition, because classmates and teachers make fewer demands on them, they tend to accept low levels of progress as their true capability. Slow track assignment makes college entrance nearly impossible and may discourage employers from offering jobs. Assignment to special education programs, thereby, may foreclose vocational options.

Special education labeling may result in the formation of a new status hierarchy within the created group, with frustration for those who are perceived as being on the bottom of the order. One "pecked at" by those higher in the pecking order may, like fowl in the barnyard, peck at those seen as weaker and lower than themselves. The result is name calling and rejection, modeled after the larger group whom the special education children aspire to join. It is not unusual for those belonging to a stigmatized in-group to hold the same prejudices of outsiders who hold them in contempt. Black, Jewish, Asian, and native Americans know that members of their own groups hold the same prejudices that the majority group holds against them, at times even more strongly. It is not surprising, therefore, to witness class status consciousness and hostility among pupils in special education.

Children in special education classes, then, absorb the attitudes and values of the larger society toward them. They were involuntarily grouped under a label which carries negative connotations and thereafter do not see themselves as members of society's mainstream. Labels such as learning disabled and educable mentally retarded have presumably been necessary to acquire funds for children with special learning styles. For all the good this labeling has done, however, there has been incalculable and unnecessary harm.

The consequences of segregating "labeled" children are minimized when students are assigned to regular classrooms and leave only for periods of specialized instruction that can be provided better on an individual or small group basis. Each child then has a "prescription" for learning prepared by both regular classroom and specialized educational teachers. The prescription is based upon each child's social, emotional, and academic needs and sets specific objectives that can be periodically evaluated. Segregated special education programs should be reserved for those with compelling special needs and those who will be incapable of mainstream functioning in adult life (Anderson, 1973).

Outside of school, people live and interact with each other largely without planned, deliberate segregation. Obviously, there are many forms of *de facto* segregation; however, the thrust of our society is to break down barriers among people of differing abilities, interests, and backgrounds. It is important for children to learn how to relate to people who differ from themselves in the pace-setting environment of the schools. The mainstream of education ought to be comprised of people of all kinds of abilities, handicaps, and interests, as is the broader community. Where they spend their time in academic tasks can be related to their educational capacities. To socially segregate children with handicaps from children who do not have them during their educational years contradicts the realities of social living. Adults all live, work, and play together in our communities, and children should live, work, and play together in our schools. To do otherwise, as we have done through classifying and segregating children, is to produce adults who classify others, and themselves, on the basis of ability as they learned to do in school.

Some form of classifying children in schools is inevitable because of the educational system's need to deal with groups of children in different ways responsive to their needs. Moreover, the funding of special programs depends upon identifying their recipients. At the present time, however, the practice of classifying children still has a strong etiological thrust, as if the causes of a child's problems offer a basis for educational management. This approach is appropriate in the health system, in which effective treatment depends upon knowledge of the cause of a disease. It is not necessary or helpful in education, however, because it both focuses attention on something "wrong" with the child and assumes that something "wrong" needs to be corrected.

More to the point in education is to base classification on educational objectives so that specialized services can be directed to those children who have special requirements. For example, rather than the classifications of mentally retarded, emotionally distrubed, or learning disabled, it is more realistic to program for children who need to learn self-care, basic vocational skills, social skills, and basic academic skills. With such an approach it is not necessary to place a "label" on the child. All that is necessary is simply to identify what the child needs educationally and offer the child that program. It is no more necessary to label a child mentally retarded, emotionally disturbed, or learning disabled than it is to divide the larger mass of students into those who are bright, average, or dull. Furthermore, the labeling of deficits in children does not in itself lead to effective ways of remedying them.

RECORD KEEPING IN THE PUBLIC SCHOOLS

Records are kept in the schools for only one reason—to facilitate the education of each child. Their purpose is not solely to gather data in itself. Legally, the records belong to the school but for the most part they are open to the inspection of parents and children (Federal Regulations, 1974). The day has passed in which school records can be made and kept without the knowledge and approval of the persons affected by them. It is important, then, to prepare and process all records, with the expectation that they will be shared with parents and children.

Even the practice of reporting a child's progress directly to parents and bypassing the child overlooks the child's need for the information. When that has been done, children have not felt the degree of responsibility for their school life that comes when they are included in the reporting process. Many children have understandably interpreted their exclusion from the evaluation and reporting process as evidence that schooling is something expected of them by their parents and, therefore, not their own responsibility. Schools have also inordinately expected parents to change their children's behavior, almost as if little could be accomplished directly with the child. Including children in record keeping and reporting conveys the clear message that children do have a central role in their own education.

More specifically, Hobbs makes a number of suggestions about records and record keeping in the schools (1975). He points out that school records have archival and communicational functions and are often handled by staff not in direct contact with the children. As a result, he calls attention to the following considerations:

1. Privacy—Information that is not actually needed for educational purposes should not become part of the school's record keeping system. Information which limits opportunities of the child in the future might inadvertently be preserved and communicated inappropriately.
2. Confidentiality—Records must be protected so that only those who need and have a right to know can have access to the information.
3. Due process—The content of records and their interpretation must be visible to the persons affected and subject appropriately to their control.

These considerations lead to the recommendation that each school system should follow responsible and ethical practices, monitored by a policy board composed of appropriate professional people, legal counsel, and parents or their representatives. This board would:

1. develop guidelines and procedures for record keeping;
2. monitor and review procedures;
3. make decisions to release information outside the agency in instances where prior consent of the parents and child is not possible or feasible;
4. hear complaints;
5. impose sanctions for the misuse of records.

Recommendations are also made especially for the parents of children with special educational needs:

1. Parents and legal representatives of children in special education should be given periodic notice of the information collected and maintained about their children, the purposes for which it is maintained, its uses, the period for which it will be retained, and the persons and agencies to whom it is available.
2. Parents and legal representatives of exceptional children should be given access to records maintained about their children. Information could be withheld under special circumstances only under the authorization of the relevant records policy board, which also must operate under the scrutiny of the courts.
3. Parents and legal representatives of exceptional children should be afforded opportunities to contest the accuracy or completeness of records maintained about their children.
4. The contents of information held in a computer system should be periodically printed out and provided to the parents in complete detail. The system also should record the name, agency, date and content of information shared for each time information is provided.
5. All information should be reviewed by the parents and the school at least each ten years. Any information to be retained must have the joint agreement of the person and the school. All other information should be removed.

Although in the past public school records have not been seen as highly pertinent to later life, the likelihood that they will be in the future through computerized systems makes the foregoing principles imperatives.

THE IMPORTANCE OF VALUES IN EDUCATION

Because children identify with adult models, it is vital that people in positions of influence over children recognize that, whether we like it or not, children look for guidance and cues to the values of their teachers and school administrators (Sugarman, 1973). Children do seek ethical and moral values and tend to adopt those of their parents and their teachers. Every child has experience with at least several teachers who exert a significant influence on personal value choice and personality development. This cannot be overlooked, and efforts to denude the public school system of values ignore the developmental needs of children. To raise children in an educational system without manifest values is to raise children in a vacuum and convey the message that values are unimportant. It is through a value system that the child and adult link the past and the future, freeing them from preoccupation with the immediate satisfaction of their immediate needs.

During the troubled 1960s schools and universities abdicated their moral leadership. Today they confront many problems of immoral behavior—from cheating and stealing to drug taking and illicit sex. Concerned social scientists ask what the schools can do to help teach moral standards and self-discipline to the nation's growing generation.

In the face of the trend to remove religious and patriotic influences from the schools, it is helpful to identify basic values about which disagreement does not exist in a democratic society. Although ideals to be sought after and seldom fully achieved, the following have emerged as qualities that result from generally acceptable values: honesty, integrity, altruism, independence, trustworthiness, lack of prejudice, friendliness, wisdom, and responsibility. The lack of these qualities is apparent enough in our society today, and although the schools cannot bear full responsibility for the situation, it is likely that the "neutral" stance taken by many educators has been interpreted by some children as evidence that values are not as important as getting high grades and succeeding at any cost in school.

Although the function of education is often seen as to prepare students for success in life, the best test of an education is how it equips them to cope with failure. Most of us can meet success with equanimity, but failures and disappointments are challenges to personal integrity. Insofar as we are successful in life—by whatever standards we may choose to judge success—we should give proper credit to our educational opportunities. Yet we can never estimate the value of our education until we know from experience how it has prepared us to meet adversities and the frustration of cherished ideals and ambitions.

An important implicit value in schools is that making mistakes is "bad," leading to a generally experienced "error phobia." Rather than recognizing that learning is inevitably a trial-and-error process, children tend to view errors as avoidable and as an indication of failure. To make a mistake has grown to be regarded as "bad." Consequently, children come to value themselves in terms of whether or not they are "good" in school, which means making few mistakes and achieving high grades. Furthermore, to be "wrong" on a test question is equated with being bad rather than simply lacking the knowledge or skill required to answer the question correctly. Rather than a stimulus to find the correct answer, the error is a cause of discouragement and a sense of failure. Some children react by losing interest in school. Others resort to cheating or other means of concealing their potential errors. Most children, however, are embarrassed when they make mistakes.

An important antidote to this "error phobia" is modeling by adults who can readily admit errors and demonstrate ways of rectifying them. Another aid is to promote the attitude that tests are checks on self-knowledge and skills and to provide for learning the lacks identified by the test.

A promising recognition of the educational system's role in the acquisition of values is illustrated by the approach of Simon and Howe in their method of values clarification (Simon, 1972). This method encourages students through a variety of structured techniques to examine their ideas, choose values, recognize the importance of values, and develop ways of incorporating values into their lives. The objectives of this approach are to improve self-awareness, self-esteem, and social relationship capacities. The optimal result would be that children will be more secure, dependable, inner-directed, and less self-conscious.

An important developmental aspect of early adolescence is the growing capacity for self-awareness. It is useful, then, to stress self-discovery or "finding out about me" in a structured part of the curriculum. This can be done by encouraging the students to think about and discuss the things they like about themselves and the things they do not like. It is enlightening for them to discover that their concerns are shared by others. More specifically, the students can rate themselves on the way they look, the way they act, the way they feel, the way they think, the things they believe, and the way they think they get along with other people. The result of directing their attention to these things is discovering what they can and cannot do in terms of academic, athletic, recreational, and social skills. They can also then figure out what they can do about the things they do not like about themselves. It is important for children to find out about themselves through making mistakes and risking failure and disappointment. One cannot really know oneself unless new things are tried. A byproduct is developing the ability to tolerate frustration, an essential ingredient of maturity.

Perhaps the most controversial kinds of values are political. Greenstein's study on how children form their political beliefs, therefore, is relevant (1969). He found that children's first conception of political authority is more emotional than cognitive in nature. School age children, like many adults, have impressions that figures such as the President of the United States are important but have no clear understanding of what these individuals do. The emotional response of children to prominent political leaders is strikingly positive and unambivalent, more so than for adults. Greenstein found that children acquire party attachments before they can make more than the most fragmentary distinctions between the political parties. Moreover, children adopt the positive side of adult sentiment toward political leaders before attitudes of political cynicism.

As it now stands, efforts to increase the political effectiveness and the involvement of citizens come too late and are too generalized. The differences in the political awareness of upper and lower socioeconomic status group adults are reflected in differences in the political orientation of their children. Since most of the learning relevant to adult civic behavior takes place in childhood, before the age at which children are usually exposed to formal civic training, attention to the education of children in the political process is warranted. Typically, between the sixth and eighth grades, civic education begins, consisting largely of information about the formal machinery of government. Emphasis is on emotionally neutral, nonpartisan appeals to participate out of a sense of obligation. Research shows, however, that partisan enthusiasm is the strongest determinant of political participation and could be tapped in children. The enthusiasm of children could be captured through the stimulus of partisanship and the incorporation of the political process in their school lives. More direct involvement of children in aspects of their own governance, then, offers the most effective way of preparing them for later citizenship. This might mitigate the tendency for children to form attachments to political parties solely on the basis of their family affiliations or their teachers' preferences.

Although at times controversial and misunderstood, the schools have a role in promoting the acquisition of values by children. The problem is to find ways of doing this within the pedagogical style of education. Instruction in human sexuality, family living, and self-awareness have been utilized with varying degrees of success. These topics have been most effectively handled with the participation of professionals from the health and mental health systems. For better or for worse, however, the most potent source of values for children are those modeled by adults.

BEHAVIORAL CONTROL

Under a variety of names, ranging from classroom discipline to behavioral modification, a number of techniques have been used to influence the school behavior and performance of children (Stenhouse, 1967). From the days of corporal punishment to current applications of behavioral therapy, schools have looked for ways of influencing students beyond the pedagogical techniques of teaching (Hyman, 1977).

There can be no question about the vulnerability of the school in arbitrarily seeking students' conformity to adult defined standards of behavior. More uncertain, however, is the legitimacy of using rewards other than the satisfaction of learning and punishments other than the frustration of not learning in promoting education itself. We know that children will do things for a pleasurable material reward and not do things because of fear of displeasure. We know also that few adults can remain responsible citizens without positive and negative consequences of their actions.

There is no present answer to the dilemma of both fostering children's freedom and imposing necessary constraints on that freedom. Beyond stating that this reflects the human condition of living within a social order, we can usefully distinguish between behavioral controls that contribute to and those that hinder a particular child's development. Thus, children with weak impulse control need more structure and firmness than those who are self-inhibiting. Some children require physical contact in order to be sure that adult authority is firmly grounded or that adult affection is sincere. Most children are grateful that times and places are established for them so that they can get their work done. And all children appreciate an atmosphere in which they are not substantially distracted from their activities.

On the other hand, simply rendering an active child quiet or holding other children responsible for the action of one or a few cannot be justified as more than showing children that adults can mobilize impressive power. As a result, the experience of education has shown that, even with the most difficult children, questions of behavioral control are less when the quality of educational technique is high and the needs of each child are defined and met (Jones, 1968). Classroom control issues result when too many children are being less than adequately taught under adverse conditions.

The interest in behavioral modification as a form of behavioral control and learning facilitation is a product of applying experimental research methodology to humans outside of the laboratory. It assumes a target behavior can be identified, that an agent for changing that behavior can be found, and that before and after application of that agent measurements can be made of the success or failure of the agent. The value of this approach is that it forces precision in describing a child's behavior and focuses attention on resolving a specific problem.

The hazards of behavioral modification techniques are related to the circumstances under which they are employed, the thoroughness of their application, and the long-range results obtained. The important questions are: Who makes the judgment about which behaviors are to be influenced? Is the judgment in the child's interests? Is the behavior expressive, with its suppression leading to repercussions in the child's personality, or is it instrumental, its change merely altering a coping skill? Is the application based upon a detailed knowledge of the child, and will the technique be carried out and coordinated diligently? Will a desired behavioral change now be still desirable in later years? Or will the effort result only in temporary change, impress the child with the value of doing nothing without a reward, show the child that adults once more do not mean what they say if the program is inconsistent, or foster the child's dependency on external motivators?

All of these questions illustrate the complexity of behavior control issues, which too frequently are oversimplified (Behavioral Science Education Project, 1978). Generally, they evaporate with good teaching. Specifically, behavioral control may be useful as a part of a professionally administered special education program, when conceived and executed with specific mental health and developmental objectives for the child and not simply used to achieve conformity in the classroom.

Education of Young Children

For a variety of reasons, the education of young children is a growing and controversial industry caught between three powerful and potentially conflicting forces. First is a long tradition and experience in nursery school education developed outside of public schooling. Largely within the purview of home economics and influenced by seminal thinkers outside of education, such as the physician Maria Montessori, nursery school education has stressed the uniqueness of young children and their need for schedules, programming, and personnel that differ markedly from those appropriate for older children (1974). Nursery schools have been used and influenced by parents who have desired growth facilitating experiences for their children.

The second influence has come from a downward extension of public education to the early years of life. Based upon an awareness that group programming can be applied at earlier ages than in the past and that later education can be facilitated by earlier access to children, public schools are exploring ways of lowering the age of entry into the system. As illustrated in the growing popularity of kindergartens, the thinking and methodology of public education, which naturally does not include families or parent influence and originates in schools of education, are increasingly being applied to young children.

The third force is from the growing child care industry, which includes day care facilities and family care alternatives. Supported by federal and community funding, day care programs have schedules, activities, and personnel who do not have consistent professionalism that can draw upon the experience of nursery schools or public education. The rapid proliferation of day care, including its extension into the first year of life, has raised deep concern about the neglect of the needs of young children.

Because of the lack of deliberate and sound planning for the education of young children, we find that once more the adult world learns its lessons in child rearing slowly. Nowhere is this more apparent than in day care programming for young children. Because of the immediate profits in day care from meeting the children's day-to-day needs and minimizing the demands they place upon adults, we seem destined to repeat past mistakes and to handle children in ways that serve adults rather than children.

From the time that Robert Owen established the first English infant school in 1816 so that mothers could work, day care for children has experienced many trials but has persistently endured. In 1854 a New York hospital established nursery school programs for the children of poor women, leading in the 1870s to day nurseries for working mothers. In 1919 Grace Caldwell, representing the New England Center of Day Nurseries, called attention to the value of day programming for the children of families with problems, if social work for the child's full life could be provided. In 1965 Operation Head Start, stimulated by Julius Richmond, a pediatrician, began as a summer preschool program and progressively expanded through the country.

Two basic lessons in early child rearing, however, have been persistently ignored: (1) that extrafamily activities are useful extensions of family living for all young children, and (2) that early childhood is a unique period of life requiring specialized attention. On these two points day care planning founders and fruitless, heated debates continue over whether or not programs for young children have value and whether or not expertise is required to implement them.

Parents with adequate financial means appreciate the benefits of a nursery school program for their children between the ages of three and five. A half-day nursery school experience has broadened the horizons of their children and provided mothers with welcome opportunities to pursue their own interests. For them, a nursery school is a valuable addition to the life of the child and family, rather than a place to leave children while adults are otherwise employed.

In contrast, the children of disadvantaged parents have either been unable to experience life away from their immediate home and neighborhood or have found themselves shunted from one makeshift baby-sitting arrangement to another. These children do not have access to nursery schools and an adequate child rearing experience. It is for these children that public day care programs have been established, both to provide a more adequate child rearing environment than is available in their homes and to make it possible for their mothers to be employed. Because the day care programs tend to be seen as remediating a deficiency in the children's lives, the advantages of the nursery school aspect of day care, such as is available to better financed families, are often overlooked.

A specific illustration of a relatively new area of programming for young children is day care for infants. Since 1964 the Syracuse Children's Center has accepted the care of infants between the ages of six and 15 months. The program has shown that certain infants can benefit from this kind of day care if carefully selected and programmed for in a sophisticated manner. Children at that age can benefit from a half-day program with a staff ratio of one to each two to four infants and with the close cooperation of the mothers. These children move on to a full day from 15 to 36 months, and then into a regular nursery school program. Here, as is true in other programs for young children, extrafamily care can be useful for infants if expertly managed.

A realistic fact of day care, however, is its high cost. The provision of day care on a full day, five-day-a-week basis averages three to four times as much as a regular nursery school. The cost is higher because day care takes the place of a part of home care. The high cost argues for the use of day care only in specific situations where such an expenditure is justified for the welfare of the child. There is much evidence that young children's extrafamily needs can be met by less than a full day care program. When day care extends to a full eight-hour day or more, the needs of adults are primarily being met. Further developmental implications of day care are discussed in Chapter 5.

Day care can be a threat to the family when adults take the easy way out, even though they may later regret their action. At the present time, many women are appropriately entering the job market for economic and self-fulfilling reasons. At the same time, many women inappropriately seek a working life as a means of resolving financial and family problems. For them, easy access to employment and day care—a manipulation of their environment much like divorce—is more palatable than facing their own problems in intimate family relationships. Rather than changing themselves and their homes, they seek escape. As a result, mental health clinics are seeing a growing number of disillusioned working mothers. To the extent that day care for children provides a piecemeal approach to the management of disorganized families and does not take into account the children's need for cohesive, continuous family relationships, it joins the list of fragmented welfare programs that have promoted the undermining of family life among the disadvantaged.

In a review of day care in the United States, Steinfels concludes that: (1) day care for certain children is necessary; (2) day care programs should be normalized and seen as quality programs for children, not as devices for solving welfare problems; (3) day care programming should be expanded gradually to permit the development of new modalities, such as family day care; (4) day care must be developmental in orientation, not custodial; and (5) day care is one of many possible programs that could encourage the emergence of new child rearing patterns, new roles for women, and genuine family child-centered relations (Steinfels, 1973).

Although many short-range problems exist, it is likely that day care for children, cognizant of the developmental uniqueness of early life, will help disadvantaged children with special needs. More significantly, there may be a time when all children will simply have access to nursery schools.

The frontier of education lies with young children. As Montessori found, there is great potential for linking the learning of reading and writing to the child's natural acquisition of language during the fourth year of life. To do so, however, she pointed to several basic adult prejudices, reflecting "agism," that must be overcome. The attitude that children must be taught these skills overlooks the teacher within the child and risks stifling techniques that could rob the child of the natural opportunity to learn about the adult world of symbols through such stimuli as simply having letters of the alphabet as playthings that can be seen as tangible representations of the spoken word. Furthermore, the attitude that the child's mind is empty and must be filled ignores the boundless energy and curiosity that young children possess. Another misconception is that young children should not be expected to work—true enough if equated with forced labor, but not if play is recognized as their "work."

For the increasing large-scale programming for young children, the highest level of sophistication in child development knowledge must be applied. The plasticity and impressionability of young children heighten the responsibility of those who would supplant parents in child rearing to do a better job—and certainly to do no harm. The most important adult prejudice against small children, however, must be overcome: that little ones need the least because they are too young to know, care about, and be affected by what happens to them.

Conclusion

The educational system in America is a huge industry dominated as much by the management of its physical plant and children as by its educational mission. Originally intended to instill mental discipline, schools have been charged with creating socially efficient citizens and more recently enhancing self-fulfillment. With necessarily vague objectives for absorbing a twelve-year or more block of people's lives, the indices of success of the school system have been based upon tangible school resources rather than its impact on its graduates. Increasing attention should be paid to the results of education.

Advocacy for children in schools is needed to ensure that the cognitive, temperamental, physical, and cultural individual differences in children are recognized and capitalized upon to counter the strong tendency for these differences to unnecessarily become impediments to educational and social progress. Vigilance is further required to ensure that the classificatory labeling of children does not continue to stigmatize and fetter children who can be scarred psychologically and limited in developing coping skills. School records should also be restricted to their function in facilitating education rather than as data files which perpetuate stereotypes and potentially affect later career opportunities. There is also a need to recognize the importance of basic values modeled and articulated by adults in the schools to counter the misconception that the constitutional separation of church and state implies an amoral society. Great care is also needed in the application of behavioral control methods that are based upon conformity to the classroom rather than developmentally sound objectives.

The legal matters affecting the educational system have focused largely on the rights of children to be educated by their states, the excessive use of adult power over children, and the persistent reminder that parents have a voice in the education of their children. All of these points are necessary to ensure that schools do not remain isolated from families, communities, and other child caring systems.

The educational system holds powerful influence over the futures of children. It complements the family in preparing young people for adult lives in which there is routine, schedules, obligations, people to be pleased, and jobs to be done. However, only when seen in the context of the family, peer groups, and other social institutions does the educational system serve society's greater purposes. This is nowhere more evident than in the growing extrafamily care of young children.

Unfortunately, the educational system itself has not achieved the level of insight of wise teachers who recognize the impact of their personal influence on their charges. It is through the personalities and commitment of individual teachers to children that schools make their imprint on the citizens of the future. The challenge, then, for schools is to maintain milieus which inspire competent and dedicated teachers who can carry out their work with its inherent advocacy element. With improvement in the quality of administrators and teachers, children will have less need for formal advocacy of their interests by people from outside of the school system.

References

ANDERSON, E. M. (1973) *The Disabled Schoolchild: A Study of Integration in Primary Schools*. London: Methuen.

ANSON, R. J. AND KURILOFF, P. J. (1975) *Students' Right to Due Process: Professional Discretion and Liability under Goss and Wood*. Washington, D.C.: Capitol Publications.

ATKINSON, C., AND MOLESKA, E. T. (1962) *The Story of Education*. Philadelphia: Chilton Books.

BALLARD, J. (1977) *Public Law 94-142 and Section 504—Understanding what they are and are not*. Reston, Virginia: Council for Exceptional Children.

BEHAVIORAL SCIENCE PROJECT (1978) Ann Arbor, Michigan: Ann Arbor Community Services.

Benskin et al. v. Taft City School District (1976) *Human Behavior*, pp. 25–33, August.

BERLIN, R., AND BERLIN, I. N. (1975) "Parents' Advocate Role in Education as Primary Prevention." Chapter in Berlin, I. N. (Ed.), *Advocacy for Child Mental Health*. New York: Brunner/Mazel.

BIRCH, H. G., AND GUSSOW, J. D. (1970) *Disadvantaged Children: Health, Nutrition and School Failure*. New York: Grune and Stratton.

BLOCH, A. M. (1978) "Combat Neurosis in Inner-city Schools." *American Journal of Psychiatry*, 135:1189–1192.

BOLLAND, J., AND SANDLER, J. (1965) *The Hampstead Psychoanalytic Index*. New York: International Universities Press.

BOWER, E. M. (1972) "K.I.S.S. and Kids: A Mandate for Prevention." *American Journal of Orthopsychiatry*, 42:556–565, July.

BOYER, E. L. (1977) "A Drive for Better Schools—What the Government Plans." *U.S. News and World Report*, pp. 63–65, July 11.

Brenden v. Independent School District 742, 477 F. 2d 1292 (8th Cir., 1973).

Brown v. Board of Education, 347 U.S. 483 (1954).

BRUNER, J. S. (1961) *The Process of Education*. Cambridge, Mass.: Harvard University Press.

Children's Defense Fund (1974) *Children Out of School in America*. Cambridge, Mass.: Children's Defense Fund.

Children's Defense Fund (1975) *School Suspensions—Are They Helping Our Children?* Cambridge, Mass.: Children's Defense Fund.

COLEMAN, J. S. ET AL. (1966) *Equality of Educational Opportunity*. Washington, D.C.: U.S. Government Printing Office.

COLEMAN, J. S. (1978) "School Desegregation and City-Suburban Relations." Unpublished Manuscript, Chicago, Illinois: University of Chicago.

CROW, A., AND CROW, L. D. (1964) *Vital Issues in American Education*. New York: Bantam Books.

Dixon v. Alabama Board of Education, 294 F. 2d 150 (5th Cir., 1961).

EISENBERG, LEON (1976) "Youth in a Changing Society." Chapter in Vaughan, V. C., III, and Brazelton, T. B. (Eds.), *The Family—Can It Be Saved?* Yearbook Medical Publishers, pp. 59–66.

FEDERAL REGULATIONS, Family Educational Rights and Privacy Act of 1974, 45 Code, sec. 99.5.

FLAPAN, D., AND NEUBAUER, P. (1975) *Assessment of Early Child Development.* New York: Aronson.

GALABURDA, A. M., LeMAY, M., KEMPER, T. L. AND GESCHWIND, N. (1978) "Right-Left Asymmetries in the Brain." *Science*, 199:852–856.

Goss v. Lopez, 419 U.S. 565,95 S. Ct. 729 (1975).

GREENSTEIN, F. I. (1969) *Children and Politics.* New Haven and London: Yale University Press.

GREER, C. (1972) *The Great School Legend.* New York: Basic Books.

HARVARD EDUCATIONAL REVIEW (1969) *Equal Educational Opportunity.* Cambridge, Mass.: Harvard University Press.

HOBBS, N. (1975) *The Futures of Children: Categories, Labels and Their Consequences.* San Francisco: Jossey-Bass.

Hobson v. Hansen, 269 F. Supp. 401,490 (DDC, 1967) or 269 F. Supp. 401 (DC,D.C., 1967).

HYMAN, I. A., McDOWELL, E., AND RAINES, B., (1977) "Corporal Punishment and Alternatives in the Schools." National Center for the Study of Corporal Punishment and Alternatives, Temple University, Philadelphia, 19122.

Ingraham v. Wright (1977) 97 S. Ct. 1401, April 19.

JONES, R. M. (1968) *Fantasy and Feeling in Education.* New York: New York University Press.

KATZ, M. B. (1968) *The Irony of Early School Reform: Educational Innovation in Mid-Nineteenth Century Massachusetts.* Cambridge, Mass.: Harvard University Press.

KINDER, J. A. (1978) *Decision Making in Public Education.* Washington, D.C.: Capitol Publications.

KIRP, D. (1973) "Schools as Sorters: The Constitutional and Policy Implications of Student Classification." 121 U. Pa. L. Rev. 705, 733–737.

KIRP, DAVID L., AND YUDOF, MARK G. (1974) *Educational Policy and the Law: Cases and Materials.* Berkeley, Calif.: McCutchan.

KOLESNIK, W. B. (1962) *Mental Discipline in Modern Education.* Madison: University of Wisconsin Press.

KRUG, E. A. (1969) *The Shaping of the American High School—I—1880–1920.* Madison: University of Wisconsin Press.

KRUG, E. A. (1972) *The Shaping of the American High School—II—1920–1941.* Madison: University of Wisconsin Press.

Larry P. v. Riles, 343 F. Supp. 1306 (ND Calif., 1972).

Lau v. Nichols, 414 U.S. S. Ct. (1973).

LAWRENCE, M. M. (1971) *The Mental Health Team in the Schools.* New York: Behavioral Publications.

LAZERSON, M. (1971) *Origins of the Urban School.* Cambridge, Mass.: Harvard University Press.

LEACOCK, E. B. (1969) *Teaching and Learning in City Schools.* New York: Basic Books.

MACCOBY, E., AND JACKLIN, C. N. (1974) *The Psychology of Sex Differences.* Palo Alto, Calif.: Stanford University Press.

MARITAIN, J. (1943) *Education at the Crossroads.* New Haven: Yale University Press.

McInnis v. Shapiro, 394 U.S. 322 (1969).

MERCER, J. (1973) *Labelling the Mentally Retarded.* Berkeley: University of California Press.

MESSICK, S. ET AL. (1976) *Individuality in Learning.* San Francisco: Jossey-Bass.

Mills v. Board of Education, 348 F. Supp. 866 (DDC, 1972).

MINUCHIN, P., BIBER, B., SHAPIRO, E., AND ZIMILES, H. (1969) *The Psychological Impact of School Experience.* New York: Basic Books.

MONTESSORI, M. (1974) *Childhood Education.* Chicago: Regnery.

MORSE, W. C. (1975) "The Schools and the Mental Health of Children." Chapter in Berlin, I. N. (Ed.), *Advocacy for Child Mental Health.* New York: Brunner/Mazel.

MOYNIHAN, D. P. (1969) "Sources of Resistance to the Coleman Report." Chapter in Harvard Educational Review, *Equal Educational Opportunity.* Cambridge, Mass.: Harvard University Press.

Papish v. Board of Curators of the University of Missouri, 35 L. Ed. 2d 681,93 S. Ct. 1197 (1973).

PAUL, J. L., NEUFELD, G. R., AND PELOSI, J. W. (EDS.) (1977) *Child Advocacy Within the System.* Syracuse, N.Y.: Syracuse University Press.

Pennsylvania Association for Retarded Children v. Commonwealth, 343 F. Supp. 279 (ED Pa., 1972).

Pickering v. Board of Education, 391 U.S. 563 (1968).

Pierce v. Society of Sisters, 268 U.S. 510 (1925).

ROTHMAN, E. P. (1976) *Troubled Teachers.* New York: McKay.

San Antonio Independent School District v. Rodrigues, 411 U.S. 1 (1973).

SARASON, S. B. (1971) *The Culture of the School and the Problem of Change.* Boston: Allyn and Bacon.

SEIDEN, A. (1976) "Overview: Research on the Psychology of Women I and II." *American Journal of Psychiatry,* 133:995–1007, September; 133:1111–1123, October.

SILVERBERG, N. E., AND SILVERBERG, M. C. (1974) *Who Speaks for the Child?* Springfield, Ill.: Thomas.

SIMON, S. B., HOWE, L., AND KIRSCHENBAUM, H. (1972) *Values Clarification: A Handbook of Practical Strategies.* New York: Hart.

STEINFELS, M. O. (1973) *Who's Minding the Children? The History and Politics of Day Care in America.* New York: Simon and Schuster.

STENHOUSE, L. (1967) *Discipline in Schools.* Oxford: Pergamon Press.

SUGARMAN, B. (1973) *The School and Moral Development.* London: Croom Helm.

TALMADGE, H. (ED.) (1975) *Systems of Individualized Education.* New York: Mc-Cutchan.

TANNER, J. M. (1961) *Education and Physical Growth.* London: University of London Press.

THOMAS, A., AND CHESS, S. (1977) *Temperament and Development.* New York: Brunner/Mazel.

Tinker v. Des Moines Independent Community School District, 393 U.S. 503,515 (1969).

TYLER, L. E. (1977) *Individuality: Human Possibilities and Personal Choice in the Psychological Development of Men and Women.* San Francisco: Jossey-Bass.

U.S. *Census Bureau* (1977) "Projections of the Population of the United States; 1977–2050. *Current Population Reports*, P25–704.

VAIZEY, J. (1962) *The Economics of Education.* New York: Free Press.

WESTMAN, J. C. (1973) *Individual Differences in Children.* New York: Wiley.

WESTMAN, J. C., RICE, D. L., AND BERMANN, E. (1967) "Nursery School Behavior and Later Adjustment." *American Journal of Orthopsychiatry*, 37:725–731, July.

Wisconsin v. Yoder, 406 U.S. 205 (1972).

WITKIN, H. A. (1976)) "Cognitive Styles in Learning and Teaching." Chapter in Messick, S. (Ed.), *Individuality in Learning.* San Francisco: Jossey-Bass.

ZHAONC, R. B. (1976) "Family Configuration and Intelligence." *Science*, 192:227–236, April.

Chapter 9
Children and the Legal System

Children find their way into courts of law today for far too many reasons. Although some have committed crimes, most children are in court simply because of family problems. Most delinquents come from homes with problems. Many children, however, have done nothing to bring them into conflict with laws. One-fifth of juvenile court cases result from conflict within families in the form of truancy, incorrigibility, and running away (John Howard Association, 1977). One-tenth of the children in juvenile courts are there because they are neglected by their families (Hindelang, 1975). The rest find themselves the center of lawsuits related to their custody, economic support, and parental visitation. In divorce cases, many children are exposed to years of disputes over their custody and are torn between warring parents who use the courts to punish each other with the children as pawns—and participants—in the fray. It is evident, then, that children enter the legal system because of breakdown or disturbance in their families.

Of grave concern to society is the fact that the behavior of many minors brings them into conflict with law enforcement agencies. Youth under 21 are a significant factor in public crime, accounting for 40% of the arrests for all serious crimes in 1977 (Webster, 1978). Certain crimes are predominantly committed by youth: 71 percent of motor vehicle thefts, 71 percent of burglaries, 60 percent of larcenies, and 55 percent of robberies were committed by persons under 21. Of interest also is the fact that 35 percent of forcible rapes, 31 percent of aggravated assaults, and 25 percent of criminal homicides were committed by youth. Even more significant is the fact that the 3.6 million youths arrested in 1977 represent a small fraction (4%) of the school age young people. These youths are known in their communities, are accessible, and could be influenced if given sufficient priority by society. Even more tragically, most can be identified by the fourth grade in school, but no effective preventive action is taken.

In spite of the prominence of youth in crime, only one in six of our courts are devoted to juvenile matters (Hindelang, 1975). Although adult courts are overburdened, the situation in juvenile courts is worse. Juvenile courts review between 10 and 50 cases a day in some jurisdictions, whereas one adult case may consume days or months of court time. The grotesquely distorted situation is illustrated by the $5 million of public funds spent on the trial of Charles Manson, illustrating the high priority placed on protecting the legal rights of an adult.

In the light of all of these facts, it is no wonder that neglect of children's rights is receiving attention. It is unlikely that an eight-year-old child will ever enter a courtroom and file a lawsuit; however, the time is drawing near in which the rights of children will be buttressed by full representation of children in court. A dramatic illustration is the *Zepeda* case in Illinois, in which a child successfully sued his father for having caused him to be born out of wedlock. Courts are struggling with questions such as whether or not children can sue parents for negligence, as in automobile accidents, or bring action for damages against third parties who disrupt the family by alienating the affections of one of the parents (Wadlington, 1969).

The growing interest in children's rights is the result of a shift from the traditional view of the child as a person to be acted upon to the view that a child can act legally upon others. The prospect of children acting upon adults stimulates a variety of reactions. Beyond a latent irrational fear that children will be turned loose in courtrooms is a mélange of considerations that require adjustments in the legal system to respond fully to the rights of children. One of these adjustments is in the basic procedures of courts. Unlike adults, each child is continuously growing, with important changes taking place in relatively short periods of time. The nature of the judicial process, which is based upon the painstaking and time-consuming elucidation of a case, is calamitous for children who require swift detection and remedies for their problems.

This chapter will touch on some of the reasons why children and families do not fit well into the legal system, and why adult legal concepts do not apply to children. Hopefully, ideas may emerge which will be useful to lawyers and the courts in adapting to the special characteristics of children.

Children, Parents, and the State

First, a brief historical review will provide perspective. The law and the judicial system originated as society's first effort to deal with problems between people. Although religion offered guidelines for behavior, it did not offer practical ways of solving problems between people. Only recently has medicine, in the form of interpersonal psychiatry, begun to deal with conflicts between people. With roots in Hebrew literature and English common law, the American legal system has emerged as society's mechanism for dealing with interpersonal conflicts. Of particular significance to us is the fact that historically those conflicts have been between adults.

In the eighteenth-century English common law, the term "children's rights" would have no place. Children were regarded as chattels of the family and wards of the state with no recognized legal rights or power. Over the intervening years, the law's concern with children has been confined to those occasions when the state has intervened in families to protect or punish a child. The gradual emergence of children's rights is an outgrowth of the doctrine of *parens patriae*, which has justified state intervention upon parental prerogatives and even termination of all parental rights under certain circumstances. Alongside this concept, the law has assumed that the proper relationship between parents and the state in their joint control over a child's life is one of parental privacy.

The doctrine of *parens patriae*, literally "father of his country," stems from early English common law, in which the king was viewed as having a duty to protect those incapable of protecting themselves, and having a general duty to protect all citizens. The *parens patriae* doctrine placed the ultimate authority of the state over parental rights. Accordingly, the doctrine could lead to the denial of liberty to parents, but it could also take liberty from children. Furthermore, the doctrine permits the state to compel children and their parents to act in ways most beneficial to society. It is important to note that the doctrine never implied that the state could assume parenting functions and was limited to influencing parent–child relationships.

Generally speaking, the existence of parental rights over children has not been questioned (Kleinfeld, 1970). Adults may act as they wish with their children, except as the state imposes standards of conduct and duties upon them. The consent of children is unnecessary for the exercise of parental power, which extends to almost any area of children's lives. Some traditional categories of this broad parental power are rights to name a child, to custody, to service and earnings, to control religion and education, and to discipline. Prevalent legal theory holds that parental duties toward children are inherently accompanied by powers necessary to carry out those duties. Thus, the duty of support implies the power to make decisions about where children will live, what they will eat, and how they will dress. The duty to provide a favorable moral environment implies the power to censor the books read and movies seen by the child.

Following the principle of parental dominance over children, a series of subordination laws exist in most states and support parents in their efforts to control their children through defining incorrigibility, running away, and delinquency as causes for state intervention. Until recently the scope of parental authority has not been limited to protect the interests of children, although the law is moving in this direction. Serious questions are being raised about providing parent-invited state intervention against children who are disobedient. The informal sanctions available to parents for obtaining obedience and the disadvantages of running away, for example, are so strong that when children do engage in chronic disobedience or flight, quite likely their behavior is justified, and state intervention will not deter or prevent it through action directed solely against the child.

Strongly influencing the balance between the power of children, parents, and the state are both the right of families to privacy and the opposing right of the state to intervene on behalf of children. The current erosion of the attractiveness of assuming parental responsibilities highlights why the state has been reluctant to intervene in family affairs. Parenthood is a difficult burden and is becoming more of a voluntary option than a duty. The power of the state to further undermine the family has long-range implications for society. Increasing the burdens of child rearing may negatively influence whether or not adults choose to become parents. Even now there is a tendency on the part of some parents to wish to reduce their responsibilities for their children, leading some to support children's rights with the hope that others will assume responsibility for their children.

THE ADVERSARY SYSTEM

In an atmosphere of reluctance to interfere with parental power, we are seeing the emergence of the power of children in interaction with the power of parents and the power of society. This interaction takes place in the adversarial format of the judicial system in which concepts are tested, rights determined, and power distributed through argumentation of debated issues. Originally based upon the conception that God would strengthen the hand of the righteous, whether in a duel or in arguments before a judge, the adversarial procedure involves the presumed vigorous representation of opposing points of view in order to permit an impartial judge or jury to accomplish justice.

Employing the adversary system, a child with rights becomes a participant in a struggle for power. Because the adversary system depends upon pitting opposing forces against each other and awards children power, it is likely that a latent fear of the rebellion of children has been one of the deterrents to the full recognition of the rights of children in the past. Providing children with rights also provides them with influence and detracts from the power of parents and the state. It is this tendency of the law to cast the interaction of children, parents, and society in power terms within an adversary model that is both the strength of the law for children and its weakness.

Although power struggles are the *modus operandi* of the law, the adversary method cannot take into account the fact that children, parents, and society are mutually synergistic, interdependent, and non-competitive, each being essential to the other. The adversary model tends to heighten conflict between the adult and child generations rather than recognizing their basic interdependency. Overlooked is the reciprocal dependency of children and adults. Without children society would be extinguished, and the lives of adults would be diminished. The disadvantage of the adversary process is that it necessitates choosing between rather than harmonizing competing interests. Fortunately, much compromise and negotiation to resolve conflicts does occur within the legal system and takes place outside of the overt battleground of the courtroom.

Although the adversary model has been found to be useful in criminal, contract, and tort cases, in matters of domestic relations it distorts reality by polarizing and heightening the disparate interests of the individual members of the family rather than stressing their common interests and the rewards which can result from subordination of individual interests to those of the family as a whole. Although in troubled times the family does show interpersonal conflict, to overemphasize that aspect ignores the rewards and gratifications of cooperative family living.

THE INTERFACE OF PARENTAL AND CHILDREN'S RIGHTS

When the rights of children vis-à-vis their parents are legal issues, a useful distinction can be drawn between legal rights to *protection*, which guard children from the harmful acts of others, and legal rights to *choices*, which permit persons to make choices of binding consequence, such as voting, marrying, exercising religious preferences, and choosing whether to seek education. Clearly, children must have legal rights to protection. The development of the capacity for responsible choice selection, however, is an educational process in which growth can be stunted if unlimited freedom and responsibility are thrust too soon upon the young. Moreover, the lifelong effects of binding, childish choices can create permanent effects far more detrimental than the temporary limitations upon freedom inherent in the child rearing process. Children will outgrow their restricted state, but the important question is whether they will outgrow it with the capacity to function as mature, independent members of society. Precisely because of their lack of this capacity, minors should have legally protected rights to special treatment, including protection against their own immaturity, so that they will have the opportunity to develop the capacity to make mature choices.

In the final analysis, adults will not remain in family units if their parental authority is not ultimately supported. The nature of childhood includes the potential for tyranny of children over adults. While authority may usually be most effectively exercised through persuasion rather than through brute force, a family that operates as a true democracy is less likely to provide the security, role modeling, leadership, socializing, and limit setting essential to growth than one that is based upon ultimate parental authority. To the extent that government policies foster noncommital attitudes on the parts of parents—either because parents believe they have no right to give direction to their children or because they fear that the state will not support them—both the children of those families and society as a whole will suffer. The development of policies that encourage parental responsibility for children is in the interests of children (Hafen, 1976a).

An example of an extreme undermining of parental authority is the proposal that minority status be abolished. This would reverse the underlying presumption of children's legal incompetence and presume that children, like adults, are capable of intelligently exercising their rights and of assuming full moral and legal responsibilities until proven otherwise. The difference between a rebuttal presumption of incompetence and the presumption of competence is that the former places the burden of proof on children and their advocates, while the latter shifts it to those who challenge the children's status.

The issue of competence is always involved to a greater or lesser degree in legal work with children. This fact has brought the need for more than the usual amount of expert testimony in cases involving children. The age factor makes it necessary for some kind of assistance to courts in understanding and interpreting a child's needs and wishes. This means that inherent in children's legal rights is the relative competence of each child to exercise them. In a sense, this brings the equivalent of psychological testimony into each case involving a child. Unfortunately, to cast this matter simply in terms of "legal competence" overlooks the fact that we are really dealing with a child's capacity to assume responsibility for oneself, not a mental defect in the form of mental incompetency. By definition, children are dependent and unable to assume complete responsibility for their own lives. This point should be clarified so that we think not simply in terms of competence of mind but more accurately in terms of competence to assume responsibility for one's life course, which obviously follows a developmental pattern.

The legal adjudication of parent–child rights occurs largely when protection of the child is an issue. The state has the power to intervene and assume temporary custody or guardianship of children when neglect, abuse, or parental incompetence exists. Children can be placed in foster care, and parental rights can be permanently terminated. The state exercises responsibility for establishing custody in divorce cases, and for establishing a permanent parent–child legal relationship through adoption. Unfortunately, criteria for making these alterations are not well defined, and there is a need for statutory guidelines. The record of the judicial system is not impressive when a child's custody is contested. Generally, the practice is to exercise judicial restraint toward intervention in such matters and taking no decisive action, which tends to perpetuate the status quo and provides the easiest administrative resolution for custody problems. Because of this, adjudication of the custody of children is often drawn out over years rather than being resolved early and definitively for the child's benefit. Even worse, many youngsters spend years in foster care because no one has assumed the responsibility for making the drastic decisions that are sometimes necessary in pursuing the interests of the child.

On the other hand, historically, the courts have been accustomed to dealing with rebellious or recalcitrant youth, capable of theft, assault, and other crimes of adult proportions. Juvenile courts were established to deal with these matters. The basic presumption was that the court acts upon the child, shifting responsibility from the family, rather than acting on behalf of the child. The child has been seen as an object to be manipulated rather than as an active participant in the judicial process.

This has also been the case for children who commit "status offenses." These offenses are related to problems in schooling in the form of truancy, problems in child rearing in the form of incorrigibility, and problems in child–parent relationships as expressed through running away from home. All of these actions constitute rebellion against either parental or social control and are not offenses in adult life. Another series of legal actions relate to the legal status of children, such as illegitimacy, divorce custody, foster care, adoption, stepchild relationships, right to medical treatment, and the range of issues related to mental retardation.

Children have been victimized by obsolete laws enacted for eras dominated by "agism" far more extreme than at the present, with resulting discrimination and injustice. Furthermore, much family law intermixes the rights of children with legislation involving marriage, divorce, and child custody. As the centuries-old subservience of children in the family is being philosophically and practically protested, there is a growing awareness that children are people with rights previously ignored by statutes and courts. The result is a new concern for the child in American law. This raises the question of whether or not children should be included in family law or whether a new body of child law should be developed (Katz, 1974).

The critical issue is that children depend upon courts for recognition, nurture, and protection, not simply the administration of justice. Courts find themselves less concerned with establishing fault and more with improving human relations. Litigation involving children really should not be balancing power among children, parents, and the state, but directed toward ensuring a favorable future outcome in a child's life. Unlike criminal law, which is devoted to protecting the rights of defendants when the issue is whether or not an action occurred, litigation involving children is based upon determining and protecting a child's interests. Ascribing rights to children will not immediately solve these problems, but it will force the judiciary and legislatures to take into account the child's point of view.

Child Development Concepts Relevant to the Legal System

The most important feature distinguishing adult law from children's law is the fact that children are engaged in an ongoing process of physical, emotional, social, and psychological development, all of which continually alter their perceptions of the world and their needs. A child's developmental stage determines behavior and understanding of the world. Furthermore, each child is part of a parent–child unit. It is, therefore, conceptually impossible to deal with a child apart from the parent–child relationship. When a child has completely outgrown parenting, the child becomes an adult. Conversely, adult status is defined by emergence from the dependent condition of childhood, the completed process being referred to as "emancipation" in legal writings.

All of this means that adult law and adult court practices are oriented to an individual person, but this is not possible with children. Three crucial additional developmental principles emerge in approaching children and their caretaking units in the legal system: (1) age grading based upon changing capacity; (2) the "psychological best interest" standard with implicit promotion of a child's development; and (3) the critical importance of time in a child's life.

AGE GRADING

Age grading runs throughout the legal system. In many contexts, persons' rights, powers, duties, and disabilities under the law depend on the determination that they have "come of age." Chronological age determines whether or not a person can, or must, go to school, go to jail, marry, work, obey parents, speak freely, see a movie, inspect school records, receive parental support, provide support to parents, have counsel, testify in court, own a credit card, buy, sell, smoke, bet, drink, and drive (Simon, 1975). The most prominent of these are specified in legislation. Additional stipulations are made by public officials administering federal, state, and local laws.

Whatever the source of age-grading law—statutory, judicial, or administrative—it has special consequences for the least advantaged children: the poor and the disabled. These are the youths most likely to drop out of school at an age when attendance is compulsory; to undergo punishment or criminal or civil commitment at an age when few procedural safeguards are available; and to need some form of government assistance, often granted or withheld according to age. Moreover, these children, as a result of personal incapacity or lack of family resources, may be the least equipped to overcome or avoid government age-grading restrictions through persuasion, legal challenge, or alternative dispositions in private schools, hospitals, or other institutions.

Age grading not only has a differential impact according to socioeconomic class and health status, but its rules vary, sometimes according to sex, as children move from one legal arena to another, from state to state and town to town, and from judge to judge or from one administrator to another. Whatever its form and expression, the presence of age grading is ubiquitous and commanding.

Of no greater importance in age grading is the determination of when children are able to make decisions for themselves. The capacity to assume responsibility for decision making gradually increases as one ascends the developmental ladder. At the age of five, children assume responsibility for school attendance, at 16 they may acquire a driver's license, at 18 they may vote, and at 35 they are eligible to become President of the United States. This approach, which is based upon the biological maturation of the central nervous system, leads one to view the child as moving from a level of relative incapacity to one of competency to assume full responsibility. Because legislation must take into account masses of people, an individual's ability to assume a given responsibility is linked to the attainment of a certain birthdate rather than developmental age, without taking individual differences in developmental rates and capacities into account. There is a need for increased responsiveness of laws to individuals so that social responsibilities can be awarded to children who have demonstrated capability for more responsibility than would be allotted to them solely on the basis of chronological age. One of the burdens of childhood is waiting for a birthday in spite of demonstrated capability.

The ability of children to participate in decision making that affects their personal lives and to assume responsibility in broader social matters involves a mixture of intellectual, cognitive, emotional, social, and temperamental factors that defy generalization. The ability of children to participate in decision making regarding their custody in divorce settlements, for example, is based upon far more than an intellectual understanding of questions they are asked. A child's emotional ties to parents, immediate considerations related to the child's comfort rather than long-range goals, transient anger and resentment toward a parent, and perceptions of social attitudes toward parents may influence a child's decision in ways unrelated to that child's long-range interests. Furthermore, the developmental stage colors children's views of their parents, the reasons for their parents' divorce, and the degree to which a wish for parental reunion is dominant.

In the matter of custody, many jurisdictions understandably have adopted policies that guide them in including children in decision making regarding their parents. Some courts hold that a child over seven years of age should be permitted to register opinions regarding custody, and that a child over 14 years of age should be permitted to make the decision regarding the custodial parent. This point of view reflects the tendency of society to view children as capable of assuming responsibility at certain ages. What is not taken into account is the fact that, even though a child may be cognitively able to make a judgment and express an opinion, being placed in the position of making a choice about one's parents can unduly tax the child's relationship with both parents. Generally speaking, it is not fair to place a child in the position of making choices between parents. The child did not bring about the family discord and, therefore, should not be required to take responsibility for making decisions resulting from the divorce.

There are practical ways of including a child's point of view in custody decisions. Even though courts have generally been aware that children are more than merely interested parties in litigation that affects them, decisions regarding custody and placement have been determined largely from an adult-centered point of view. It is only recently that the parent–child relationship as a unit has been susceptible to evaluation through modern child psychiatric techniques.

As described in greater detail in Chapter 4, it is useful to think of a child's capacity for arriving at personal judgments regarding family matters in three interrelated ways: first, capacity to observe situations correctly; second, capacity to evaluate the implications of these observations; and third, capacity to express these judgments coherently to others.

The first capacity is related to the child's ability to perceive reality. An innate egocentricity heavily flavors a child's perception of reality from infancy through early adolescence. Before the onset of formal operational thinking in early adolescence, children cannot view abstractly their parental relationships. Even adolescents may be influenced by value judgments of their parents, which affect their perceptions until their own separate identities are firmly established.

The second capacity needed by a child to participate in family decision making is the ability to evaluate realistically situations once they are perceived. Children's evaluations of their parents are inevitably colored by loyalty conflicts and their own developmental needs.

The third capacity required in assuming responsibility for making choices is a child's ability to express coherently observations and evaluations. During early childhood, communication is framed in terms of meaningfulness to oneself. It is only later that communication is intended to enhance the listener's understanding. As an illustration, children frequently capitalize on hostilities between their divorced parents by making statements based on their own feelings and thus fuel the fires of discord. In these situations parental conflict is perpetuated by a child's statements and behavior, which are calculated to arouse the anger and anxiety of parents toward each other because of the child's anger toward them.

As can be seen, the act of involving a child in family decision making depends upon a judge's ability to assess the child's perceptive, evaluative, and reporting capabilities. The technical skills involved in making these assessments clearly fall within the purview of professionals trained to evaluate children. To this end, generalizations about developmental stages are less helpful than information about specific children developed in their life situations.

Optimally, a child's feelings and opinions should be incorporated into a complete picture of that child's life gained from data from a variety of sources. The question faced by courts is whether or not children are reliable, competent witnesses and to what degree children are capable of understanding the implications of their statements. The court must face, furthermore, the question as to whether or not children should be confronted with the onerous responsibility of making preferential statements about their parents.

THE PSYCHOLOGICAL BEST INTERESTS STANDARD

There is a growing statutory recognition that children's interests should be paramount in situations in which they conflict with their parents' interests while safeguarding the rights of parents to raise their children as they see fit, free from intervention by the state. When a child's placement becomes the subject of controversy in the courts, however, the parents have called attention to their inability to resolve the problem themselves and have invited others to make decisions for them. It is at this time, from the legal standpoint, that the psychological best interests of the child become an issue, not before.

Goldstein, Freud, and Solnit make the point that the "best interests" standard deserves critical scrutiny (1973). They hold that it tends to be a rationalization made by decision makers justifying their judgments about a child's future. Seductively, it implies that there is a "best" alternative for a child. This implication diverts the decision maker from carefully weighing the positive–negative impact of any decision. Recognizing the idealism of the best interests standard, they suggest another guideline for decision makers in custody cases: "that which is least detrimental among available alternatives for the child." They argue that the introduction of the idea of available alternatives should force consideration of the advantages and disadvantages of the realistic options. These options should be evaluated in terms of which is least likely to preclude the chances of the child becoming "wanted." They hold that the "least detrimental" standard is less awesome, more realistic, and thus more amenable to data gathering than the best interests standard.

When the interests of a child are contrasted with the desires of the parents, a realistic plan for a child can be developed within the context of available alternatives. An eloquent statement revealing the difficulty and painfulness of the choice lies in a decision by a fictitious Lord Baltimore (Goldstein, 1973):

> Despite my sympathetic concern for adults faced with tragedy, the choice before the court is no different, though apparently more difficult than it often seems in foster parent–common-law adoption cases. Whatever the court decides, inevitably there will be hardship. It may be the biological parents, already victimized by poverty, poor education, ill health, prejudice, their own ambivalence, or other circumstances, who are denied their child. It may be the child who is torn away from his psychological parents. It may be the psychological parents who are deprived of the child for whom they have long and faithfully cared. It may be all of them.
>
> In a court with my oath to implement the state's preference for serving a child's interests, my choice and decision are clear, though not, as they seldom

are, easy. I must decide not to disturb the child's relationship with his common-law parents. More precisely, I must even deny the biological parents an opportunity to call into question the existing placement of "their" child unless they could introduce evidence that "their" child is neglected or abandoned. Harsh as it is and as it must seem to the biological parents, their standing in court is no greater than that of a stranger.

As a judge, I have to recognize as irrelevant feelings which have been aroused in me because of my childhood experiences, my own concerns about being a parent, and my religious origins. These feelings would compel me to place the child with the biological parents, as compensation for their suffering, were it not for the guideline which stresses the child's need for continuity.

Further, to return to the problem of judicial choice as originally posed, I maintain that, once the least detrimental alternative is found, such decisions maximize known benefit and minimize known harm for all parties concerned. To leave undisturbed the relationship of the child to his common-law parents protects the well being of the largest number. To favor the biological parents would impose an intolerable hardship on both the child and psychological parents. To favor the child would be to favor as well his psychological parents. If each human being's interest is entitled to equal weight, more interest will tilt the scale toward leaving well enough alone than toward allowing the biological parents to prevail.

Arguments have been made that the winning adult will suffer guilt for depriving the other adult of the child or that the child himself will feel let down by one set of parents or the other. But to attribute to the judicial process the capacity to work out and to weigh the significance of such inponderables in the decision making is unrealistic.

Let me now address those who argue that the adult's interest, not the child's, should be paramount. Even if such a policy were adopted, the court would be hard pressed in most cases to determine whether the biological or the psychological parent or who of the divorcing parents would be most harmed by the denial of custody.

The state may, of course, assert another policy to be applied in cases of extreme hardship, resulting from major disasters approximating the Dutch situation. Parents who have been forced to relinquish their children against their wishes would have a primary and overriding right to regain their custody. The state would be committed to assist such parents in the search for their children and in enforcing their right to repossess them. It might be argued that any other policy would violate a fundamental ethic of a civilized society regardless of the individual's needs and state of mind.

But after reviewing the arguments for each of these policies, I return to the guidelines that have governed my decisions. I am convinced that, by and large, society must use each child's placement as an occasion for protecting future generations of adults by increasing the number of adults who are likely to be adequate parents. Only in the implementation of this policy does there lie a real opportunity for beginning to break the cycle of sickness and hardship bequeathed from one generation to the next by adults who as children were denied the least detrimental alternative.

THE IMPORTANCE OF TIME IN CHILD LITIGATION

The judicial process is time consuming as it ponderously moves toward its goal of justice. In many instances, the passage of time is an advantage by permitting reason to replace the heat of emotions. In the lives of adults months, or even years, may not be critical in arriving at the conclusion of a trial. For a child, however, that period of time may disrupt a parent relationship or schooling. Even several weeks for a young child may be a harsh separation from a parent with resulting emotional damage. For the adolescent a delay of even a week from the time of an offense to the time of a hearing may lessen the impact of court intervention and only impress the adolescent with the ineffectiveness of law enforcement. For children and youth, speedy adjudication is paramount. Not only does the child's concept of time differ from that of the adult, but the passage of time has critical effects on a child's development.

A related principle is the importance of ensuring continuity of a child's development so that any decision made affecting the life of a child must be monitored over time. Paradoxically, courts are in a strategic position to provide for monitoring and review, but they often have not taken advantage of that opportunity, with resulting vacillation and temporizing. It is unfortunate that few judges are able to follow through in their role as advocates for children who have passed through their courts. If the child is seen as depending upon continuous parenting rather than as a detached individual, the court's deliberations can focus on preserving the continuity of caretaking while, and after, the merits of a case are determined.

The Rights of Children

Theoretically, the interests of adults who choose to be parents and the interests of their children are complementary. This is reflected in the legal tradition that parents are the best advocates of their children's interests. As a result, little consideration has been given in the past to the legal rights of children as a discrete interest group. With the growing recognition that the child's side of the parent–child unit has not been sufficiently considered, legislative reform is moving to change children's legal status in two ways: first, by extending more adult rights to children and, second, by recognizing the unique needs of children as legally enforcible rights (Rodham, 1973).

The first approach to the rights of children through extending them adult rights is exemplified by proposals for awarding all the rights of adult criminal defendants to accused delinquents, by empowering children to obtain medical care without parental consent, and by providing children with an attorney, a *guardian ad litem*, in any situation in which their legal interests are affected (Landsman, 1978). In this light, however, practicing lawyers hold differing views about the rights of children and the rights of adults and apply different standards to juvenile clients. A lawyer may have reservations about helping a juvenile "beat a case," and, if a case is won on a technicality, may feel obliged to warn the child against the danger of future misconduct. As a representative of adult society, the lawyer may feel a responsibility to establish a model of morality for the juvenile, but may not feel the same responsibility to an adult offender. It is as if society holds hope and high expectations for children, which are relinquished when they achieve adulthood.

Another illustration of extending adult rights to children is through awarding emancipation. The fully emancipated child legally becomes an adult; the partially emancipated child is freed from certain parental controls while remaining under them in other respects. The general rule has been that emancipation is an act of parents or of the state, not of the child, and the burden of proving emancipation rests upon the minor. For example, emancipation has been adjudicated in parental actions to recover a minor's wages, so that it is now accepted that minors can keep their earnings, ending their parents' rights to their wages. On the other hand, in cases of child support, courts have been unwilling to declare emancipation when it would mean depriving the minor of support. Another area of reluctance to emancipate is in the ability to execute contracts. The general rule has been that emancipation does not affect a minor's incapacity for contractual liability. On the other hand, during the past decade, most states have lowered the age for voting to 18. Still other legislation enables minors to consent to medical treatment for venereal disease, drug abuse, and medical emergencies.

A second general approach to children's rights is based upon the assumption that, even if all adult rights were granted to children, this would not guarantee that the critical developmental needs of children would be met. This line of reasoning is reflected in a variety of "bills of rights for children," including both psychological and physical categories, the latter being easier to define. Although closer to the developmental realities of childhood, these "bills of rights" tend to be idealistic and attribute magical power to the law, expecting what is far beyond its means. While the law may claim to establish conditions, in fact it cannot create them.

The conditions mentioned in bills of rights for children are illustrated in the following list adapted from Foster (1974).

The right to preparation for life through being a wanted child free from preventable disability through adequate family planning, genetic counseling, prenatal, perinatal, and postnatal health care.

The right be regarded as a person within the family, at school, and before the law.

The right to receive parental love and affection, discipline and guidance, and grow to maturity in a home which enables the child to develop into a mature and responsible adult.

The right to be supported, maintained, and educated to the best of parental ability, in return for which children have a moral duty to respect their mothers and fathers and have reciprocal duties to their parents.

The right to a positive social identity through name and ethnic identification.

The right to a safe and secure environment in the form of adequate shelter and recreational facilities and freedom from harmful pollutants.

The right to adequate nutrition and health care, including the prevention of illness. A controversial corollary is the right to seek and obtain medical care and counseling without parental consent. Many adolescents are faced with difficulties in the realm of pregnancy, contraceptive information, venereal disease, drug abuse, and emotional disturbance about which they are reluctant to confide in their parents. As a result, they do not receive adequate medical care. This is a complicated issue, however, because the option always exists that adolescents could be helped therapeutically to communicate with their parents to the benefit of both. Any policy that bypasses the possibility of improving communication within the family runs the risk of driving a wedge between family members, rather than helping to resolve conflicts within the family.

The right to earn and keep their own earnings and to be emancipated from parental authority when they are qualified to do so and their interests would be served.

The right to a relevant education to develop each child's potential on an equal access basis and free of legal constraints, except where such are necessary and protective of children's interests. Compulsory school attendance and child labor laws are an intolerable burden for many minors, forcing them into the limbo of "dropout" status. Compulsory school attendance illustrates the complexity of these issues because it is related to the right to an appropriate education of quality. Minors would not drop out of school if their education suited their needs; thus a legal issue could be resolved by improving education.

The right to receive fair treatment and to be listened to by adults with authority. This includes the right to have standing in legal proceedings and to assert claims of interest with the assistance of legal counsel.

The right to receive special care, consideration, and protection in the administration of the law so that the child's interest is always paramount. This applies especially to custody determinations, but also includes the rights of students to form organizations, to determine their own dress, to have free speech, to arrange assembly, and to use school facilities.

As is evident, these fundamental "rights" of children extend beyond those constitutionally guaranteed for adults. The presumption is that children deserve to be reared in accordance with the ideals of society. Each of these "rights" has been encountered in some form in the courts.

Current trends in the practical determination of the rights of children are illustrated in a series of Supreme Court decisions. These decisions have generally made children more visible in the judicial process and have established for them the right to counsel, to due process, to the reasonable adjudication of majority, and to the right to an education. The Supreme Court has further confirmed the validity of juvenile courts, as distinguished from criminal courts, while it has mandated due process to protect children from abuse by juvenile courts.

The Supreme Court established policy regarding due process for children in court through three landmark decisions: *In re Gault*, *In re Winship*, and *McKeiver* v. *Pennsylvania*. The *Gault* decision brought due process guarantees from the 14th Amendment into state juvenile proceedings on a case-by-case basis. Subsequently, *In re Winship* declared that proof beyond a reasonable doubt as a due process requirement in adult criminal cases applies to juveniles as well. In *McKeiver* v. *Pennsylvania*, the Supreme Court held, however, that a jury trial in the juvenile courts adjudicative stage is not a constitutional requirement and "refrained from taking the easy way of a flat holding that all rights constitutionally assured for the adult accused are to be imposed on the state's juvenile proceeding." The Court's reasoning was that if a jury trial were required it would turn the juvenile proceedings into a full adversary process, destroying the ideal of an informal protective proceeding and possibly ending the juvenile court as a separate institution.

While *Gault* recognized the child's right to counsel, questions continue on the issues of when that right may be waived and what constitutes effective counsel. The question of the point at which the right to counsel comes into existence also has aroused controversy. *Gault* did not clearly extend the right to the preadjudicatory phases of the juvenile proceedings and declared that the substantive advantages of the juvenile process must not be eliminated by the imposition of due process.

McKeiver acted as a brake on the application of constitutional rights to juvenile proceedings by emphasizing the differences between juvenile and adult trials. *McKeiver* not only supported the right of the states to maintain their own juvenile court systems, but returned to the state some power to determine the rights of the child. In the future each state must develop a sound philosophy for its juvenile courts, which incorporates some due process rights while retaining aspects of the original *parens patriae* theory. In effect, the Supreme Court is encouraging each state to experiment with its juvenile justice system to provide for both due process rights and rehabilitation of the juvenile.

Because of the criminal–civil dichotomy that has long prevailed in the courts, the *Gault* decision did not reach into family litigation because it was confined to an incident occurring in the juvenile courts. The necessity for protection through legal counsel for children in custody cases, however, is urged on the same basis that due process was introduced into the juvenile courts. The philosophy of *Gault* would extend the right to counsel previously reserved for adults through all proceedings involving juveniles. The precedent of *Gault* could result in mandatory provisions for legal counsel for children in all custody contests, as it now does in some states. In 1968 the National Conference of Commissioners on Uniform State Laws (1968a) adopted the Uniform Child Custody Jurisdiction Act, designed further to end jurisdictional conflict and competition in interstate custody cases and to provide a model for state legislation.

Several specific areas deserve special mention because many children do not have a legal foundation from which to assert their rights. They are children who do not have established legal status with parents. One group are those referred to as "illegitimate" children. The U.S. Supreme Court in *Levy* v. *Louisiana* and *Glone* v. *American Guarantee and Liability Insurance Company* has addressed this problem, establishing the principle that an illegitimate child is the legal equivalent of a legitimate child in most areas of the law. The Court invalidated much legislation dealing with illegitimacy, creating a gap which state legislatures have not filled.

In another vein, *Stanley* v. *Illinois* and *Rothstein* v. *Lutheran Social Services* affected routine adoption processes by requiring termination of the parental rights of known unmarried fathers. As a result of these Supreme Court decisions and legislative inactivity, the law related to illegitimacy is in a state of confusion. The Revised Uniform Adoption Act proposed by the National Conference of Commissioners of Uniform State Laws (1971) is intended to fill this vacuum. The Act's guiding principle is to award full equality to all children, legitimate and illegitimate, in their legal relationships with both parents. The act provides ways of identifying the father for children born out of wedlock and also contains provisions for setting a level of child support, for the enforcement of judgments, and for other issues such as custody. In addition, it sets up a procedure whereby the rights of a disinterested, remarried father may be terminated with a minimum of delay and interference with the adoption process. Because children have been buried in marriage and divorce legislation concentrating on adult aspects of the family, more specific child laws to complement family law are needed.

Another neglected group of children are the increasing numbers of stepchildren. For the children of divorce, the stepparent relationship is often a source of chronic frustration and difficulty. In common law, the term "stepchild" refers to the child of one of the spouses by a former marriage. However, in common law, the mere establishment of a step relationship imposes no legal obligation on a husband to support the children of his wife through a previous relationship. The rights of stepchildren have been established very slowly through the years, always in direct opposition to common law. Where *in loco parentis* relationships have been established between the stepchild and the spouse who is not the natural parent, the only legal obligations of the stepparent are the duty to support, the right to have services rendered to the child, and the right to participate in suits for the child involving third parties. Other areas, such as workmen's compensation, are controlled by statutes which often withhold from a stepchild any right to benefits from the stepparent relationship. Legislative solutions are needed in order to establish a definition and an overall policy for stepchildren.

In summary, work on the legal rights of children is based upon the adaptation of adult rights, upon the developmental needs of children, and upon the concept that adults should "set good examples" for children. Running through these themes is recognition of a need for guiding and protecting children from hurting themselves through actions that would be regretted in later years. Both through its expectations of parents and its hopes for the young, society appears to stress ideal models for its developing children. The social foundation for promoting and protecting the interests of children is solid. The challenge, then, is at the level of implementation.

The Juvenile Court System

Although the target of relentless reformers since the turn of the century, the number of juvenile delinquents has steadily increased, doubling since 1957 to presently include 4 percent of children between 10 and 17 years of age and to account for almost half of all the crimes committed in the United States (Corbett, 1974). It appears that juvenile delinquency as a socially defined phenomenon is tightly woven into our social fabric. At any rate, our loosely related system of juvenile court, correctional, foster care, and probation services has not made inroads into the problem of juvenile delinquency. As a result, public attention is focused on the juvenile court system today (Davis, 1978). Some advocate its expansion, others its elimination.

In desperation, many communities are remanding older adolescents to adult courts. A survey carried out by the Children's Defense Fund found 350 children in 449 jails (Children's Defense Fund, 1976). Twelve percent were jailed because of property offenses, such as theft, and 18 percent because of status offenses. One boy was jailed simply because he had no other place to go; one girl was there because her mother was in the hospital; and another girl was in jail as protection from her father, who had committed incest with her.

Dissatisfaction with the juvenile justice system exists throughout the nation. The complaint is that it neither protects the public nor helps the child. There is disagreement, however, about the causes of the system's unsatisfactory performance. Some believe that a separate system of juvenile justice has failed and will continue to fail because it is not directed at the causes of delinquency and at the rehabilitation of the delinquent. Others advocate managing juvenile offenders more as we do adults (Juvenile Justice Standards Project, 1977). Still others believe that the system has not failed but, rather, has never been given an adequate trial because it exists only in form rather than substance. Others believe that the less than 3,000 juvenile courts in the United States are simply too few to do the job. The failure, in their view, is not the system's but the failure of communities to provide the personnel, facilities, and funds necessary for individualized juvenile justice.

Whatever the current state of juvenile courts, they bear the brunt of criticism, to the extent that some people seem to feel that juvenile crime is a result of the juvenile court system itself. In one sense, beleaguered juvenile courts promote juvenile crime. They certainly stand as ineffective models and, although helping milder cases, do not dissuade hardened delinquents who may view the juvenile judge as a challenge or as a source of entertainment.

Underlying the ineffectiveness of the methods and procedures of the juvenile court system over the years has been a tendency to equate understanding with "permissiveness" and character development with "treatment." Awareness of the difficult life situations of delinquents has frequently led to a sympathetic, soft approach that has failed to set needed limits for the youth. Moreover, just as the adult correctional system has used the euphemism of "treatment" for the operations of its penal system, the conception of the juvenile court as a "treatment" instrument of delinquency has overlooked the obvious psychiatric, social, economic, and racial factors that contribute to juvenile crime.

One of the unfortunate aspects of the juvenile court system has been a tendency to protect adolescents from full realization of the gravity of their offenses and an appreciation of the consequences of their actions. Law enforcement officers are well aware of offenders who return to the streets with the sense that they have "conned" the system, only to try bigger and better things until their actions force intervention again. Many teenagers use the arena of the community to provoke limits that they have not received at home. Unfortunately, the courts' responses replicate their parents', and amount to either inappropriate leniency or too severe punishment.

Many young offenders consider the juvenile court to be a "joke" and continue their lawbreaking road to becoming adult criminals. When hard-core delinquents laugh at a court, and the community as a whole has little confidence in it, the system itself must be carefully scrutinized. Actually, the system's problems are obvious, including delays in hearings, lack of follow-up, excessive caseloads, lack of standardized procedures, inadequate social service staffs, the advent of defense attorneys in juvenile cases, and the use of plea bargaining, which rewards a minor for manipulating the system in the hope of "getting off easily."

The message that many youngsters receive from the juvenile court system is of greatest importance. They hear the court say "Don't do it again," but they find that there is little follow-through. When a troubled boy is in and out of court with little happening to him each time, he is harmfully affected because the message is at best mixed. It is confirmation that there are no significant consequences if he does it again. The following case report is not unusual and illustrates the problem:

> John, fifteen, had forty offenses on his record, most of them burglary and theft. He was referred to the court two years before for a number of these offenses. He admitted the offenses, but the case was referred to another county to which his family had moved. He decided to plead not guilty to the offenses there, and no action was taken. He moved back to the first county and was referred again for other offenses. His social worker did not bring the case to court. Six months later, he committed a rash of offenses. The judge ordered him placed in a treatment center. The social worker felt it was not appropriate and did not follow through. Five months later, John was assigned to a new social worker when the social services department was reorganized. The new worker brought him back into court, where the judge again ordered that treatment center placement be arranged. Before he could be placed, John was arrested for stealing a minibike. When the prosecutor asked that John be kept in detention until the next day when he was to be placed, a court administrator refused because the offense did not justify holding him. The following day John left the state and was lost to the court's purview thereafter.

On the other hand, the potential of juvenile courts for overreaction is exemplified by the United States Supreme Court ruling in the landmark case of *Gault*: a 15-year-old boy was placed in a correctional institution, where he could remain until the age of 21, because he made an obscene phone call for which an adult would have been punished by a fine of $5 to

$50. The Supreme Court called attention to the fact that juvenile court decisions can be capricious and that the rights of adolescents to due process procedures must be taken into account. On the one hand, the protective, presumably helpful, shield of the juvenile court has been relied upon to guide adolescents through transient antisocial behavior resulting from the dependent, still immature sides of their development. On the other hand, it is clear that all juvenile court practices cannot be relied upon to be benign and helpful. The harshness of the *Gault* disposition led the Supreme Court to link the need for due process to the potentially drastic interventions available to the juvenile court rather than to the Court's abstract concern for due process for juveniles.

It is clear that adolescents need protection from heavy-handed management by insensitive or vengeful adults. It is also clear that the community needs protection from the manipulation of the courts by exploitative minors. The following cases illustrate this point:

> Jerry, 16, was charged with ten thefts and seven burglaries. He pleaded not guilty to the charges at the first hearing two months later. Jerry's attorney brought 32 legal motions for the judge to rule on thereafter. Six months later the case still had not been scheduled for trial.

> Bob, 15, and four other youths were involved in a series of burglaries. Because the prosecutor had to sort out all the interconnecting participation, four months elapsed before a formal charge on seven burglaries was lodged. When brought to trial, Bob's attorney moved that the case be dismissed because of lack of a speedy trial. One year after the arrest that motion was denied. Meanwhile the other boys admitted their involvement in court and were placed on probation. The judge ordered restitution for them, however, it could not be calculated until Bob's case was tried. Bob's attorney again appealed the case on the grounds of a lack of a speedy trial.

The National Conference on Commissioners on Uniform State Laws (1968b) has written a Uniform Juvenile Court Act in an effort to implement recent Supreme Court decisions. The model act is based upon the assumption that if departures in juvenile court from criminal procedure are to be justified when delinquent conduct is alleged, involving what for an adult would be a criminal act, the juvenile court proceedings and dispositions must be governed by the objectives of treatment and rehabilitation. If the approach is punitive, the procedures should adhere to the constitutional requirements for criminal proceedings.

At the present time juvenile courts generally lack treatment and rehabilitative resources. In a study of 1,214 juvenile courts, 58 percent provided no medical, psychological, or psychiatric examinations or services. An additional 25 percent were able to provide them in less than 10 percent of the cases. Since one-third of the delinquent population and almost three-quarters of their parents show clear evidence of serious psychopathology, juvenile courts cannot expect rational approaches to delinquents' behavior to be successful (Lewis, 1976). Even in courts with mental health professionals on their staffs, their recommendations are often not followed, in large part because of lack of treatment facilities (Ferster, 1975).

Frequently, the disposition of a juvenile is dictated by financial considerations. In 1977, in Wisconsin, the comparative monthly costs of care were as follows: state inpatient psychiatric unit, $3,300; county hospital, $2,100; child caring institution, $1,500; state training school, $700; and probation, $60. The financial attractiveness of probation is evident.

More sobering is the experience of a juvenile court functioning under ideal circumstances. Ferster's study of that model court supported the ultimate usefulness of a juvenile court, but simultaneously recognized its ineffectiveness. His conclusion was that a major handicap pervaded that entire court system; it was the erroneous unspoken presumption that making no action, which was termed "giving a child a chance," was helpful to the minor. Furthermore, there was the belief that directing a child to "go to school," "mind his parents," or "stop stealing" would have an effect on behavior. This pattern of responses to offenders was observed in all parts of the system, in which the police, social workers, judges, and probation officers all gave the child "another chance" and little else. The failure to take action stemmed not from indifference but from a feeling of helplessness in changing the children's home lives, school situations, or emotional difficulties. Of at least equal significance was the almost total lack of recognition of the rights of children, not only in the juvenile justice system, but in the community. Even in this optimal setting, 54 percent of the juveniles were recidivists, and the general perception of the court by the community was that it was not meeting the community needs.

Ferster's study concluded that the claim that the juvenile system cannot work at all is invalid. What must be taken into account is society's attitude toward juvenile courts. The greatest problem at the present time is that communities look to juvenile courts to solve problems. The direction should be reversed. The juvenile court should act as a mechanism to assist families and communities in resolving their problems. It should act as a facilitator in bringing together the offender and the victim in a growth producing experience so that the offender feels the realistic impact of the offense on the victim and can experience the event as a learning experience. To the extent that the court becomes a place to which schools, parents, the police department, and other aspects of the community can simply "send their problems," the potential value of the juvenile court to achieve conflict resolution between young people and adults cannot be realized.

The juvenile court should not be an extension of parents as it is forced to become when families are unable to control, motivate, or rear their children. This misuse of the court system has permitted parents to readily turn their problems over to society with the statement, "We can't do a thing with him." This means that status offenses, such as incorrigibility, running away, and truancy should be handled in other ways that can support families in their child rearing efforts.

The juvenile court does have an important role to play as a specialized arm of the community which can be brought into play when the community is adversely affected by the behaviors of minors or when a family unit itself breaks down. Even then, however, the court should apply its resources either to repairing the child's family or providing a new family unit for the child.

The following case is a glaring example of the ineptitude of state intervention when brought in to solve a family problem:

> Cynthia Snyder, a 15 year old girl, was temporarily taken to a juvenile court receiving home by her father because of her rebellion against her parents' restrictions on her smoking, dating and other activities. She showed no delinquent behavior. Cynthia later filed a petition alleging that she was incorrigible with the hope of being placed in a foster home. This was granted. Two years later, the Washington Supreme Court upheld the decision. Realistic hopes for salvaging the parent–child relationship were lost during the two years of litigation. After she turned 18 her parents filed a claim against the State of Washington for alienation of affection. In this case the state intervened in a family problem and represented the child against her parents. This costly and time consuming approach which left family relationships aggravated can be contrasted with what might have happened if a mental health approach, such as family therapy, had been employed, rather than a legal remedy (Hafen, 1976b; *Snyder*).

Juvenile courts need to relate to treatment institutions to heal the emotions and minds of young people and their families; however, they can draw upon their own authority to ensure that the misdeeds of children and youth are resolved within the neighborhood, family, and school. No greater learning experience occurs for a young offender than to make restitution to the victim either through the repair of damage or compensation for injury. When the delinquent offense is taken from the arena of exciting defiance and selfish plunder into concrete reality, the young offender becomes aware that a specific person was injured by specific actions that must be restituted. What for so many delinquents is a dehumanized ritual of vandalism, as an example, is suddenly converted into a human experience between real people with real consequences and with potential for deepened understanding, character growth, and wisdom.

Where the juvenile court system has gone astray is in providing a convenient mechanism for dehumanizing juvenile offenses so that the young offender has lost the opportunity to absorb real consequences for personal actions and to witness mature adults attempting to resolve realistic human problems. It was the lack of these very opportunities in many delinquents' backgrounds that spawned their antisocial behavior.

Contrast the experience of the delinquent who vandalizes a house and subsequently comes in contact only with police officers, attorneys, juvenile court social workers, judges, and ultimately fellow offenders in a reformatory, with the experience of the delinquent who vandalizes a house, faces the victim, admits his wrongdoing, cleans up and repairs the damage, and works to earn money to pay for the remaining damage, thereby establishing a relationship with the people injured. In the latter instance the delinquent's contact with professionals in the community is limited to a brief encounter with a police officer, a social worker, and a judge who set up a contract between the offender and the victim. The first instance is dehumanized, the second is an intimate personal growth experience for the offender—and the offended.

The most significant criticisms of the juvenile courts relate to the lack of coordination between them and schools, community resources, and families. The opportunity to bring children and parents into contact with each other around juvenile offenses in a constructive way is seldom utilized. The power of families to resolve these problems is greater when backed up by the court than most people realize. This can be done through formally charging parents with responsibility for their children's behavior, and holding them accountable if they themselves are unable to assume this responsibility. Support for the parents can be both positive or penalizing, depending upon the circumstances.

Unfortunately, the juvenile court system has been struggling with inadequate legal and treatment models. Because it has focused on the individual child, it has overlooked the essential dependency of juveniles on their family units. It has recognized the importance of family pathology in the genesis of antisocial behavior, but has been unable to deal with those forces.

As an outgrowth of the Progressive Movement at the turn of this century, the juvenile court was conceived as a confidential system adapted to the needs of children. Because of inadequate or nonexistent community resources, it also attempted to provide rehabilitation and treatment for youthful offenders. Increasingly, juvenile courts assumed a social agency flavor over the years, with dilution of their judicial purpose. As a result, they have foundered within the judicial system.

Delaney envisions the juvenile court of the future as one from which status offenders are removed, and one in which children have the best of both worlds, namely, due process and therapeutic safeguards administered by competent judges who have enough time to do their work. Standards for the future should include upgrading the status of the juvenile courts from salary, prestige, and power points of view. There should be family court specialization, and there should be referees to share the work. There should be neighborhood branches, and the court should function in both formal and informal ways (Delaney, 1976).

The juvenile court system is needed in order to provide continuity of care for children, but it cannot operate realistically within the crisis-oriented, adversarial general court system procedures. The dependent status of children with their built-in need for integration of services and continuity of care must be recognized. Under ideal circumstances, the juvenile court system can provide continuity of supervision for dependent children in the role of parent supporter, but not parent surrogate. The juvenile court itself cannot provide treatment for children. It can facilitate, plan, and carry out genuine advocacy functions for over-burdened and pathogenic families who are unable to cope with children in need. For the many burdensome, unwanted children who require some mechanism for providing structure for their lives, the juvenile court can provide that structure. Mental health services can provide the thera-peutic, treatment-oriented support in order to promote family competen-cy. At times, however, when this is not possible, and a new family en-vironment is needed, the only effective mechanism available for this is the court system with its authority to arrange for placement and termination of parental rights.

The legal system can intervene when society needs to provide a youngster with a more suitable child rearing environment. It cannot in-duce people to provide more competent parenting functions, however, and must function in collaboration with other children and youth-oriented agencies. The juvenile courts should be the legal arms of mental health, health, and welfare networks of services for children. Diverting cases to more appropriate agencies can significantly reduce the legal system's burden (Lemert, 1976). Just as mental health services cannot provide the protection or support needed in a child's life situation, the juvenile court cannot assume responsibility for changing lives.

Fortunately, a realistic and effective objective exists for juvenile courts to stimulate neighborhood participation in identifying and working with juvenile offenders whose parents can be induced to cooperate with their neighbors. In many neighborhoods it becomes evident that there are in-adequate recreational facilities for adolescents, whether they be skating rinks, community centers, or other places for young people to congregate. When the problems are dealt with on this level, so that offenders and the offended have face-to-face relationships with each other, there are few that cannot be solved. The juvenile court can be instrumental in facili-tating this end.

A change is required in the juvenile court's approach to minimize the handling of delinquency out of context in an impersonalized way through the law enforcement, juvenile court, correctional system, which remains apart from the mainstream of the community and makes it extremely difficult for the delinquent—becoming criminal—to reintegrate. If we treat delinquent youths as junior criminals, we enhance the possibility that they will assume this identity and become adult criminals (Snyder, 1978). The juvenile court, then, must be oriented not only to work with individual children and families, but with various components of the community. We have known since the 1920s that the answers to delinquency lie in human engineering (Healy, 1969). Just as psychiatry developed community psychiatry as a field, it appears that the legal system should promote integration of juvenile courts within community child caring networks.

Family Law

Although there is much dissatisfaction with the juvenile court system, it is in the area of family law that more public reform through divorce legislation and revisions in children's codes has taken place. There is growing awareness that the legal system is struggling with too much when it attempts to define and resolve family problems. Furthermore, the administration of family law is usually dispersed throughout general courts, without the consistent availability of specialized family court services (Argo, 1977). Judges often find family litigation to be the most taxing aspect of their work.

Family problems come into courts legitimately not because of antisocial or criminal behavior, but because marriage is a legal contract with statutory controls. Most marital conflicts, however, are based less on contractual issues and more on personal unhappiness. Practicing attorneys feel ill equipped to handle these psychological and emotional matters and recognize the fact that more than legal skills are required to understand and aid people involved in family litigation (Carter, 1976).

As a result of the obvious limitations of the legal system in addressing family conflicts, efforts have been made to revise the role of courts in family matters through such steps as removing divorce from the adversarial model by creating "no fault" divorce; through adding counseling resources to specialized family courts (Argo, 1977); or through defining the courts as part of the social welfare system for the enforcement of minimum social standards (Mnookin, 1976). Most lawyers and judges are torn between their humanistic impulses to aid foundering families constructively and their professional roles, which limit them to the use of their legal skills.

Although they recognize that family problems involve other professional disciplines, the courts zealously guard their decision-making power and have not found effective ways of functioning within a broader network of human services. In part, this may be due to the legal system's natural reluctance to relinquish authority in any established area, if only based upon inertia. In addition, however, society tends to define family problems in legal terms, appears unwilling to entrust decision or enforcement power to the behavioral sciences without due process safeguards, and expects the courts to solve family disputes. As a result judges find themselves resorting to legal solutions because they lack better answers, and people continue to "call the police" and turn to judges when things go wrong in their homes.

CHILD REARING RESPONSIBILITIES

The aspects of family law that predominantly affect children hinge on fixing responsibilities for child rearing. In this respect courts are caught between increasing tensions that exist between society's expectations of parents, parents' own desires and capacities, and—now—the interests of children. Supposedly, the court balances the interests of the state, parents, and children; however, it is weighted toward maintaining the dominant, local social conceptions of child rearing. Society expects parents to raise and socialize children, and parents optimally seek self-fulfillment through child rearing in the context of their efforts to achieve satisfaction in work, play, and personal growth.

The current trend is toward increasing society's role in child rearing, one that some elements in government greet because of the resulting increase in their power; however, the consequent increase in the tax burden creates a counter-force to turn responsibilities back to parents. The tension between society and parents is heightened when parents seek to avoid expected child rearing responsibilities. The essential point is that society is ambivalent: the state's power is increased by more involvement in child rearing, but the increased cost invokes fiscal constraints. Historically, these constraints have not deterred increased government expenditures so that the ambivalence is steadily tipping toward increasing the role of government in child rearing. All of this means that the courts, although reluctantly and inappropriately, will play an increasing role in family matters—both because people turn to them and because child rearing is becoming more of a social endeavor.

The final common denominator in family law issues affecting children is the question of who has the responsibility for rearing a specific child. The issues of financial support, guidance, and promoting parent–child relationships turn upon who has legal custody of the child.

Mnookin provides a useful framework for analyzing American custody law by identifying three historical strands (1976). First of all is the law related to divorce custody, second is the law related to guardianship, which involves decision making but no legal duty to support the child, under the supervision of welfare or probation agencies, and third is the law related to the termination of parental rights in order to permit adoption.

DIVORCE CUSTODY CONTESTS

Generally, in arriving at custody decisions, courts lack necessary information and are confronted with impossible choices that lead to indeterminate results. Questions placed before courts regarding a child's custody relate to the probable outcomes resulting from a series of available alternatives. The problem is to determine what the outcome will be for each alternative. Under circumstances of a dispute between two parents, the choice is easy when one of the parents is clearly harmful. Ordinarily, however, the choices are not clear cut. They depend upon selecting the alternative least detrimental to the child's interests. In doing so, the greatest challenge is to devise criteria that can be used in order to make these determinations. Such factors as a child's happiness, religious training, economic productivity, stability, security, intellectual stimulation, warm relationships with parents, and discipline are commonly used. In Chapter 4 more objective criteria are proposed related to social competence as the ultimate goal of child rearing.

Because child custody matters are handled largely through general courts, the orientation of the law toward custody has been adult centered. In an effort to facilitate the operation of general courts, family court commissioner offices, or family court divisions in themselves, have been established to provide investigative and counseling services, particularly for people experiencing divorce. In some states an attorney for the child, a *guardian ad litem*, is appointed whenever custody is contested (Landsman, 1978). The overlap between family courts and juvenile courts is also significant in that families going through disruption are more likely than others to have children coming to the attention of the juvenile authorities. It is remarkable that one court deals with one side of a family problem related to parental divorce, and another court deals with another side because one member of the family is a juvenile offender. In contrast with the juvenile court, however, the family court is basically an adult court with a strong emphasis on administering financial settlements in the form of child support and alimony. Although decisions regarding child custody and visitation and child support are made in these courts, the administrators, judges, *guardians ad litem*, and social workers do not ordinarily have training in understanding or coping with problems related to children.

At this point a brief review of the pertinent aspects of marriage and divorce law is appropriate. Long ago, John Stuart Mill pointed out that marriage is a three-way contract between husband, wife, and unborn child, reflecting society's underlying view that marriage is for the purpose of procreation and child rearing. Much of the current controversy regarding marriage hinges on whether or not one wishes to, or inadvertently will, assume the responsibilities of raising children.

When divorce occurs, those with children are more complicated than those simply involving two adults. In 1974, 60 percent of divorces in the United States involved children (Carter, 1976). Placed in perspective, approximately 26 percent of American children were living in homes affected by divorce (Carter, 1976). The upward trend in divorces has been consistent since 1960, more than doubling from 2.2/1,000 to 5.0/1,000 in 1978. This is offset to a degree by a parallel increase in the marriage rate from 8.5/1,000 to 10.1/1,000. In absolute numbers there has been a 100 percent increase in divorces, a 20 percent increase in marriages, and a 30 percent increase in remarriages.

There has been a gradual shift in emphasis in American courts regarding policies affecting child custody determinations (Derdeyn, 1976). Throughout the last century the father's superior right to custody of the child reflected the tradition of English law. Even to the present time fathers are rarely exempted from child support. Gradually, the father's advantage in custody contests eroded so that until recently the mother of the child was favored. For young children, the "tender years presumption" later strongly influenced custody toward the mother. In the 1960s, 90 percent of contested cases were awarded to the mothers. Influencing the courts also has been whether or not the parent is "culpable" or "innocent" in the divorce proceedings. Over the last decade there has been a tendency to remove the sex of the parent from primary consideration as a result of the equal rights movement. Only recently has the psychological interests of the child criterion appeared in legislation, although the concept has influenced some jurisdictions since the early 1960s (Hansen, 1964).

The child's interests have received increasing emphasis because of the mounting evidence that divorce is a stressful experience for children and can have both negative and positive repercussions. Clinical studies show that psychiatric disorders are somewhat higher for children who have experienced divorce than for those who have not (Kalter, 1977). Even without the result of a psychiatric diagnosis, divorce can affect the attitudes, personalities, and subsequent relationships of involved children. Persons who divorce tend to have histories of divorce in their families (Carter, 1976). It is likely that divorce is disadvantageous for one-quarter of the affected children but advantageous for one-quarter, with the other half affected neither way (Brun, 1973). Beyond these possibilities is the fact that divorce is frequently a family affair and that it brings about major changes in the lives of children. Accordingly, knowledge of the impact of divorce upon children should be expanded and it is clearly essential for those involved in custody determinations (Westman, 1971).

When the child's interests are taken into account, fundamental questions arise about how to determine those interests and to evaluate parental abilities to meet them. In the past, evaluations of the child's interests have frequently been made from an adult point of view rather than taking into account the actual experience of the child. Children's placements with their mothers have been made solely upon evaluations of maternal fitness based upon psychological studies of a mother's personality, soundness of mind and moral attributes, and inferred mothering capacities. As a further example, court decisions have removed children from their mothers who were regarded as emotionally disturbed, when in fact their abilities to function as mothers were impaired, and the children's interests were not served.

A more effective way of determining the psychological interests of each child is through defining a child's needs and then making specific judgments as to whether or not a parent can meet those needs (Westman, 1975, 1978). The abstract question of maternal fitness is replaced by ascertaining concretely whether or not the mother can meet the psychological needs of a child. From this perspective, a mother who has been successfully treated for mental illness through medication, and in that abstract respect judged to be fit as a mother, might not be able to meet her child's psychological needs because of her unresponsiveness to her child while under the influence of the medication. Her symptoms might be in abeyance, but her ability to fill her child's needs impaired.

Criteria for arriving at custody decisions should take into account the demonstrated child rearing capacities of each party, the nature of the parent–child relationships, the priority the child has in each party's life, the capacities of each party to provide guidance and examples for the child, the capacity of each parent to provide developmental and educational resources, and the capacity of each parent to maximize stability and continuity during the dependent years. Optimally, all of these factors should be evaluated in the context of a life plan for the child developed by each of the competing parties. Examples of criteria are as follows (Adapted from Michigan Compiled Laws, 1978):

> The emotional attachment existing between the child and the competing parties and the prior responsibility for the child demonstrated by each competing party.
> The capacity and commitment of each competing party to provide the child the affection, guidance, sibling relationships, if any, education and community life appropriate to ensure the continuity of the child's development.
> The capacity and commitment of each competing party to provide the

child with food, clothing, shelter, medical care or other remedial care, and other material needs.

The capacity and commitment of each competing party to further the child's moral development through example and education.

The mental and physical health of the competing parties, the minor children and other persons living in a proposed custodial household.

The child's prior home, school and community adjustment.

The availability of child care facilities to each proposed custodial home.

The stability and continuity of the family unit in the present and proposed home.

The reasonable preference of the child, if the court deems the child to be of sufficient age and the expression of preference is not detrimental to the parent–child relationships.

The fact that ensuring continuity of a life plan for a child once a custody award has been made requires judicial monitoring and supervision is illustrated by the continued rancor between many parents after the divorce settlement. Approximately one-third of divorced families are involved in financial, visitation, and custody disputes (Westman, 1970).

More dramatically, the cases of "child snatching" bring out the state-by-state nature of custody decisions and the lengths to which some parents will go to achieve their ends. Some parents who live in other states and cannot win legal custody in a court of law resort to "kidnapping" their own children. The problem is that most state courts do not recognize custody decrees from other states, despite the "full faith and credit" clause in the Constitution. Where both parents want a child, depending on which side of what state line one stands on in the eyes of the law, each can gain legal support of their case.

> For example, two children were awarded to their father in the state of Alabama through declaration of the mother as unfit, but the mother with whom they lived won custody in Massachusetts. The father tried to have his case heard in federal court unsuccessfully. Their mother moved them out of their home and moved in with friends, but their father "kidnapped" them after school and took them to Alabama, and in turn, she took them back to Massachusetts. The father tried twice more to "snatch them" from Massachusetts, but was stopped by the local police, who were not bound by his Alabama custody order. Both parents appeared to realize that the children were afraid of being abandoned from both sides. The mother said that they tried to look happy because they feared abandonment: "The last time I got them back, one had a bleeding ulcer and the other forgot how to talk, but there were smiles on their faces."

As this case demonstrates, what happens after the custody award is sadly neglected by our present approach to custody matters, which operates virtually without mechanisms for follow-up and monitoring decisions.

GUARDIANSHIP FOR NEGLECTED CHILDREN

To highlight further the problems that children face, in the United States 400,000 children are now in foster care, largely arranged through juvenile courts, because their mothers and fathers either do not want them or cannot care for them. For a few it is, as labeled, a temporary and appropriate stopgap during parental illness or family distress. For most, it is a state of limbo continued to the age of maturity.

Agencies and courts maintain the fiction of temporariness in deference to the rights of parents who, though they may visit infrequently or not at all, continue the pretense of parental concern and refuse to permit adoption because of the potential injury to their self-image represented by open admission of their disinterest in, or incapacity for, parenthood. As Eisenberg points out, the view of foster care as temporary inhibits the foster family from fully investing its affections in a child who may be summarily removed from their home by agency workers. As a result, a child is deprived of the security of being wanted and needed by the foster family. The problem exists primarily because of a preoccupation with the legal rights of biological parents to the detriment of their offspring, a heritage of the time when children were regarded as chattel. Even worse, the foster home system is perpetuated by agencies through the temporary concept, and foster parents are either prohibited from or discouraged from adoption because the agency might lose viable and easily accessible foster homes.

Further, many foster families would prefer to adopt a child, but are unable to do so since initiation of the action may lead the supervising agency to remove the child because their attachment to the child is "too close." It is difficult to imagine a greater distortion of professional judgment when the need of the child is for the reality, not the façade, of a devoted family. Others wishing to adopt a foster child might receive a sympathetic hearing but lack the resources to accept full financial responsibility for the child. The significant reimbursement for foster care has added a financial inducement which is lost through the more permanent and satisfactory life for the child of adoption. Here the remedy lies in subsidized adoption, no revolutionary innovation since tax law already recognizes the legitimacy of income transfer when dependency is involved. In a time when growing numbers of young people decide not to give birth yet desire the pleasure of parenthood, liberalized adoption practices offer bilateral benefits to individuals and to society.

There are unusual situations under which permanent foster placement could optimally meet the needs of some older children who have unbroken emotional ties to the biological parents (Derdeyn, 1977). If the foster parents are willing and able to make a long-term commitment to a child, permanent foster placement can provide both current stability and the continuity of the child's relationships with the biological parents. Permanent foster placement requires that custody by placed with foster parents rather than with agencies, for agencies sometimes pose the same threat to the stability and continuity of foster parent–child relationships as do biological parents. Permanent foster care, like adoption, has no clear legal tradition in common law and requires enabling legislation.

An additional point should be made about foster care. If foster placement leads too readily to termination of parental rights and adoption, the foster care system might be threatened since parents would be reluctant to have their child placed in foster homes because of the fear that they might lose that child. This might mean that when temporary parental incapacity intervenes, parents would be reluctant to relinquish their children during that time. A counterargument can be made in those situations that homemaker services might preserve the home and eliminate the need for foster placement. The fact is that foster placements are made frequently without significant efforts to help the child's home. Unfortunately, removing children seems easier than improving their homes.

Because the assumption that parents have the right to raise their children without state interference is a widely held American precept, there is increasing public concern that children are too freely judged neglected and placed in foster care. The decision to disrupt a family is very serious. Overlooked all too frequently is the fact that families can be treated and rehabilitation of the original home can be undertaken. The lack of effective clinical resources is largely the reason why many homes are not adequately reconstituted. In practice, the use of foster home placement with children is usually an indication that adequate treatment resources are not available to the family.

A more detailed discussion of foster care can be found in Chapter 10.

TERMINATION OF PARENTAL RIGHTS

The resistance to initiating action to terminate parental rights as a step toward adoption is powerful. Because parents can and do change, agencies are frightened by the prospect of terminating parental ties with the later possibility of regret. Because presumably it is an irreversible decision, parental rights should be terminated only when there is solid evidence and clear indication that a better life can be found for the child. The weight of the decision is such that a combination of social agency, clinical, and legal expertise is needed to ensure that a sound decision is made. Conversely, this places on clinicians the responsibility to avoid inaction in cases in which they can make useful recommendations regarding termination of parental rights.

A typical situation illustrating the varying points of view in termination cases is portrayed in the matter of N.M.S., heard before the Family Division of the Superior Court of the District of Columbia (N.M.S., 1974).

This case pitted the rights of the biological parent against those of the foster parents who had reared a nine and a half year old child, M, who lived all but the first eight days of her life with them. When the biological mother sought return of her daughter, the agency to whom M was committed for foster placement recommended that M be returned to her. The foster parents opposed the recommendation and urged the court to award custody to them. The child personally and through court appointed counsel strongly rejected the idea of living with her biological mother and wished to continue living in the only home she had known.

The court considered various alternative dispositions. One was to permit M's adoption by the foster parents. Another alternative was to continue commitment of M to the agency, but in that instance the court was advised during the trial that it would have no authority to direct the agency to continue placement of M with the foster parents. The court seriously considered placing M with the biological mother for a period of six months and monitoring the case closely to observe its effects on M. The court decided against that alternative because it was unfair and potentially damaging to experiment with a child in order to satisfy the mother's desire to have M with her. In its opinion, the court recognized that in her own way the biological mother would try to do what was best for M, but it was a question of too little too late. Time had worked against the reunion because the foster parents became the child's psychological parents, and the child needed continuity of that relationship. The court considered the biological mother's legal position and her desire for her child and ruled that the child should remain in contact with her mother. With the help of counseling and the security of knowing she would not be removed from her foster home, the child could develop a mature relationship with her mother.

The court concluded: "M is to remain with the foster parents, and legal custody with the agency is terminated and placed with the foster parents. The foster parents are to participate in counseling if determined necessary or useful by the forensic psychiatry office. The natural mother may visit the child every six weeks, but only in the foster home. These visits are to be arranged in advance, and the mother is also directed to receive counseling. The forensic psychiatry office is to submit to the court periodic reports on the nature of the adjustment of the child to her foster parents and to her mother."

Adoption is a relatively recent historical development in the law which continues to be influenced by the concept that children are the property of their biological parents. Voluntary termination of parental rights can be made quite readily and is a significant way of resolving the birth of children to young parents who are unable to assume parenting functions. Over the years a series of statutes have emerged for terminating parental rights on an involuntary basis. Originally, the exclusive ground for termination of parental rights was abandonment, defined as evidence of an intent to sever permanently the parent–child relationship by the parent.

More recently, additional grounds for termination of parental rights have been enacted. Today parental rights may be terminated not only for abandonment, but also for evidence of the parents' failure or refusal to perform parental duties to a child for a requisite period, usually six months to one year. Further grounds exist when there is evidence of the parent's continued incapacity, abuse, or neglect which causes a child to be without the necessary parental care, control, and support necessary for the child's mental and physical well-being, and there is evidence that such a situation cannot be remedied. In most states, laws governing termination of parental rights are incorporated either in the child abuse reporting legislation or in adoption legislation. In all states, proof is required to effect the termination of parental rights. Unlike custody cases, in which decisions are open to review, the termination of parental rights means an irrevocable end to parental rights and responsibilities for a child.

Adoption in the United States is a legislative creation, with each state having its own adoption statute. While many parts of the law relating to adoption are valid reflections of society's attitudes and will remain entrenched in the law, some aspects of adoption practices should be changed. One of the problems in a court's decision to terminate parental rights is the need to determine not only parental abandonment or unfitness, but also the intent to commit fault. The courts are concerned with the intent of the parents, and sometimes will not find an intent to abandon in spite of demonstrated lack of care and concern on the part of the biological parents. Unfortunately, in spite of well developed relationships with the child by prospective adoptive parents, the expressed intent of the biological parent is often given greater weight. Courts have difficulty in distinguishing what is said by parents from what they have done. It would be helpful to minimize passing judgment upon parents or determining their intent through placing the emphasis on the interests of the child. If the child's welfare were the most important concern of the court, the need to assign fault and to arrive at findings derogatory to the parents would be minimized and resistance to termination of parental rights diminished.

Some states have enacted provisions granting courts the discretion to waive the need for parental consent if it is being withheld contrary to the best interests of the child. Such a provision could obviate the need for showing unfitness or abandonment when voluntary parental consent is not forthcoming (Derdeyn, 1977b).

In those instances in which careful study determines that termination of parental rights is in the interests of a child, it is also often in the interests of the parents. When parental rights are involuntarily terminated, the parent is not forced to abandon the sense of pride that made it impossible for the parent to relinquish voluntarily responsibility for the child. It is most difficult for a parent to admit inability to raise a child. Although it is possible in some circumstances to work therapeutically with the parent for whom termination of parental rights is to occur, more often it cannot be handled therapeutically until the court has actually made the termination. It is difficult for a parent to give up a child. It is easier to say that the judge "took my child away from me."

In spite of the reasonable statutory grounds that provide for the termination of parental rights, and in spite of the public attitude that deplores neglect of children, the judiciary is frequently paralyzed and unable to act in situations in which termination of parental rights is clearly indicated. One explanation for this difficulty in child neglect cases, for example, is that parents are consciously unimpressed by their neglect of a child because of the unconscious defense of denial. It is extremely difficult to work with the defense of denial, as experience with alcoholics and drug addicts bear out. Although it is possible for a judge to confront a criminal with the fact that he will face life in prison, or even execution, it is most difficult for a judge to confront parents with the fact that they are incapable of being adequate parents when they insist that they are adequate.

Another factor is a general social reluctance to attack the self-esteem of another person. It is most painful to confront people with their weaknesses. It is one thing to tell persons that they have committed a crime and are to be punished for it, but it is another thing to tell persons that they have failed in an area that is noncriminal and that is vital to their self-esteem, specifically being a parent. This is especially difficult in court, where a neglecting mother may sway the judge as she tearfully pours out her desire to have her children and the pain that will result if her child is taken away from her. At this point the judge desperately needs professional evaluation of the mother's true relationship with her child.

Derdeyn calls attention to the reluctance of courts to terminate parental rights, even in obvious situations of neglect and abuse (1977a). The typical situation is when a court finds that termination of parental rights is not warranted, but that the child requires continued foster care. All too frequently the child remains in limbo, subject to subsequent shifts in environment. To avoid this ambiguity, the decision to remove a child for all but brief and carefully supervised separations should be the point at which the weight of parental rights should be exerted, in order to allow the parents to keep the child if the state cannot establish that they cannot care for their child adequately.

The decision to remove children from their homes has important implications for the rehabilitation of the parents, for the agencies attempting to help them, and above all for children who are affected by separation from old, and required to form new, attachment bonds. Vigorous efforts to rehabilitate parents are clearly warranted up to the time of the child's removal. Once past the child's removal, except in cases where the separation is time-limited and carefully carried out, parental rights and the child's needs may diverge widely. Then the burden should shift to the parents to establish that their rights should not be terminated and that they are capable of caring for the child.

Wald favors developing guidelines to aid judges in arriving at dispositions that reflect the best available knowledge of child development (1976). Procedurally reasonable efforts should be required to improve the home while the children are still there. When children are removed from their homes, there should be a means of assuring continuous stability for them through monitoring at least at six-month intervals. There should be a fixed period after removal from their homes when the condition of the children's home of origin is reviewed. For children under the age of three, this could be six months, for children over the age of three, it could be 12 months. In either case, after that period of time, if the home is not suitable for the child's return, there should be a speedy termination of parental rights. This approach properly recognizes the gravity of removing children from their parents, an action that frequently is taken precipitously, at moments of crisis, without regard for the needs of the child or the rights of the parents.

The Neglected Children Committee of the National Council of Juvenile Court Judges has proposed the following model statute for termination of parental rights (Lincoln, 1976):

> The purpose of this act is to provide a judicial process for the termination of all parental rights and responsibilities in situations set forth in this act; to delineate mandatory, but not exclusive, criteria for judicial consideration; to acknowledge that the time perception of children differs from that of adults; to provide stability in the lives of children who must be removed from their homes and to make the ongoing needs of a child for proper physical, mental and emotional growth and development the decisive considerations in permanent custody proceedings. Proceedings shall be civil in nature and governed by rules of civil procedure.
>
> 1. The Court may terminate parental rights when the Court finds the parent unfit or that the conduct or condition of the parent is such as to render him or her unable to properly care for the child and that such conduct or condition is unlikely to change in the foreseeable future. In determining unfitness, conduct or condition the Court shall consider, but is not limited to, the following:
>   a. Emotional illness, mental illness or mental deficiency of the parent of such duration or nature as to render the parent unlikely to care for the ongoing physical, mental and emotional needs of the child.
>   b. Conduct toward a child of a physically, emotionally or sexually cruel or abusive nature.
>   c. Excessive use of intoxicating liquors or narcotic or dangerous drugs.
>   d. Physical, mental or emotional neglect of the child.

e. Conviction of a felony and imprisonment.

f. Unexplained injury or death of a sibling.

g. Reasonable efforts by appropriate public or private child care agencies have been unable to rehabilitate the family.

2. Where a child is not in the physical custody of a parent, the Court, in proceedings concerning the termination of parental rights, in addition to the foregoing, shall also consider, but is not limited to, the following:

a. Failure to provide care, or pay a reasonable portion of substitute physical care and maintenance where custody is lodged with others.

b. Failure to maintain regular visitation or other contact with the child as designed in a plan to reunite the child with the parents.

c. Failure to maintain reasonably consistent contact and communication with the child.

d. Lack of effort on the part of the parent to adjust circumstances, conduct or conditions to meet the needs of the child.

3. Where a child has been placed in foster care by a Court order or has been otherwise placed by parents or others into the physical custody of such family, the Court shall in proceedings concerning the termination of parental rights and responsibilities consider whether said child has become integrated into the foster family to the extent that his or her familial identity is with that family, and said family or person is able and willing to permanently so integrate the child. In such considerations, the Court shall note, but is not limited to, the following:

a. The love, affection and other emotional ties existing between the child and the parents, and his or her ties with the integrating family.

b. The capacity and disposition of the parents from whom he or she was removed as compared with that of the integrating family to give the child love, affection and guidance and to continue the education of the child.

c. The capacity and disposition of the parents from whom the child was removed and the integrating family to provide the child with food, clothing, medical care and other physical, mental and emotional needs.

d. The length of time the child has lived in a stable, satisfactory environment and the desirability of maintaining such continuity.

e. The permanence as a family unit of the integrating family or person.

f. The moral fitness, physical and mental health of the parents from whom the child was removed and that of the integrating family or person.

g. The home, school and community record of the child, both when with the parents from whom he or she was removed and when with the integrating family.

h. The reasonable preference of the child if the Court deems the child of sufficient capacity to express a preference.

i. Any other factor considered by the Court to be relevant to a particular placement of the child.

4. The rights of the parents may be terminated as provided herein if the Court finds that the parents have abandoned the child or the child was left under such circumstances that the identity of the parents is unknown and

cannot be ascertained, despite diligent searching, and the parents have not come forward to claim the child within three months following the finding of the child.

5. In considering any of the above bases for terminating the rights of a parent, the Court shall give primary consideration to the physical, mental or emotional condition and needs of the child.

Many aspects of this model already exist in the statutes of most states. The problem lies in their application. The fact that courts are burdened with situations that go on for years and that lead to immense cost to society because of reluctance to act in terminating parental rights points to a defect in the system (Steketee, 1977). There is a structural need for a child advocate to bridge the health, welfare, and legal systems at this point. No one discipline is in a position to evaluate the needs of a child. Because the legal system has its own rules and techniques, a *guardian ad litem* or a legal counsel for the child facilitates action within the legal arena (Hansen, 1964). The gravity of terminating parental rights dictates a comprehensive clinical assessment and unity of clinical opinion with respect to the child's interests. It is the lack of sufficient data about and representation of the child's needs and lack of available alternative placements that accounts for judicial reluctance to terminate parental rights.

Ultimately, the law is a reflection of social policies, whether they be expressed through legislation or social values. In the realm of family law, it is well to recognize that society's charge to the legal system is ambivalent. On the one hand, the autonomy and privacy of the family is paramount. On the other hand, a sizable segment of society would call the police and use the courts as an extension of their personal power. Others abdicate family responsibilities to the state, either by desire or by default. The social backing for legal interventions in families is complicated and capricious. Realistically, the practice and adjudication of family law is for the courageous.

Legal and Mental Health Teamwork

Lawyers and judges are confronted routinely with responsibility for making decisions in the lives of children without possessing the necessary knowledge and tools. The heavy, ill-managed family and juvenile court caseloads are mute testimony to the inability of the legal system in itself to protect and promote family living and the development of children. Courts can enforce laws and manage family disputes over property and money; however, they are not designed to effect a meeting of the minds of parents and children and are clearly not prepared to help parents discharge their responsibilities to their children.

The nature of the legal system leads it to assume responsibility for family decision making when parents, if capable, could do so themselves with long-range benefit. This is seen particularly with adults who avoid personal responsibility by using courts as surrogate parents to make decisions for them while simultaneously they sabotage and rebel against the very judges to whom they have shifted responsibility. Thus, the court becomes an arena for acting out the drama of family pathology. Judges and lawyers are acutely aware of their limitations in managing family relationships, and daily they bear the frustrations of attempting to deal with social and emotional crises associated with disintegrating families. As a result, they increasingly turn to mental health professionals for assistance.

A growing role for the mental health system is to aid courts and families to arrive at rational decision making for their children. The mental health system offers unique advantages in minimizing the adverse effects of family conflicts on children because it is prepared to support people who are temporarily overwhelmed by turbulent circumstances. Especially in custody disputes, parents lack the objectivity required to make constructive decisions, because they are at the mercy of the prejudices and discontents that led to their divorce in the first place. It may be helpful, therefore, for parents to turn to mental health professionals for aid in understanding and promoting the psychological interests of their children.

In particular, the approach of child psychiatry offers an integrated interdisciplinary assessment based upon knowledge of a child, siblings, parents, school, and community. The evaluation process is based upon as much contact with children and significant people in their families, schools, and communities as is necessary to gather comprehensive information. Although, optimally, child psychiatrists should be brought into cases through the court on behalf of a child, the advantage of their approach is their commitment to helping people to help themselves, rather than to exercise authority over them. The confidentiality of the psychiatric relationship is also of value. Furthermore, even though child psychiatrists may temporarily assume responsibility for making recommendations to courts, their basic commitment as physicians is to aid the parents and the affected children. Ultimately, the legal system resolves custody conflicts between parents through the adversarial procedure in the courtroom. In contrast, the mental health system aids parents to arrive at agreement out of court and opens channels of communication to permit them to handle subsequent matters that affect their children. In many instances, courts have been forced to assume responsibility for family decision making when it would be preferable for the parents to be encouraged to use the aid of the mental health system in managing their own families.

With legal and mental health collaboration, courtroom proceedings can take place in a matrix of supportive and therapeutic forces, so that the overall result is to help families function more effectively, rather than reinforcing adversarial splintering of family relationships. Furthermore, mental health professionals can provide courts with essential data on the developmental needs of children, parent–child bonds, family dynamics, and the children's perceptions and attitudes.

Several specific examples of interdisciplinary work in a legal–mental health system network can be cited. Kalogerakis describes the role of a clinician–advocate as a member of a court staff (1975). He recognizes that adversarial procedures are the foundation of the legal system; however, he points out their conflicts with knowledge of child development. As an illustration, a juvenile who does not desire psychiatric hospitalization has a right to a lawyer who supposedly will vigorously prevent that result if possible. A lawyer who fails to do that might be regarded as behaving unethically. The lawyer's ethical position, to further the wishes of the client, may interfere with the long-range interests of the client. The lawyer, therefore, may not be in a position to advocate a child's interests. The evaluation of an adolescent's needs, based upon the stage of development, cognitive functioning, personality organization, and presence or absence of psychopathology, and the implications of these factors for the court, is the province of mental health. If these issues are critical to establishing what is in the interests of a child at any given point, one cannot reasonably expect a lawyer alone to serve as an advocate for a child, particularly if ethics dictate furthering client wishes rather than needs.

A clinician–advocate would be equipped to assess the true meaning of a child's assertions, evaluate conflicting wishes, deal with ambivalence toward parents, and weigh the implications for personality development. A child psychiatrist, psychologist, or social worker, trained to understand fully the workings of the courts, could fill such a role. Unless an attorney as well, the clinician–advocate would be unable to argue the case, so the continued presence of an attorney is essential. However, the latter's function would then be to assure due process, with the task of arguing for the child's interests falling upon the clinician–advocate. Kalogerakis believes that, short of such a solution, true advocacy for children in courts will continue to be elusive. This proposal is in line with the historical use of forensic psychiatrists within the legal system, and runs counter to the current trend of decreasing the extralegal functions of courts.

Wallerstein and Kelly describe another approach in the form of a model clinical service outside of the legal system for divorcing families (Wallerstein, 1977). The service was used by attorneys and courts as divorce counseling for families with children. A three-month period with an average of 14 hours of counseling time was found to be useful between one and six months following parental separation. They found that the steps of separation and legal filing were necessary to separate marriage from divorce counseling. Also, if delayed beyond six months of separation, the counseling was too late to affect the decision-making process, was resisted by consolidation of parental antipathy, and was complicated by unnecessarily extending the confusion and suffering of both parents and children. Divorce counseling is an example of a clinical means of meeting the needs of a population segment likely to be temporarily disabled in parenting capacity because of the formidable tasks and stresses that accompany divorce.

In Chapter 11, a practical means of introducing interdisciplinary teamwork into the legal system is described for child abuse cases.

In another vein Rodham has proposed, as did Kubie long ago, that community boards of persons representing children from the milieu in which a family lives be established to evaluate a child's needs (Rodham, 1973). The board membership would include parent and professional representatives and would be responsible for periodically reviewing child placements and making recommendations about terminating parental rights and visitation matters. This proposal assumes that courts do not have sufficient wisdom and that expert witnesses cannot bring such wisdom to the court. It places responsibility for evaluating children and monitoring their progress upon community elements. Although probably impractical, the concept has merit because it invokes the responsibility and perspective of the community in supporting family life and highlights the need for follow-up.

At the national level, the Mental Health Law Project is an example of interdisciplinary cooperation in protecting the legal rights of the mentally handicapped and improving conditions for their care, treatment, education, and community living. Sponsored by a variety of mental health, legal, and social organizations, the Project provides a vehicle for bridging disciplinary concerns in the mental health field.

The increasing availability of child psychiatrists, trained family counselors, and community mental health services for children offers the potential for increased collaboration between the legal and mental health systems. The technical skills involved in assessing a child's developmental needs fall within the purview of mental health professionals trained to evaluate children and systems impinging upon them. Because many children suffer from shifting, temporary resolutions of crises in their lives, it is necessary that adequate information and practical guidelines be established to develop a long-range life plan based upon the psychological interests of each child. The fact must be faced that the legal system alone is not prepared to do this and to fulfill a complete advocacy role for children.

The Role of the Legal System in the Lives of Children

The legal system is obviously limited in its ability to resolve problems in human relations. Not only is the adversarial process ill equipped to resolve conflict between parents and unable to deal with the child as an inseparable part of at least a two-person unit, but judges and attorneys are not trained or prepared for helping families to cope with problems in living.

A source of confusion in family law has been the customary orientation of the attorney to become the "expert" in preparing a specific case. This is based upon the principle that the most effective application of legal skill is for the lawyer to be the "sole expert" for a client, drawing upon the knowledge of other experts but having the unique expertise of applying that knowledge to the resolution of a specific courtroom issue. This model breaks down in family law where the issues relate to ongoing parent–child relationships, continuity of development for the affected child, follow-up and monitoring of decisions, and support of parents and children. The lawyer can be the "sole expert" in fact finding, the common aim of criminal and civil law practice. The lawyer cannot be the sole expert, however, in family law where helping people cope with problems in living, or treatment, is the predominant need. The "counselor" aspect of the practice of law includes elements of human wisdom; however, the attorney is not trained for, or ordinarily interested in, therapeutic human relations counseling.

Another problem is that courts cannot always be trusted to be benign and helpful. Too frequently, people must be protected from harm by the legal system itself. Many of the recent changes in juvenile courts, for example, have been to protect juveniles from abuse by the court system. Similar concern has arisen about the practices of general court judges in determining child custody and visitation. Personal preferences and prejudices play more of a role than do objective guidelines in many child-related adjudications made in general courts (Levy, 1976; Mnookin, 1976). Because of its adversarial nature and emphasis upon due process, the legal system also tends to fractionate and disrupt families. Due process procedures should be reserved for those situations in which they are truly indicated, such as when parents are obviously in conflict with the interests of their children. All of these points indicate that the legal system should foster and support, rather than undermine, families.

Beyond these considerations is the fact that in the United States lawyers are playing an increasingly important role in the governance of society. Lawyers have been trained to operate the legal system as well as to improve the substance and method of law. As law has become more effective as a social instrument, it has taken on more and more functions, increasingly attracting able people into the profession. This, in turn, has made law still more effective and useful. It is through such a gradual and lengthy process that lawyers have become pervasive and influential in contemporary American society. By now, even if society wanted to reduce the role of law and lawyers, the task would be difficult to carry out—unless the lawyers themselves take the lead (Li, 1977).

Because of the ability of individuals to bring every matter to court, the judicial system is already overloaded to the point of near paralysis in urban areas. In the long run, in order to cope with this deluge and to devote more time to the interests of children, the judicial system will have to be greatly expanded or the courts will need to change their roles to reviewing the decisions of families, local groups, and administrative agencies (Bazelon, 1976). It is in the area of family problems that many cases now subject to court action could be handled more appropriately and effectively outside of the legal system.

Of greatest significance for the future of the courts, however, is Bazelon's point that the courts can improve their role in the decision-making process and remove themselves from making personal decisions for families by functioning within the community network of human services. He holds that courts should reserve their decision making for monitoring processes at an administrative level. The courts should develop procedures to ensure the accountability of social institutions and parents for the implementation of life plans for children devised in conjunction with welfare and mental health supporting services. The questions that courts can raise and appropriately adjudicate in human relations situations are: (1) was there a full and fair opportunity for exploration of facts and opposing views? (2) was there adherence to the requirements of the law? and (3) was information rationally applied to reach the ultimate conclusion? This means that courts should review administrative decisions rather than make those decisions themselves. This would mean that courts would shift from the individual to small groups and broader social systems in their emphasis.

We are, however, a long way from achieving more appropriate roles for the courts. Unfortunately, the legal process is so slow that at times the children named as plaintiffs grow up without needed services before their cases are completed. Speeding up of the legal process is essential in matters affecting children. Furthermore, all too often in social cases a judicial decree is handed down, but no change occurs and time is lost until enough evidence of lack of compliance is gathered and the judge is notified. A typical case is the celebrated *Mills* v. *Board of Education* of 1972, in which the District of Columbia has still not developed a plan to provide suitable education for all handicapped children, as ordered by the court.

Stated in another way, the law is highly developed in individual adversarial decision making, but it needs to exercise its influence at broader levels within society itself. The legal system can be a potent instrument for not only changing social systems, but also for making sure systems do what they are supposed to do. On the other hand, even though courts can attack unfairness, they cannot straighten out lives twisted by the ravages of poverty, deprivation, and maltreatment. The courts can play a role in the administration of public and private services for children, and they can provide the legal aspect of comprehensive advocacy for children.

The complexity of the role of law in the lives of children was captured by Bazelon (in *Haziel*): "Many children need, above all, a stable home such as they never enjoyed. They need parents, or, what may be heartbreaking, they need better parents. This the court can never provide. Our failures with children merely reflect the failure of social justice in America. Until we take some steps toward eradication of the malignancy of social injustice, 'child advocacy' may remain a hollow promise, an empty phrase, 'full of sound and fury, yet signifying nothing.'"

Conclusion

The stark fact that almost one-half of the arrests in the United States are of youths under the age of 21 accompanies the fact that most children enter the legal system because of breakdown or disturbance in their families. Unfortunately, the legal system is ill prepared to cope with these family problems.

The legal system came into being as society's method of resolving conflicts between people. Because those conflicts were between contesting adults, the adversary procedure evolved as a practical means of deciding which party was right and which party was wrong. Conflicts could be resolved through the vigorous assertion of two points of view, with one emerging as the victor. To this day the adversary method deeply infuses all legal proceedings.

The adversary method has not proved to be appropriate in family law, however, where the need is for harmonizing the interests of family members and negotiating conflicts between the rights of parents and the rights and developmental needs of children. In family law the predominant need is not to establish guilt but to work out complex interpersonal, economic, and social problems.

When legal issues arise regarding children, special considerations are involved beyond those encountered in dealing with adults. Inevitably, the age of a child plays an important role in how that child is regarded, treated, and involved in legal proceedings, giving rise to the legal concept of age-grading responsibilities for the young. The psychological interests of children have also received special consideration because of the role of the courts in protecting the developmental courses of children. Furthermore, there is a growing recognition of the importance of speedy adjudication of matters involving children because of the special developmental importance of time in their lives.

Shifting from a time in which children were regarded as the property of their parents, there is now a growing recognition of the legal rights of children. These rights are based upon extending certain rights of adults to children and protecting and meeting their developmental needs.

Juvenile courts were established to create a milieu in which children could be managed apart from the procedures of adult criminal courts. They were intended to provide for the rehabilitation, rather than simply the punishment, of juvenile offenders. The impotence of juvenile courts has led to allegations of their failure. More accurately, there is a pressing need for juvenile courts to function as the legal arm of community networks of services for children and to mediate between offenders and the offended.

Family courts have emerged in recognition of the special nature of legal issues in family law. They concentrate upon fixing responsibility for child rearing when the custody of children is contested, when guardianship for neglected children is indicated, and when termination of parental rights is in the interests of children and parents. The major problems in family law result from a lack of decision making and appropriate intervention in the lives of children to ensure that each child has permanent, dependable parents regardless of biological relationships and the wishes of adults unprepared to meet child rearing responsibilities.

Because legal matters involving children and families result from problems in human relations, closer collaboration between the legal and mental health systems is essential. The legal system can provide the authority required to ensure implementation and monitoring of reasonable life plans for children; however, the aid of the mental health system is useful in determining what this life plan should be in the light of the developmental needs of a specific child.

The most appropriate role for courts in the lives of children is to review administratively and monitor the work of professionals skilled in human relations in devising and therapeutically managing reasonable life plans for children. Only the legal system can protect the rights of parents and children. However, the legal system cannot make personal decisions for people or resolve the complex problems of family living and child rearing. Even more fundamentally, a shift in public attitude is required so that the first recourse for families in trouble is to call a counselor rather than a lawyer or the police.

References

ARGO, J. M. (1977) *An Overview of Family Courts*, National Memorandum, Center for State Courts, 1660 Lincoln St., Denver, Colo. 80203, April 22.

BAZELON, D. (1976) "Reflections on Child Advocacy." Chapter in Westman, J. C. (Ed.), *Proceedings of the University of Wisconsin Conference on Child Advocacy*. Madison: University of Wisconsin–Extension, Health Sciences Unit.

BRUN, G. (1973) *Children of Divorce*. Copenhagen, Denmark: Gylendals, Boghandel.

CARTER, H., AND GLICK, P. C. (1976) *Marriage and Divorce: A Social and Economic Study*. Cambridge, Mass.: Harvard University Press.

CHILDREN'S DEFENSE FUND (1976) *Children in Adult Jails*. Washington, D.C.: Washington Research Project, December.

CORBETT, J., AND VEREB, T. S. (1974) *Juvenile Court Statistics, 1974*. Pittsburgh: National Center for Juvenile Justice.

DAVIS, S. (1978) *Rights of Juveniles: The Juvenile Justice System*. New York: Clark Boardman Company.

DELANEY, J. J. (1976) "The Juvenile Court: Where We Were; Where We Are; Where We're Going." Chapter in Westman, J. C. (Ed.), *Proceedings of the University of Wisconsin Conference on Child Advocacy*. Madison: University of Wisconsin–Extension, Health Sciences Unit.

DERDEYN, A. P. (1976) "Child Custody Contests in Historical Perspective." *American Journal of Psychiatry*, 133:1369–1376, December.

DERDEYN, A. P. (1977a) "Child Abuse and Neglect: The Rights of Parents and the Needs of Their Children." *American Journal of Orthopsychiatry*, 47:377–387, July.

DERDEYN, A. P., AND WADLINGTON, W. J. (1977b) "Adoption: The Rights of Parents Versus the Best Interests of Their Children." *Journal of Child Psychiatry*, 16:288–295, Spring.

EISENBERG, L. (1975) "The Ethics of Intervention: Acting Amidst Ambiguity." *Journal of Child Psychology and Psychiatry*, 16:93–104.

FERSTER, E. Z. (1975) "The Juvenile Court." Chapter in Allen, R. C. et al. (Eds.), *Readings in Law and Psychiatry*. Baltimore: Johns Hopkins University Press.

FOSTER, H. H., JR. (1974) *A Bill of Rights for Children*. Springfield, Ill.: Thomas.

Gault, 387 U.S. 1 (May 15, 1967).

Glone v. *American Guarantee and Liability Insurance Company*, 391 U.S. 73 (1968).

GOLDSTEIN, J., FREUD, A., AND SOLNIT, A. J. (1973) *Beyond the Best Interests of the Child.* New York: Free Press.

HAFEN, B. C. (1976a) "Children's Liberation and the New Egalitarianism: Some Reservations About Abandoning Youth to Their Rights." *Brigham Young University Law Review,* 1976 (3): 605–658.

HAFEN, B. C. (1976b) "Status Offenses and the Status of Children's Rights: Do Children Have the Legal Right to Be Incorrigible?" *Brigham Young University Law Review,* 1976 (3):659–691.

HANSEN, R. W. (1964) "Guardians ad Litem in Divorce and Custody Cases: Protection of the Child's Interests." *Journal of Family Law,* 4:181–184.

Haziel v. *U.S.,* 404 F. 2d 1275,1279 (DCCir., 1968).

HEALY, W., AND BRONNER, A. F. (1969) *Delinquents and Criminals: Their Making and Unmaking.* Montclair, N.J.: Patterson Smith.

HINDELANG, M. J., DUNN, C. S., SUTTON, L. P., AND AUMICK, A. L. (1975) *Sourcebook of Criminal Justice Statistics, 1975.* Albany, N.Y.: Criminal Justice Research Center.

HOWARD, JOHN, ASSOCIATION (1977) *Juvenile Court Services: A Statewide Master Plan and Study.* Chicago: John Howard Association, March.

JUVENILE JUSTICE STANDARDS PROJECT (1977) Recommendations. Volumes 1–24, New York: Institute of Judicial Administration.

KALOGERAKIS, M. G. (1975) "Symposium: Children's Rights—Psychiatry and the Law." *Journal of Psychiatry and Law,* 3:475–499, Winter.

KALTER, N. (1977) "Children of Divorce in an Outpatient Psychiatric Population." *American Journal of Orthopsychiatry,* 47:40–51, January.

KATZ, S. N. (1974) *The Youngest Minority.* Chicago: American Bar Association.

KLEINFELD, A. J. (1970) "The Balance of Power Among Infants, Their Parents and the State." *Family Law Quarterly,* 4:410–443.

LANDSMAN, K. J., AND MINOW, M. L. (1978) "Lawyering for the Child: Principles of Representation in Custody and Visitation Disputes Arising from Divorce." *Yale Law Journal,* 87: 1126–1190.

LEMERT, E. M. (1976) *Instead of Court—Diversion of Juvenile Justice.* Washington, D.C.: U.S. Government Printing Office, DHEW Publication No. (ADM) 76–59.

Levy v. *Louisiana,* 391 U.S. 68 (1968).

LEVY, R. J. (1976) "The Rights of Parents." *Brigham Young University Law Review,* Vol. 1976:693–708.

LEWIS, D. O., AND BALLA, D. A. (1976) *Delinquency and Psychopathology.* New York: Grune and Stratton.

LI, V. H. (1977) *Law Without Lawyers.* Stanford, Calif.: Portable Stanford.

LINCOLN, J. H. (1976) "Model Statute for Termination of Parental Rights." *Juvenile Justice,* 27:3–8, November.

McKeiver v. *Pennsylvania; In Re Burrus,* 403 U.S. 528, 29 L. Ed. 2d 647,915.Ct.1976.

MENTAL HEALTH LAW PROJECT, 1220 Nineteenth St. N.W., Washington, D.C. 20036.

MICHIGAN COMPILED LAWS (1978) "Child Custody Act of 1970." Volume 37, 722–23.

Mills v. *Board of Education*, 348 F. Supp. 866 (DDC,1972).

MNOOKIN, R. H. (1976) "American Custody Law: A Framework for Analysis." Chapter in Westman, J. C. (Ed.), *Proceedings of the University of Wisconsin Conference on Child Advocacy.* Madison: University of Wisconsin–Extension, Health Sciences Unit.

NATIONAL CONFERENCE OF COMMISSIONERS ON UNIFORM STATE LAWS (1968a) *Uniform Child Custody Jurisdiction Act.* Chicago: National Conference of Commissioners on Uniform State Laws.

NATIONAL CONFERENCE OF COMMISSIONERS ON UNIFORM STATE LAWS (1968b) *Uniform Juvenile Court Act.* Chicago: National Conference of Commissioners on Uniform State Laws.

NATIONAL CONFERENCE OF COMMISSIONERS ON UNIFORM STATE LAWS (1971) *Revised Uniform Adoption Act.* Chicago: National Conference of Commissioners on Uniform State Laws.

N.M.S. (1974) Family Division, Superior Court of the District of Columbia, January 14.

RODHAM, H. (1973) "Children Under the Law." *Harvard Education Review*, 43:487–514, November.

Rothstein v. *Lutheran Social Services*, 31 L. Ed. 2d 786 (1972).

SIMON, J. (1975) Personal Communication, Yale Law School, February.

Snyder, 85 Wash. 2d 182, 532 P. 2d 278 (1975).

SNYDER, P. R. AND MARTIN, L. H. (1978) "Leaving the Family out of Family Court: Criminalizing the Juvenile Justice System." *American Journal of Orthopsychiatry*, 48:390–393.

Stanley v. *Illinois*, 405 U.S. 645 (April 1972).

STEKETEE, J. P. (1977) "Concern for Children in Placement: Planning for Children's Futures." *Juvenile Justice*, 28:3–45, May.

WADLINGTON, W. (1969) *Children*, 16:138–142, July–August.

WALD, M. S. (1976) "State Interventions on Behalf of 'Neglected' Children: Standards for Removal of Children from Their Homes, Monitoring the Status of Children in Foster Care and Termination of Parental Rights." *Stanford Law Review*, 28:627–706, April.

WALLERSTEIN, J. S., AND KELLY, J. B. (1977) "Divorce Counseling: A Community Service for Families in the Midst of Divorce." *American Journal of Orthopsychiatry*, 47:4–22, January.

WEBSTER, W. H. (1978) *Crime in the United States—1977.* Washington, D.C.: Superintendent of Documents, U.S. Government Printing Office.

WESTMAN, J. C. AND CLINE, D. W. (1971) "Divorce is a Family Affair." *Family Law Quarterly*, 5:1–10.

WESTMAN, J. C. (1975) "Guidelines for Determining the Psychological Best Interests of Children." Chapter in Allen, R. C. (Ed.), *Readings in Law and Psychiatry*. Baltimore: Johns Hopkins University Press.

WESTMAN, J. C., CLINE, D. W., SWIFT, W. J., AND KRAMER, D. A. (1970) "Role of Child Psychiatry in Divorce." *Archives of General Psychiatry*, 23:416–420, November.

WESTMAN, J. C., AND LORD, G. R. (1978) "Model for a Child Psychiatric Custody Study." Presented at the 1978 Annual Meeting of the American Academy of Child Psychiatry, San Diego, Calif.

Winship, 397 U.S. 358 (March 1970).

Zepeda v. *Zepeda*, 379 U.S. 945 (1964).

Chapter 10

Children and Social Services

Dennis Smith, a 17-year-old California youth, said:

> If I'd known I was going to have to spend the first sixteen years of my life this way, I'd rather have been dead. I'd have wished my mother could have aborted me.

With the help of attorneys from the local youth law center, Dennis filed suit against Alameda County for $500,000 in damages. Relinquished at birth by his mother, he became a legal dependent of the county, which never arranged for his adoption. Instead, he was shunted between foster homes and institutions, an average of once each year for a total of sixteen moves. Dennis summarized the effect upon him:

> It's like a scar on your brain; every time something bad happens, you wonder if you're going to another home.

Dennis' precedent-setting suit held that Alameda County had a legal, as well as a moral, obligation to find him adoptive parents who could have provided a suitable child rearing environment. Since it did not, the lawsuit alleged the county was negligent and guilty of breach of contract.

Unfortunately, the story of Dennis Smith is not unusual. Four hundred thousand children are in foster care in the United States, and too many stay there through their dependent years. Unusual is the fact that action was taken to call Dennis' plight to public attention in an effort to bring about changes in welfare practices. Dennis' case highlights the dilemma of children for whom the state has assumed a parental role without the capability of ensuring an adequate family life for them. On the contrary, state and federal laws have consigned many children to lives not only without means but also without hope of acquiring the skills needed to become productive members of society (Kraus, 1973).

Many children like Dennis have been harmed by an inadequate national, state, and local child welfare system. In fact, increased expenditures, approaching $2 billion annually, have brought diminishing returns (DHEW, 1976). For example, the federal Aid to Families with Dependent Children Program involving over 7 million children often does not serve its purpose. Desertion and illegitimacy characterize more than 40 percent of the AFDC families. The method of AFDC funding has made it obvious that having more children is the route to increased income, and the absence of a father through parental desertion is a way of ensuring eligibility for aid. The welfare system's damaging consequences for men in households is particularly striking. The welfare payments make the man superfluous by removing his economic function. Welfare competes with a man's low earning ability, and the more generous the welfare program, the worse he makes out in this competition. He then removes himself from family responsibilities and drifts away from home. The questions are raised: How many middle-class families would survive if the mother and children were guaranteed the father's income without the father's presence? And how many middle-class fathers would stay in their less-than-interesting jobs under those circumstances?

A more specific indictment of the welfare system was made in a report of the Group for the Advancement of Psychiatry (1973). They found that the welfare system may damage the self-esteem of clients, create a sense of hopelessness and helplessness, and promote dependency. Even in those instances in which a welfare department functions as well as constraints permit, the system itself may predispose to unhealthy personal and family development.

The working conditions of public welfare personnel further illustrate the ill effects on mental health of the welfare system. Most workers have unwieldy caseloads, so that they cannot give their individual clients more than passing attention. Workers are assigned largely to screening applicants for funding eligibility and to investigating cases to make sure that administrative practices are observed. Welfare workers spend much of their time trying to persuade clients to work, to plan budgets, and to limit family size. In general, the welfare worker's watchdog rather than service role is stressed. As a result, the welfare system tends to approach the welfare client in a punitive, restrictive, and nonsupportive way, which discourages the progress of clients toward personal and family autonomy. Welfare workers, then, are burdened with impossible tasks that create frustrations which seriously undermine their morale and effectiveness.

The Origins of the Welfare System

The reasons for the welfare system's problems today can be understood by an examination of the system's background, for poverty, sickness, and suffering have existed throughout history.

In the Middle Ages refuges for the poor were first established under the aegis of the church in monasteries for the old and sick, the handicapped, and the homeless. Under those circumstances, mendicancy grew throughout Europe, since begging for alms was not only an easy way of living, but also a respected practice of monks and missionaries. An opposite trend emerged later, however, as European states enacted repressive statutes imposing brutal penalties in an effort to wipe out vagrancy.

Following the English Elizabethan Poor Law in 1601, efforts were made to meet the needs of the poor more systematically through alms and workhouses, usually with high-sounding intent but harsh implementation. The persisting problem of limiting welfare, however, so that it did not become a substitute for working led then to vacillation between ideals of welfare and the realities of administering it, as is true today. The pervasive attitude toward the poor, including children, was one of disdain and contempt, establishing a foundation for modern attitudes toward the disadvantaged. Dependency was thought to result from personal fault, idleness, drinking, or vice, and was considered an aberration that could be remedied simply by increased personal commitment to constructive endeavors. Although this may have been true for some of the dependent poor, most became poverty stricken because of economic depressions in the wake of industrialization. Furthermore, the philosophy of individualism and free enterprise assumed that the common good would be served if individuals were responsible for their own economic security with minimal interference from the state.

The Industrial Revolution created new social problems that the older human institutions—the family, neighborhood, church, and community—could no longer meet. In response to humanitarian, Judeo-Christian precepts, a public sense of responsibility stimulated the development of charitable services to assist those who needed help. First in England and then in the United States, problems of poverty were attacked by charity societies. Originating in London over a century ago, the charity societies sought to help the poor efficiently and to avoid waste of funds, competition, and duplication of services among relief agencies. This form of organization was widely imitated in the United States, so that by 1880 charity societies were active in all the major cities in America.

The founders of the charity organization movement represented bourgeois benevolence. They realized that factors other than the characters of indigent clients contributed to their destitution. These factors included low wages when work was available and the total absence of income in times of depression. Such glimpses into the life situations of the poor stimulated a gradual shift in perception concerning the causes of poverty and were instrumental in shaping more benevolent attitudes toward the poor. An awareness emerged of the relationship between social structure and the individual which called for distinguishing between individual and societal causes of poverty.

During the last quarter of the nineteenth century, the workers of the charity societies were influenced by the recognition of widespread economic and spiritual distress among the masses of low-paid manual laborers, the sick, and the unemployed in the large industrial cities. They saw the lack of helpful, constructive relief from public authorities who were apathetic toward the suffering of the destitute. The charity societies accepted Thomas Chalmers' theory that public financial relief for the poor was not effective in itself, and that clients needed rehabilitation so that they could support themselves and their families. They sought to achieve this goal by making personal visits to the poor, and giving advice and admonitions in addition to financial aid. In each case rehabilitation of poor persons was to be carried out after a careful investigation of their respective conditions. This was the beginning of social casework (Hamilton, 1974).

A noteworthy experiment in the United States was the settlement house movement, symbolized by Hull House, established in Chicago by Jane Addams. Her plan was not to form a new charity, but to build a settlement house as a place for immigrant working people in which they might enjoy life in the new country. She hoped to develop moral and intellectual qualities and values of living suitable for a democracy and to make good citizens out of underprivileged slum families. As a mechanism for integrating immigrant groups, the settlement house proved to be a successful model for transcultural integration. More important, from the settlement houses came the call for slum clearance, for juvenile courts, for the consumers' league to help homemakers, and for protection of the health of the family.

Historically, social work was first a movement for social reform and later a helping profession (Friedlander, 1974). Accordingly, social work has been as strongly influenced by prevailing political climates as by professional knowledge, fluctuating between periods of emphasis upon either society or individuals. During the Progressive Era at the turn of the century, social reform was hoped for through social legislation. In the more conservative political climate of the post–World War I era, interventions were for individuals who were assessed and treated by psychoanalytically oriented techniques. During the Depression, when ways had to be found to maintain the millions of people out of work, there was a return to social reform through legislation that gave a measure of security to selected groups. After World War II the focus was again on individual centered counseling. The War on Poverty of the 1960s saw a return to programs for the benefit of groups in communities rather than individuals. In more recent years, the academic discipline of social work has shifted from a casework approach to systems manipulation, in part because welfare agencies do not have the resources to provide individualized attention and in part because aspects of the social system must be changed in order to help individuals. Currently, we are in the midst of a reaction against community developed programs, based upon the lack of tangible results from social action efforts of the previous decade. Lacking in previous conceptions of approaching poverty either through the individual or society has been an emphasis upon supporting the family—the actual unit of living.

As can be seen, the welfare system began because of concern about indigent adults and has not yet specifically accommodated to the needs of children or to the idea that support of the family is essential, both for adults and children. Defeating the purposes of the welfare system is the fact that we are still struggling with the Elizabethan "Poor Law" dilemma. When income derived from welfare is equal to that earned from low-paying work, the number of people on welfare increases, despite the availability of work. Consequently, amid widespread prosperity during the last decade, the welfare rolls continued to increase (Weinberger, 1974).

The Welfare System Today

The welfare system is comprised of a mélange of laws, programs, licensing and regulatory functions, benefits, and services which are intended to assist handicapped and economically disadvantaged citizens at the federal, state, and local levels. The welfare system over a decade serves 7 million women alone (Rein, 1977) with a total annual expenditure on child welfare of $2 billion. Of the funds going into the welfare system from federal, state, and local sources, approximately 50 percent is devoted to programs that include children (DHEW, 1976).

In order to understand the present welfare system, it is helpful to note how it differs from the health and legal systems. The health and legal systems are devoted to solving problems through the methods of science and human wisdom. In contrast, the welfare system is not designed to solve problems but, rather, to carry out legislated policies. The welfare system, accordingly, does not have a built-in test of effectiveness, as through determining the correct diagnosis and treatment in the health system or the determination of facts in a court of law. Instead, opinions about the effectiveness of the welfare system are influenced by the prevailing political climate. This lack of intrinsic testing capacity tends to lead to the perpetuation of welfare programs, once established. Furthermore, welfare programs involve doing things for people, and do not involve action on the part of recipients other than demonstrating eligibility. The welfare client is under the control of the system, in contrast with the patient who uses the health system and the legal client who is represented through the legal system.

In theory, social welfare has a basic advocacy function, namely, that of promoting the interests of the disadvantaged. On the other hand, its activities tend to be based upon the idealistic rhetoric of social conscience, tempered by the prevailing political climate. In practice, society's ambivalence toward welfare is reflected in the magical wish to eliminate poverty through welfare programs and a concomitant reluctance to fund them adequately. This has been expressed through ill-fated simplistic theories such as providing people with money in order to remove them from poverty. Another early theory about child rearing was that providing a hygienic atmosphere, as in an orphanage, was preferable to life in a dirty home. A later theory was that providing children with foster homes was better than leaving them in "bad" homes. For children, these theories have generally been implemented through removal of a child from one place to another, as pointed out by Margaret Mead. All of these policies have been compounded by the low status of the welfare clientele and, consequently, have tended to place welfare agencies, and welfare workers as well, in a low social status.

In recent years the basic mission of the welfare system has been under thoughtful scrutiny (Wilensky, 1975). From one point of view, the welfare system should be oriented toward "abnormal" emergency functions, to be used when normal mechanisms of the economy break down. Another viewpoint is that social welfare is a necessary, "normal," preventive function of a complex interdependent society through which individuals are helped to realize their potentials through optimal use of available resources. The "abnormal" point of view is one that dominated the field prior to the Depression of the 1930s; it represents the current prevailing public view. The "normal" model became increasingly visible in the wake of the New Deal; it represents the current view of welfare professionals. The argument has been advanced that, just as the health system is a permanent and necessary part of the social system, the welfare system is also a needed and permanent institution, both for the prevention and treatment of social ills. This logic holds that institutions beginning with a treatment orientation must ultimately include prevention as a function. Whether or not one prefers the abnormal or normal view, it is evident that the welfare system is a significant part of our society. Even if poverty were to vanish, it is unlikely that the welfare system would cease to exist. It is this point that highlights the distinction between the narrower field of welfare administration and the broader field of social services.

The greatest problem in the welfare system today is the lack of professionalism in social work that would at least ensure the competence of workers within the constraints of the system. This is nowhere more apparent than in the field of child welfare, in which there has been a patent deterioration in the quality of services. For children and families, social welfare programs have never been adequate, and they are currently deteriorating through widespread merging of caseloads and generalized assignments for all social service workers. This has diffused the time of experienced and trained child welfare staffs, which have not been replaced by others with equivalent background or training. Moreover, educational and experiential criteria for child welfare personnel have been reduced or eliminated. Minimally trained personnel enter the system and are rarely provided appropriate in-service training or staff development. Program specialists, consultation, and skilled and appropriate supervision have been reduced. As a result, even available resources and proved techniques of helping children and their families are poorly utilized (DHEW, 1976).

Most welfare workers have not had graduate social work training and lack background for their work. More ominous, however, is the fact that the current education of social work students is impeded by the lack of fieldwork agencies with qualified supervisors and exemplary facilities. Generally, agencies lack experienced caseworkers and have a high staff turnover. A two-year tenure in one position is now regarded as a long time. Furthermore, it is most difficult to evaluate the successes and failures of social work practices. Consequently, social workers are inclined either to look upon each client as a unique phenomenon or to make unwarranted generalizations because they lack professional experience.

The development of more professional welfare policies and programs can be fostered by an understanding of attitudes toward the poor and by recognizing that communities are adversely affected by welfare programs that are not soundly administered. Thus, the rapid increase of individuals applying for welfare benefits in the 1960s occurred because the level of eligibility was raised. Migration to metropolitan areas has been stimulated by welfare benefits that frequently exceed income for low-paying jobs in rural areas. Moreover, organized campaigns to make living on welfare more attractive have encouraged applications for assistance benefits (Kristol, 1974).

On the positive side, in order to remedy these deficiencies, the field of social work reflects the following trends in casework practice: (1) increased emphasis on social diagnosis and treatment in relation to the facilities of agencies; (2) increased skill and understanding of clients' tensions, fears, and frustrations in their social and economic environments; (3) increased awareness of the need for reduced caseloads; (4) understanding of the importance of preventive individual and family counseling; (5) awareness of the importance of interdisciplinary teamwork; (6) working with the family, groups, and the community in addition to the individual client; and (7) assuming advocacy roles with clients (Ad Hoc Committee on Advocacy, 1969).

Glazer points out that, although Great Britain and Sweden place more emphasis upon social welfare systems than the United States, there is also considerably less question of the primacy of the family in child rearing (1974). Family independence in those countries is the acknowledged goal of social welfare, whereas this concept has not been promulgated in the United States. Because of the absence of such a unifying concept, America faces a dilemma that goes beyond the experience of any other technological society. For the resolution of this dilemma, Glazer urges return to such traditional value patterns as family solidarity and the positive influence of work in promoting personal satisfaction and meaning in life. This is reminiscent of Freud's basic ingredients of mental health, the ability to love and the ability to work. The challenge for government programs since Elizabethan England has been to tap the human need to love and to work.

Another problem in America is that the thrust of social welfare interventions has been to assimilate ethnically diverse minorities in a culture that can best be described as white, Anglo-Saxon, Protestant, and middle class. Although acceptance of the differences between ethnic groups that vary in skin color, physical characteristics, language, and religious practices has been the manifest intent of social work, in practice there has been a lack of appreciation of distinctive cultural groups. The fact that many social workers are estranged from their own ethnic and religious roots furthers this notion. The emergence of ethnic awareness, as among black people, has set up a massive chain reaction in the self-perception of minority groups, such as Puerto Ricans, Mexican-Americans, Asians, and American Indians. As a result, intergroup relations are now more abrasive than in the past, as different minorities engage in the sometimes painful process of finding their identities. In so doing, vehement assertion of distinctiveness as well as similarities between ethnic groups ensues. The current focus on ethnicity, however, should not overshadow the significant interrelationships between social class and race. Both variables are essential for an understanding of clients.

An important development in the field of social welfare as a response to ethnic and social class awareness and the critical shortage of manpower has been the emergence of large numbers of community workers (GAP, 1975a). Originally conceived as a solution to the manpower problem, later supported as a method of employing the poor, and at times seen as instruments for social and institutional change, community workers have begun to demonstrate their value by reaching people previously inaccessible to welfare personnel. The community worker occupies a strategic position for child advocacy at the intersection of all the systems in which community life is enmeshed: health, mental health, education, welfare, housing, employment, and law enforcement.

The community worker tends to view the basic cause of the client's difficulty as deriving less from inner stress and more from external disadvantage rooted in the inequities of the social and economic order. A recognition of this view of etiology is essential in understanding the approach of the community worker. As seen through the eyes of the community worker, the major problems are: (1) the need for milieu reliability, including dependability of relationships and cultural sustenance; (2) the need for role definition and permeability through reality orientation and problem-solving assistance; (3) the need for personal fulfillment through freedom of expression and choice and role evolution; and (4) the need for performance rewards through opportunities for achievement and group support.

Problems have been encountered between community workers and professionals in supporting systems. These difficulties have resulted when community workers feel misunderstood and unappreciated and the backup professionals feel they are not being utilized. It is important in collaboration between the community worker and professionals to recognize several critical factors. First, the community workers' functions must be clearly defined, giving primary importance to their indigenous status, the value of which should not be lost in the delivery of services. Second, they must be appropriately remunerated for services rendered. Third, they need appropriate backup. Ideally, the end product would be that community workers would have sufficient security in their work so that they could use the consultation and supervision of a full spectrum of professional disciplines without demeaning their own position and without status concerns. With that capacity community workers could provide key bridging roles between health, mental health, legal, welfare, and educational services, and through their visibility and accessibility a focus for pressure to effect community change.

The increased availability of medical care has also brought more psychiatrists into clinical contact with welfare clients. The resulting collaborative relationship between psychiatrists, community, and social workers makes it possible for clients to receive coordinated support during psychiatric treatment. Psychiatrists can also bring specific mental health principles into the operation of social agencies in consultation roles. The knowledge and skills of mental health professionals can be helpful in policy making and in institutional reform as well (Group for the Advancement of Psychiatry, 1975b).

Another major problem for social welfare is the wide disparity between current knowledge, actual practice, and even research studies. For example, a paper written in 1975 concludes that better coordination of services and continuity of care is desirable in the treatment of drug abusing mothers whose children are in foster care (Fanshel, 1975a). The study presents data which shows that the children of drug abusing mothers tend to be locked into foster care at a disproportionately high rate, suffering continual placement from one setting to another. Because of the high investment of funds required to sustain children in foster care, the author suggests that these resources could be made available more profitably for more intensive treatment of the addiction problem of their mothers. He also asks if there is a need for a closer working relationship between agencies offering foster care services and those with expertise in addiction services. These ideas are presented as new, even though they have been key professional concepts for years. This example is a prime illustration of the fact that even the current professional literature contains rediscovery of the long apparent lack of coordination and continuity of services for children and families.

A systems point of view can be used to clarify the problems of the welfare system. All complex systems include a series of interlocking and interdependent subsystems. In carrying out its functions, each subsystem draws sustenance from, as well as helping to support, other subsystems. Although the goal of the welfare subsystem of American society is to provide support for persons who cannot support themselves, it also works with other subsystems to maintain the integrity of society. Whether a necessary and permanent ingredient or a dispensable part of our society, a large body of our population is in need of supportive services. If these people can be better served by other systems, the welfare system will be affected. If society deals effectively with the social and ecological causes engendering the need for support, the welfare system will be affected. In any event, collaboration with the other systems reciprocally influences the character of the welfare system. Unlike the health and legal systems, which deal with abnormal states of people that require rectification, the welfare system aims to help people carry out the basic tasks of living. It is no wonder, then, that society is ambivalent toward welfare programs and that the welfare system lacks a solid foundation of its own.

In summary, the existing welfare system has grown "like topsy." It is based upon administering categories of aid, with different social workers dealing with each specific aid program. It is not based upon long-range planning but is the result of fragmented, crisis-oriented responses to pieces of social problems, with resulting fragmentation of services and a lack of support for families and children. The quality of services for children is deteriorating rather than improving. There is a pressing need for increased professionalism in social work, so that welfare programs can be administered more effectively and the broader range of social services can be appreciated and utilized.

The Family and the Welfare System

Students of the social scene conclude that the primary purpose of all social welfare should be to strengthen family life (Costin, 1972; Bazelon, 1976; Eisenberg, L., 1975). In fact, it is the lack or breakdown of family functions that creates social welfare caseloads. The image of happy, healthy children having opportunities to achieve their full potentials within a stable family and community is a goal to which the majority of American citizens would subscribe. This idealized image reflects the belief that children's best chances for happiness and optimal development are within their own families, with parents who rear their children according to their own values without outside interference.

Following this line of reasoning, support of the family is the first line of defense for the development of a child. Family income maintenance, homemaker services, adequate housing, and marital counseling to preserve family integrity become preconditions for the development of many children. Included in these services should be universal accessibility for family planning, for frequently it is the unwanted child or the additional child who detonates family disintegration as well as becoming its principal victim. With more than half the mothers having children between the ages of six and 17 in the U.S. work force, good day care and after-school services are essential if children are to have stimulating environments in which to grow.

Furthermore, the gradual dispersion of the extended family and the growing tendency to isolate children into narrow age groups demands new social measures at school and at work to reintroduce those essential interactions with juniors and seniors, as well as agemates, that traditional society automatically provided. At the turn of the century, 50 percent of the homes in Boston contained parents, their children, and at least one other adult—a grandparent, aunt, or other relative. The comparable figure today is 5 percent. The elderly can rediscover their personal usefulness by the reinvention of grandparenthood. We could wish no greater bonus for today's children than that they could share the warmly remembered, gratuitous, and undemanding love with which grandparents enveloped past generations' early lives (Eisenberg, L., 1975).

At this time, because a national social policy to support the family does not exist, many public actions undermine family life. Because any one social institution or government function is related to the others, policy formulation in any one area becomes significant to the others. Thus, varying state and federal programs have an impact on family life even though family concerns were not directly considered in the formulation of the policies. When government acts ineffectively to prevent the pollution of lake waters by industrial waste, scarce recreational areas which are important to family life are lost. Also, urban renewal programs have cleared unsightly and overcrowded areas of the city and constructed modern buildings, but in so doing they have ignored the established patterns of neighborhood life important to families and children. Public housing policy does not always coincide with family needs, as when a mother is denied access to housing because she is unmarried or because her son is on probation. The lack of a comprehensive family policy is related not only to the shifting balance toward the state absorbing parenting functions, but also to a lack of appreciation of the developmental needs of children. National family policies should balance the interests of children, parents, and the state. If combined with the principle that children are generally helped more effectively through their own parents, the result would be more service to families and a shift in attitude for community institutions and social agencies to working on behalf of parents instead of against them.

As Kadushin points out, private lives in the United States are predominantly family centered; however, public policy formation is not (1976). He feels that respect for the right of a family to privacy and freedom from external control and intrusion is more apparent than real. In most instances, when public agencies are called upon to help a child in need of protection, the parents are hurt as much as the child. Only a fraction of social agency cases require legal intervention if families are approached with acceptance rather than condemnation.

On the other hand, running counter to a national emphasis on the family is the fact that parenthood is increasingly becoming an unselected option because of society's growing acceptance of childlessness as a viable life style. The result is that parenthood, which is difficult enough under the best circumstances and about which people are generally ambivalent, is seen as an avoidable burden by many young people. From this point of view, the current emphasis upon children's rights may increase the problems of being a parent because parental rights may be perceived as threatened. Moreover, in a subtle way, the children's rights movement makes it easier to abdicate parenthood by calling attention to the need for the community to assume greater responsibility for children. Although not the only way, parenthood is one of the best ways of making people human. Adults are at their caring and sharing best when enacting the role of parenthood. In a society in which more and more people become less and less involved in child rearing, Kadushin fears that society will be less human, less understanding, and less compassionate.

A social policy supporting the family's role in child development would focus the responsibilities of society in several ways. The purpose would not be to support families blindly, but to ensure that each child has an adequate family in which to develop. One way would be through the state's use of regulatory powers. The state can regulate child placement procedures, standards for professional training and practice with children and families, licensing of children's facilities, and the determination of parental fitness. A second way is to intervene in the relationship of a parent and a child. When parental care falls below a level allowed for by law, or when a child or young person engages in delinquent acts prohibited by law, the state can intervene as a protector and use its power to require a better level of care or treatment for the child within the family or elsewhere. A third way is to legislate various child welfare services and tax benefits for child rearing. For example, the federal government can subsidize states to aid in the development of local social services for children and families, and more realistic tax deductions for parents can be allowed.

The high level of competence needed in order to function as a parent in modern society places much stress on families. The availability of opportunities for children outside of the home has also eroded the sense of responsibility of some parents. When families malfunction, the welfare system becomes involved. Because the welfare system fundamentally administers legislation, it will only be responsive to those families if guided by a unifying national policy supporting child development within the family. The current piecemeal approach to children lacks the purposeful support of family life. The effects of that lack of direction are obvious in the large number of children who have not had parents with whom to identify, as the case of Dennis Smith dramatically illustrates.

Child Welfare Services

Since the beginning of this century a wide variety of welfare services has been developed for children. These services are basically intended to

(1) support, (2) supplement, or (3) substitute for the care given to children by their parents. Because each of these services has been added at a particular time and because of a specific piece of legislation, the general pattern is one of separate staffs, buildings, and priorities for each categorical service. Different social workers and departments offer services independently to the same child and family. As a result uncoordinated, fragmented approaches are dictated by the nature of the system and cannot relate coherently to the entire life needs of an individual child.

Before devoting attention to each category of child welfare service, it is of interest to note Carsten's statement (Kadushin, 1974):

> Child welfare has acquired significance that is so broad and vague that it has come to be applied to almost every effort in social and community work that is likely to benefit children. If the term child welfare includes every activity that either directly or indirectly promotes the welfare of children, we would include most of the significant activities engaged in by a society. We would include the sanitary engineer working toward a physically healthier environment for children, the traffic engineer working for a reduction in automobile accidents, the research scientist studying congenital anomalies, and the military guarding the country from attack.

A more specific definition of child welfare is based on society's delegation to the profession of social work responsibility for helping certain problem situations encountered by children. The Advisory Council on Child Welfare Services of the U.S. Department of Health, Education and Welfare defined child welfare services as

> those social services that supplement or substitute for parental care and supervision for the purpose of protecting and promoting the welfare of children and youth, preventing neglect, abuse and exploitation, helping overcome problems that result in dependency, neglect or delinquency, and when needed, providing adequate care for children and youth away from their homes, such care to be given in foster homes, adoptive homes, child caring institutions or other facilities.

In a sense, the fact that child welfare has been seen as the purview of social work has permitted society to deflect its responsibility for children to social workers. They have been given a mission doomed to failure and, thereby, have been subjected to unfair scapegoating. Just as it has been possible for society to feel that it is caring for the disadvantaged because there are welfare programs, it has been possible to feel that it is caring for vulnerable children because there are child welfare workers. In contrast, the child advocacy concept reverses the direction of flow, shifting the responsibility for vulnerable children from a specific professional discipline to all professionals and nonprofessionals who work within child caring systems. From a systems point of view, society has tended to displace its responsibility for children upon the beleaguered subsystem of child welfare and absolved itself of its responsibility for meeting the needs of vulnerable parent–child units.

SUPPORTIVE SERVICES FOR PARENTS

A major part of the funding of child welfare is administered through the Aid to Families of Dependent Children program. Although in original intent designed to be more than financial aid, the implementation of the program is largely through the disbursement of funds and determining client eligibility to receive them. The fact that more than financial aid is needed by these children is illustrated by a survey of AFDC children. It disclosed that 35 percent had personality disorders and 65 percent could be helped by improved educational and employment opportunities (Eisenberg, J. G., 1976). Other forms of categorical financial aid are also administered for parents and children with specific handicaps.

A second child welfare service is more or less available depending upon staff resources, but ideally infuses all functions. In this category are direct individual, family, and group casework services to help parents fulfill their parental, vocational, and social roles.

A third category of service is to unmarried parents to help them make decisions for the care or relinquishment of their children and to assist them in problems associated with unmarried parenthood. From a child's point of view, it is desirable to proceed quickly to termination of parental rights and adoption. This can be done with a mother who has not become involved in child rearing, but it is difficult for those who, because of their own immaturity, depend upon a child for their integrity and, although unable to care for the child, are unwilling to entrust the child to others. Because the pool of adoptable babies is decreasing, the number of people who are willing to adopt children is high. This means that there are many adults who would be willing to adopt children if agency practice and legal intervention could be arranged to ensure the swift and effective placement of children. It is an unfortunate fact that in this area the interests of the children have received little attention and the emphasis has been upon the wishes of the unwed parents.

A fourth category is broadly described as protective services designed to intervene on behalf of children who live under conditions seriously detrimental to their physical, emotional, and social welfare. Most states have enacted child abuse and neglect legislation, but the definition of emotional neglect has been vague and, although even more detrimental to the child's development than physical abuse, has been given low priority in practice. Ideally, if parents are viewed as needing aid, therapeutic intervention with the family can be carried out. The unfortunate fact is that social workers are overburdened by excessive caseloads and untrained in therapeutic skills, leading to the more typical disposition of removing the child from the home, paradoxically the more drastic, yet more easily accomplished, technique. More desirable is the development of prevention and therapeutic programs, such as community networks aimed at specific groups of parents with problems who need to be identified and helped, such as for abusive parents as described in Chapter 11.

SUPPLEMENTARY SERVICES FOR PARENTS

Homemaker services have been provided on a temporary basis for families undergoing crises or needing concrete guidance in both planning and carrying out day-to-day child rearing responsibilities. This service should be expanded as one of the most effective ways of maintaining children in their own homes while parents are temporarily unable to do so.

A growing area of welfare activity, particularly through licensing and funding, is day care for children. Day care centers, family day care homes, and small group homes operate to strengthen and support parental roles under ideal circumstances. Even though it is true that parents usually send children to nursery school because they wish to and send children to child care centers because they must, day care of high quality can be supportive in child rearing.

Licensing, regulation, and supervision of day care for children is a vital welfare function because of the tendency for day care to be of low quality. Unlike nursery schools with their foundation in early childhood education, day care centers may have little professionalism and may employ inexperienced, transient staffs. Furthermore, the day care center schedule is apt to be congruent with the working day and serves people from the lower socioeconomic groups, whereas the nursery school is for a more limited period, and serves middle-class families. Unfortunately, a child's experience of day care has not been given sufficient attention. Ten or 12 hours a day is a long time to be in competition with peers. It is a long time to share a teacher with other youngsters of the same age. It is a long day to be in the same room with 15 to 20 people. Simply the pressure of people and noise, even happy noise, can be wearing. And children do wonder where their mothers are (Auerbach, 1975).

The long hours in day care also result in a tendency to shift parental responsibilities to the day care center staff. An example is one mother's request for health services in day care: "I don't see my kid too much during the day, just in the morning when he's still sleepy, and at night, when he's tired from a long day. I can't tell whether his health is O.K. The ones who can are at the Center, because they see him all day and can compare him with other kids" (Auerbach, 1975).

The Children's Bureau, in a 1962 national survey of licensed day care facilities, defined day care as parenting protection for children, either during the parents' working day or part of the day and for reasons not necessarily connected with parental employment. Nursery schools and kindergartens were not considered to be day care facilities within the meaning of this definition because their chief purpose was education. More recently, the tendency has been to blur the distinction between these two programs as the quality of day care improves.

We need data on the effects of day care on children. The evidence is that day care can be beneficial or harmful, depending on the kind of mother, the kind of child, and the kind of family. It depends, among other things, on why the mother works, how much she works, what she does, what work does to her or for her, how old her children are, what provisions she makes for them while she works, and how a child perceives the fact of her working. There is a general lack of certainty as to whether day care is a social, educational, or health responsibility, and the unfortunate fact is that often it is administered by the dictates of limited budgets. Accordingly, there is a need for setting higher standards than are currently applicable (Steinfels, 1973).

SERVICES SUBSTITUTING FOR PARENTS

Because they involve such drastic interventions in the lives of children and because there is a considerable body of child development knowledge bearing upon them, the substitute parenting functions of child welfare will be treated in greater detail. They include foster care, adoption, and group care facilities. Before doing so, the vital issue of where the legal custody of a child is lodged when parental substitution is invoked will be highlighted.

GUARDIANSHIP

Although there is wide variation, depending on state statutes and judicial practice, it is customary for judges to assume temporary guardianship of children when there is parental incapacity or unwillingness to participate in a court-designated program. A parent may relinquish custody voluntarily or a court may order involuntary termination of parental rights for statutory reasons after due process has been observed. The guardianship of a child may be awarded to an agency or an individual on a temporary basis, with the expectation that it will be returned to the parents when no longer indicated. Although a useful mechanism that permits the community to intervene to protect a child's interests, guardianship can be abused when required administratively in order to obtain services and consequently invade a parent–child relationship without justification.

Temporary guardianship can be transformed into permanent custody, either to a state agency or to individuals through adoption of the child. When this is done the intervening step of termination of parental rights, both for the mother and for the father, is necessary. Rarely is it in the child's interests to have permanent custody lodged with an agency since no institution can be a psychological parent. The matter of termination of parental rights is discussed more fully in Chapter 9.

Because of the ease of removing children from their homes, the Carnegie Commission has recommended the following guidelines for the placement of children in substitute care (Keniston, 1977):

1. Before any child is removed from home for more than a brief emergency period, there must be clear and convincing demonstration with due process that the child is in imminent danger of serious physical, psychological or emotional harm.
2. There must be a strong presumption in favor of children remaining in their natural home or with relatives. Courts should be required at the earliest possible stage of any legal proceeding to determine whether or not a salvage operation is possible.
3. Before removal the court must find that the place the child is sent will be less damaging than remaining at home.

In the matter of adoption, several specific considerations are important in current procedures related to termination of parental rights. The courts have not fully considered the problems created for the infant, whose adoption may be delayed in order to secure consent of putative fathers, as currently required by both judicial decree and state statutes. For example, the State of Wisconsin requires that the unwed biological father be notified of the mother's termination of parental rights before adoption can occur. If the court cannot identify the biological father, however, it may terminate his rights after at least 30 days have elapsed since the birth of the child (Wisconsin State Laws, 1973).

Concern about the rights of the unwed father was clearly expressed in *Stanley* v. *Illinois* when two "illegitimate" children were taken from their father's custody and made wards of the state following the death of their mother, since Stanley was presumed unfit because under Illinois law a father of an illegitimate child was not defined as a parent. The U.S. Supreme Court ruled that under the Equal Protection Clause of the 14th Amendment all parents were entitled to a due process hearing on their fitness.

The application of the principle of an unwed father's rights to social agency practice occurred in *Rothstein* v. *Lutheran Social Services of Wis-*

consin and Upper Michigan. In this case the parental rights of the mother of an illegitimate child had been terminated and the child was adopted by a married couple. Rothstein petitioned the court, claiming to be the natural father and requesting the child's custody. The Wisconsin Supreme Court held that fathers of "illegitimate" children had no right to custody of such children. The U.S. Supreme Court vacated the Wisconsin Supreme Court's judgment. The Wisconsin Supreme Court then ruled that adoption could not take place without termination of the father's rights.

Because the pursuit of the rights of parents could, and often does, delay the speedy resolution of custody issues, the National Conference of Commissioners on Uniform State Laws (1971) prepared the Revised Uniform Adoption Act. In order to protect a child from technicalities related to rights of biological parents, the model act stipulates that parental consent is not required of a parent who has abandoned a child, a parent who has failed significantly and without justifiable cause for one year to communicate with the child or provide for the care and support of the child, and a parent judicially declared incompetent or mentally defective. Furthermore, consent to adoption could not be withdrawn after the entry of a decree of adoption, and would be withdrawn only prior to the decree if in the best interests of the individual to be adopted.

FOSTER CARE

Foster home placement involves a total reallocation of the care of a child so that someone else takes over all aspects of parenting, but without possessing legal guardianship which may reside with an agency or the child's parents. The fact that foster parents do not have legal guardianship of a child has implications for the nature of the relationship between the foster child and the foster family, and it does permit the return of the children to their homes of origin at any time.

Foster home placement is a form of drastic social surgery and should be resorted to only after efforts to keep the child's home intact have been exhausted (American Academy of Pediatrics, 1975; Stone, 1969). The importance of this point is underscored by the National Council of Adoptive Parents Organization in their statement: ". . . foster and institutional placement should be only a temporary stop-gap on the way to biological family rehabilitation or legal adoption." In practice, however, foster placement is often the first, and easiest, disposition at a time of family crisis. All it involves is transporting a child from one house to another. The number of children in foster family care is increasing. In 1962 there were 176,000. The number in 1977 was estimated to be 400,000 (Child Welfare League of America). More reliable and definitive criteria for placing a child in foster care are clearly needed (Wald, 1976).

The concept of foster care is a *temporary* placement when parents are unable to care for their children. The fact that foster care may not be temporary, however, is exemplified by the 1957 Mass–Engler Survey of children in foster care (Mass, 1959). That study of 422 children found that one-half spent six years or longer in foster care, and almost one-third were in care 10 or more years later. The children in long-term care were distinguished by their below-average intelligence, their nonwhite status, and the poverty of their parents. Twelve years later, Mass' study of 4,281 children disclosed that no more than one in four of the foster care children returned home (1969). A more recent study suggests that the situation might be improving. A five-year longitudinal study of over 600 children in foster care in New York City found that 64 percent had returned to their homes by the end of five years (Fanshel, 1978). Of greater concern is Kadushin's analysis of eleven foster care studies, which indicates that 23 percent of the children had three or more placements (1979). The Child Welfare League's current estimate is that foster placements average four to six years and that most children remain in foster care throughout their dependent years.

Although Kadushin's follow-up study of foster care indicates that 70 to 80 percent of the children generally grow up satisfactorily (1974), Gruber found that 40 percent of his series had significant problems (1973, 1978). Long-term placement is not necessarily disadvantageous to the child, but the child lacks the guarantee of permanence provided by a legal relationship with adoptive parents. Foster homes have certainly failed to fulfill their purpose of temporary refuge. The problem, then, lies in the fact that the temporary intent of foster family care conflicts with the actual situation. Agencies are trying to reduce the tendency to drift into long-term foster care by requiring reassessment of foster homes at frequent intervals. One agency achieved a gradual, consistent drop in the number of children in foster care over two years by instituting follow-up. It is likely, however, that judicial guardianship and review will be necessary for all but the most evident temporary placements.

One of the reasons why foster children do not return home is that little or no services are offered to their parents (Jenkins, 1966). In theory, a child's parents should be helped to make whatever changes are necessary to permit the child to return home, but 35 percent of the parents of the children under public auspices and 23 percent of the parents of the children under voluntary agency auspices did not receive casework services in one study. More to the point is the finding that of 30 children in foster care, in only two cases did the child's parents receive casework that met standards of adequacy (Boehm, 1958; Kadushin, 1974).

Another significant problem is that many foster children are not free for adoption. The "permanently neglected child" is defined as a child in foster care whose parents, notwithstanding the efforts of the agency to encourage and strengthen the parent relationship, fail substantially and continuously for a period of more than one year to maintain contact with their child, although physically and financially able to do so. In these cases either no, or insufficient, efforts are made to terminate parental rights appropriately and release the child for adoption.

One of the most troubling aspects of foster care is the picture of confused self-identity which many foster children reflect. The multiple relationships they are expected to manage, many of them successive, temporary, and unsupportive, take a toll in terms of their well-being. They often need mental health services because of the confused and frightening emotions that attend the experience of placement separations. Social workers have encountered repeated evidence that foster children need their own parents; however, once a child is in care, contacts between the biological parents and the agency and child are infrequent.

Fanshel reported on a sample of 624 children who were studied in a five-year longitudinal investigation of foster care in New York City (1975). In two out of five cases, parental visiting was either consistently low or declined over time. Sixty-six percent of the children who received no visits during the first year of care were still in care five years later. He recommended that agencies should be held accountable for efforts to involve parents in responsible visitation, and if they do not do so, this should be taken as an indication of neglect, and termination of parental rights considered.

An important contributing factor to the frequent multiple placements of foster children is the common phenomenon of "testing the placement." Because they often have backgrounds in which relationships with their own parents have been strained, foster children tend to come into conflict with foster parents more than can be expected because of differences in personal habits and customs. In addition to these understandable sources of friction, foster children test the sincerity and commitment of their new parent surrogates, frequently during the middle half of their first year of placement. At that point, the child's behavior problems may lead to a change in foster homes rather than a successful "passing" of the test. When this occurs the second time, and thereafter, the children confirm their underlying convictions that no one really cares about them, and life-long impairment of human relationships may result.

Foster care should really be regarded as a form of institutional placement. Rather than a response to children without parents who can be readily handled through adoption, foster placement is ordinarily a response to family disorganization or to a child's behavior problems. The old idea was that "all the child needs is a good home." In fact, foster children too often remain emotionally tied to their parents by unmet needs and unresolved conflicts. Because they are unable to live with their parents, they are trapped in a future which promises only a succession of foster homes or institutions. It is evident that treatment of the child's original family is far superior to that of removal to a foster home, unless foster care is temporary, with a specific plan for the child's return home. The indication is clearly for increased family supportive services (Clifton, 1976; Weissman, 1978). One of the obvious alternatives is to provide homemaker services for a family in difficulty and thereby to strengthen the home, rather than to remove a child from the family and permit it to disintegrate further.

As one of the consequences of being disadvantaged, foster care is used largely for lower-class children. Middle-class children have housekeepers, grandparents, and others to care for them in emergency situations. Foster care is the only option the poor mother has for her children during a crisis. Paradoxically, some mothers fear that if they place their children in foster care, even with temporary intent, they may lose them. Accordingly, they keep their children in inadequate care and resist foster home placement even when it might be beneficial.

More and more people are becoming financially dependent on being foster parents. The current trend is to increase foster care (Thomas, 1977). In fact, some foster parents are now becoming group foster parents as a full-time occupation. Under these circumstances, it is less desirable for foster parents to think in terms of adoption, and more desirable to think in terms of the number of children they care for to increase their reimbursement. All of this highlights again the fact that the only adults who can be expected to be primarily committed to a child's development are those legally responsible for the child. We must face the fact that children are financial responsibilities, and only a committed parent is willing to assume that burden. It is difficult to ask another person to do this without pay, and if paid, that person cannot truly be a parent substitute when the relationship of the child is colored by the associated income.

Under some circumstances, the possibility of permanent subsidized foster care has merit (Derdeyn, 1977a). This is useful for children who may be unable to function in family settings. These children should be identified and placed in closely supervised foster homes in order to determine what their long-range potential is for family living. Adoption is not an equitable expectation under circumstances in which an ultimately unfavorable outcome is likely. A second instance in which permanent foster care is indicated is for older children who have already made substantial psychological identifications with their parents, who for the remainder of the child's dependent years are unable to fulfill child rearing responsibilities. Under these circumstances it is useful to preserve a relationship between a child and parents, even though legal responsibility for the child is assumed by permanent foster parents.

It should be recognized, however, that, from a child's point of view, the ideal resolution is adoption. When a child is capable of family living, subsidized adoption is preferable to permanent foster care because many people are reluctant to adopt a child when it means assuming financial responsibility with inordinate medical, educational, or psychiatric costs (Gallagher, 1975). Parenthetically, care must be taken to ensure that a permanent foster care relationship is not entered inappropriately because of the reluctance to face a child's parent with termination of parental rights.

Another problem is that there is no clear-cut definition of the foster parent's relationship to agencies, so that foster parents are sometimes regarded as clients, sometimes as paid employees, and less commonly as colleagues (Katz, 1976). A new use of the foster family is as a treatment resource, reflecting a trend toward the greater disturbance of children being placed in foster care.

In a sense, foster parents have more duties than privileges (Katz, 1971). Moreover, the development of an emotional bond between themselves and their "temporary" children may be discouraged by agencies. In one case a girl was removed from her foster parents and placed with her biological mother, even though she had seen her biological mother only twice in three years of placement; her emotional attachment to her foster parents and theirs to her were disregarded. The critical question for judges in making dispositions when there is a legal tug-of-war between social agencies and foster parents is to decide in what setting and with whom the child will develop physically and emotionally to optimum benefit. It must be recognized that children in foster care are more vulnerable than those reared by one set of parents, and expectations of foster children must be tempered by the facts of each case. For children who have long relationships with their foster parents, the concept of "foster care with tenure" should be considered wherein the foster parents, rather than the biological parents, are favored for legal custody and their psychological parenting of the child is thereby legally validated (Goldstein, 1973).

Special problems are associated with children of minority groups. In the United States, three in every 100 children live outside their homes of origin. In North Dakota, South Dakota, and Nebraska, however, one in every nine Indian children is in a foster home, adoptive home, or boarding facility. In a survey of 16 states, 85 percent of all Indian children in foster care were placed in non-Indian homes. They are also at risk in later development, particularly in adolescence, when they are subject to ethnic confusion and a pervasive sense of abandonment (American Academy of Child Psychiatry, 1977).

An illustration of the complex problems confronting agencies is the current controversy over placing children with single or homosexual foster parents. Variations in life style surfacing in recent years raise moral questions. In the absence of evidence on the results of such placements, the question of the long-range impact of placing children under these unique circumstances remains unknown and subject to judgment regarding each case.

On the positive side, some children receive the care they need in foster care through access to temporary family living away from their own homes. On the negative side, a costly and self-perpetuating foster care system has led to the detachment of children from permanent adult relationships and conflicts for foster parents who wish to adopt children for whom they have become psychological parents while legally prevented from doing so. Above all, there is the continued, usually unsuccessful, struggle to provide children with committed adults who are not their legal parents. All considerations point to compelling reasons for salvaging each child's family when possible and, when not, finding a new permanent family through adoption.

ADOPTION

In contrast to the relatively recent phenomenon of foster care, adoption is an ancient legal process whereby a parent–child relationship is established between persons not so related by birth. It will be discussed in detail because it is the prototype of a substitute parent–child relationship. Originally, adoption was solely for the benefit of the adopter, largely to continue the bloodline of a family. This factor persists in the motivation of adopting parents to have a child when unable to do so biologically.

Adoption for the benefit of children is a recent historical development. The first English adoption law was enacted in 1926. In the United States general adoption statutes became widespread much earlier after Massachusetts enacted the first adoption law in 1851. Adoption in the United States is wholly a legislative creation, with each state having its own statute. Since there was no historical precedent for adoption in the English common law, the courts have tended to follow the legislatively prescribed course rather narrowly. A continuous amendment process, therefore, has been necessary to ensure that the broad goal of fully integrating a child into an adoptive family is accomplished for all purposes, including such a clear-cut matter as inheritance.

The shift toward emphasizing the benefit to children of providing adoptive parents who will nurture them has been reflected in the replacement of informal, "black market" adoption with public or private social agency placement. Most states now forbid adoptive placements made by other than the natural parent, guardian, relative, or authorized agency; prohibit independent placement except with relatives; and require that all adoptive placements with others than stepparents or blood relatives be made by licensed social agencies or departments of welfare. Emphasizing the child's benefit has led to the employment of screening procedures to qualify adults for the role of adoptive parents. In fact, the screening procedure is so extreme at times that it is overdone. For example, so much emphasis can be placed upon the qualifications of the adoptive couple that when they do receive the child, they feel under continuous scrutiny, creating tension in the adoptive parent–child relationship.

An accurate current statistical profile of adoptions is not available since the federal government ceased gathering information in 1971. In 1971, of the 169,000 children legally adopted during that year, 51 percent were adopted by relatives, and 49 percent by nonrelatives. At the present time there are approximately 1.5 million adopted children in the United States, reflecting a fairly consistent prevalence of 2 percent in recent years. In 1971, almost two-thirds of the children adopted were born to unwed parents; however, these children were only one-third of the total number of children born out of wedlock that year (Child Welfare League).

A major consideration in adoption is the developmental level of the child under consideration. For example, recognition of the need for immediate placement after the birth of a child and for the constructive handling of the biological mother's separation from the child has increasingly influenced placement practice. Before the shift in emphasis to the welfare of the child, infants were held in temporary foster care until their physical and neurological status was known. This led to inappropriate withholding of placement because of the mistaken belief that long-range prognosis could be determined during the first months of life. Subsequently, there has been a shift away from the concept that children are adoptable only if they are in good health or developing normally.

Information about children adopted from foster care was obtained in Boehm's study that found that children who remained in foster care differed significantly from those who moved into adoptive homes (1958). The greatest difference between the two groups was their emotional adjustment. Foster children more often than adopted children evidenced behavior problems, conflict about parent relationships, and confused self-identity as a product of their extended foster care status (Toussieng, 1962). Still a disproportionate number of adopted children were seen in psychiatric clinics, where a 15 percent to 30 percent incidence of adoptees were found in contrast with a 2 percent general population incidence (Schechter, 1970; Wieder, 1977a). The most disturbing finding was that the adoptability of children changed during their years of foster placement. Many children labeled "hard to place" would have been adoptable when they first became known to the court or social agency if there had been a more realistic evaluation of their family situation, immediate casework attention to planning for their future lives, and aggressive steps to find suitable adoptive homes. Many children in foster care might have been adoptable if there were a systematic evaluation of their parents' capacity to handle their return. Children who have been regarded as unadoptable become that way simply because of the failure of social agencies to understand and monitor them over time. They have been made unadoptable by multiple foster home placements.

Consensus exists, then, on the desirability of adopting children at early ages based upon such evidence as: (1) research on maternal deprivation and the efficacy of continuity in mothering; (2) evidence from a number of follow-up studies of adoption which has been in favor of the earlier placed children (Tizard, 1978); (3) the low predictability of infant developmental scales, no longer regarded as worth delaying a child's placement in order to match parent and child; (4) the expressed wish of many adoptive applicants to receive an infant or a very young child; and (5) savings in agency administrative costs when children are placed early. Of greatest importance in this respect is recognition of the fact that a risk is assumed by parents who adopt a child, just as when one has a biological child for whom there is no guarantee of outcome.

A specific contribution to handling the adoption of a newborn baby is to provide for advance termination of parental rights by the mother on a voluntary basis and to arrange for the placement of the child as soon as possible after birth. There is a question as to whether or not the baby should be seen by the biological mother, and whether or not the biological mother should meet the adoptive parents. Although there may be exceptions, from the biological mother's point of view, it is important for her to achieve closure of her conception and pregnancy through actual contact with her baby. It has been feared that if a mother has contact with the baby, she will change her mind or will be disturbed. Even if such an immediate reaction occurs, it can be therapeutically managed, and the mother does need to have closure of the biological process of birth through having physical contact with her baby.

By the same token, it is important for a biological mother to have a concrete image of the adoptive parents, just as it is important for the adoptive parents to have a concrete image of the biological mother. If the choice is between leaving these matters to fantasy, or providing reality, there is justification for linking the human experiences of giving birth and beginning to raise a child. The issue is how much knowledge adoptive parents and biological parents should have about each other. On the one hand, there is the argument that if there is no knowledge other than that which is necessary for medical purposes, the adoptive parents have a more distinct feeling of their role without the distraction of awareness of the child's biological parents. On the other hand, adoptive, biological parents and adoptive children throughout their lives entertain fantasies about the biological parents which may be diminished in importance through actual knowledge.

An important issue for adopted children is curiosity about their origins. The Adoptees' Liberty Movement Association presumes that truth about one's origin is the birthright of every person. The organization aims to open birth records for all adopted adults and helps biological parents to find their children after the age of 18 as well. The fulfillment of an adopted child's curiosity depends upon how much information is provided by agencies to adoptive parents as a basis for informing their child. It is difficult to discuss adoption with children without implying that they have been rescued from inadequate parents, an implication which is difficult for adopted children, who to some extent form fantasied identifications with their biological parents. During adolescence another problem arises. Many adoptive children are aware that they were born to unwed parents. Identification, to whatever limited degree, with biological parents who engaged in illicit sex of which they are the living evidence confronts adolescents with the question of resolving the tendency to think of their own sexuality—"like father, like son; like mother, like daughter." The desire of adopted children to trace their biological parents is now accepted as one that may be acted upon when they reach late adolescence.

Another area is assessing the motivation of potential adoptive parents. The screening process has been important in order to assure that a child is being sought for reasons related to the child's interests, in addition to serving the adoptive parents' needs. This has been coupled with a range of considerations that relate to the qualifications of the prospective adoptive couple. Several generalizations can be made about adoptive parents. Adoptive mothers adopt their first child later in life than most parents, and the marriage has been childless longer. This means stable patterns of parental interaction exist that may be more difficult to change in response to the incorporation of a child into the adults' lives. Although there is conflicting evidence, after the adoption of an infant, a woman is more apt to conceive a biological child. When this happens, the adopted child is often the oldest child in a biologically related sibling group.

In predicting parental potential in adoption, there seems to be little association between positive factors and favorable outcome; however, a few indicators of potential "bad" parenting can be identified. These negative factors relate to uncertainties about the motivation for adoption, in addition to health and energy limitations of the adopting mother. A trained social worker's judgment in identifying serious impediments to satisfactory parenthood is probably reliable. The application process, however, is fraught with problems for potential parents because of its tendency to label them in terms of their acceptability or unacceptability. To qualify for a child is to pass, and not to qualify is to fail one of the few "tests" of eligibility for parenthood.

Kadushin cites one study that illustrates the special problems that adoptive parents face during the first years (1974). It found that adopters were particularly anxious about their approach to child care and discipline, were unsure about how to interpret adoption to their child, and were concerned about the possibility that their child would later seek out the biological parents. All of these factors point to the importance of reassuring and supporting parents early in the adoption process rather than continuing to place them in a position of insecurity about failing their trial as parents. In contrast with biological parents, all adoptive parents must work through the emotional issues of adoption (Kent, 1976; Schechter, 1970).

Another important area relates to informing children of their adoption. Social workers agree that, for the healthy development of self-identity, children must be helped to know about and understand their adoptive status. Because of unfortunate experiences in which adolescents discovered their adoptive status, it has been held that a child should know about adoption from the earliest years and should learn about it from the adoptive parents. There is more recent evidence, however, that the developmental level of the child must be taken into account. Knowledge of adoption is confusing for children prior to their ability to think in cause-and-effect terms, which occurs at about the time of school entry. The practice of introducing a child to adoption through the use of such books as *The Chosen Child* is currently questioned. What is not taken into account is the ability of the child to understand what adoption means.

Schechter recommended that children be introduced to the idea of adoption when they are of early school age and can comprehend the concept without the negative connotation that is experienced prior to that time (1964). At the age of three or four a child only senses that "adoption" means being different and, therefore, "bad."

Wieder found that lasting damage to self-esteem resulted from disclosure of adoption to children prior to the age of three (1977a). As children listened to stories of their adoptions they felt the adoptive mothers were trying to "get rid" of them as shameful, disgusting, or bad. They held the distorted belief that their biological mother had cast them out to die and that they were "found" by the adoptive mother. Because they were abandoned once, they feared abandonment again by their adoptive parents. An ambivalent attitude toward the adoptive mother developed because she was the "savior" to whom the child clung for survival and also the bearer of bad news toward whom the child directed hatred felt for the abandoning, unreachable biological mother. He concluded that preschool children are not equipped to comprehend and master knowledge of their adoption.

The following principles, clearly distinguishing sex education from adoption interpretation, for informing a child of adoption are useful: (1) the child's receptivity to adoptive status is best assured if the parents accept it themselves; (2) the time to inform the child is not when inquiries begin about how babies are born; (3) there are many opportunities to inform the child as the child enters school and enquires about family relationships; (4) the child should be told only as much as can be understood and digested at any one time; and (5) repetition in different contexts is useful, just as with sex education.

Overemphasis on adoption has dangers because it may make a child feel atypically special and burdened with living up to excessive expectations, particularly when the child has the impression of being "chosen" from among others available. This occurs particularly when there are biological siblings whom the adopted children feel were "just born" and have no special responsibilities, whereas they do because they were "selected."

Biological and adopted children differ in their management of the "family romance" fantasy (Wieder, 1977b). The family romance fantasy is a common developmental solution during middle childhood to conflicts with biological parents in the form of the wish to be an adoptee and thereby have a set of ideal parents elsewhere. The fantasy solution of the biological child's conflicts—adoption—is a *fait accompli* for the adoptee. The adoptee's wish, in contrast to the biological child's, is to deny adoption, establish a fantasized blood tie to the adoptive parents, and thereby erase repeating the humiliation of rejection by one's biological parents that adoption implies. The dependence on their adoptive parents and anger at them for inevitable real life disappointments carry fearful possibilities of retaliatory reabandonment. This makes the developmentally appropriate fantasy of having been adopted an unacceptable and dangerous wish for adopted children. Whether adopted or biological, children benefit from opportunities to express and talk about these fantasies so that they are not secretly harbored and buried and lost to the correcting influences of reality.

The existence of fantasies about biological parents is dramatically illustrated in Rod McKuen's book, *Finding My Father* (1976). He describes the moment at which he became aware he was born out of wedlock:

> I was nearly sixteen . . . after I had spent my savings, my aunt had little use for me and one day in a rage called me a bastard. My answer was equally graphic, and her reply was, "No, you really are a bastard." Raising her voice even louder, she told me that I had been born out of wedlock, that nobody even knew who my father was, and I likely never would know.
>
> I didn't say anything right away. I pretended not to hear. I couldn't even look at her. Finally I asked her to repeat what she had said. On hearing the words the second time, I felt as though someone had kicked me in the stomach. On reflection I am never even sure why. Maybe because in reality, having nothing to go on in the way of tangible evidence of my father—no photographs, no ideas as to color of hair or eyes, height, weight, occupation—I had been able to invent and elaborate upon the absolutely perfect father whenever I needed him. Over all the years he'd assumed various guises, various occupations. He was the captain of a ship or sailing vessel, the

engineer or brakeman on a train. He was an actor who made movies, and most of the time he was a cowboy or a big, hardy man who worked out of doors. Now in a single sentence, a moment, he was no one. He didn't exist and as I walked out of my aunt's house for the last time the truth hammered me dead. I would probably never know him now, never see or find him, and he would never find me. It didn't occur to me that my aunt might be lying. She had been so vicious in her statement, so positive, I must have known at once, intuitively, she was telling the truth. And anyway, I received the news almost as if I had been expecting some kind of revelation—a revelation that at last, however mean and inappropriate, had been given to me. I felt unhappy, betrayed, cheated, empty, lied to, all at once.

Although research in the social sciences is imperfect at best (Lawton, 1974), some data is provided on adoption in Eldred's study of 216 adopted subjects who were compared with a matched control group of biological children (1976). The majority of the subjects were born outside of marriage and were placed with childless couples who had been married an average of eight years at the time of the child's placement. With an average age of 34 years, the group of adoptive mothers was 10 years older than the biological mothers. The adoptees learned of their adoption at the average age of 11 years with one standard deviation of six years, most receiving the information from their adoptive parents. One-half of the adoptees reacted to the information with indifference or positive emotion, but the rest manifested negative reactions of shock, upset, and unhappiness at not having been told earlier or dissatisfaction with the adoptive parents. The subjects who learned about their adoption from their adoptive parents were more likely to report reacting positively to the information than when learning about it from others.

A majority of the subjects in Eldred's study said they had never consciously thought or wondered about their biological parents. Only 5 percent of those knowing of their adoption took some action to trace their biological parents and another 5 percent were tempted to do so, but did not. Significantly, however, 21 percent had personal contact with their biological parents either in person, or by mail or phone. In some cases, the biological mother was an "aunt" who visited the home during childhood, with the subject subsequently learning who she was. In other cases the parent or subject initiated contact during the subject's adolescence or adulthood, and additional meetings followed. This study raises an unmentioned side of adoption, namely, the interest on the part of biological mothers to find their children. This study suggests that mothers take more of an initiative in locating their children than children do in locating their mothers.

Subjects in this study did not show a high interest in their biological parents, but it was greatest when there were poor relationships with the adoptive parents, negative reactions to learning about the adoption, or having a biological or adoptive parent who had been hospitalized for mental illness. In this study those who had had some contact with their biological parents did not generally differ from the remaining adoptees in either the degree of their psychopathology or the quality of their relationships with their adoptive parents. The findings of this study provide no evidence to discourage contact with biological parents on the grounds that it might be harmful to the child. A subsequent study of adoptees reunited with their biological parents found the experience to be mutually satisfying in 90 percent of the cases (Sorosky, 1976 and 1978).

Legal cases related to the rights of adoptive versus biological parents have been heartrending because of the common failure to consider the interests of the child. In *Sampson* v. *Holton*, a woman surrendered her child at birth to her doctor for adoption, but when the child was 18 months old, petitioned to have the child returned to her. The court held that Iowa requirements for consent to adoption had not been met, and that the child, now over 18 months old , should be returned to the natural mother, irrespective of the fact that the adoptive parents were her psychological parents. In a New York case, a three-year-old boy was awarded to the biological mother and carried from the courtroom "screaming for the only mother (his adoptive mother) he had ever known." The child had been surrendered at birth by his biological mother under her family's pressure, which she ultimately rejected.

The irony in the adjudication of cases such as these is that the courts allowed—indeed, almost required—losing sight of the welfare of the child. The appeal of the *Sampson* case was because the court precluded itself from considering the welfare of the child by characterizing the issue as one of adoption instead of custody and ruling only on the technical requirement of consent to adoption. It is evident, therefore, that statutes must be made to bend instead of the child (Iowa Law Review, 1971). In the final analysis, parents as adults can adjust to heartbreak more readily than small children. The wisdom of King Solomon did not lie in the fact that he awarded a child to the biological mother after offering to give half of the child to each contestant. What was awesome in Solomon's case was that, when placed in the position of bearing the pain of loss to save her child's life, the biological mother withdrew and was willing to make the supreme sacrifice.

Another technical legal risk is that some courts have held that the consent to adoption of a child can be withdrawn at any time after an adoption decree is entered. In *Hendricks v. Curry* a child, after living the first two and a half years of her life in an adoptive home, was returned to the care of her biological mother. At issue was the principle that the natural mother had an unqualified right to withdraw the consent to adopt. In *Moreland v. Kraft*, a three-month-old boy was given to adoptive parents with a written surrender for adoption. Three years later they petitioned for final adoption to which the biological mother did not consent. A lower court stated that the withdrawal of consent came too late; however, the reviewing court ruled that the consent was invalid and returned the boy, who was almost four years old, to the biological mother because of her right to withdraw consent at the time of the adoption hearing.

In these cases, the technicality of informed consent overrode the interests of the child. Unfortunately, the court's attention was misdirected to terminating parental rights, and the evident reluctance to do so had an important relation to the fact that parental intent and fault are considered in findings of abandonment and unfitness. Courts are concerned with the intent of the parents, and often will not find an intent to abandon in spite of demonstrated lack of care and concern on the part of the biological parents. Because of the preponderance of parental rights expressed in laws, the courts do not make objective findings regarding children. The requirement of intent to abandon, in addition to findings derogatory to the parent's character, add to the reluctance of courts to terminate parental rights. Under present laws the child's welfare is not primary. Changes in state statutes are needed to make the interests of the child the most important concern in all adoption contests (Derdeyn, 1977).

As the only way of assuring a child an opportunity for development outside of a biological family, statutes should be oriented toward strengthening the adoptive family and toward realization of the child's interests. Adoptive parents should be protected from technical considerations arising from the rights of the biological parents as observed in the Revised Uniform Adoption Act drafted by the National Conference of Commissioners on Uniform State Laws (1971).

Knowledge gained from adoption experience demonstrates that parenthood is not endowed or automatically instituted by the fact of birth but is earned over time. One of the most important questions to an adopted child is, Who is "my real" parent? From the child's point of view, the only thing that matters is who are really "my mom" and "my dad.'" This has led to the helpful distinguishing between a child's biological parent, who may simply have become a parent through the accident of pregnancy, and the parent with whom the child has identified: the psychological parent. Work in the adoption area has led to the conclusion that from a child's point of view one can usefully talk in terms of a biological parent, who may have little or no relevance in a child's life except when the child evidences interest regarding biological origin. The adoptive parent who has earned psychological parenthood of a child is the child's "real" parent through a child's identification with the parent who has identified with that child as well.

From the point of view of agency practices, additional current problems regarding adoptive services are (Kadushin, 1974): (1) the "hard to place child," (2) ambiguity regarding the adoptive parent role, (3) residual negative feelings regarding adoptive status, (4) controversy over agency and independent placements, and (5) religious qualifications held for adoptive parent applicants.

From the point of view of indicated changes, agencies must continue to modify their requirements and study procedures so that the placement process is transformed to an evaluative judgment of applicants in relation only to those parental qualities which at the present stage of knowledge can be assessed with confidence. A planned process to enhance the adoptive parents' ability to perform well in the task of adoptive parenthood should then follow. Postadoptive counseling to individuals or groups of adoptive parents who desire guidance at various stages of adoptive parenthood should be provided. The trend toward more active collaboration among child placing agencies should be extended. Perhaps most needed is for agencies who handle adoptions to become more involved in the problems of other agencies and community institutions as part of a network of services for children and families.

GROUP CARE

Group care for children, particularly for adolescents, refers to a range of facilities from hospital-like institutions to family-like group homes. In between are emergency shelter and detention facilities, child caring institutions, residential treatment centers, training schools and institutions for the blind, deaf, and mentally retarded. As is true for other welfare programs, this conglomeration of services arose from several theories regarding child care, reduced to practical solutions for difficult problems posed by children.

One theory was that special treatment could be provided for children who could not function in their homes because of special problems in group settings with specialized services, just as treatment could be more effectively provided in hospitals for certain illnesses. Another theory, particularly applicable to adolescents, was that less stimulating group living away from the stresses of family life would enable certain teenagers to function more adequately. But the dominant force behind the development of group facilities has been to provide a place to put young people who create problems for their families and communities.

There is great variability in the ways that states approach institutional placement for children. At one extreme are states that attempt to close all institutions and force communities to cope with their own problems. At the other extreme are states that place children in institutions in other parts of the country. It is estimated that some 20,000 children have been placed in institutions outside of their home states. Scandalous case reports have led to lawsuits based upon states' efforts to find the least expensive disposition for problem children without concern for the quality of care. This situation led the Carnegie Commission to recommend that a state should be held accountable, as are parents, for children who are their wards (Keniston, 1977). Indeed, the state should be held to a higher standard for it cannot plead ignorance or lack of resources:

1. state laws should explicitly recognize the rights of institutionalized children to healthy growth and development;
2. state laws should recognize the right of institutionalized children to be housed and cared for in small, home-like settings;
3. the civil rights of institutionalized children (free speech, movement and association) should not be curbed without a standard of reasonableness.

The field of institutional care remains controversial. There has been a decided movement away from large institutions and a commitment to community-based group care programs. Yet it is difficult to point to research which justifies such a change (Kadushin, 1979).

On the positive side, the trend toward small group homes integrated in communities and capable of providing therapeutic milieus, access to specialized educational services, and psychiatric treatment increases the likelihood that the young person's family will be involved in the treatment program. Ideally, group homes should provide the living atmosphere of a home with stable adults and an age range of peers, a therapeutic program for each child and growth facilitating experiences including the child's family: all within the young person's community (Westman, 1971). The group home as part of a community treatment network holds promise for ending an area in which troubled youngsters have been removed from their natural living environments, isolated from the mainstream of community living, graduated from one correctional institution to another and ingrained in a life style devoid of intimate relationships, and epitomized by the tattoo worn by many: "Born to lose" (Whittaker, 1979).

Reform of the Welfare System

No one questions the need for reform of the welfare system. In fact, there is talk of *abolishing* the welfare system. There is no doubt that the sheer bulk of the welfare system with its built-in vested interests institutionalizes the very problems it is intended to resolve, just as our law enforcement system has elements that tend to perpetuate crime. Whether or not people will accept the welfare system as a "normal" part of society, or continue to see it as an "abnormal" response to social problems expected to disappear, only time will tell.

Without question, the public welfare system can be more efficiently and humanely administered if income support is disbursed automatically to all citizens at a level below that of the minimum wage at the same time that social, rehabilitation, and medical services are readily available to all who need them. This basic maintenance income could be either through a guaranteed annual income for all, a negative income tax guaranteeing a certain level of income, or family allowances. Such a program would encourage the poor to develop more autonomous functioning and greater self-esteem and to become less disaffiliated from society and less resentful of their circumstances. Another advantage of such income maintenance is that public welfare workers and administrators would be removed from the burden of eligibility determination and financial administration and freed to do their jobs as professional social workers. As can be seen from the contents of this chapter, if the interests of children are to be served, there will be no shortage or work in the future.

Conclusion

In an effort to move beyond its origins in charity organizations and the administration of politically legislated welfare policies, the field of social work is striving to develop professionalism to permit the translation of knowledge of human development and social systems into practices and programs that will support those who have problems in meeting their basic physical, emotional, and social needs. The current state of the welfare system is desperate, particularly for children and families. Even its objective of supporting people without removing the incentive to work is no closer to achievement than it was at the time of the Elizabethan Poor Law. Rising welfare costs are matched by deteriorating services.

Welfare programs have been addressed to individuals for specific categories of aid, either on the theory that money paid to individuals is the approach to eradicating poverty or simply an expedient to relieve immediate financial distress. Lacking in social welfare theories and practice is application of knowledge of child development, human motivation, and the importance of family life. The results are frustrated and demoralized welfare clients and workers in a system unable to deliver services of proved effectiveness and high quality.

The field of social work has developed a range of child welfare services that are available in public and private agencies in widely varying quantity and quality. Although too often delivered without an appreciation of child development knowledge and family dynamics, they generally aim to support, supplement, or substitute for parental care. In whatever form, too little attention is devoted to fixing legal responsibility for each child's interests, resulting in large numbers of children who have no legal parent devoted to their care. Consequently, there is a pressing need to determine as soon as possible whether parental rights should be terminated and to establish for each child a plan for early return home or to a newly created family.

Because the easiest and most available solution for children with social problems is transporting them from one house to another, foster care is increasing to become a massive industry. Although conceived as a temporary solution to families in distress, too many children in foster homes remain there throughout childhood. More grimly, almost 25 percent of them move from one foster home to another and become unadoptable through no fault of their own.

Even creating a new family for a child through adoption is fraught with obstacles. The reluctance of courts to terminate parental rights even under circumstances of gross neglect has been hampered by the need to demonstrate intent to abandon. More recently, the additional requirement of obtaining the consent of putative fathers prior to adoption has further complicated the speedy provision of permanent, committed care to children through the security of legal adoption. Even when adoption occurs, an inordinate emphasis upon informing children of their adoption too early in life has unduly complicated the lives of adoptive families.

The greatest problems have been encountered with children who have been placed in inappropriate, or denied appropriate, institutional care. The lack of an understanding of individual children's needs has led them either to be "expelled" from communities and placed in the least expensive institutions or has denied them access to therapeutically effective, but temporarily costly, residential treatment facilities.

Without an understanding of the needs of each child and each family, the welfare system will continue to operate ineffectively. The removal of the financial element from welfare through ensuring every citizen's right to basic financial maintenance below the minimum wage level would free social services from the administration of piecemeal categorical aid programs so that the personal needs of their clients could be met through the application of our current knowledge of child development and family life.

References

AD HOC COMMITTEE ON ADVOCACY OF THE NATIONAL ASSOCIATION FOR SOCIAL WORKERS REPORT (1969) "The Social Worker as Advocate: Champion of Social Victims." *Social Work*, 14:16–22, April.

ADOPTEE'S LIBERTY MOVEMENT ASSOCIATION, 157 W. 57 St., New York, N.Y.

AMERICAN ACADEMY OF CHILD PSYCHIATRY (1977) *The Placement of American In-*

dian Children—The Need for Change. Washington, D.C.: American Academy of Child Psychiatry, April.

AMERICAN ACADEMY OF PEDIATRICS (1975) "The Needs of Foster Children." *Pediatrics*, 56:144–145, July.

AUERBACH, S., AND RIVALDO, J. A. (1975) *Rationale for Child Care Services: Programs vs. Politics.* New York: Human Sciences Press.

BAZELON, D. (1976) "Reflections on Child Advocacy." Chapter in Westman, J. C. (Ed.), *Proceedings of the University of Wisconsin Conference on Child Advocacy.* Madison: University of Wisconsin–Extension, Health Sciences Unit.

BOEHM, B. (1958) *Deterrents to the Adoption of Children in Foster Care.* New York: Child Welfare League of America.

CHILD WELFARE LEAGUE OF AMERICA, 67 Irving Place, New York, N.Y. 10003.

CLIFTON, P. M., AND RANSOM, J. W. (1976) "An Approach to Working with the 'Placed Child.'" *Child Psychiatry and Human Development*, 6:107–117.

COSTIN, L. B. (1972) *Child Welfare: Politics and Practice.* New York: McGraw-Hill.

Department of Health, Education and Welfare (1976) *Child Welfare in 25 States—An Overview.* Washington, D.C.: Children's Bureau, DHEW Publication No. (OHD) 77-30090.

DERDEYN, A. P. (1977a) "Dependent, Neglected and Abused Children: A Case for Permanent Foster Placement." *American Journal of Orthopsychiatry*, 47:604–614.

DERDEYN, A. P., AND WADLINGTON, W. J. (1977b) "Adoption: The Rights of Parents versus the Best Interests of Their Children." *Journal of Child Psychiatry*, 16:228–295, Spring.

EISENBERG, J. G. ET AL. (1976) "A Behavioral Classification of Welfare Children from Survey Data." *American Journal of Orthopsychiatry*, 46:447–463, July.

EISENBERG, L. (1975) "The Ethics of Intervention: Acting Amidst Ambiguity." *Journal of Child Psychology and Psychiatry*, 16:93–104.

ELDRED, C. A. ET AL. (1976) "Some Aspects of Adoption in Selected Samples of Adult Adoptees." *American Journal of Orthopsychiatry*, 46:279–290, April.

FANSHEL, D. (1975a) "Parental Failure and Consequences for Children: The Drug Abusing Mother Whose Children Are in Foster Care." *American Journal of Public Health*, 65:604–612, June.

FANSHEL, D. (1975b) "Parental Visiting of Children in Foster Care: Key to Discharge?" *Social Service Review*, 49:493–514, December.

FANSHEL, D., AND SHIM, E. B. (1978) *Children in Foster Care.* New York: Columbia University Press.

FRIEDLANDER, W. A., AND APTE, R. Z. (1974) *Introduction to Social Welfare.* Englewood Cliffs, N.J.: Prentice-Hall, 4th Edition.

GALLAGHER, U. M., AND KATZ, S. N. (1975) "The Model State Subsidized Adoption Act." *Children Today*, 4:8–10, November–December.

GLAZER, N. (1974) "The Limits of Social Policy." Chapter in Weinberger, P. E. (Ed.), *Perspectives on Social Welfare: An Introductory Anthology*, 2nd Edition, New York: Macmillan.

GOLDSTEIN, J., FREUD, A., AND SOLNIT, A. J. (1973) *Beyond the Best Interests of the Child.* New York: Free Press.

GROUP FOR THE ADVANCEMENT OF PSYCHIATRY (1973) "The Welfare System and Mental Health." Vol. 8, Report 85, July.

GROUP FOR THE ADVANCEMENT OF PSYCHIATRY (1975a) "The Community Worker: A Response to Human Need." Vol. 9, Report 91.

GROUP FOR THE ADVANCEMENT OF PSYCHIATRY (1975b) "The Psychiatrist and Public Welfare Agencies." Vol. 9, Report 94, November.

GRUBER, A. R. (1973) *Foster Home Care in Massachusetts: A Study of Foster Children—Their Biological and Foster Parents.* Commonwealth of Massachusetts, Governor's Commission on Adoption and Dependent Care.

GRUBER, A. R. (1978) *Children in Foster Care: The Destitute, Neglected and Betrayed.* New York: Human Sciences Press.

HAMILTON, G. (1974) *Theory and Practice of Social Case Work.* New York: Columbia University Press, pp. 17–33.

Hendricks v. Curry, S.W. 2d 796 (1966), p. 800.

IOWA LAW REVIEW (1971) "Natural vs. Adoptive Parents: Divided Children in the Wisdom of Solomon." *Iowa Law Review*, 57:171–198.

JENKINS, S., AND SAUBER, M. (1966) *Paths to Child Placement: Family Situations Prior to Foster Care.* New York: Department of Welfare and the Community Council of Greater New York.

KADUSHIN, A. (1974) *Child Welfare Services.* New York: Macmillan.

KADUSHIN, A. (1976) "Some Doubts About Child Advocacy." Chapter in Westman, J. C. (ed.), *Proceedings of the University of Wisconsin Conference on Child Advocacy.* Madison: University of Wisconsin-Extension, Health Sciences Unit.

KADUSHIN, A. (1979) "Children in Foster Family Care and Institutions." Chapter in Mass, H. (Ed.), *Five Fields of Social Work Practice.* New York: National Association of Social Workers.

KATZ, S. N. (1971) "Legal Aspects of Foster Care." *Family Law Quarterly*, 5:283–302.

KATZ, S. N. (1976) "The Changing Legal Status of Foster Parents." *Children Today*, 5:11–13, November-December.

KENISTON, K. (1977) *All Our Children: The American Family Under Pressure.* New York: Harcourt, Brace, Jovanovich.

KENT, K. G., AND RICHIE, J. L. (1976) "Adoption as an Issue in Casework with Adoptive Parents." *Journal of Child Psychiatry*, 15:510–522.

KRAUS, H. D. (1973) "Child Welfare, Parental Responsibility and the State." *Family Law Quarterly*, 7:377–403.

KRISTOL, I. (1974) "Welfare: The Best Intentions, The Most of Result." Chapter in Weinberger, P. E. (Ed.), *Perspectives on Social Welfare: An Introductory Anthology*, 2nd Edition. New York: Macmillan.

LAWTON, J. J., AND GROSS, S. Z. (1974) "Review of Psychiatric Literature on Adopted Children." *Archives of General Psychiatry*, 11:635–644, December.

MASS, H. S. (1969) "Children in Long Term Foster Care." *Child Welfare*, 48:321–333, June.

MASS, H. S., AND ENGLER, R. E., JR. (1959) *Children in Need of Parents*. New York: Columbia University Press.

MCKUEN, R. (1976) *Finding My Father*. New York: Coward, McCann and Geoghegan.

Moreland v. Kraft, 244 So. 2d 37 (1971).

NATIONAL CONFERENCE OF COMMISSIONERS ON UNIFORM STATE LAWS (1971) *Revised Uniform Adoption Act*, Chicago, Ill.

NATIONAL COUNCIL OF ADOPTIVE PARENTS ORGANIZATION, Adoptive Parents' Committee, 210 Fifth Ave., New York, N.Y.

REIN, M., AND RAINWATER, L. (1977) "How Large Is the Welfare Class?" *Challenge*, September–October.

Rothstein v. Lutheran Social Services of Wisconsin and Upper Michigan, 405 U.S. 1051 (1972). Decision, April 1975.

Sampson v. Holton, 185 NW 2d 216 Iowa (1971).

SCHECHTER, M. D. (1970) "About Adoptive Parents." Chapter in Anthony, J., and Benedek, T. (Eds.), *Parenthood*. Boston: Little, Brown.

SCHECHTER, M. D. ET AL. (1964) "Emotional Problems of the Adoptee." *Archives of General Psychiatry*, 10:37–46.

SOROSKY, A. D., BARAN, A., AND PANNOR, R. (1976) "The Effects of the Sealed Record in Adoption." *American Journal of Psychiatry*, 133:900–904, August.

SOROSKY, A. D., ET AL. (1978) *The Adoption Triangle*. Garden City, New York: Anchor Press.

Stanley v. Illinois, 405 U.S. 645 (1972).

STEINFELS, M. O. (1973) *Who's Minding the Children? The History and Politics of Day Care in America*. New York: Simon and Schuster.

STONE, H. D. (1969) *Reflections on Foster Care: A Report of a National Survey of Attitudes and Practices*. New York: Child Welfare League of America.

THOMAS, G., POLLANE, L., BRANSFORD, R., AND PARCHURE, S. (1977) *Supply and Demand for Foster Family Care in the Southeast*. Athens, Ga.: Regional Institute of Social Welfare Research.

TIZARD, B. (1978) *Adoption : A Second Chance*. New York: Free Press.

TOUSSIENG, P. (1962) "Thoughts Regarding the Etiology of Psychological Difficulties in Adopted Children." *Child Welfare*, 41:59–65.

WALD, M. S. (1976) "State Intervention on Behalf of 'Neglected' Children: Standards for Removal of Children from Their Homes, Monitoring the Status of Children in Foster Care and Termination of Parental Rights." *Stanford Law Review*, 28:623–706, April.

WEINBERGER, P. E. (ED.) (1974) *Perspectives on Social Welfare: An Introductory Anthology*, 2nd Edition. New York: Macmillan.

WEISSMAN, H. H. (1978) *Integrating Services for Troubled Families*. San Francisco: Jossey–Bass.

WESTMAN, J. (1971) "Myths About Children, Families and Child Care Programs." Chapter in Kuhn, R. (Ed.), *Child-Care Challenges*. Madison: University of Wisconsin–Extension, Department of Social Work.

WHITTAKER, J. K. (1979) *Caring for Troubled Children: Residential Treatment in a Community Context*. San Francisco: Jossey-Bass, Inc.

WIEDER, H. (1977a) "On Being Told of Adoption." *Psychoanalytic Quarterly*, 46:1–22.

WIEDER, H. (1977b) "The Family Romance Fantasies of Adopted Children." *Psychoanalytic Quarterly*, 46:185–200.

WILENSKY AND LABEAUX (1975) "Conceptions of Social Welfare." Chapter in Friedlander, W. A., and Apte, R. Z. (Eds.), *Introduction to Social Welfare*, 4th Edition. Englewood Cliffs, N.J.: Prentice-Hall.

WISCONSIN STATE LAWS, Chap. 263, Laws of 1973.

Chapter 11
Children and Health Care

       The health care system is undergoing a fundamental reassessment. A sense of impending change fills the air. In the past, the miracles of medical science were seen as bringing triumph over dreaded diseases. In the last decade, however, the social, economic, legal, and moral problems of medicine have occupied the center of public attention.

       In the 1960s the premise was that America would benefit from more medical care—more hospitals, more personnel, and more elaborate technology. More recently, the prevailing assumptions in health planning have been revised. Now the emphasis of federal Health Systems Agencies is on reducing the number of hospital beds, consolidating duplicated facilities, and decreasing dependence upon medical technology. The reasons for this shift in emphasis are primarily financial. Between 1960 and 1976 the nation's expenditures on medical care rose from 5.2 percent to 8.6 percent of the Gross National Product. By 1981 it is estimated that the figure will be 10.2 percent (Starr, 1978). In the eyes of some, that is too much for a nation that has not yet achieved adequate health care for all its citizens.

For many American children, health care poses special problems of an advocacy nature. Access to the health care system is the first step toward getting health care services. Yet many children never make it through the front door. Twenty-five percent of children between the ages of one and five and 38 percent between six and 17 have not seeen a physician during the past year. The unserved children live largely in urban and rural areas of poverty. Even when services are available, however, they are often not used or used well. For example, immunizations can be obtained free through public health departments. Yet, in 1974, one of every three American children between one and four were not fully immunized against polio (Children's Defense Fund, 1976). Prenatal care is also available at no cost, but 28 percent of pregnant women received no care during their first trimester in 1975 (National Center for Health Statistics, 1977). As a result, the American Medical Association has stressed the need for outreach workers to overcome the communication, motivational, and educational barriers to receiving health care. Experience with the federal program of Early and Periodic Screening, Diagnosis and Treatment for Medicaid eligible children has confirmed the importance of this kind of advocacy contact with families (Comptroller General, 1975).

Another important point is that children can be cared for more efficiently by comprehensive, prevention-oriented services rather than by episodic care. After an initial increase because of backlog, hospitalization rates decreased significantly for children receiving continuous care in demonstration Children and Youth Projects, which provided outpatient continuous care as is available in private pediatric practice. The total number of hospital days decreased from 113,000 in 1968 to 98,000 in 1970. Hospitalization rates as low as 25 per 1,000 enrollees have been achieved in contrast to a national average of 62.5 per 1,000 (Seligman, 1975).

Because children are inseparably related to their mothers during early life, adequate prenatal and postnatal care is the first stage of essential health care for children. Still, in 1977 the United States ranked fourteenth in the UN survey of infant mortality rates (United Nations, 1979). Problems for the newborn are reflected in mothers' use of substances toxic for the fetus during pregnancy and in the lack of prenatal and perinatal care among the disadvantaged. Furthermore, the general tendency in our society to view childbirth as a medical incident rather than as a natural phenomenon distorts the need to balance technical advances against the advantages of "natural" approaches. The fact that many children born in this country are deprived of a harmonious delivery experience in which the parents and infant experience birth as a creative, exciting act may result in infants who are insufficiently stimulated during the neonatal period. A cultural resistance to breast feeding also deprives infants of the psychological advantages of a natural relationship with their mother's body, and the biological advantages of breast milk. Much of the responsibility for this can be attributed to a lack of emphasis upon the interpersonal and physical facilities required to enhance birth as a natural human experience.

Another example of a special problem in health care for children is the conflict between parental wishes or beliefs and the provision of preventive or therapeutic health services for their children. The withholding of immunizations and blood transfusions, the refusal to authorize surgical or medical care because of religious scruples, and ignorance or apathy may lead to the intervention of a juvenile court in securing services for a child on the grounds that the interests of a child ultimately take precedence over the right of parents to family autonomy and nonintervention by the state. Such matters highlight conflicts between children's need for medical care and the wishes of adults responsible for them. The health care of children is dependent upon the wishes and beliefs of their parents, who may or may not be able to promote effectively their children's interests. In these cases the need for individual case advocacy is clear. This is particularly critical for the adolescent who lies in the transitional position between parental dependency and self-responsibility.

Health Education

Beyond the problems related to the availability of health care for children is the long-range need to foster a healthy citizenry. The health of children is inextricably related to the health of adults since the roots of many adult illnesses lie in childhood experiences, attitudes, and habits. As a consequence, the orientation of children toward major causes of disease and ways of maintaining health should receive high priority.

Knowles calls attention to the need to develop attitudes and habits that promote health (1977). More than half the reduction in mortality rates over the past three centuries has been due to improved nutrition and the reduction of communicable diseases through advances in sanitation. A relatively smaller contribution was made by the introduction of medical and surgical therapies in the twentieth century. Today, the major health problems in the United States are the chronic stress-related diseases of middle and later age: heart disease, strokes, and possibly cancer. Most death and disability in middle age are preventable. For young adults, the leading causes of death are accidents, heart disease, cancer, homicide, and suicide. For those under 25 years, accidents are by far the most common cause of death, followed by homicide and suicide. Of deaths at all ages in the United States in 1976, 47 percent were due to heart disease and strokes; 20 percent to cancer; and 8 percent to accidents. But death statistics tell only a small part of the story. For every successful suicide, an estimated ten others have made attempts. For every death due to accidents, many more are injured and some are permanently disabled. The implication is clear. Improved mental health and health attitudes during early life may substantially alter premature death rates in later life.

Modern medicine has brought spectacular benefits to individuals through the cure and containment of disease and the alleviation of suffering. Surprising, however, is the fact that the increasing allocation of more people, money, and machines to health care has affected mortality and morbidity rates only marginally. If current trends continue, the diminishing returns from expeditures for health care loom as a major economic problem for America.

An attitude that deserves close scrutiny is our faith in progress through science, technology, and industrial growth. Overlooked is the fact that most of us are born healthy and become ill as a result of personal misbehavior and environmental conditions. At this point, the solution to the problems of ill health in modern American society involves individual awareness and responsibility for one's health and public responsibility for improving the quality of life (Saward, 1978).

Unfortunately, most individuals do not become concerned about their health until they lose it. Attempts at healthy living are thwarted by the temptations of an economy that depends on high production and high comsumption. Furthermore, fatalistic attitudes hurt many people. Parental genes are seen as deciding one's fate, no matter what one does. For others, there is the reassuring story of someone who has led a temperate, viceless life and died of a heart attack at the age of 45. Even more reassuring is the case of Winston Churchill, who lived to be 90. He drank brandy, smoked cigars, eschewed exercise, and was grossly overweight. With the aid of such rationalizations, most of us ignore our health.

The message is clear today. The prevention of disease means forsaking things that many people enjoy—overeating, excessive drinking, pill taking, staying up at night, engaging in promiscuous sex, driving too fast, and smoking (Belloi, 1973). Maintaining health means special effort—exercising regularly, going to the dentist, practicing contraception, ensuring a harmonious family life, and submitting to screening examinations. More fundamentally in recent decades, we have steadfastly sanctified individual freedom while progressively narrowing it through relying more heavily upon a beneficent state. The idea of individual responsibility has been submerged by emphasis upon individual rights, to be guaranteed by government and delivered by public and private institutions. As a result, the costs of sloth, gluttony, alcoholic intemperance, reckless driving, sexual indulgence, and smoking have become a national burden. In truth, the "right" to health depends upon the personal obligation to preserve one's own health almost as a public duty. Accordingly, individuals should expect access to health information and services of quality without unmanageable financial barriers. Unfortunately, people have been led to believe that national health insurance, more doctors, and greater use of high-cost, hospital-based technologies will improve the health of the nation. As can be seen, none of these can replace individual attention to health (Farquhar, 1978).

All of these factors suggest that the behavior of American adults might be changed if there were adequate programs of health education that stressed the pleasures of health in primary and secondary schools and colleges. The view that children have of health is couched largely in negative terms with stress on health hazards and prohibitions. Children tire of "scrub your teeth," "don't eat that junk," "go to bed," and "get some exercise." Almost in a contrary fashion, by the time they are sixteen, they expect to have cars, to drink, to smoke, and to become sexually active. If they demur, they may be regarded as "sissies." Peer group pressure to "do wrong" is hardly balanced by the limp protestations of permissive parents, nervously keeping up with the Joneses in homes crammed with snacks and bars. There is little counterbalancing emphasis on the satisfactions and pleasures of physical well-being.

The barriers to the assumption of individual responsibility for one's health are a lack of sufficient interest in and knowledge about what is preventable and about the pleasures of health. Meanwhile, the idea of individual responsibility has been eroded by stress on individual rights, the responsibility of society-at-large, and the steady growth of production and consumption. Changing human behavior involves sustaining and repeating an intelligible message, reinforcing it through peer pressure and approval, and establishing clearly perceived rewards which materialize in as short a time as possible. Advertising agencies know this, but it is easier to sell deodorants, cosmetics, and automobiles than health.

Knowles holds that people must become aware of the fact that the perpetuation of the present high cost of treatment-oriented medicine will result only in higher costs and greater frustration. The next major advances in the health of the American people will be determined by what individuals are willing to do for themselves and for society-at-large. If we are willing to follow the principles of healthy living, we can extend our lives and enhance our own and our nation's productivity. If parents can reassert their authority with their children, they can promote their offsprings' optimal mental and physical development. If we participate fully in private and public efforts to reduce the hazards of the environment, we can reduce the causes of premature death and disability. If we are unwilling to do these things, we can anticipate steadily rising costs of health care, with little improvement in health. Individuals can either remain the problems or become the solutions to them (Knowles, 1977).

Knowles suggests a number of practical steps that could be taken to promote the health of our future adult population:

1. Support the best possible integration of health education into the school system, stressing measures that the individual can take to preserve personal health and minimize environmental hazards. Children are impressionable and their attitudes, knowledge, and habits will determine the health of the nation. In the majority of schools, health education is assigned low or no priority. Curricular materials need to be developed, health educators recruited and trained, and courses on health education given central importance.

2. Support expanded physical education that will meet the daily activity needs of children and ensure that each child learns enjoyable athletic and recreational skills during elementary school. Failure to acquire these skills shuts off valuable opportunities for recreation and physical fitness in later life.

3. Support a greater national commitment to research in health education and preventive medicine with emphasis on epidemiologic studies, cost-benefit analysis, and the most effective and least offensive ways of changing human behavior. The less than 0.5 percent for health education and 2.5 percent for preventive medicine of the total national health expenditure should be increased to at least 5 percent and preferably 10 percent of that total.

4. Support increased taxes on the consumption of tobacco and alcohol, public education programs on the hazards of their use, restriction on advertising, and subsidies to help producers in agriculture and industry shift to other products.

5. Devote more attention to the family as the basic social unit of the nation. Parents should be helped to use genetic counseling and family planning, to promote the proper intellectual, emotional, and physical development of their children, both at home and in school, and to set an example of individual responsibility in their own life styles.

The shadows of disease and unhealthy habits follow poverty and ignorance. The greatest benefits can be obtained through preventive medicine and health education measures aimed specifically at impoverished minority groups in urban as well as rural areas. Quite beyond these direct measures, total health depends on the eradication of poverty and ignorance; the availability of jobs; adequate transportation, recreation, and housing; the level of public safety; and an aesthetically pleasing and physically benevolent environment. Improved health follows those elements which are central to the quality of life.

Knowles points out that individuals have the power—indeed, the responsibility—to maintain their own health. However, individuals are powerless to control disease-provoking environmental pollutants, except as they become knowledgeable enough to participate in public debate and to support government controls. Here we must depend on the wisdom of experts, the results of research, and a national will to legislate controls for our protection in the face of short-term adjustments in our national economy.

All of these considerations highlight the importance to adult society of health education for children. If we are to reach children successfully, however, it is essential to bring their point of view into the health care system. Collaboration between the health and educational systems is needed in order to develop effective strategies and methods for health education and to counteract peer and advertising pressure to engage in health threatening activities.

Medical Ethics

Before enumerating the apecific advocacy issues in health care for children, some traditional positions of thinkers in medical ethics should be noted (Dedek, 1975; Reiser, 1977). The venerable Oath of Hippocrates stresses the obligation of the physician to do no harm. More recently, the World Health Organization spelled out the ethical responsibilities of physicians in the 1948 Declaration of Geneva, largely in reaction to the abuse of the physician's role in Nazi Germany. Subsequently, in 1964, the Declaration of Helsinki made more explicit principles regarding the ethics of research, and the 1970 Declaration of Oslo was addressed to the ethics of abortion (Bliss, 1975).

Although these ethical statements were not specifically designed for children, they do offer general guidelines for the application of medical ethics. Bliss and Johnson recommend specifying treatment aims in a given situation, and then ascertaining whether or not the aims are right in principle and whether or not the aims are in conflict among themselves. They suggest that methods of applying the aims be examined critically from the point of view of whether or not they are workable, whether or not the method fulfills the aims, and whether or not the method itself is morally right. They then encourage examination of the long-term results, whether or not there is a morally unacceptable spinoff, whether or not the results invalidate the aim or the method, and whether or not there is a limit to a physician's responsibility for the later results of present actions. They further call attention to the checks and balances on medical practice in the form of professional codes, ethical committees, laws, religious beliefs, and other cultural values.

These points lay the foundation for the physician's responsibility to clearly define diagnostic and therapeutic strategies in the light of the patient's interests. More than the other child caring systems, the ethical base of medicine, then, is a firm foundation for the additional step of assuming degrees of responsibility for children through both individual and class advocacy. Pediatricians, in particular, are focusing attention on their roles as advocates for children (Seidel, 1976; Task Force on Pediatric Education, 1978). As illustrations of current advocacy issues, four topics will be touched upon: the long-range impact of medical interventions, the effects of hospitalization, informed consent, and the confidentiality of health records for children.

The Long-Range Impact of Medical Interventions

Increased attention is being devoted to the rights of the unborn child. These can be stated positively in terms of a child's right to be born a "healthy child" or a "wanted child," or, negatively, as a child's right not to be born defective or "unwanted." The central issues are birth control, which eliminates conception and the possibility of life, through contraception or sterilization of adults to abortion of a living fetus. In the broadest sense, population control hopes to create an environment that is hospitable to the existing population and for children yet to be born. Although there has been a movement to provide abortion simply at the request of a pregnant woman, the trend has been to regard abortion as a decision to be made between physician and patient when it is not morally repugnant to either.

The controversial nature of birth control makes it a major political and constitutional issue. When abortion is performed because of the likelihood of a devastating inherited disease, a decision can be made for the unborn child to eliminate the possibility of living with that disease. The ethical standards applied to genetic counseling in these cases are clearly within the realm of advocacy, in that the interests of the unborn child are assessed and taken into account. The thesis is that a child has the right not to be born as a disabled organism. Just as some defective fetuses are naturally aborted through miscarriage, medicine can also eliminate the prospect of live birth of the fetus through the act of therapeutic abortion. The ethical and emotional issues are obviously complex, including the long-range effects of abortion on the parents (Francke, 1977).

In the matter of unwed teenage pregnancy, the psychological futures of both the young mother and the unborn child are at stake. Whether abortion is in the interests of both or whether giving birth to the child and raising or placing the child are more desirable alternatives raises critical advocacy issues. Health personnel are placed in a direct role, not of prescribing management in these situations, but of helping the affected young mother, father, and their parents devise a solution. The application of advocacy skills is particularly important in these situations, in which it is imperative that the people concerned be helped to make a decision that will be in the interests of all, including the unborn child.

A related area, from the point of view of the newborn, is that of euthanasia. The criteria used in determining whether or not a defective baby receives life-saving efforts or is actively deprived of life have yet to be defined. In practice, the use of euthanasia is widespread, but some believe that even a profoundly retarded and defective infant should have the benefit of whatever existence lies in store. In these cases the physician is placed in the position of advocating life or death for the organism. It is evident that such decisions are often based upon spot judgments without a clear rationale. Professionally developed guidelines are needed.

Another area of potential threat is genetic engineering, which places judgment in human hands about the nature of a human being. The most serious of all human problems created by biological research is the imminent power to alter the genetic structure of the species. This is a matter of extreme importance in terms of class advocacy for children, and for society generally.

Another area of current concern is screening for genetic disorders. The matter of screening children for presence of the XYY genotype was brought to public attention dramatically. When the association of an extra Y chromosome with tall stature, mental retardation, and aggressive behavior was first made, the finding had a profound impact on the scientific community, the legal and medical professions, and the public at large. The reason for the excitement was unclear because only 11 cases were reported in the world literature of what was then considered a rare syndrome (Jacobs, 1965). Other investigators began to look for persons with the extra Y chromosome among tall retarded inmates of institutions for criminal offenders, discovering more than a hundred of them in a scant four years. The instant appeal of these findings was partly because the possible defense against punishment for violent behavior was obvious (Jarvik, 1975).

The novelty of the XYY approach was that aggressive behavior could be regarded as an inherent predisposition (Witkin, 1976). This idea led to screening for this genotype early in life by a Harvard project (Culliton, 1975). Overlooked was the fact that home environment, early upbringing, and a host of social-cultural factors have either reinforcing or inhibiting effects on genetic predispositions. The project was discontinued because of the likelihood that the financial, emotional, and social costs of screening were contrary to the interests of the affected children. In other genetic disorders the same question arises: Is it in the interests of individuals to know that they possess genetic predispositions? Are the benefits of such knowledge to society sufficient to override the individual's interests? Because these questions must be answered in both categorical and individual ways, screening for genetic disorders of any kind deserves extremely careful consideration.

Another controversial issue is raised by procedures that change the sex of a child because of the presence of abnormal genital organs or injury to them, such as to the penis. At the present time there is a trend toward the surgical conversion of children with ambiguous genitalia during early life in the belief that if this is done prior to three years of age, the psychological gender of the child can be molded so as to correspond to the surgically created gender. Recent evidence suggests that gender identity begins during the second year of life. The long-range implications of sex change, from the point of view of the child and later adult life, are complicated by the changing state of knowledge and surgical techniques, in addition to considering the question of what that child as an adult would have desired (Westman, 1975).

Another area is the long-range impact of routine surgical interventions on children. Whether a circumcision or a tonsillectomy, one needs to take into account the long-range social and psychological effects of procedures that may or may not have medical benefits. The history of past routine tonsillectomies which were found to be medically unjustified illustrates the point. Similar questions have been raised about the true benefits of routine circumcision, which is a direct assault on the phallus at a time when the infant is extremely susceptible to conditioning. Moreover, the long-range psychological impact of the loss of the foreskin for the male has not been established (Kaplan, 1977; Thompson, 1975).

The Impact of Hospitalization on Children

Nothing has been more surprising to the public than that the interests of children have been ignored in children's hospitals themselves. An extensive literature has developed on the effects of hospitalization on children, particularly during the early years. Although much progress has been made in using that knowledge to reduce the adverse effects of hospitalization, it is still true that the convenience of adults more than the interests of children influence the physical structure, operations, and milieus of children's hospitals. There are notable exceptions, but the fact that they are exceptions signifies that, in general, hospitals and physicians have yet to apply knowledge of the impact of hospitalization on children.

The adverse effects of hospitalization vary with the age of the child. Even at birth, only recently have widespread efforts been made to promote emotional bonding of mothers and infants (Annexton, 1978). During the first three years of life even brief separations from parents can have significant long-range effects. Extended periods of separation, particularly from the ages of eight to 18 months, can influence the course of personality development through the sapping effects of an anaclitic depression. In addition to the disruption of family and home life, various aspects of the hospital experience engender phobic responses and traumatic anxiety. In a broader sense children's needs for recreational and educational activities are often not met in hospitals. And frequently the staff and parents do not effectively interpret the facts of illness, surgery, diagnostic and treatment procedures and prognosis, leaving children at the mercy of their fantasies (Robertson, 1962; Bergmann, 1965; Haller, 1967; Vernon, 1965).

Informed Consent and Children

The doctrine of informed consent reflects the ancient concern of Anglo–American law with the individual's right to be free from the conduct of others that affronts bodily integrity, privacy, and individual autonomy. In the medical setting, the doctrine originated primarily with respect to surgery.

The systematic examination of informed consent ethics began after the Nuremberg trials of World War II when the brutal research conducted on concentration camp victims was revealed. In part because of that extreme situation and later events, such as the maldevelopment of the upper extremities resulting from the use of thalidomide in Europe in 1962 and 1963, and the injection of mentally retarded children with hepatitis virus at Willow Brook State School on Staten Island in 1966, rules for proxy consent for children involved in federally funded research have been mandated by the Department of Health, Education and Welfare. These rules include rigorous requirements that such research be reviewed by committees when there is a risk for a child.

Before beginning a discussion of obtaining informed consent for treatment or research with children, it is appropriate to note that serious questions are being raised in the literature about the possibility of ever obtaining informed consent even for adults. Informed consent procedures have been described as "elaborate rituals," in which messages sent often do not correspond to messages received, resulting in the passage of words, but not in what could be called a comprehending, understanding, informed state (Ingelfinger, 1972). If there is credibility to the idea that adults are not giving truly informed consent, even though it may appear that they are so doing, the matter becomes even more complicated for children.

Strictly speaking, informed consent for minors has been equated with parental permission for actions involving people below the age of majority, now 18. The term "consent" implies actions involving oneself, as for a child, whereas "permission" may imply acting on behalf of another, as by parents. The presumption is that the relationship between parents and child is a normal, loving one. When this is not the case, a nonparental guardian is sometimes the source of permission. It is evident that parental permission and the direct consent of minors overlap in a gradient that relies completely upon parental permission during the early years and includes the possibility of sole consent as the minor nears the age of majority. Under certain circumstances, where physical insult to a child is significant and where the parent's conflict of interest is overt, such as for organ donation, parental permission alone does not constitute adequate protection and a child may participate in the decision making, in some instances with the aid of a court-appointed advocate.

In actual practice under English common law, minors under the age of 12 are not deemed capable of consenting to medical or psychiatric treatment or investigative research. Thus, unless in a life-threatening emergency, or if the minor is emancipated, a doctor who treats a child without parental permission risks liability for assault and battery. To facilitate medical care for adolescents, many state laws now allow minors to consent to treatment for specific kinds of medical problems, such as venereal disease, drug or alcohol abuse, birth control, and abortion.

The state statutes that permit minors' consent to health care are in response to four situational categories (American Academy of Pediatrics, 1974b):

1. The health need is of such a sensitive and private nature that youths are unlikely to tell their parents until either the condition or complications have progressed to the point when they no longer can be hidden, for example, venereal disease, alcoholism and drug abuse.
2. Runaway youths who will not seek care because to do so would reveal their whereabouts to their families.
3. Youths who have acute illnesses or injuries when away from home or when parents are otherwise unavailable and to delay emergency care would prolong pain, suffering, risk complications or endanger life.
4. Youths who have assumed an adult life style and are partially or fully "emancipated," such as those who work and substantially support themselves. Included are those who are married and are serving in the armed forces.

None of these state laws requires a physician to treat youths solely on their own consent, but they enable care when necessary to protect health. It is important, therefore, that a concerted, but noncoercive, effort be made to assist the dependent teenager ultimately to involve parents to obtain the benefit of their support and guidance. The health professional may well serve as an intermediary in restoring interrupted intrafamily communication and unity which could not have come about otherwise.

In some states, the "mature minor" doctrine is evolving in response to the needs and rights of "emancipated" youth. The following criteria can be helpful in determining whether that doctrine applies in marginal cases (American Academy of Pediatrics, 1974b).

1. The minor makes most decisions about the conduct of daily affairs.
2. The minor independently moves to and from home.
3. Even though supported by parents, the minor earns personal expense money and manages day-to-day financial matters.
4. The minor makes medical appointments independently and can state needs, and is able and motivated to follow recommendations.
5. The minor appears to understand the risks and benefits of proposed procedures, and can give informed consent.
6. The minor is unable to communicate with parents about thoughts and concerns.

The ultimate conflict in matters of minors' consent is between the basic rights and responsibilities of parents concerning their children and the emerging concept that youths have the right to make decisions relating to their bodies and their care. When the preservation of privacy and confidentiality affects the utilization of health care by youth, the conflict must be resolved. The resolution should not be entered, however, without full awareness of the implications of privileged communication which can readily be abrogated by court order. Confidentiality is discussed in detail in Chapter 12.

When informed consent is obtained from a minor, the matter of confidentiality between the minor and the physician vis-a-vis the parents is automatically raised. The complex nature of confidentiality is illustrated by Wigmore's four criteria for determining whether a particular relationship is judged to merit protection by privilege (Slovenko, 1966):

1. The communications must originate with the expectation that they will not be disclosed.
2. Confidentiality must be essential to the full and satisfactory maintenance of the relation between the parties.
3. The confidential disclosure must be one which community opinion sedulously fosters.

4. The injury that would accrue to the relationship by the disclosure of the communications must be greater than the benefit thereby gained for the correct disposal of litigation.

These principles emphasize the gravity of invoking privileged communication under any circumstances, but particularly that which shuts off communication between parents and children. Consequently, states have enacted statutory protection so that youngsters can invoke confidentiality in order to secure treatment for venereal disease or drug abuse without the knowledge of their parents. The controversial issues of teenage pregnancy, abortion, and the dissemination of birth control information do not ordinarily have that kind of statutory privilege.

Of extreme importance in matters involving youth is the fact that withholding information from parents inherently jeopardizes the parent–child relationship. Most of these situations can be handled therapeutically, and information can be brought to the awareness of the parents, strengthening the child–parent relationship. If it is necessary to invoke confidentiality in a way that excludes the parents, there is not an open relationship between the youngster and the parents. This fact in itself indicates the need for therapeutic intervention, and, if sensitively handled, the information may be a stimulus to improving the relationship. The premature invocation of statutory confidentiality is often based upon a failure to understand the parent–child relationship and to unduly emphasize protecting the child from painful disclosure and punishment or misunderstanding at the hands of the parents. To withhold this information from the parents might in the long range continue a pathological relationship and replace the possibility for therapeutic intervention with a greater problem in the parent–child relationship. Put another way, it is usually in the youth's interests to promote communication within the family on significant matters.

A more detailed consideration of the concept of informed consent is in order before proceeding. This applies to both parental permission and to the consent of a child deemed capable of doing so. Four elements of informed consent in making decisions regarding treatment or participating in a research investigation are as follows (Meisel, 1977):

1. Voluntariness—patients must be free from coercion and from unfair persuasion and inducements.
2. Information—patients must be informed of the risks, discomforts and side effects; the anticipated benefits; the available alternatives and their risks, discomforts and side effects and the likely consequences of no treatment. All of this must be provided in simple language.
3. Competency—patients are presumed to have the capacity to comprehend information to the extent that a "reasonable" person

would do so. If the patient is not "competent" or of "sound mind" any decision is invalid.

4. Understanding—this can be construed to mean that as long as a "reasonable" person would have understood the information, understanding can be assumed. Or it can be construed to refer to whether or not the patient actually understood. Courts thus far have followed the first principle.

When all of these elements have been satisfied, the parents and child can be considered "informed," and thence in a position to give or withhold permission and consent.

Understandably, criteria for research on children that may lead to new knowledge and benefit to them and others have received special attention (Duffy, 1973; Romano, 1974). There is general agreement that the information to be obtained through the research must warrant whatever risks are involved for the child. Furthermore, the investigation must be conducted by properly qualified persons, all of the criteria for informed consent must be satisfied, and the welfare, safety, and comfort of the subject must remain paramount and, should the subject require special aid, it must be available.

The more fundamental question of whether nontherapeutic research should be done at all on uncomprehending subjects who are unable to give consent has been addressed. English common law has been construed by some to hold that a child, even with parental or guardian permission, should not be subjected to research unless there is a direct potential benefit for the child. Curran and Beecher state, "Where the research is therapeutic, a minor may be included if informed consent is obtained from the parents or guardian. Where the research is not therapeutic, minors may be included if 14 years of age or older and if intelligent and mature enough to give informed consent. Parental consent is also required for discernible risks or hazards. Children under 14 may participate in clinical investigation which is not for their direct benefit where the studies are sound, promise important new knowledge and pose no discernible risk" (1969).

Campbell points out that non-beneficial research on children has been permitted in England and the United States when four conditions have been met:

1. The use of children as a "last resort," that is, legally competent subjects are either not appropriate or unavailable.
2. There is no significant risk.
3. There is a firm medical basis for expecting a significant benefit for others.
4. Consent is provided by a legally authorized representative of the subject.

In the light of these principles, it is evident that informed consent for research is problematic for children of all ages, particularly the very young. Accordingly, the National Commission for the Protection of Human Subjects of Biomedical and Behavioral Research has substituted "assent" by the child for consent and "parental permission" for the consent of parents. In general, the Commission felt that children with normal cognitive development become capable of meaningful assent after the age of 7. These children should be provided with a "fair explanation" and invited to sign a form analogous to that used for "informed consent." In most cases the deliberate objection of a child should be construed as a veto, except when the only way a child might receive a diagnostic or therapeutic modality is by participating in the research project. Under these circumstances, the parent or guardian may make decisions that override the school age child's objections. In some situations, however, the objections of teenagers to parental decisions might prevail (NCPHSBBR, 1977).

Because of the complexity of obtaining informed consent that appropriately includes parental permission and assent of the child, a third party may be useful in an advocate role to aid the child and parents in arriving at a decision. Thereby, the parents, the child, and the professionals can be assisted in understanding the mutual concerns and intentions.

A specific clinical area in which informed consent is especially complex is in a child's donation of an organ, specifically a kidney (Fost, 1977). In these cases simple parental permission is insufficient. There has been a general reluctance to permit organ donation by children because of their incapacity to authorize it knowingly and the possibility that, when they attain maturity, they might have a different view about having lost a kidney during their childhood. On the other hand, it might be contrary to the best interests of the child to be deprived of the opportunity to donate a kidney. The following considerations can be applied to a potential child donor situation:

1. Renal donation can be justified when there is likely benefit to the donor, or the donor is capable of giving informed consent, or analysis suggests that a rational person, in the situation of the prospective donor, would agree.
2. Age is not a meaningful index of the capacity to give informed consent in this area.
3. Children have the same potential benefits from renal donation as adults and should not be categorically excluded.
4. Because of the overt conflict of interests faced by parents in sibling donations, the use of a *guardian ad litem* and court proceedings is indicated in assuring the validity of a minor's organ donation.

The principle that the donation must be of likely benefit to the donor or in the best interests of the donor is the most important (Katz, 1972).

Thus, a Massachusetts court authorized a renal transplant from a sibling at Peter Bent Bringham Hospital on hearing testimony that the donor would probably suffer "serious emotional impact" if his brother died and concluded that the operation was "necessary to the donor's future welfare and happiness." Having found the procedure to be beneficial to the donor, parental consent was considered valid, and the hospital was protected against future vulnerability. There was also direct testimony from the donor, a 14-year-old twin, who demonstrated his understanding of the significant facts, his close relationship with his brother, and his desire to have the operation done. His only question, in fact, was why it was any of the court's business.

Confidentiality of Health Records for Children

There is widespread concern about the confidentiality of children's medical records. Proposals for reporting systems that would permit government monitoring of various conditions of childhood have been made for the collection of useful data. At the same time, there is concern about the possible short- and long-range adverse effects on children of transmitting information beyond the confidential patient–physician relationship. Public knowledge of neurological and mental disorders poses significant hazards of stigmatizing the affected person. In response to these concerns, the American Orthopsychiatric Association adopted a policy statement on the confidentiality of health records (American Orthopsychiatric Association, 1975; Schuchman, 1978).

In the view of the American Orthopsychiatric Association, the compilation and computerization of data on individuals by government agencies, health and social service providing agencies, and insurance carriers has become an increasing threat to the privacy and security of the individual. The availability of such data to those beyond whom it was initially and knowingly given by the individual has become especially threatening because it is frequently impossible to assure or verify the accuracy of data collected by computers, and the data can too readily be obtained by others without the individual's knowledge or consent.

The providers of health and social services need to create some record of their evaluation, diagnosis, treatment, and results in order to provide continuous quality care. This information is highly personal, especially in the provision of services for emotional problems. Treatment in this area involves disclosing personal information, intimate feelings, and attitudes. It is critical that society maintain at least one place for the individual to share and discuss feelings with another individual with assurance that these matters will be kept private and confidential. In order to meet the need for records and to protect the individual, the following principles should be observed:

1. No distinction should be made in both rights and responsibilities for the maintenance of privacy and confidentiality of health and social services records among those who are providing the care. This includes nurses, psychologists, social workers, and all related service providers who participate in the delivery of services.

2. All materials in the record should be shared with the consumer, who shall be informed of the implications of the materials to be shared, and who shall have the right to decide what information may be shared with anyone beyond the immediate provider of service. At no time shall any part of the record be available without the consumer's written consent or that of legal guardian.

3. Only that data required for a given legitimate purpose should be requested and provided. Service providers have a responsibility to ensure the specificity, accuracy, and validity of data shared with third parties. Data should not be consumer-identifiable when provided for actuarial and other research purposes, and in other situations in which consumer identity is not required.

4. Where the primary consumer or patient is a child or adolescent, the interest of the child shall be paramount and take precedence over those of others. When a family is involved as a unit, the rights of each must be safeguarded while joint problems are handled. Thus, for example, financial or sexual information about the parents should not be available to the child or adolescent; the child's experience with drugs or sex equally should be unavailable to the parents except as such matters are dealt with during the conjoint therapeutic process. The provider of service has the responsibility to maintain records in a current and relevant condition and to expunge material which is out-of-date and no longer appropriate. The contents of the record shall be discussed with the parent and child, as appropriate, and those parts kept separate which should remain the property of each family member separately.

5. Institutions, agencies, and private providers should reevaluate their processes for data requesting, sharing, and handling and make them specific to the person and situation being dealt with. In short, the record stands in place of the person and should be approached and treated with the same consideration due to the consumer as a person. Consistent with the implications of third-party payment procedures, as well as the need to protect the service provider, records should be used only in the provision of service and on the behalf of the consumer. Under no circumstances should it be possible or acceptable to use a clinical record in any criminal procedure

or investigation, or for credit or employment purposes, without the informed and specific consent of the consumer.

6. A dual record system, utilizing working notes and a health care record (or a social service record) is appropriate and should be instituted by health care and social care providers. The working notes are the work product of the provider and should be the property of and maintained in possession of the provider. They should contain all the information necessary to the provider for serving the consumer, including tests, diagnoses, treatment, speculations, doubts, possibilities, and questions to be dealt with at another time. These notes should not be available to any other person or institution; they should not be subject to disclosure or discovery procedures and should be destroyed when no longer relevant to current service delivery.

7. Health and social service records should be separate from academic performance records in school systems.

It is evident that once information passes from the person with whom a patient has a confidential relationship, there is little sense of personal responsibility to protect that information. At that point sensitivity to the personal significance of the information is lost. Furthermore, disclosure of confidential information can be required in a court of law. Those who keep health records are well advised to prepare them to be read by their patients and for possible later public exposure. In Chapter 12 a more extended treatment of confidentiality is offered.

Child Abuse and Neglect

The syndrome of child abuse and neglect will be used as an example of an interdisciplinary approach to a clinical program requiring advocacy. It is a useful example because the public response to child abuse and neglect dramatically illustrates the manner in which society responds to a community problem by dealing with surface manifestations rather than causes (Soman, 1974). Through an interdisciplinary approach, the health system can strike at the causes of this complex social problem (Martin, 1976).

Because it has been more clearly defined, child abuse will be our central focus, although only one in five neglected children are also physically abused. Child abuse has existed for centuries with varying degrees of acceptance by society. In earlier times, the destruction of children considered undesirable for religious, political, or economic reasons, or because they were defective or female, was culturally approved. In Biblical times,

Herod destroyed an entire sector of male infants in his district. During the fourteenth century, unwanted babies were thrown into the Thames River without significant interference by society; and during the Industrial Revolution young children were beaten and forced to perform dangerous and unhealthy tasks for long hours in filth-ridden environments. The works of Dickens, Hardy, and the Brothers Grimm vividly portray the lot of children exploited by adults.

The first systematic legal intervention on behalf of an abused child occurred in the United States in 1874. Ironically, the outcry was raised by the American Society for the Prevention of Cruelty to Animals. The child involved in this case, who was malnourished and regularly beaten by her adoptive parents, obtained legal protection on the basis that she belonged to the animal kingdom.

In a broad sense, violence against children is rooted in culturally determined practices of child rearing, with a higher reported incidence among the lower educational and socioeconomic strata of society and broken families (Lystad, 1975). Gil significantly concluded, however, that the most serious form of child abuse is still inflicted by society rather than by parents. He points to societal abuse of children as signified by infant mortality, hunger and malnutrition, poverty, inadequate medical care, and poor education in addition to sanctioned corporal punishment in schools. The American culture encourages the use of a certain measure of physical force in rearing children. For Gil (1970), child abuse is a reflection of a society that condones violence. He holds that as long as society models the abuse of children through permitting them to grow up in poverty and deprivation, parents who subject them to violence will continue to reflect the broader social abuse of children. Although the opposite is also true—society reflects the behavior of its adults—the point that child abuse and neglect cannot be viewed outside of their social context is certainly valid.

Although the radiological clues were reported earlier, child abuse was first brought dramatically to the attention of the medical profession at the 1960 annual meeting of the American Academy of Pediatrics when Kempe identified the "battered child syndrome" (1962). He described the most severe form of abuse to children who were physically battered with resulting injuries such as fractured bones. Since that time a spectrum of maltreatment has been included in the syndrome of child abuse and neglect (Fontana, 1973). A strict definition of child abuse is limited to children who suffer from serious physical harm or sexual molestation inflicted by other than accidental means by those responsible for their care or others exercising temporary or permanent control over children. Neglected children are those whose physical or mental condition is seriously impaired as a result of the failure of those responsible for their care to provide adequate food, shelter, clothing, physical protection, or medical care necessary to sustain the life or health of the child (Department of Health, Education and Welfare, 1968).

A more inclusive definition of child abuse and neglect is the failure to provide a child with the care that circumstances demand. This is broad enough to take in all forms of child maltreatment, whether willful or not; whether physical or emotional; whether acts of omission or commission; and whether affecting the body or the mind, or both. In this light, physical abuse and the various forms of neglect are on a continuum ranging from the most to the least obvious. Each case must be determined on the facts: the age and the physical and mental condition of the child; the act or omission, or a combination of both; the reasons therefore, and whether an isolated occurrence or repetitive; and the impact on the child (Delaney, 1976).

STATISTICAL DATA ON CHILD ABUSE AND NEGLECT

Patterned after the 1963 Model Child Abuse and Neglect Reporting Law (DHEW, 1968; OCD, 1974), all 50 states rapidly enacted child abuse reporting laws which require physicians, nurses, teachers, social workers, and others to report suspected child abuse or neglect either to a social service department or to the police. At this time the current level of reported cases of child abuse and neglect remains incomplete because of the lack of uniform reporting between states (Katz, 1975). In 1977, a total of 466,940 children were reported in the ratio of two neglect cases to one abuse case. Of the cases investigated, 47 percent were substantiated and 53 percent were not found to warrant intervention by social agencies (American Humane Association, 1979). In addition, studies have shown that approximately 10 percent of all injuries seen in emergency rooms in children under the age of three are due to inflicted rather than accidental trauma. Furthermore, other studies suggest that 30 percent of all fractures seen in children under two years of age are inflicted by others (Kempe, 1975).

A profile of child abuse and neglect can be obtained from the 1977 national data collected by the American Humane Association (1979). The types of abuse reported were: minor physical injuries (contusions, abrasions), 51 percent; major physical injuries (fractures, subdural hematomas, internal injuries), 2 percent; sexual abuse, 11 percent; burns, scalding, 3 percent; congenital and environmental drug addiction, .1 percent; and unspecified physical abuse, 33 percent. The types of neglect reported were: physical neglect, 78 percent; medical neglect, 9 percent; emotional neglect, 8 percent; and educational neglect, 5 percent. A sense of the ages of children, equally divided between males and females, can be gained from the 1977 American Humane Association data: under the age of 2, 18 percent; from 3 to 5, 18 percent; from 6 to 8, 18 percent; from 9 to 11, 17 percent; from 12 to 14, 16 percent; and from 15 to 17, 13 percent. Males were somewhat higher in the lower age groups and females in the older groups. Families in which abuse occurred are likely to be larger and with children closer in age than average families.

The 1977 American Humane Association data indicated that of the persons reporting child abuse, approximately 33 percent were agency sources (public and private social agencies, schools, law enforcement, and hotlines); 11 percent were medical sources (hospitals, physicians, nurses, and coroners); 40 percent were individuals (neighbors, friends, relatives, siblings, victims, and self-referrals); and 16 percent were unspecified others. The 1977 American Humane Association data gives further details for individual referrals: parents themselves, 5 percent; relatives, 15 percent; neighbors, 17 percent; the affected child, 2 percent; and others, 1 percent. When the perpetrators of physical abuse were analyzed, the data disclosed the following: fathers, 26 percent; mothers, 57 percent; stepfathers, 4 percent; stepmothers, 1 percent; adoptive fathers, .1 percent; adoptive mothers, .1 percent; siblings, .4 percent; other relatives, 3 percent; sitters, .5 percent; and unknown, 8 percent.

CHARACTERISTICS OF ABUSING PARENTS

In a study of over 1,000 abusive and seriously neglecting families, Kempe found that deliberate, premeditated, and willful abuse—clear-cut "cruelty to children"—accounts for only 5 percent of the entire group (1975). Those parents had lifelong aggressive personality disorders unlikely to change through psychiatric intervention. In another 5 percent, one of the parents was suffering from psychosis, and the children were part of a delusional system to their great peril. The prognosis for establishing a reasonable parent–child relationship in those cases was poor. The remaining 90 percent of the abusive parents studied appeared to belong to a variety of nonspecific personality types.

The childhood experiences of the 90 percent of the abusing parents do set them apart from most parents. The majority of these parents were individuals who had received little nurturing love from their own parents. These abusive parents were exploited by their parents from their earliest childhoods, had to conform to rigorous standards of behavior, and had to support their own parents emotionally. Some were abused themselves (Jayaratne, 1977). In short, the abusing parents lacked childhoods with early dependency followed by gradual emancipation. These individuals missed adequate parenting experiences in their own childhoods and became distrustful of their own good qualities, feeling themselves inferior and deserving of punishment. They continued to seek a loving relationship and often married at a young age in the hope of gaining support from their spouses. Unfortunately, they tended to marry someone similarly deprived. The result was two needy individuals who clung to each other like struggling nonswimmers, with the result that both drowned emotionally.

Whether or not physical abuse occurs in a particular family depends upon the interaction of at least four factors (Kempe, 1972; Helfer, 1976):

1. Both parents, regardless of financial or social status, were themselves emotionally deprived children.
2. One child in the family is seen in a special, unrealistic way. The child is seen as demanding, unattractive, willful, spoiled and not living up to the parents' standards. The child also may possess personality or physical qualities making child rearing unusually stressful.
3. The parents experience a crisis, such as loss of job or an unwanted pregnancy. In this context the child's behavior, such as prolonged crying, may be interpreted as accusatory: "If you were a good mother or father, I wouldn't be crying like this."
4. Generally there is no lifeline or rescue operation available to the parents. They have no close friends, relatives or neighbors to whom they can turn in moments of stress.

In extreme cases, a study of murdered children and their killers found a pattern of long-term parental child maltreatment extending to the siblings and continuing after the murders (Kaplun, 1976). The victims were usually preschoolers born out of wedlock; the assailants, usually the mothers or their paramours, had backgrounds of assaultiveness and social deviance and killed in impulsive rage. These parents were refractory to counseling or treatment. The assault that killed the child was unpremeditated and impulsive, and similar assaults were directed against siblings or spouses before and after the killings.

Abuse by siblings as a factor in fully understanding the actual events in child abusing families has been increasingly recognized (Tooley, 1977). Older siblings may be implicated in repeated serious assaults on young children. Parents may hesitate to report or even to recognize such attacks for reasons which may vary considerably. In order to maintain intrafamilial solidarity, they may make a preconscious decision that the assault was "accidental" or normal "horseplay" overdone. Another kind of family arrangement is one in which parents placate an older child in order to forestall temper outbursts and attacks. That child then assaults a younger child, who is the family's "sacrificial lamb" and bears the brunt of physical punishment and deflects abuse from other family members. The parents refuse to recognize the resulting damage to the younger child, or they shrug it off. A third and more serious family pattern involves an older child acting out a parent's unconscious wish to be rid of a younger child, which can lead to life-endangering extremes and serious psychological sequelae.

A connection between alcoholism and physical abuse of children appears repeatedly in research reports on abused children. In examining situations in which child abuse and neglect are most likely to occur, families are found to be socially isolated, to have youthful and inexperienced parents, and to have a history of greater than average complications with pregnancies (Smith, 1974; Kent, 1975). It is interesting to note that these factors are common in alcoholic families.

Kempe maintains that alcohol plays a part in approximately one-third of child abuse cases (1972; Barton, 1978). In many more cases, alcohol can be related in some way to the family problem that led to the child abuse. Alcohol may play a major role in specific types of child abuse. For example, in a study of incest victims, alcohol abuse frequently seems to be a factor in father-daughter incest occurrences (Browning, 1977).

Personality characteristics associated with child abusers are also strikingly similar to the personality characteristics of alcoholic persons. Both alcoholics and child abusers are often described as having a low frustration tolerance, low self-esteem, impulsivity, dependency, immaturity, depression, problems with role reversals, difficulty in experiencing pleasure, and lack of understanding of the needs and abilities of infants and children (Spinetta, 1972).

In spite of all these negative characteristics, it is important to note that most abusing parents have affectional bonds with their children, who in turn depend upon and are loyal to them (Steele).

CHARACTERISTICS OF ABUSED CHILDREN

Although easily overlooked, children who are abused play a variety of roles in the violent behavior directed toward them. In Gil's 1967 survey, 29 percent of the children revealed deviations in social interaction and general function, 14 percent suffered from deviations in physical function, and 8 percent revealed deviations in intellectual functioning during the year preceding the abusive incident (Gil, 1970). Whether these factors precipitated the abuse or emerged as a consequence is not known. The evidence is, however, that prematurity, mental retardation, language delays, physical handicaps, behavior disorders, and physical illness occur more frequently than would be expected in abused children (Buchanan, 1977; Friedrich, 1976; Green, 1977). Temperamental factors are also important.

More significant is the fact that abused children are enmeshed in webs of family interactions in which they may play witting and unwitting provocative roles both as children and in later life. A study covering three generations of families of abused children supports the theme that children who experience violence during their childhoods have the potential of becoming violent members of society in the future (Silver, 1975). That study also found that some abused children cope with the emotional stress of physical abuse through identification with the aggressors. Their models for identification and later imitation show weak impulse control in general and direct physical expression of aggressive impulses in particular. In contrast, there are abused children who develop identities as "victims." Rather than becoming delinquents or criminals, they become victims. At an early age some children who are repeatedly battered learn to sense when it is time to leave or to be quiet. There are other children, however, who under similar circumstances perform the act or say the word that precipitates a beating. These children seem to have learned that love is equated with being hurt, and they establish a pattern of inviting assault and becoming victims.

EVENTS PRECIPITATING ABUSE

Child abuse results from the interaction between a child and a parent (or parents), with a stressful event serving to catalyze the actual episode of abuse. Given the predisposing characteristics of a parent and a child, stresses are likely to precipitate violence. A professional dealing with an incident of abuse initiated by a number of clearly definable crises may be tempted to believe that resolution of the problems creating the stress will, in turn, completely resolve the problem of abuse. This is a dangerous assumption. Resolution of a particular crisis may stop abuse for a time, but unless the family receives some form of support and therapy, abuse will probably recur with each subsequent crisis (McNeese, 1977).

The definition of a stressful event varies. An event viewed as a crisis by one family may be tolerated by another without resort to abuse. Although an abusive episode can be triggered by a trivial occurrence, it is more likely that the actual contributing event is genuinely emotionally stressful.

Emotional stresses that commonly initiate abuse are a death in the family, physical or mental illness in one or both parents, a major developmental change in a family member (e.g., a child becomes a rebellious adolescent or a parent faces a midlife crisis), or divorce or separation of the parents. A crisis may also be situational, but with clear emotional effects. Loss of a job or income, a move to a new community, or poverty and inadequate housing can tax a parent's emotional resources to the extent that violence results.

The following case history describes various circumstances that can bring about an incident of abuse (McNeese, 1977). A distinction is made between the stresses that contributed to the episode of abuse and the actual precipitating events. It becomes obvious that, although a seemingly minor event can trigger abuse, a complex of factors may play a contributing role.

A 19 year old mother called her obstetrician reporting she had hit her 6 week old baby and was afraid that she would really hurt him if she did not speak to someone.

Child Factors. The baby had been detained in the hospital after birth for treatment of bacteremia. After he was discharged, he had many minor illnesses including colds, moniliasis, and diarrhea. He was a fussy child and needed medication and special care.

Parent Factors. As a child, the mother had been abused by her own mother repeatedly. She spent time in child shelters from the age of 8 to the age of 18, when she married. Her parents disapproved of her husband. She had no experience in child care and had been ill with urinary tract infections during her pregnancy. At the time of evaluation, she still had an infection.

The father had a supportive family, but he ran away from home to join the armed forces at the age of 16. He had a quick temper and occasionally drank excessively.

Stresses. The car would not start. The telephone was disconnected because a friend had used it and left them with a $200 telephone bill. The father was under pressure at work and quit his job to return to school. A move to a new area was to take place in two weeks.

Precipitating Events. The parents had a fight, and the father stormed out of the house. The air conditioner broke down. The mother then repeatedly struck her baby.

THE IDENTIFICATION OF ABUSED CHILDREN

Because of the gravity of the problem and the obvious danger to children, as well as the hazards and injustice of unsubstantiated accusations, the diagnosis of child abuse is a matter of extreme importance and must be carefully established (Helfer, DHEW; Helfer, 1973). There is a delicate balance between protecting children and protecting parents from unwarranted instrusions into family privacy. There is also a continuum ranging from physical battering to emotional neglect, although the two may coexist. Inevitably, the distinction between appropriate physical discipline and abuse arises as well. The most severe instances of child abuse in the form of the "battered child" are most likely to be present in hospital emergency rooms and clinics; however, all health personnel should be alert to the possibility of child abuse.

A child who has one or more fractures which are in different stages of healing, or a head injury, bite marks, unusual burns, or injuries around the mouth is a possible abuse victim. Because of the deceptive stories given by parents about the injured child, the following crucial points in the history should be explored before accepting parents' explanation of a child's injury: (1) there may be a delay between the time that the injury occurred and the time that help is sought; (2) the history may be discrepant with the physical and X-ray findings; (3) a history may be elicited of previous accidents; and (4) the parents' reaction to suggested medical assistance may be inappropriate, for example, they may refuse indicated hospitalization. Additional factors that suggest child abuse are: (1) a history of violent practices used in rearing the parents; (2) the parents' negative attitude toward the child; (3) the presence of a precipitating crisis, such as intractable crying, an unwanted new pregnancy, or loss of job; and (4) the presence of parental social isolation.

Adult patients involved in or threatened by the possibility of committing child abuse may develop acute functional symptoms that result in their seeking emergency medical care. The possibility should be explored with parents who present functional symptoms, especially psychogenic weakness or paralysis (Mogielnicki, 1977). Another recently reported form of child abuse is through parental falsification of illness in a child or through production of illness, as in the case of a 14-month-old child who died from excessive feeding of salt (Meadow, 1977).

Although the usual statutory requirement is that suspected child abuse or neglect be reported to social protective services or law enforcement agencies, there is growing recognition that a thorough investigation before the diagnosis of child abuse is established should be carried out by an interdisciplinary child protection team (American Academy of Pediatrics, 1974a). For hospitalized children, accessibility to such a team can be easily arranged; however, the same approach can be used profitably with nonhospitalized suspected cases. An example of such an approach to suspected child abuse and neglect is the child abuse team established in 1968 at Children's Hospital in Pittsburgh (Evans, 1975). The child abuse team is made up of pediatricians, psychiatric social workers, attorneys, and child psychiatrists. The team not only aids in understanding a specific child's situation, but it can also carry out a treatment program which may include legal intervention. In the health system a team approach can be employed just as are renal, cardiological, and other specialty teams. The advantage of having a team based in the health system is not only that child abuse usually involves physical injury to the child, but also that the evaluation of child development is an area of expertise in the health system. The need is less protecting the child from further injury and more promoting the child's growth and development.

Child abuse is such a grave situation that it should be carefully diagnosed and treated on an individual case basis (Green, 1976; Kempe, 1976). The social service system alone is not prepared to make the diagnosis, nor are law enforcement officers. The health system is and should be involved in each case. Not only is there a 50 percent chance of social service nonverification of child abuse, but the adverse effects of false accusation, particularly if transmitted to a state or national register are tragic. In Milwaukee, Wisconsin, a young couple were reported as abusers by the county welfare department because their infant son had unexplained fractures. The department filed a petition to remove the baby from their custody because "they were shaking the child so hard they broke his bones." The parents were finally exonerated when medical testimony established that their child suffered from a rare metabolic defect which was associated with fractures in the absence of serious trauma. The parents' attorney pointed out that "we had a switch from child abuse to parent abuse." The mother said, "No one would listen to us or believe us, and everyone was accusatory. We're upset about the way it was handled, and we think our rights were violated."

A further indication of the need for the study of suspected child abuse within the health system is the complicated matter of sexual abuse of children (Walters, 1975). Although often regarded as involving attacks by strangers, similar to the rape of adolescent and adult women, the sexual abuser of a younger child is usually not a stranger, but the father, uncle, grandfather, or brother. Ambiguity enshrouds this area because incest may be a culturally condoned pattern and borders on sexual explorations that are a part of family life. Defining sexual child abuse is no easier than defining abuse in general.

The sexual abuse of children deserves special attention because numerous complex, multidetermined variables must be considered (Rosenfeld, 1977; Herjanic, 1978; Summit, 1978). Because sexual abuse in this context usually involves family members, it is really incest. A useful general definition of sexual abuse is exposure of a child to sexual stimulation within a given social-cultural context that is inappropriate for the child's age and level of development, ranging from seduction and sex play to sexual intercourse.

One problem in assessing sexual abuse is obtaining the facts. Initially, Freud theorized that childhood sexual molestation was a trauma suffered by all of his hysterical patients. He later concluded that the experiences reported by his adult patients were really memories of fantasies. It is, therefore, important that the status of the relationship between the child and the adult and the nature of the acts committed be verified.

Another vital consideration is the nature of family relationships and life style. There appear to be two types of incestuous families: (1) the ingrown family, whose members find it difficult to cultivate relationships outside the family and relate primarily to each other; and (2) the promiscuous family, in which sexual attitudes are poorly defined and sexuality is permitted with few limits. In many instances the incestuous relationships are distorted searches for caring and warmth on the part of the family members. The needy child or adult attempts to obtain nurturance through sexuality which overshadows the genital aspects. For example, some children try to prevent abandonment through holding their parents' marriage together by complying with invitations to sexual activity. The conscious or unconscious participation, or even initiation of the seduction, of the child is frequently described.

Because incest has been practiced under certain cultural circumstances, questions about its adverse effects have been raised. Although "normal adult adjustments" have been reported in sociological follow-ups of incestuous relationships, the adverse effects in our culture have been substantiated at both obvious and subtle levels. The outcome may be related as much to the family setting as the event itself. These are in the form of later prostitution and illegitimate pregnancies or adult frigidity or depressions, and behavior and learning disorders in children. Clinical work with children also discloses intense guilt and anger toward the parent who overtly or tacitly condones the incestuous acts.

While the child has been viewed as the abused party and one adult has most often been singled out as the abuser in legal cases, an understanding of the nature of family interactions indicates that the entire family must be evaluated in order to arrive at a useful treatment plan. Ultimately, the child is the "innocent" victim, but the resolution of the problem must take into account the child's role. It is evident that a strictly legal definition of sexual abuse is insufficient and careful diagnosis is required.

The most compelling reason for dealing with child abuse within the health system is that beyond an accurate diagnosis the greatest need is for treatment programs. The growing number of self-identifying child abusers points further to the need for easy access to interdisciplinary professional services. Through interdisciplinary teamwork, social workers learn about the limitations of hearsay evidence; physicians learn about expert testimony; lawyers learn about medical syndromes, such as "failure to thrive"; police learn about nonpunitive ways of helping families; and all professionals learn each other's language. The team approach permits the establishment of a diagnosis and of individualized, nonstigmatizing help for the family.

THE TREATMENT OF ABUSING FAMILIES

A professional person or team with sufficient knowledge, background, and understanding to put together the facts about a child's life experience and what will meet realistically the child's needs is required to coordinate a treatment plan. There is a critical need for an early decision as to whether a therapeutic or legal intervention is more appropriate (Schmitt, 1978). Care must be taken to ensure that additional child abuse and "parent abuse" does not take place through premature or inappropriate removal of the child from the family (Derdeyn, 1977). To determine the small, but significant, number of cases in which a new family and life is needed for the child, the following criteria suggest an unfavorable prognosis for treatment:

1. recurrent severe injuries of the child;
2. parental lack of concern about injury;
3. parental personality disorder (isolation, alcoholism, drug abuse, criminality);
4. child seen as intrinsically evil or bad by parent;
5. child not seen as separate entity by parent;
6. general lack of parental impulse control.

In Kempe's experience, 90 percent of abusive parents are treatable by reconstituting their sense of trust and by giving them support over a crucial period of a year or so. Four key treatment modalities are used in Kempe's program (1975):

1. Lay therapists to provide mothering to the needy family and a life line in moments of stress.
2. Parents Anonymous which is a group of abusive parents who meet in a group setting to derive help from each other.
3. A crisis nursery which can be used at any time, day or night, with no questions asked, for those hours or days of stress when the child can be quickly removed to a place of safety.
4. A therapeutic day care center where abusive parents can see their children *vis a vis* other children and where they can exchange feelings and experiences with other parents who are working out their difficulties. In those cases where the abused child has been in foster care for a period of time, the decision to safely return the child to the parents is based upon the parents' achievement of better self images, positive views of the child, learning to use life lines and successfully managing a crisis themselves.

Insight therapy appears to be contraindicated with many abusive parents because, if they relive their own deprived childhoods in the treatment process, they may become intensely depressed and suicidal. These parents are also so threatened by authority figures that individual psychotherapy may not be possible (Blumberg, 1977).

In Kempe's program within eight months, 80 percent of the families have their children back in their home permanently, 10 percent require more time, and in 10 percent of the cases termination of parental rights is recommended. The issues involved in the early and decisive termination of parental rights are discussed in Chapter 9.

In addition to programs for the parents, the need for direct therapeutic intervention with the child should not be overlooked (Green, 1978).

Early psychiatric involvement in cases of child abuse is indicated to determine both the child's role in provoking and reacting to the abuse. Because the children have been traumatized and because their own personality development has been affected, individual psychotherapy is frequently indicated. Psychotherapy can also be helpful in resolving the child's ambivalent feelings toward the abusing parent. Because some may be destined to become battering parents themselves, they deserve treatment to prevent the recurrence of the same situation in their later lives. Removal from home does not resolve a child's reactions to the abuse and creates an additional problem because of separation from parents. Unfortunately, most cases of child abuse are handled by social service departments simply through the decision for removal or nonremoval from the home and involvement of parents in rehabilitative work for themselves, overlooking the therapeutic needs of the child.

It is paradoxical that the dramatic national concern for protection of abused and neglected children has not been accompanied by an appropriate investment in restoring healthy developmental progress for them. These children live in frightening circumstances without sufficient help, doing their best to survive behind the walls of privacy which surround their families. More attention should be devoted to the well-being of the victims rather than simply mirroring the tendency of society to be concerned only with the control and rehabilitation of the aggressors.

CHILD ABUSE AND NEGLECT REGISTRIES

The early literature on child abuse and neglect emphasized the need for legislation to protect people who were required to report their suspicions regarding child abuse in relatively broad terms. As an extension of reporting procedures, state registries were developed and a national registry was proposed. As experience has accumulated with state reporting systems, however, it has become apparent that reporting systems can invade and harm the lives of children and their parents as easily as help them, if only through the stigmatizing effect of labeling people.

The major purpose of reporting legislation is to protect and help children. That protective purpose cannot be realized, however, until sufficient effort and funds are invested to improve the level of services available to the child and the family. Undue emphasis on reporting directs attention away from the pervasive social problems, such as poverty, of which child maltreatment is but one symptom. An emphasis on reporting also leads to the belief that once a report is made, care and treatment will automatically follow, which is not true in most cases (Sussman, 1975).

One reason for keeping a public record of child abusers was the early view that litigation would be needed against abusive parents. Experience has shown, however, that legal interventions are not needed in most instances. In Wisconsin, of statutorily reported child abuse cases, no court referral was needed in 82 percent of the cases; 78 percent of the children remained in their homes, only 12 percent were moved to foster homes, and 1 percent were institutionalized (Wisconsin Department of Health and Social Services, 1977).

Another purpose of state and national abuse registries was to keep track of the movement of abusive parents. A national registry was seen as facilitating the discovery of repeated injuries, increasing the likelihood that child abuse would be detected. Growing experience, however, shows that a direct transmission of reported cases from the state level to a national registry probably might lead to inaccuracy in 50 percent of the cases (American Humane Association, 1978). This degree of uncertainty argues against the validity of any large-scale registry.

Another purpose of a federal child abuse registry is the collection of data to guide federal planning and expenditures. This kind of information is already available through organizations such as the American Humane Association, illustrating that data can be collected without the need for an additional individual case reporting mechanism at the federal level.

In spite of evidence to the contrary, the illusion is still prevalent that child abuse and neglect are problems of poor people exclusively. Children of more affluent families, who receive their medical care in private practice settings where the relationship of the clinician to family, the payment structure, and the ethics of treating personal information are quite different, are more likely to have their injuries characterized as "accidents." It is easier to make the diagnosis of child abuse in an inner-city hospital where calling a poor minority mother a "bad parent" is acceptable. Thus, many middle-class child abuse and neglect cases do not appear in registries or journal articles. Any reporting system, thereby, runs the risk of discriminatory treatment of disadvantaged minority groups (Newberger, 1977).

A community cannot deal with child abuse unless it is known, so that some kind of reporting system is necessary. However, to be effective, such a system should be more than a case registry or a person to call. It should be based upon a community attitude that makes abuse and neglect a concern of everyone and rewards the reporter and the family by positive responses which both protect the child and help the parents. The existence of the national organization Parents Anonymous offers parents an increased opportunity to seek help in their communities.

Still, each community should develop a channel through which child abuse cases can be handled (DHEW, 1976). It is incumbent on each community to organize a skilled staff encompassing the talents of medicine, law, social service, nursing, homemaking, and child care for the benefit of families at risk. Early recognition, diagnosis, treatment, and, if necessary, legal intervention can be accomplished most effectively through integrated interdisciplinary collaboration. Economic savings of such a program to communities could come from reduced expenditures for foster home, court, and, later, prison costs. The savings in life and prevention of injury and disability would be immeasurable. Above all, the reduction of abuse and neglect in the next generation by preventing it in this one would be a major medical and psychosocial achievement.

SUMMARY

In summary, abusive parents are often lonely, isolated, and frustrated people. They probably received inadequate parental care in their own formative years. They usually single out one child for maltreatment, a child who constitutes a special source of irritation, who under stress loses self-control. The children at risk must be protected; however, children and abusers alike need understanding and treatment to permit the children to live and develop within their families without fear of brutality or neglect. The emphasis should be upon the developmental progress of the children, not simply upon eliminating the abuse.

Mandatory child abuse reporting in the states should lead to early diagnosis, treatment, and reaching out to potential abusers (Kempe, 1976), not just identifying child abusers and protecting children from them. Beyond that, abusing and neglecting parents should be encouraged to seek help for themselves voluntarily through such organizations as Parents Anonymous. Schools should be sensitized so that earlier intervention can take place prior to the battering that is detected in health care facilities. Generally, support is further needed for the improvement of the economic and social condition of families and, specifically, for providing lifelines and emotional support for abusing parents. The management of child abuse should seldom involve the courts, but should fall upon child protective services and health treatment resources. To the extent that child abuse can be diagnosed and managed within the health care system, the most appropriate, effective, and helpful care can be given. Prompt and effective legal intervention should be available in those few cases in which termination of parental rights is indicated.

The child abuse experience can be regarded as the beginning of a widening range of family support mechanisms. The health system is in a unique position to assume leadership in utilizing the processes of diagnosis and treatment in managing this social problem. As this happens, it will become evident that this approach to child neglect is an entree to helping many kinds of parents who are not fully meeting the emotional and developmental needs of their children.

Conclusion

This rising costs of health care have focused public attention on the problems and benefits of the health care system. Still, for too many American children, there are communication, motivation, educational, and financial barriers to adequate preventive and therapeutic health care. Furthermore, when available, health care for the young should be continuous with a preventive, developmental orientation. Episodic care is inefficient, costly, and omits preventive medicine for children.

Of greatest importance is the fact that many life-threatening conditions of childhood and adulthood are preventable. Just as sweeping changes occurred in the control of communicable diseases through the advent of sanitation in the previous century, the next major breakthrough could come because of the commitment of individuals to preserve and maintain their health through reducing the consumption of noxious substances and minimizing environmentally induced stresses.

At the present time many children are exposed to peer and mass media seductions into life styles that emphasize product consumption, passivity, and risk taking. Greatly needed are counterbalancing health education, parental, and social supports for attitudes favoring physically and mentally stimulating, pleasurable activities. These are needed to reduce the self-defeating aspects of life, currently expressed in the form of high levels of personal stress and substance abuse by both the young and the old.

The fundamental answers to the health of the nation lie less in expanding treatment facilities and more in preventing disorder through greater individual responsibility for one's health. In addition, public responsibility for minimizing environmental hazards to health, removing financial barriers to health services, and ensuring standards for quality care must be recognized and implemented. The aim is to increase and strengthen the capacity of communities, parents, and children to act on their own behalf as both health consumers and advocates.

A series of specific issues highlight the advocacy role of health care workers. Among them are the long-range implications of medical interventions, such as the rights of the unborn child, euthanasia, screening for genetic disorders, and sex change surgery. The impact of hospitalization on children brings out the need to consider carefully indications for hospitalizing children and orienting hospital milieus and personnel to the special requirements of children. Of great importance in medical and surgical treatment, research, and special situations such as organ donations are the issues involved in balancing informed parental permission and the consent of children of varying ages. The exposure of health records to computerized systems, the courts, and patients themselves necessitates treatment of the health record as an extension of the patient and calls for rearranging existing record-keeping approaches.

The syndrome of child abuse and neglect has been used as an illustration of the power of an interdisciplinary health-oriented clinical approach to a complex social problem requiring both individual and class advocacy. Because of the need to understand the circumstances of abuse and to help both abusing parents and the abused child through a coordinated and continuous treatment program, legal and social services alone cannot alleviate the causes of child abuse. Furthermore, the emphasis should be upon the developmental progress of the abused child and the integrity of the family, not simply the elimination of abusive behavior. For these reasons, each community should develop a parental assistance network with access to an interdisciplinary child protective team and a complementary range of therapeutic resources. Such a network opens the door to helping many kinds of parents who are not meeting the emotional and developmental needs of their children.

References

AMERICAN ACADEMY OF PEDIATRICS (1974a) *A Descriptive Study of Nine Health-based Programs in Child Abuse and Neglect.* Evanston, Ill.: American Academy of Pediatrics, April.

AMERICAN ACADEMY OF PEDIATRICS (1974b) "The Implications of Minor's Consent Legislation for Adolescent Health Care: A Commentary." *Pediatrics,* 54:481–485, October.

AMERICAN HUMANE ASSOCIATION (1979) *National Analysis of Official Child Neglect and Abuse Reporting.* Englewood, Colo.: American Humane Association.

AMERICAN ORTHOPSYCHIATRIC ASSOCIATION (1975) "Policy Statement of Confidentiality of Health Records." *Newsletter, American Orthopsychiatric Association,* Vol. 19, No. 1, August.

ANNEXTON, M. (1978) "Parent–Infant Bonding Sought in 'Birthing' Centers." *Journal of the American Medical Association,* 240:823–826.

BELLOI, N. B., AND BRESLOW, L. (1973) "Relationship of Health Practices and Mortality." *Preventive Medicine,* 2:67–81.

BERGMANN, T. (1965) *Children in the Hospital.* New York: International Universities Press.

BLISS, B. P., AND JOHNSON, A. G. (1975) *Aims and Motives in Clinical Medicine.* London: Pitman Medical.

BLUMBERG, M. L. (1977) "Treatment of the Abused Child and the Child Abuser." *American Journal of Psychotherapy,* 31:204–215.

BROWNING, D. H., AND BOATMAN, B. (1977) "Incest: Children at Risk." *American Journal of Psychiatry,* 134:69–72, January.

BUCHANAN, A. AND OLIVER, J. E. (1977) "Abuse and Neglect as a Cause of Mental Retardation." *British Journal of Psychiatry*, 131:458–467.

CAMPBELL, A. G. M. (1974) "Infants, Children and Informed Consent." *British Medical Journal*, 3:334–338.

CHILDREN'S DEFENSE FUND (1976) *Doctors and Dollars Are Not Enough.* Washington, D.C.: Children's Defense Fund.

COMPTROLLER GENERAL OF THE UNITED STATES (1975) *Improvements Needed to Speed the Implementation of Medicaid's Early and Periodic Screening, Diagnosis and Treatment Program.* GAO Report No. 1, MWD-75-13, January 3.

CULLITON, B. J. (1975) "XXY: Harvard Researcher Under Fire Stops Newborn Screening." *Science*, 188:1284–1285.

CURRAN, W. J., AND BEECHER, H. K. (1969) "Experimentation in Children." *Journal of the American Medical Association*, 210:77–83.

DEDEK, JOHN F. (1975) *Contemporary Medical Ethics.* New York: Sheed and Ward.

DELANEY, J. J. (1976) "New Concepts of the Family Court." Chapter in Helfer, R. E., and Kempe, C. H. (Eds.), *Child Abuse and Neglect: The Family and the Community.* Cambridge, Mass.: Ballinger.

DEPARTMENT OF HEALTH, EDUCATION AND WELFARE (1968) *The Child Abuse Reporting Laws: A Tabular Review.* Children's Bureau. Washington, D.C.: U.S. Government Printing Office.

DEPARTMENT OF HEALTH, EDUCATION AND WELFARE (1976) *How to Plan and Carry Out a Successful Public Awareness Program on Child Abuse and Neglect.* Washington, D.C.: Superintendent of Documents, Publication No. (OHD) 77-30089.

DERDEYN, A. P. (1977) "Child Abuse and Neglect: The Rights of Parents and the Needs of Their Children." *American Journal of Orthopsychiatry*, 47:377–387, July.

DUFFY, J. (1973) "Research with Children: The Rights of Children." *Journal of Child Psychiatry and Human Development*, 4:57–70.

EVANS, S. L., FISHER, G. D., AND REINHART, J. B. (1975) "Experience with a SCAN Program in a Children's Hospital." Presented at the 1975 Annual Meeting of the American Association of Psychiatric Services for Children.

FARQUHAR, J. W. (1978) *The American Way of Life Need Not Be Hazardous to Your Health.* Stanford, Calif.: Stanford Alumni Association.

FERSTER, E. Z. (1975) "The Excess Y Chromosome—How Should the Law Respond?" Chapter in Allen, R. C. (Ed.), *Readings in Law and Psychiatry.* Baltimore: Johns Hopkins University Press.

FONTANA, V. J. (1973) *Somewhere a Child Is Crying.* New York: Macmillan.

FOST, N. (1977) "Children as Renal Donors." *New England Journal of Medicine*, 296:363–367, February 17.

FRANCKE, L. B. (1977) *The Ambivalence of Abortion.* New York: Random House.

FRIEDRICH, W. N., AND BORISKIN, J. A. (1976) "The Role of the Child in Abuse: A Review of the Literature." *American Journal of Orthopsychiatry*, 46:580–590, October.

GIL, D. G. (1970) *Violence Against Children: Physical Child Abuse in the United States.* Cambridge, Mass.: Harvard University Press.

GREEN, A. H. (1976) "A Psychodynamic Approach to the Study and Treatment of Child-abusing Parents." *Journal of Child Psychiatry,* 15:414–429, Summer.

GREEN, A. H. (1977) "Psychopathology of Abused Children." *Journal of Child Psychiatry,* 16:92–103.

GREEN, A. H. (1978) "Psychiatric Treatment of Abused Children." *Journal of Child Psychiatry,* 18:356–371.

HALLER, J. A. (1967) *The Hospitalized Child and His Family.* Baltimore: Johns Hopkins University Press.

HELFER, R. E. *The Diagnostic Process and Treatment Programs on Child Abuse and Neglect.* DHEW Publication No. (OHD) 75–69.

HELFER, R. E. (1973) "The Etiology of Child Abuse." *Pediatrics,* 51:777–779.

HELFER, R. E., AND KEMPE, C. H. (1976) *Child Abuse and Neglect: The Family and the Community.* Cambridge, Mass.: Ballinger.

HERJANIC, B., AND WILBOIS, R. P. (1978) "Sexual Abuse of Children." *Journal of the American Medical Association,* 239:331–333, January 23.

INGELFINGER, F. J. (1972) "Informed (But Uneducated) Consent." *New England Journal of Medicine,* 287:465–466, August 31.

JACOBS, P. A., PRUNTON, M. ET AL. (1965) "Aggressive Behavior, Mental Subnormality and the XYY Male." *Nature,* 208:1351–1352.

JARVIK, L. F., KLODIN, V., AND MATSUYAMA, S. S. (1975) "Human Aggression and the Extra Y Chromosome: Fact or Fantasy?" Chapter in Allen, R. C. (Ed.), *Readings in Law and Psychiatry.* Baltimore: Johns Hopkins University Press.

JAYARATNE, S. (1977) "Child Abusers as Parents and Children: A Review." *Social Work,* 22:5–9.

KAPLAN, G. W. (1977) "Circumcision—An Overview." *Current Problems in Pediatrics,* 7:1–33, March.

KAPLUN, D., AND REICH, R. (1976) "The Murdered Child and His Killers." *American Journal of Psychiatry,* 133:809–813, July.

KATZ, J. (1972) *Experimentation with Human Beings.* New York: Russell Sage Foundation, pp. 964–972.

KATZ, S. N., HOWE, R. W., AND MCGRATH, M. (1975) "Child Neglect Laws in America." *Family Law Quarterly,* 9:1–372.

KEMPE, C. H. (1975) "Child Abuse—The Battered Child Syndrome." Chapter in Allen, R. C. (Ed.), *Readings In Law and Psychiatry.* Baltimore: Johns Hopkins University Press.

KEMPE, C. H. (1976) "Approaches to Preventing Child Abuse: A Health Visitor's Concept." *American Journal of Diseases of Children,* 130:941.

KEMPE, C. H., AND HELFER, R. E. (1972) *Helping the Battered Child and His Family.* New York: Lippincott.

KEMPE, C. H., SILVERMAN, F. N., AND STEELE, B. F. (1962) "The Battered Child Syndrome." *Journal of the American Medical Association,* 181:17.

KENT, J. T. (1975) "What Is Known About Child Abusers?" Chapter in Harris, S. B. (Ed.)., *Child Abuse Present and Future*. Chicago: National Committee for Prevention of Child Abuse.

KNOWLES, J. H. (1977) "The Responsibility of the Individual." *Daedalus*, 106:57–80.

LYSTAD, M. H. (1975) "Violence at Home: A Review of the Literature." *American Journal of Orthopsychiatry*, 45:328–345, April.

MARTIN, H. P. (ED.) (1976) *The Abused Child: A Multidisciplinary Approach to Developmental Issues and Treatment*. Cambridge, Mass.: Ballinger.

MCNEESE, M. C., AND HEBELER, J. R. (1977) "The Abused Child: A Clinic Approach to Identification and Management." *Clinical Symposia*, Vol. 29, No. 5.

MEADOW, R. (1977) "Munchausen Syndrome by Proxy: The Hinterland of Child Abuse." *Lancet*, 2:343–345.

MEISEL, A., ROTH, L. H., AND LIDZ, C. W. (1977) "Toward a Model for the Legal Doctrine of Informed Consent." *American Journal of Psychiatry*, 134:285–289, March.

MOGIELNICKI, R. P., MOGIELNICKI, N. P., CHANDLER, J. E., AND WEISSBERG, M. P. (1977) "Impending Child Abuse: Psychosomatic Symptoms in Adults as a Clue." *Journal of the American Medical Association*, 237:1109–1111, March 14.

NATIONAL CENTER FOR HEALTH STATISTICS (1977) *Vital Statistics of the United States 1975, Volume I—Natality*. Washington, D.C.: U.S. Government Printing Office.

NATIONAL COMMISSION FOR THE PROTECTION OF HUMAN SUBJECTS OF BIOMEDICAL AND BEHAVIORAL RESEARCH (1977) *Report and Recommendations: Research Involving Children*. Washington, D.C.: DHEW Publication No. (OS) 77-0004.

NEWBERGER, E. H. (1977) "Child Abuse and Neglect: Toward a Firmer Foundation for Practice and Policy." *American Journal of Orthopsychiatry*, 47:374–376.

OFFICE OF CHILD DEVELOPMENT (1974) "Child Abuse and Neglect Prevention and Treatment Program." *Federal Register*, 39:43936–43941, December 19.

REISER, S. J., DYCK, A. J., AND CURRAN, W. J. (EDS.) (1977) *Ethics in Medicine: Historical Perspectives and Contemporary Concerns*. Boston: MIT Press.

ROBERTSON, J. (1962) *Hospitals and Children: A Parents-eye View*. London: Gollancz.

ROMANO, J. (1974) "Reflections on Informed Consent." *Archives of General Psychiatry*, 30:129–135.

ROSENFELD, A. A., NADELSON, C. C., KRIEGER, M., AND BACKMAN, J. H. (1977) "Incest and Sexual Abuse of Children." *Journal of Child Psychiatry*, 16:327–339.

SAWARD, E., AND SORENSEN, A. (1978) "The Current Emphasis on Preventive Medicine." *Science*, 200:889–894.

SCHMITT, BARTON D. (1978) *The Child Protection Team Handbook: A Multidisciplinary Approach to Managing Child Abuse and Neglect.* New York: Garland STPM Press.

SCHUCHMAN, H. (1978) "Toward Assuring Confidentiality of Records in Large-Scale Assessment Programs." *American Journal of Orthopsychiatry,* 48:71–76.

SEIDEL, H. M. (1976) *Legal Change for Child Health: The Report on a Wingspread Conference.* NAPS Document No. 03046. New York: Microfiche.

SELIGMAN, F. (1975) "Children and Youth Projects: Past, Present and Future." Presented at the Annual Meeting of the American Orthopsychiatric Association.

SILVER, L. B., DUBLIN, C. C., AND LOURIE, R. S. (1975) "Does Violence Breed Violence? Contributions from a Study of the Child Abuse Syndrome." Chapter in Allen, R. C. (Ed.), *Readings in Law and Psychiatry.* Baltimore: Johns Hopkins University Press.

SLOVENKO, R., AND USDIN, E. (1966) *Psychotherapy, Confidentiality and Communication.* Springfield, Ill.: Thomas.

SMITH, S. M., HANSON, R., AND NOBLE, S. (1974) "Social Aspects of the Battered Baby Syndrome." *British Journal of Psychiatry,* 125:568–582.

SOMAN, S. C. (1974) *Let's Stop Destroying Our Children.* New York: Hawthorn Books.

SPINETTA, J. J., AND RIGLER, D. (1972) "The Child Abusing Parent: A Psychological Review." *Psychological Bulletin,* 77:296–304.

STARR, P. (1978) "Medicine and the Waning of Professional Sovereignty." *Daedalus,* pp. 175–193.

STEELE, B. F. *Working with Abusive Parents from a Psychiatric Point of View.* (National Center for the Prevention and Treatment of Child Abuse and Neglect) DHEW Publication No. (OHD) 75–70.

SUMMIT, R., AND KRYSO, J. (1978) "Sexual Abuse of Children: A Clinical Spectrum." *American Journal of Orthopsychiatry,* 48:237–251.

SUSSMAN, C. (1975) *Reporting Child Abuse and Neglect.* Cambridge, Mass.: Ballinger.

TASK FORCE ON PEDIATRIC EDUCATION (1978) *The Future of Pediatric Education.* Evanston, Illinois: The Academy of Pediatrics.

THOMPSON, H. C. ET AL. (1975) "Report of the Ad Hoc Task Force on Circumcision." *Pediatrics,* 56:610.

TOOLEY, K. M. (1977) "Young Child as Victim of Sibling Attack." *Social Casework,* 58:25–28.

UNITED NATIONS (1979) *1977 Demographic Yearbook.* New York: United Nations.

VERNON, D. T. A., FOLEY, J. M., SIPOWICZ, R. R., AND SCHULMAN, J. L. (1965) *The Psychological Responses of Children to Hospitalization and Illness.* Springfield, Ill.: Thomas.

WALTERS, D. R. (1975) *Physical and Sexual Abuse of Children: Causes and Treatment.* Bloomington, Ind.: University of Indiana Press.

WESTMAN, J. C., AND ZARWELL, D. (1975) "Traumatic Phallic Amputation During Infancy." *Archives of Sexual Behavior*, 4:53–63.

WISCONSIN DEPARTMENT OF HEALTH AND SOCIAL SERVICES (1977) "A Five Year Statistical Comparison of Child Abuse Reporting in Wisconsin."

WITKIN, H. A. (1976) "Criminality in XYY and XXY Men." *Science*, 193:547–555, August 13.

Chapter 12
Children and Mental Health Care

As is true with mentally ill adults who are called criminals, alcoholics, and vagrants, emotionally disturbed children are often not recognized as such because they are disguised by labels, such as mental retardation, learning disability, delinquency, and drug abuse. Furthermore, emotional disturbances in children are concealed by many overriding social conditions, including family disturbances, racism, poverty, cultural differences, and educational inadequacies. Because of these broad social, cultural, economic, and familial influences, the individual emotionally disturbed child is frequently overlooked.

As a society we are only beginning to become aware of the true extent of mental illness and emotional disturbance in children, now estimated at 15 percent of the population (President's Commission on Mental Health, 1978). As primary care professionals gain greater sensitivity to the emotional and mental disorders of childhood, increasing numbers are being

375

uncovered. Thus, the full scope of children's mental health service and manpower needs is yet to be appreciated.

Even when an emotionally disturbed child is identified, there is a strong tendency to seek simple, short-range solutions to solve the problem, all too frequently postponing the full-scale intervention that is required. In fact, because of the complex developmental and current life factors contributing to children's problems, the most important ingredients of treatment are the coordination and long-term continuity of services.

The field of children's mental health is the most recently developed of the systems included in this book. The Juvenile Psychopathic Institute, founded in Chicago in 1909, was the first psychiatric clinic for children. On a nationwide scale, mental health services for children appeared in the form of child guidance clinics sponsored by the Commonwealth Foundation in the 1920s. A body of knowledge was assembled in the first textbook on child psychiatry in 1935 by Leo Kanner. The field was organized on a national level in 1947 through the formation of the American Association of Psychiatric Services for Children. The status of child psychiatry as a medical specialty was affirmed in 1959 through the institution of certification in child psychiatry by the American Board of Psychiatry and Neurology. More recently, the crisis in child mental health was brought to public attention in the reports of the Joint Commission on the Mental Health of Children in 1969 and the President's Commission on Mental Health in 1978.

In only one sense are psychiatric services for children older than for adults. It is in the concept of community psychiatry which began in child guidance clinics and later reached adults through community mental health centers instituted in the 1960s, many of which absorbed existing clinics for children (Hetznecker, 1976; Tulchin, 1964). Unfortunately one of the byproducts of establishing community mental health centers has been a reduction in children's services that were replaced or absorbed by them, In 1970, only 30 percent of 205 community mental health centers had services for children (Health Resources Statistics, 1970). More specifically, a NIMH survey of eastern New York State reported in 1976 disclosed that an average of 25 percent of CMHC admissions were children with some catchment areas reporting as low as 10 percent (NIMH, 1976).

Paradoxically, within the mental health system itself it is now necessary to point out that services for children differ in a number of respects from those needed by adults. This is because the crisis intervention and brief treatment orientation of community mental health centers are not adapted to the coordination and continuity of care functions essential for the management of children's problems (Berlin, 1977). There are even questions about the effectiveness of brief, specific interventions generally (Polak, 1975). Two cases illustrate this point:

Case No. 1

At the age of three a boy was diagnosed as hyperactive and seen one time at a community mental health center. His mother thought he would outgrow this, but five years later she was seen again for several family counseling meetings at the center because of his behavior problem. During adolescence he appeared in juvenile court and was placed in a child caring institution for two years. At the age of 17 he was arrested again because of his delinquent behavior. Intensive treatment of the child and his family at the first admission could well have averted this outcome.

Case No. 2

In kindergarten a boy was said to be hyperactive. Because an older brother was placed in an educable mental retardation class, this boy was regarded as mentally retarded. He received several medications without help. In the third and fifth grades, he was referred to two community mental health centers. He finally was admitted to a child caring institution for three years. Thereafter, when returned to his home, he received special education in junior high school but was soon suspended from school. At no point in his 14 years had he received a child psychiatric evaluation.

Children require a spectrum of services, as do adults. They include outpatient, inpatient, emergency, day treatment, consultation, and community education. In addition, interdisciplinary teams are necessary to meet the mental health, health, legal, educational, and social needs of emotionally disturbed children. It is important to recognize that child mental health professionals have used interdisciplinary and community oriented techniques for years and are aware of their limitations and strengths (Rafferty, 1976). Child mental health professionals have been conservative in ambitions and claims and selected patients for each treatment modality with a meticulousness that later became antithetical to the ambience of community mental health centers. Unfortunately, child guidance clinics were judged as failures by some because they did not meet the mental health needs of all children. That goal was never claimed nor was it possible with the limited resources available then or now. As time has passed, experience has borne out the continued need for specialized services for children.

The Heritage of Children's Mental Health Services

There are many important differences between the delivery of mental health and health care, particularly from the point of view of community expectations. A brief examination of the background of the relationship between public psychiatry and society will help to clarify these differences.

In the early part of the last century humanitarian impulses led society to transfer responsibility for caring for social "misfits" from the jails to asylums. At that time public psychiatry unwittingly entered an ill-fated covenant by accepting society's charge to handle its unacceptable citizens. What was originally conceived of as treatment was in fact a euphemism for the segregation of people from the mainstream of society. In shifting the disposition of the mentally ill from jails to asylums, the practices and policies of criminal confinement were transformed into commitment laws for the admission of patients to mental hospitals. The hope of the community was that psychiatrists would treat or rehabilitate the mentally ill, but the means and knowledge for doing so were not available (Stone, 1976; Barton, 1978).

Rather than as a field of medical practice, then, psychiatry came to be seen as an agent for handling society's deviants. An inevitable disenchantment by communities that used psychiatric facilities as a means of resolving social problems resulted. There was also an equally inevitable rebellion of "patients" who found themselves receiving less than promised. All of this frustrated the healing impulses of psychiatrists. The end result was that psychiatric treatment became the target of society's prejudice against social deviants, and a sense of "badness" was associated with mental patients. The overdramatized stigmatization and loss of freedom associated with psychiatric hospitalization today is based upon the fact that many psychiatric facilities were, and still are, woefully inadequate and, according to prevailing health system standards, intolerable.

We are in the midst of a judicial reversal of that which the judiciary created. There are now many right-to-treatment and right-not-to-be-treated lawsuits based upon the ill effects of institutional mental health care. More accurately, we are shifting away from the presumption that people are treated by simply placing them in mental hospitals toward a more sophisticated expectation that patients receive quality services. Stated in another way, courts initially sent people to asylums to relieve the community of offensive behavior. Now courts are releasing people from hospitals with the hope that they will receive more effective community-based treatment at less cost.

This general background of social prejudice against the mentally ill plays a role in the ambivalence of communities toward mental health services for children (Rexford, 1969). In addition, a number of specific attitudes stand in the way of establishing adequate services for children (Lippit, 1973; Adams, 1976):

1. the belief that making children conform or adjust is all that is needed;
2. the assumption that simple causes and remedies to children's problems can be found;
3. the view that if given the opportunity all children will develop normally;

4. the view that young people cannot participate in decisions that affect them;
5. the attitude that each one of the variety of professionals knows what is best for children;
6. the idea that minors know what is best for themselves.

The ambivalence of communities toward children influences public opinions, beliefs, and actions. If this underlying ambivalence is ignored and rational explanations of why people differ so widely in what they believe is best for children are relied upon, frustration, suspicion, and litigious "philosophical" confrontations occur between community groups and even within mental health center staffs over programming for children (Newman, 1966).

One legacy of psychiatry's early, unwitting covenant with the legal system through accepting a role in the segregation of society's deviants is the sense today among children that to be "mental" is to be "bad." Another legacy is the large number of institutions of poor quality for children. In the area of mental health services for children, the aid of the legal system to ensure quality care is needed (Koocher, 1976; Polier, 1976).

The Right to Treatment

The report of the Joint Commission on the Mental Health of Children used the most conservative estimates and stated that there were 1,400,000 children under the age of 18 needing psychiatric care in 1966. Nearly 1 million of those children did not receive adequate treatment. Furthermore, the admission of teenagers to state hospitals rose 150 percent from the previous decade. Instead of being helped, many were worse for the experience. From all of this, the Joint Commission concluded that there was not a single community in this country which provided an acceptable standard of services for its mentally ill children. As the currently estimated 3,920,000 emotionally disturbed children attest, that remains the case today. As a result, litigation attacking the quality of care in public facilities is increasing.

A series of landmark judicial decisions have clearly supported the right of people of all ages to quality mental health care. In the case of *Rouse v. Cameron*, Judge Bazelon ruled that an adult criminally insane patient had the right to be spared cruel and unusual punishment, the right to due process, and the right to treatment. In Alabama the case of *Wyatt v. Stickney* established minimum standards of care for mental hospitals, requiring the discharge of patients who did not receive treatment if they were held involuntarily, and requiring the state to fund adequate treatment. In *Donaldson v. O'Connor*, the U.S. Supreme Court ruled that patients who were not dangerous could not be confined against their will if they did not receive treatment and awarded a former patient $20,000 in damages assessed against state hospital physicians who were found to have infringed upon his freedom. In *Dixon v. Weinberger*, the District of Columbia was ordered to create community facilities to permit the discharge of patients from St. Elizabeth's Hospital to the "least restrictive care" appropriate for their treatment. All of these cases indicate a trend toward holding psychiatrists responsible for inadequate treatment in institutions. This is the reward of the present-day institutional psychiatrist for psychiatry's earlier acceptance of responsibility for society's "misfits." Understandably, the public expects that psychiatrists should not tolerate inadequate treatment facilities at peril to themselves.

There is no constitutional guarantee of treatment of any kind; however, most states statutorily assure treatment in mental hospitals. The "right-to-treatment" issue has been raised by the civil commitment of patients to institutions. Except as provided for in state statutes, however, there is no "right to treatment" for those who are involuntarily committed (McGough, 1977).

As Bazelon pointed out in *Rouse v. Cameron*, there are only two types of confinement sanctioned by society: confinement in a prison as punishment for the offender, and confinement in a mental institution for treatment. When treatment is not afforded, a hospital becomes a prison.

Further specifications of the treatment that mental hospitals must provide were set forth in *Wyatt v. Stickney*. In those cases, Alabama Governor Wallace argued that confinement for custodial care in itself was valid. This argument was rejected. Instead, standards for evaluating the quality of treatment were established. These standards included a provision against institutional peonage, ensuring a humane psychological environment, minimum staffing standards, detailed physical plant standards, minimum nutritional requirements, provisions for individualized evaluations of residents, habilitation plans and programs, a release provision ensuring transitional care and the right to treatment in the least restrictive setting necessary for habilitation (*Wyatt v. Aderholt*). Unfortunately, these standards are limited to the structure and process of institutionalization rather than to methods of treatment.

The "least restrictive alternative" approach propounds the idea that if patients can function in some setting other than a mental hospital, the court has the responsibility to place them in that setting. Many patients are held in hospitals because of the lack of community facilities. Furthermore, supporting the patient's need for normalization means developing aftercare for many patients who have not previously lived in communities. The extent to which a judicial decision can stem the antipathy toward mental patients that exists in communities is being tested through this doctrine.

Legal cases are beginning to be raised specifically for minors. *Morales v. Turman* is a right-to-treatment case which was brought against the Texas Youth Council on behalf of youths in Texas juvenile delinquent institutions. The case illustrates the complexities of the legal process. The contention of the plaintiffs was that children in institutions have a right to rehabilitative treatment and may not be held in a custodial or punitive situation. In August 1974, a federal district court upheld the right to treatment and to protection from harm for juveniles in six Texas state reformatories. Progress began toward developing community-based rehabilitation facilities during the appeal, and one of the reformatories was closed. In July 1976, the Fifth Circuit Court of Appeals reversed the judgment, stating that the trial should have been before a three-judge court instead of a single judge. In 1977, the U.S. Supreme Court overrode that decision and remanded the case to the Fifth Circuit for proceedings on its merits.

Wald makes the ironic point that minors whose custody has been assumed by the state under neglect, delinquency, mental illness, or retardation laws are unlikely to receive effective treatment. This contradicts the intent of statutes dealing with juvenile offenses which were based on the concept of rehabilitation, not punishment. Thus, juvenile law is on common theoretical ground with statutes which prescribe treatment for the adult mentally ill. Accordingly, courts have insisted in specific cases that once minors are found to need treatment, adequate resources must be on hand to implement that treatment. Thus far, however, no viable legal theory for a general right to treatment for all children has emerged.

It can be argued that a child's dependent status is a creation of society, through compulsory education laws, child labor laws, and restrictions on minors' ability to contract. That dependent status, in turn, contributes to minors' inability to secure treatment for themselves. Hence, society should have an obligation to provide such treatment. Moreover, parents can be prosecuted under state criminal law for neglect if they do nothing to improve conditions injurious to their children. The state as *parens patriae* could be equally guilty under the 19th Amendment of the U.S. Constitution when it fails to provide necessary physical and psychological nurture for its wards (Pyfer, 1974).

In another vein, there may be an emerging right to mental health treatment as an adjunct to the "right-to-education" laws mandating that children with any kind of handicap, including emotional or mental problems, are required to be given an education at public expense. In the District of Columbia, this has been interpreted to mean that where education is possible only in conjunction with treatment, the school system must pay for or arrange for psychiatric treatment as well (*Mills v. Board of Education*).

Ensuring treatment for children faces a long, difficult road. Even with the aid of parent lobby groups and visibility through the President's Commission on Mental Retardation which has existed since the Kennedy administration, we must note the plight of the mentally retarded. The initial difficulty lies in classification. Many moderately retarded persons have been erroneously classified as profoundly retarded and institutionalized for life. Even those correctly diagnosed as severely retarded can respond to love and careful training. Where retardation is moderate or mild, and where treatment could make possible a life of self-support and respect, some states still do not provide adequate services for retarded children. Mandatory education laws are now remedying this problem in most states. Still, a long, tortuous course follows, translating legislative and judicial intent into action for individual children (Kindred, 1976).

The Right to Refuse Treatment

For adults, there is little question that treatment may be refused on the grounds of religious scruples or personal philosophy, as long as the public interest is not endangered by an untreated condition. If an adult is not mentally competent, however, the approach has been the same as with children who have been regarded as incompetent to make decisions regarding health. Courts have exercised a *parens patriae* responsibility over the refusal and objection of a parent or guardian (McGough, 1977) and interceded to allow prescribed medical treatment for incompetent adults and children in life-threatening situations.

In spite of the *parens patriae* doctrine and acknowledged parental decision-making responsibility, controversy rages today over whether or not minors have the right to refuse treatment. On the surface, this appears to accord adult rights to minors, a logical inconsistency. The matter, however, is much more complicated than that.

First of all is the presumption that, although later in life adults are responsible for their health, even abusing it if they wish, it is prudent to postpone that choice for children. To permit a child to decline essential treatment might prevent that youngster from reaching adulthood. In other words, a child ought to be able to enter adulthood in optimal physical and mental health. Accordingly, the presumption is that children should receive necessary health and mental health care and no one—the child's parent, society, or the child—should interfere with that aim.

Behind the right to refuse treatment, however, is an even deeper problem, namely, that adequate treatment is often not available. There is reason for giving minors the opportunity to refuse treatment which may be harmful or inadequate. Most of the concern about the right of minors to refuse treatment is really based upon the fact that treatment facilities are inadequate. It is one thing for a minor to refuse to be helped, and it is another thing for a minor to be spared a destructive fate. The tragic fact is that standards for mental health care for children are lower than for physical health care. This is largely a result of the lack of trained professionals in the field of children's mental health.

These cases illustrate the ineffectiveness, if not the frank damage, of "treatment":

> A 21 year old girl functioning at the moderate mental retardation level had many years of diagnostic studies, hospital placements, and attempts to integrate her into public school. Ultimately she remained at home with her parents who always suspected that she was not really retarded, a fact finally confirmed by psychological tests, but her progressive disability persisted.

> A 15 year old boy was admitted to a state penal institution for adults. His family with six children lived in poverty. At the age of six he was hospitalized with adults for the first of three times in county hospitals. He was placed in a reformatory at the age of 13 after having been previously "served" by 25 different agencies.

In another vein, it is becoming increasingly clear that minors do have a legal right to challenge decisions subjecting them to certain kinds of medical treatment. Courts have generally prohibited parents from unilaterally sterilizing their children, insisting on or refusing to consent to abortions or to donating children's organs for transplants to siblings. Underlying these decisions is the principle that a child can suffer from parents' fallible judgment. The direction is also toward greater participation of minors in decision making about mental health treatment, especially extreme therapies (Ellis, 1974; Wald, 1976). Consequently, physicians and parents must increasingly take into consideration their minor patients' attitudes and desires. Most important, the degree of risk of harm from treatment or nontreatment has a direct bearing on whether or not a minor's attitude toward treatment becomes a legal question. The more serious the intervention, the more important it is that children's interests be protected when their verbalized wish is to refuse treatment.

The case of *Kremens v. Bartley* brings out the complex issues involved when parents decide to hospitalize their child (Watkins, 1976; Ferleger, 1976). The case became moot when a new Pennsylvania law was enacted providing that children 14 to 18 years old who were subject to commitment by their parents should be treated essentially as adults. The U.S. Supreme Court did not rule on the issue, stimulated by concern that when parents are motivated by intrafamily conflicts, frustration, and hostility, a child can be scapegoated and hospitalized more because of the parents' desires than the child's interests. It is difficult for a lawyer to deny such children the protection of judicial overseeing of their admission to hospitals.

What happens, however, if parents and child cannot coexist in the same house, but a hearing decides that hospitalization is inappropriate from a child's point of view? What effect will the courtroom alignment of parents and doctors against lawyer and child have on the child's emotional problems? Due process hearings introduce an adversarial stance into the therapeutic relationship of doctor–patient as well as into the relationship between parent and child. Who will continue therapy if a child wins the battle against parents and doctors? In sum, the state, however well motivated, may have to show that it can commit resources to treat a child properly before it can override parental authority and permit a minor to refuse treatment.

In practice, the question of refusing treatment usually arises with adolescents from troubled families, clouding objectivity in all quarters (Wilson, 1978). In the past, two paths have been followed into treatment institutions: placement by an adolescent's parents or by the juvenile court. Both routes gave the adolescent no legally sanctioned voice in the matter. Regardless of whether the adolescent wanted such a placement or contested it, adult authority made the decision. New rules are now being offered which mitigate parental authority by stipulating that hospitalized adolescents may protest their placement and obtain court review and representation by appointed attorneys.

A new ethos holds that courts should take custody of an adolescent only to protect society, never solely to protect adolescents from themselves or their families. The critics of the old policy begin by pointing to the manifest inadequacies of public institutions for adolescents, particularly those under the aegis of juvenile courts. But these critics sweep beyond these well justified targets to include all psychiatric hospitals for children. If this line of reasoning is accepted by courts and legislatures, the result would work against adolescents who need psychiatric services, as well as their families and the rest of society. These critiques rest on a fundamental misconception of adolescent psychology and the fact that there are therapeutic possibilities in psychiatric treatment without the verbalized consent of adolescents.

There are three inaccurate assumptions prevalent in legal circles today:

1. The parents of disturbed adolescents are inclined to be too ready to have them institutionalized. The clinical evidence is to the contrary: actually it is inordinately difficult for parents to resolve to maintain their children in needed residential care.
2. Psychiatrists keep children in hospitals for unnecessarily long periods of time. There is no evidence for this belief, which is based

upon outdated conceptions of mental hospitals. The disappearance of a problem in the hospital setting does not mean that the adolescent is ready to live in the community.

3. Adolescents mean what they say. There is a developmentally determined discrepancy between the words and actions of troubled teenagers.

A more rational approach to residential treatment for adolescents should not be based solely on the severity of symptomatic behavior, but on how successfully that behavior can be contained within the context of relationships with parents, therapists, other adults, and peers in the community (Miller, 1977a, 1977b). Such placement should not be made solely on the grounds that the community must be protected from the adolescent. Such a view equates the hospital with a jail. For adolescents who are drug dependent, absconding from home or school, or seeking sexual promiscuity, outpatient interventions fail unless very rapid attachments to therapists are made. For this cluster of problems, psychiatric hospital care can remove adolescents from noxious environments and permit the initiation of problem solving which could not begin while they remained in their communities.

One legal concept seems to be that juveniles have the right to decide on actions affecting their lives and freedom, unless they are found to be incapable of doing so. The thinking appears to be that adolescents' rights will be protected by holding court hearings for those patients who protest verbally against the initiation or continuation of treatment. This makes it possible for some adolescents to pit legal authority against medical authority as a means of manipulating adults against each other, as they have previously done so skillfully in their homes and communities. Unless someone takes the initiative in demonstrating legally valid grounds for treatment in courts, the result is that adolescents who could be effectively treated in inpatient psychiatric facilities may not get it there or anywhere else.

In *J.L. & J.R. v. Parham*, a Georgia federal district court held that permitting parents or guardians to hospitalize children without a legal hearing does not satisfy due process. Although there is reason to require due process procedures for admission to a state hospital with inadequate resources—in this case, Milledgeville State Mental Hospital—a blanket requirement fails to recognize the essential responsibilities and rights of parents for the upbringing of their children and the harm involved in requiring due process adversary hearings in all cases.

Because of the possibility of requiring due process procedures for all psychiatric hospitalizations of children, the Michigan Association for Emotionally Disturbed Children found it necessary to defend the right of children to voluntary hospitalization. The MAEDC held that disturbed children should have voluntary access to hospitalization just as adults do. Mental health professionals should make the final decision about hospitalization, as do physicians in other areas of health care. If the voluntary aspect of a child's admission is not upheld, and it is necessary to commit each child involuntarily through the adversarial process to a hospital, children would be required to secure a commitment order from juvenile court in order to be hospitalized and details of the court proceedings would be open for public inspection. The courts, not qualified mental health professionals, would determine clinical indications for admission. Of the children now hospitalized, most would be denied treatment because they would not meet the requirements for court commitment. The MAEDC holds that it is ironic in this day that the rights of children to voluntary treatment in children's psychiatric facilities must now be defended after the long campaigns to establish this right.

Overlooked in the current fray over the right to refuse treatment is the fact that if parents are not able to make constructive decisions regarding the mental health treatment of their children, then they are neglecting the health of their children. Under those circumstances there should be court guardianship. Either the parents are, or they are not, capable of decision making for their child. If they are not, the court should assume that responsibility, and there is no need for an intermediate stage in which the minor is given responsibility for decision making. Excessive legal intervention in psychiatric conditions interposes too much outside authority in family matters and magnifies parent–child conflicts.

The voluntary hospitalization of minors for psychiatric treatment should not require due process any more than the voluntary hospitalization of adults. When the community does need protection from an adolescent, due process is appropriate because the community is depriving the adolescent of freedom for its own reasons. Under those circumstances, due process should determine that justice is being served through the process of involuntary commitment.

In order to ensure access to available treatment, the involuntary commitment of a person should include a determination of partial incompetency to refuse or consent to treatment at the time of commitment. The commitment order would then be an authorization to treat the patient with accepted therapies. The separation of civil commitment and treatment now permits the virtual imprisonment of patients, who thereafter do not receive treatment. This is a clear-cut usage of mental hospitals as prisons. If a person is in such a state that commitment to a hospital must be involuntary, it follows that this person may also refuse treatment. Only an authorization for treatment at the time of commitment will ensure that the person receives treatment (Roth, 1977).

As becomes evident, the fundamental issue is really not the right of children to refuse treatment, nor is it that most children need protection from malevolent parents. The basic problem is that many institutions for children do not provide adequate treatment and sometimes are harmful. There should not be a blanket reaction against all residential facilities, however. The real issue is the right of children to receive effective treatment.

One way of focusing public attention on obtaining treatment for children is through forcing communities to deal with inadequate facilities by preventing the admission of children to them through legal review. Litigation can produce test cases, draw attention to unserved children, and lead to judicial orders for adequate treatment programs and staffing in deficient institutions. The price of this approach, however, is that the affected children may receive no service, and families will be forced to cope with the situation. Years may pass while courts attempt to enforce orders to create adequate treatment programs. Although others may benefit in the future, the children for whom litigation occurs will languish without help.

A second approach is through legislation which can be used to close public institutions with orderly arrangements for alternatives (Holden, 1976) or to increase funding for institutions. An unfortunate byproduct, however, is that legislatively created programs necessitate bureaucracies which in part are responsible for the existing impersonal nature of public institutions.

A third approach is to educate the public to the problems of institutions and educate professionals in alternatives to institutional care. When a community has adequate trained professionals and an adequate network of services, institutional care is needed infrequently.

A fourth, and more immediately practical, route is to enforce standards for institutions. At the present time the Joint Commission on the Accreditation of Hospitals sets standards for mental health and mental retardation facilities (Accreditation Council for Psychiatric Facilities, 1974). These standards can be used by courts or communities to determine whether or not a particular institution can provide desired services. Children could then be placed voluntarily only in accredited facilities.

All of the above remedies should be used without burdening individual children with "an overdose of due process" by requiring judicial review of admissions to all children's residential treatment facilities in order to save some children from ineffective institutions. The following approach includes all of these considerations, reserving due process for appropriate situations:

1. Require review when voluntary admission is to a facility not accredited by qualified standard monitoring mechanisms, such as the Joint Commission on the Accreditation of Hospitals, as a residential treatment facility for children. Periodic judicial review should follow.
2. Avoid discriminating against the child who needs service in an

accredited residential treatment facility by not imposing judicial review and highlighting loss of freedom any more than for children who are admitted to hospitals for medical and surgical treatment.

3. Educate the public to conditions in institutions which are not accredited. This can be done through publicizing cases which reach judicial review that exposes inadequate treatment programs.

4. Educate professionals in all disciplines and at all levels in alternatives to institutional care for children.

Informed Consent for Mental Health Treatment

As can be seen, much of the concern about children's right to refuse treatment really addresses the right to escape from useless or harmful "treatment." When that factor is removed, the matter of the child's right to informed consent emerges as a legitimate issue. In the past the informed consent of mental patients to treatment has generally received little attention. So both because of mental disorder and developmental immaturity, minors have not been thought of as participating in informed consent decisions.

The general matter of informed consent for treatment, research, and organ donations has been dealt with in detail in Chapter 11. To date, relatively few legal cases have tested the issue of informed consent in the context of psychiatric treatment (Meisel, 1977).

Several principles appear to be emerging in this complex field. Society seems to want minors to have needed treatment, does not want them to be exploited by charlatans, and intuitively recognizes that their judgment cannot be trusted. The intent of society, then, is that minors should have access to mental health treatment and that laws should take into account their developmental stages in determining their capability to participate with their parents in consenting to treatment.

Occasionally, there are situations in which an adolescent desires psychiatric treatment and the parents oppose it. More typically, however, when an adolescent seeks treatment, the family supports it. Although lowering the age of majority to 18 has eliminated the issue of minority for them, one common area in which older adolescents seek and receive treatment on their own, frequently without the knowledge of their parents, is through college mental health services. This is the time in which the adolescent's capacity to give informed consent is most likely to be appropriate, now technically taking place during adulthood (Farnsworth, 1957).

In practice, most adolescents do not desire treatment, many actively oppose it, and many parents are reluctant to support treatment. The greatest problem is with families in which neither the adolescent nor the parents wish treatment, to society's ultimate disadvantage. It is at those times that intervention, sometimes through court mandated treatment, is desirable in order to ensure that the adolescent's verbal opposition does not overshadow the behavioral cry for help, and that strenuous efforts are made to overcome concomitant parental opposition to treatment. In clinical adolescent psychiatric practice, the need to motivate families is a commonly recognized first step toward treatment.

The matter of informed consent is a problem for any adolescent, particularly those who most need mental health treatment. Informed consent carries the implication that present actions have future consequences. Young people may have difficulty in evaluating the consequences of their actions because, until the middle stage of adolescence, they are likely to be highly concrete thinkers and have little sense of the future. A particular problem is that most psychological difficulties during adolescence present as behavior disorders. The individual may be the victim of driven behavior designed to avoid internal tension or to gratify impulses with no recognition of the future significance of present actions. Those who need treatment the most are the least likely to request it consciously (Miller, 1977a).

In approaching the matter of motivating an adolescent for treatment, a useful distinction can be made between the words "authoritative" and "authoritarian." To be *authoritative* presupposes that the attitudes and expectations of an individual are entitled to credit or acceptance on the basis of specialized knowledge. To be *authoritarian* implies exercising power over others through coercion or force. Because the nature of adolescence includes a special sensitivity to authoritarian behavior, it is particularly important that power issues be separated from expertise.

Even in situations in which a court ultimately mandates involuntary commitment and treatment, mental health professionals bear the responsibility to follow the procedures for obtaining informed consent, as outlined in Chapter 11. Although young patients may not be able to understand and cooperate fully in the process, forming a treatment relationship depends upon establishing rapport and earning their trust. Following the principles of informed consent is an important step toward establishing a therapeutic relationship because they convey an inherent respect for the dignity and integrity of even the most troubled youth and family. For hospitalized adolescents, a documented mutual agreement in the form of a signed contract for parents and patient signifying an understanding of the techiniques, procedures, and limitations of the treatment program is useful.

Confidentiality in Mental Health Care

Especially puzzling for mental health professionals is the issue of confidentiality for children and families. What secrets can children withhold from parents and what right do children have to expect confidential relationships with their therapists? Naturally, children fear exposure of their inner thoughts and desires and, further, have varying capacities even to understand what confidentiality means. All of these special considerations for children are embedded in a general misunderstanding of confidentiality and the right to know in professional circles (Grossman, 1977).

Although confidentiality and privileged communication tend to be used interchangeably, a useful distinction can be made between them (Group for Advancement of Psychiatry, 1960). *Confidentiality* is an ethical concept related to the social role that exists between professional and patient or client. A confidential relationship is one in which persons assume that their disclosures to a professional person will not be divulged to others, except under certain circumstances for their benefit. The ethical codes of the professionals are the basis for this relationship, not the law. *Privileged communication* presumes an ethical commitment to confidentiality but has its basis in law, either in the form of common law or legislated statute. Privileged communication is a legal right that belongs to patient or client, not the professional person, and is legal recognition and protection of a professional confidential relationship.

Confidentiality is substantially different for psychiatrists than for other physicians, and for child psychiatrists is further compounded by the nature of children's services, which include communication about children with schools, courts, and agencies. Mental health professionals are not sufficiently informed of their rights, duties, and privileges with respect to confidential patient communications and records. Many psychiatrists, for example, are surprised to learn that there is no privileged communication for physicians or psychiatrists under English common law.

An illustration of the extent to which society can intrude upon confidential patient–psychiatrist communications is the case of *Tarasoff v. The Regents of the University of California*. In this decision, the California Supreme Court enunciated the doctrine "protective privilege ends where public peril begins." It ruled that psychotherapists must warn authorities specified by law as well as potential victims of possible dangerous actions by their patients. It reflects an alignment of psychotherapists with the goal of protecting society and assumes that they can accurately predict dangerous actions. This decision illustrates the tendency of the legal system to expect psychiatrists to protect the public from deviant behavior, a clear and additional public responsibility beyond that of a healer. The analogy for this position is the communicable disease model for disease control in which physicians have the responsibility of reporting serious contagious diseases (Gurevitz, 1977).

As *Tarasoff* illustrates, the privacy of patient–psychiatrist communications cannot be considered separate from the social position, role, and function of the psychiatrist. The importance of confidentiality must be weighed against the importance and necessity of society's investment in the treatment, the significance of confidentiality for the treatment process, and the need for the public to have access to information.

A brief review of the history of the physician–patient privilege concept is appropriate at this point (DeWitt, 1958). In England the long-standing tradition was to compel witnesses to appear in court and testify. This was based on the principle that the administration of justice was of benefit to all members of the community, and every competent person was obliged to further justice as a matter of public duty. As time went on, the courts were persuaded that the exclusion of classes of persons from testifying in court was necessary in order to bar persons believed to be biased, unstable, or untrustworthy from appearing as witnesses. Criteria of race, sex, minority, condition of servitude, religion, relationship, interest in the outcome of the litigation, mental illness, or conviction for crime were used to exclude witnesses. At the beginning of the nineteenth century, this policy of exclusion had progressed so far that it almost reached the realm of absurdity.

The oldest of these exclusionary privileges was the confidentiality accorded to attorneys and clergymen which appears to have been unquestioned as far back as the reign of Elizabeth I in the 1500s. In England at the present time the right of an attorney or clergyman to decline to reveal confidential communications is recognized by custom in the courts, and in America statutory privileged communication is provided for these two disciplines in most states. On the other hand, in England the courts have refused to extend a similar privilege to physicians. Without a basis in English common law, most states in America, however, have provided some form of statutory privilege for physicians and patients.

The first law establishing a physician–patient privilege was passed in New York in 1828. But in the intervening years, with the exception of a few states such as Connecticut, California, Georgia, Illinois, and Maryland, the privileged position of the psychiatrist, as a physician, has little standing before the law and is under erosion from many sources. As an illustration, typical of state statutes is the Wisconsin law on physician privilege:

> A patient has a privilege to refuse to disclose and to prevent any other person from disclosing confidential communications made or information obtained or disseminated for purposes of diagnosis or treatment of his physical, mental or emotional condition, among himself, his physician or persons, including members of the patient's family, who are participating in the diagnosis or treatment under the direction of the physician. The exceptions to this privilege are in relationship to hospitalization for mental illness, when a judge orders an examination of the physical, mental or emotional condition of the patient, when the patient relies upon a condition as an element of his claim or defense of litigation, in relationship to homocide, and in matters of child abuse or injury.

Prior to recent decades, there was little question about medical privilege because it had limited economic importance. With the development of life and accident insurance, workmen's compensation, and common carrier liability, powerful economic interests came into conflict with medical privilege. Authorities came into conflict with medical privilege. Authorities on the law of evidence, such as Professor John Wigmore, became decidedly unsympathetic, and physician privilege laws became so riddled with exceptions in case law interpretations that they have questionable meaning in actual application.

DeWitt (1958) explains why this has occurred by pointing out that the principal reasons advanced in support of physician–patient privilege are not convincing. The traditional theory that persons suffering from serious diseases or painful injuries would hesitate to confide in physicians unless they had the complete assurance of confidence that cannot later be revealed has been discredited. The fallacy of the theory is that one must assume that the prospective patient knows about privilege and specifically expects the protection it affords. Such an assumption appears to be unwarranted.

Another discredited theory is that the injury to the relationship of physician and patient through disclosure of confidential information is greater than the injury to the cause of justice so that, in the interest of public health, medical confidences must be protected against disclosure. DeWitt feels there is no evidence that privilege tends to improve the public health. He points out that the citizens of 17 states in America and persons in the British Commonwealth freely consult their physicians with no assurance whatever that, should their state of health or injuries become the subject of litigation, their confidences cannot be revealed by their physicians. The level of public health in these jurisdictions has not, for lack of a physician–patient privilege, been lowered below that of other jurisdictions which have adopted it.

On the other hand, there is abundant evidence that the physician–patient privilege undermines the very foundations of justice. In the vast majority of reported cases where privilege has been claimed, the patient or the party objecting to the testimony of the attending physician did not invoke privilege to protect the patient's right to privacy or to prevent the disclosure of matters which would humiliate or disgrace the patient. Rather, the primary motive was to use privilege as a procedural device for the purpose of excluding relevant and material evidence from a lawsuit which, were it admitted, would tend to reduce, if not defeat, chances for a favorable verdict.

Privilege, then, accomplishes little but the concealment and suppression of facts. Honest patients might fear disclosure of their state of health by their physicians. Their real concern, however, is not that their physicians may someday be compelled to disclose the truth in a court of law, but that they will involuntarily reveal the facts to friends or relatives or make their afflictions the subject of articles in medical journals or public addresses. The physician–patient privilege affords no protection against these kinds of dangers.

It is ironic that much of the erosion of medical privilege is because of dilution by the very legislators who enacted it. A growing number of exceptions to privilege are included in statutes so that today few medical confidences can really be kept secret. Honest patients have little fear, for they will not hide the truth, whether a privilege exists or not. DeWitt feels it is high time to abolish the physician–patient privilege or, as in North Carolina, to permit judges to waive privilege when they feel the cause of justice warrants it. From this background it is evident that there is a trend away from physician–patient privilege because in issues involving health matters complete medical testimony is needed in order to execute justice.

On the other hand, there does seem to be a growing indication that privilege is important in the practice of psychotherapy. The points are made that privileged communication is essential to the success of psychotherapy and that the information gained in that process is not relevant in court.

Slovenko builds on Professor Wigmore's classic formulation governing the recognition of privilege and demonstrates that communications between psychotherapist and patient are made with the expectation of confidence, that violation of this expectation of confidence is detrimental to the purpose of the relationship, and that injury to the therapeutic relationship is greater than the benefit of justice that could be derived from public disclosure of the communication (Slovenko, 1966).

Furthermore, communications to a psychotherapist during treatment are generally assumed by the public to be confidential. The essence of psychotherapy is based upon personal revelations about matters which the patient is ordinarily reluctant to reveal or disclose. A patient makes statements to a psychotherapist which he would not make to the closest members of his family. Intensive psychotherapy involves exploration into the most hidden apsects of personality, probing matters unknown even to the conscious mind of the patient. Therapists have such intimate relationships with their patients that they learn of aspects of their patients not accessible to other people. In order to achieve such a relationship, the therapist should be scrupulously honest and trustworthy. The invulnerability of confidence in the therapist is essentail to the achievement of the purpose of treatment. As Freud said, "The whole undertaking becomes lost labor if a single concession is made to secrecy." Speaking freely is difficult for anyone and essential in psychotherapy.

Another point is that psychotherapist–patient confidentiality should be fostered because public attitudes toward the topics disclosed in psychotherapy tend to be negative. Important to the status and prestige of psychotherapy is protection through the unique confidentiality of that relationship. Moreover, information if revealed would produce fewer benefits to justice than the consequent injury to the individual and to the entire field of psychotherapy. Psychiatrists and others have pointed out the great social harm that may be done to countless numbers of patients, ex-patients, and future patients by even a rare subpoena of a psychotherapist to testify. Most important, the information obtained during the process of psychotherapy is not reliable for use in court because it does not consist of "facts," but of attitudes, feelings, and fantasies. The information is of little value in the practical reality of the court and would be excluded as irrelevant and immaterial anyway.

This point of view is substantiated by the report of the Group for the Advancement of Psychiatry (1960), which concluded that the social value which effective psychiatric treatment has for the community far outweighs the potential loss of evidence resulting from withholding testimony by a psychiatrist about a patient. The absence of privilege would obstruct the public need to have unencumbered access to psychiatric treatment. As is evident, convincing arguments can be made for privileged communication for psychotherapists.

In relating confidentiality to the family, the policies of college student mental health services can be cited. On the issue of informing parents of college age students about psychiatric involvement, Farnsworth makes the point that the condition of the patient must determine the approach that the authorities take (1957). Good practice requires that no one is told about treatment unless the student's permission is obtained or there is a problem involving suicide, potential homicide, or some kind of behavior which markedly handicaps the student or his parents.

Taking all of these factors into consideration from the point of view of the child mental health professional, then, it is likely that confidentiality should apply outside of the family system; however, there is no need for rigorous confidentiality within the family system. It is in the interests of the child to promote communication within the family system on significant matters related to the realistic state of the child. Still, children do need the opportunity to talk freely about fantasies, some of which relate to their parents. Children are encouraged to speak freely in psychotherapy about things which may be largely irrational. In a therapeutic context, these fantasies can be ultimately and appropriately shared with parents. The growing use of child-oriented family psychotherapy tends to bring more and more of the irrational fantasies of both children and parents into the open so that they can be dealt with and "disarmed."

In the final analysis, it is difficult to justify as a general position "secrecy" as essential in work with children. In contrast with a psychiatrist–adult patient relationship where dangerous misunderstanding could arise if there is free disclosure of the adult's fantasies, the opposite is true with children because the ultimate goal of free disclosure of the child's fantasies within the family system is essential to the child's welfare through the therapeutic aim of improving communication and enhancing understanding of the child at all levels within the family. Although there may be justification for short-range secrecy, it is likely that long-range "open disclosure" is in the interests of children.

Still, an element of confidentiality under certain circumstances is important for children. For example, Jimmy, a seven-year-old boy, told his psychiatrist that he did not want to have to choose between his mother and father for his custody. As he put it, "If I say I want to live with my father, my mother will be hurt. If I say that I want to live with my mother, my father will be mad. I love each one." Although Jimmy communicated to the psychiatrist that he saw custody with his father as preferable to that with his mother, he did not want to go on record as stating a preference. In these situations the child's disclosure to the psychiatrist should be treated in confidence between the child and the psychiatrist. In this case the judge honored the confidential communication between Jimmy and his therapist on this issue, and it was not introduced into the court divorce hearing.

Confidentiality is an essential prerequisite for adequate diagnosis and treatment of mental and emotional disorders, and society supports the psychotherapist–patient relationship as desirable (Love, 1974). Wigmore's criteria for privileged communication are met. In court tests, in the cases of *People v. Wasker* and *People v. Leyra*, the psychotherapist privilege was upheld. The creation of a psychotherapist privilege does impede the discovery of facts in a few circumstances; however, it is clear that the relationship is one which society both needs and expects (Kennedy, 1973). To be effective, the relationship requires free and unguarded communication which is aided by confidentiality. The states in which psychiatrist–patient privilege exists are Connecticut, Florida, Georgia, Illinois, Kentucky, and Maine. Twenty-seven states, including the District of Columbia, provide a privileged relationship for psychologists (Ferster, 1975). The trend, then, is toward statutory recognition of privileged communication between psychotherapists and patients.

The Misuse of Psychiatric Diagnosis with Children

The public translation of medical concepts has always been a treacherous matter. Although such straightforward things as sanitation and immunization to prevent disease have been successful, problems arise when government systems embark upon diagnosing and managing specific diseases and defects. Typically, an unmet social need is recognized, such as mental retardation, juvenile delinquency, or mental illness. Then legislation is passed appropriating funds to deal with the problem. The expectation is that children will be found with the problems which can be treated, remediated, or removed. What follows is a complicated and costly process of identifying individual recipients of the program. In the process a label is applied to each child in order to gain eligibility for the program. Unfortunately, the model is defective because the problems to be attacked are but surface manifestations of deeper issues involving the individual, family, school, community, and ecology.

Furthermore, legislated approaches to individual problems, without awareness of the full programmatic implementation required to solve them, not only lulls the public with a sense of having solved the problem but creates complications that in the long range may be harmful to children. The pattern of flow of government funding is along categorical lines; however, children do not exist in categories; they are whole persons living in families, schools, and communities. It is not possible to resolve a child's problem through a statute that provides for the remediation of mental retardation—for example, without taking into account the impact and genesis of the problem within the family and the school system itself. Not infrequently, at the level of the school system, the learning problem is the result of faulty education. To place the onus of "mentally retarded" on a child suffering from that deficiency unfairly stigmatizes the child and deflects attention from the school.

Unlike adults who may receive a diagnosis without repercussions, the labels we apply to children affect their entire lives in their schools, peer groups, and communities. The funding and programmatically motivated labels attached to children become a part of their records. Once a diagnostic label is attached, it is difficult to change it and, even when changed, the image remains with the child. Once this kind of label is attached to a child, the school system and the child so react that a self-fulfilling prophecy develops. Consequently, these children develop images of themselves as disabled, and their self-esteem is undermined.

Of even greater importance is the fact that labels may be inaccurate; 85 percent of the children labeled mentally retarded are not mentally retarded in the full sense of the term. The diagnosis may have been made simply on the basis of a psychometric test administered by an inadequately trained person.

A child was diagnosed at the age of six as brain injured and mentally retarded and placed in an institution for the mentally retarded. When seizures appeared later, she was treated with anticonvulsant medication. The parents transferred her to a private school in another state for several years. They felt that getting help for children was a "do it yourself" matter. They found that they had to be their own "general contractor" in getting aid for her. Finally at the age of 10 she was admitted to a child psychiatric center where a complete diagnostic study identified the emotional nature of her problem and a community based treatment program was outlined.

Another example is the label of "autistic child," which has been applied to far more children than demonstrate the syndrome when proper diagnostic procedures are carried out.

The defamation of character implicit in the misapplication of labels is a potentially explosive arena for litigation as this fact becomes more widely known. This is a most serious matter because the later lives of many children are permanently disfigured through mismanagement during early life. It should be noted that the government in its *parens patriae* role does assume responsibility for being a "good parent." When this is not achieved, the state is as culpable as are the parents. Children can be abused not only by their own parents but by the state as well.

When a child's diagnosis is made public, as occurs through placement in institutions or in special classes, there is a demeaning identification that leads to both formal and informal sanctions from the peer group and from others in the community. Once children enter institutions or special classes, not only may other children shun them, but the parents of other children may not wish such children to associate with their own. This is an illustration of the subtle ways in which labeling can affect the lives of children, which becomes even more critical during the adolescent years when dating and social activities are important.

All of this leads to the conclusion that if we do use labels to correspond with government funding patterns, at least the labels should have meaning and be accurate. In Chapter 8, alternatives to individual labeling of children are suggested. For children who do need individualized diagnostic understanding, the only systems equipped to do this are the health and mental health systems. The educational, welfare, and legal systems are not designed to provide the depth of individual understanding and the breadth of interdisciplinary integration needed to achieve an accurate and realistic diagnosis and treatment for each individual. The mental health system has the capacity to integrate and coordinate care for children over an extended period of time. As a health-oriented system under optimal circumstances it has the staffing pattern, backing, and permanence needed for this purpose.

The Dangers of Psychiatric Treatment with Children

Public concern about psychiatric treatment has been justified by the limitations of some facilities and the partial use of certain techniques outside of the mental health field. One prominent area of public concern has been about the use of medication with hyperactive children. In Omaha in the 1960s, local concern was translated into public sanctions against the prescription of psychoactive drugs by physicians for children. A position statement made thereafter by the Office of Child Development served to clarify this problem and stands as a landmark (OCD, 1971). It pointed out that following careful diagnosis, the sophisticated use of medications is an invaluable adjunctive agent in the total management of certain behavior problems in children. The prescription of medication without adequate diagnosis, follow-up, and addressing the personality, family, and educational aspects of the child's problem, however, was regarded as hazardous to children (Weithorn, 1976).

Another area of concern is the use of behavioral modification or conditioning techniques. These are not specific mental health techniques, but are often so identified in lay circles. When applied without taking the child's needs into account, any conformity inducing procedure poses threats to the unfolding of children's individual differences in personality and skills. The risk is that the aim of conformity in behavior will suppress transient behavior but adversely affect personality development, particularly during the preadolescent and early adolescent years. Furthermore, adult judgments of what children's behavior should be modified is often related more to the convenience of adults than to an awareness of the needs of children. As is true with medication, behavioral therapies have value when used within a comprehensive treatment plan for certain children, but should not be used out of context as the sole treatment.

Another important area of potential risk is family therapy, which can be carried out without awareness of the uniqueness of the different generations within the family. A child can be both traumatized and neglected in the process of family therapy that is conducted without knowledge of child development. For example, children's respect for their parents can be undermined by excessive exposure of adult weaknesses in family therapy. In addition, children can be burdened inappropriately with a sense of responsibility to aid their parents and thereby unduly tax their own development.

The greatest hazards to children are the adverse effects of institutionalization (Alt, 1960). The inappropriate use of institutions that in themselves foster dependency can lead to "hospitalism." The result is a young person who becomes dependent upon custodial environments. Within public institutions, efforts are being made to "normalize" life for patients through attention to "patients' rights." This concept has not been adapted to children; however, for adults it involves providing for (Coye, 1977):

1. counsel and due process in involuntary commitment proceedings and in release;
2. legal assistance and counsel when necessary in legal matters related to family and property matters;

3. assistance in translating and exercising basic constitutional and statutory rights in institutional settings;
4. assistance in assuring additional rights one may have because of disability.

There are several ways to assure that patients' rights are recognized and protected—through litigation, legislation, advocacy, and administrative procedures. Some states are taking steps to protect patients' rights through administrative structures outside and within the department responsible for institutions. Michigan's approach to protecting patients' rights is based upon the state's statutory guarantee of their right to services suited to one's condition; to a safe, sanitary and humane living environment; to protection from abuse; to communicate and visit with persons of one's choice; to have personal property and access to one's funds; and to freedom of movement. A state office of recipient rights was established within the Michigan Department of Mental Health and rights advisors were designated in each of the Department's institutions. A procedure informs recipients of their rights on admission and provides a series of steps for the filing and redress of complaints. Complaints were received in a ratio of one to every 30 patients during the first 17 months of the program. Thirty percent were found to be justified and resulted in corrective action by institution directors.

The Michigan experience suggests that 90 percent of all patients' rights complaints can be dealt with by administrative grievance procedures within the state mental health system and need not involve litigation or legal representation. This assumes involvement of the state department of mental health and a rights protection mechanism with enough independence from providers of service to challenge them when necessary (Coye, 1977).

Advocacy in the Psychiatric Treatment of Children

For the mental health professional, advocacy means elaborating upon a role function that is already a basic part of effective child psychiatric practice (Berlin, 1975; Paul, 1977). The work of a child psychiatrist includes prevention, diagnosis, treatment, education, and consultation, in addition to the advocacy functions of ensuring the coordination and continuity of a child's treatment that lies outside of the mental health system: the child's home, community, and school. In taking the realistic life situation of a child into account, the emphasis is upon identifying the child's problems in relationship to the child's individual differences, the family structure and dynamics, the school situation, and other sources of stress or vulnerability in the community. Actually, advocacy is essential to the success of child psychiatric treatment which has as its goal strengthening parental advocacy for the child as well.

The following example illustrates what happens when advocacy functions are not included in treatment:

> As a young child, a boy was described as "just an active child" even though his head banging produced bruises. At the age of seven he was admitted to a county hospital where he was injured by another patient. He was in and out of special classes, and his custody was finally placed with the welfare department. He spent three years in institutions where the parents were unable to visit. His siblings rejected him. In his present institutional placement the social worker who works with the mother does not see the child. The child sustained a back injury, and the parents were unable to determine how it occurred, and were not satisfied with the explanation of the institution's staff. The mother is permitted to see her son one hour a month. The parents who remain devoted to their child feel helpless.

An important aspect of modern psychiatric knowledge is the fact that many children identified as mental patients are responding to disturbed family situations. Not only do other members of the family have significant psychiatric problems, but the identified child may represent only the "tip of an iceberg." The mental health professional then must face the responsibility of dealing with the other family problems. Because of the tendency to focus only upon the "primary patient," many families remain spawning grounds for both adult and child community problems.

> A family has three troubled children, two diagnosed as emotionally disturbed and one with a learning disability. Over seven years they have received the attention of 30 professional people. One of their children was placed in residential treatment at the age of eight and is now functioning reasonably well. Their six year old recently was suspended from school and placed on homebound tutoring, however, he later was admitted to a child caring institution, and placement in a foster home was recommended because of impending family disintegration. The mother remarried after a divorce. At the present time the first boy is in a foster home, and the second boy was returned to his home where he is taunted and teased by siblings, because a foster home could not be found for him. The third son is in a special education class. The mother is bewildered by all that has transpired and says that she never intended to hurt her children, but she has found it difficult to get help in her community.

All levels of mental health care for children and adolescents must be intimately related to each other. The earliest primary care and the most specialized tertiary services must function in a network based upon each child's home, school, and neighborhood. In order to ensure coordination of services and continuity of care, clinical responsibility for each child should be assigned to a specific case manager or designated advocate. The services and facilities required for children's mental health services vary according to the age of the children. Infants, toddlers, school age children, and adolescents require different kinds of care furnished by distinct groups of professionals. The mental health care of children and adolescents should be related to their developmental stages and cannot be adequately provided through adult services and facilities.

All of this highlights the fact that mental health services for children must include their families and involve people not ordinarily regarded as mental health workers. Because children and adolescents do not usually ask for help directly, they depend upon teachers, physicians, nurses, and other significant adults to seek aid for them. The prevention and early detection of emotional disorders depends upon sensitizing all adults in contact with children to their emotional and mental needs.

Conclusion

Because they are concealed by social and family problems, children with emotional and mental problems exist in much larger numbers than are known today. Adequate mental health services are not available to most children even when identified. Because the long-range development of such children is at stake, they require more intensive coordination and continuity of care than do adults. Because the young cannot fully make decisions that will ensure that their treatment needs are met, they depend upon others to make sequential decisions for them in a complicated, often incomplete, array of services.

The U.S. Constitution does not speak to the right of citizens to treatment; however, social policy generally holds that young people, whether in mental hospitals or correctional institutions, should receive treatment. Litigation also increasingly is focusing on the right of involuntarily committed young people to treatment of reasonable quality. The current emphasis on the question of whether or not minors can refuse treatment hinges more on the practical matter of the adverse effects of inadequate institutional facilities than on the theoretical issue of a minor's right to refuse treatment.

In the practice of mental health care for children, motivating parents and children for treatment is a fundamental first step. Few young people request treatment, and many families, understandably, would prefer to avoid the inconvenience and burdens of participating in treatment themselves. Accordingly, the matter of obtaining informed consent for mental health treatment is a complicated process, but necessary for establishing an effective foundation for the participation of young people and their families.

Fortunately, for children and families who use mental health services, the legal system appears to be moving in the direction of assuring confidentiality in psychotherapy and psychiatric treatment. In contrast to their treatment of physician–patient privilege, which is being gradually eroded, courts are recognizing the importance of protecting the privacy of personal exposure so necessary to effective mental health service. This trend may be particularly beneficial to children whose records and community images can be deleteriously affected by public knowledge of their special problems.

For those young people who do need mental health services, growing awareness of the hazards of the indiscriminant use of medication, conditioning procedures, family therapy, and institutionalization offers hope for the public expectation of comprehensive treatment of high quality. Unlike other health fields, standardized specific clinical techniques that can be applied in relatively uniform styles do not exist in children's mental health. There is no single mode of therapy around which other services can be built. The dominant consideration is establishing an individually tailored, comprehensive treatment program based upon each child's family, school, and community.

In a general sense, promoting the mental health of children involves promoting the development of children and the welfare of their families. More specifically, training for all who work directly with children is needed to ensure their sensitivity to social and psychological factors that affect children and the effective use of mental health consultation in identifying children in need of mental health services.

There is a critical shortage in the United States today of trained people with the knowledge and ability to carry out these objectives. The most conservative estimates indicate the current need for at least three times as many trained specialists in the fields of child psychiatry, clinical child psychology, child psychiatric social work, and child psychiatric nursing. In many communities none of these are available today. Children's mental health personnel are needed to provide services directly, to educate non–mental health workers, to provide consultation to other child caring agencies, to carry out clinical research, and to influence social policy to accommodate to the needs of children and their families.

References

ACCREDITATION COUNCIL FOR PSYCHIATRIC FACILITIES (1974) *Accreditation Manual for Psychiatric Facilities Serving Children and Adolescents.* Chicago: Joint Commission on the Accreditation of Hospitals.

ADAMS, P. L. (1976) "Local Community Change for Service to Children." *Child Psychiatry and Human Development,* 7:22–30, Fall.

ALT, H. (1960) *Residential Treatment for the Disturbed Child: Basic Principles in*

Planning and Design of Programs and Facilities. New York: International Universities Press.

BARTON, W. E. (1978) *Law and Mental Health Professions*. New York: International Universities Press.

BERLIN, I. N. (Ed.) (1975) *Advocacy for Child Mental Health*. New York: Brunner/Mazel.

BERLIN, I. N. (1977) "Child Psychiatry Perspectives: Professional Competence, Public Confidence and Children's Rights." *Journal of Child Psychiatry*, 16:748–752.

COYE, J. L. (1977) "Michigan's System for Protecting Patients' Rights." *Hospital and Community Psychiatry*, 28:375–379, May.

DeWITT, C. (1958) *Privileged Communications Between Physician and Patient*. Springfield, Ill: Thomas.

Dixon v. Weinberger, 405 F. Supp. 974 (DDC, 1975).

Donaldson v. O'Connor, 493 F. 2d 507 (5th Cir., 1974), 422 U.S. 563 (1975).

ELLIS, J. W. (1974) "Volunteering Children: Commitment of Minors to Mental Institutions." *California Law Review*, 62:840–916.

FARNSWORTH, D. (1957) *Mental Health in College and University*. Cambridge, Mass: Harvard University Press.

FERLEGER, D. (1976) "*Kremens v. Bartley*: The Right to Be Free." *Hospital and Community Psychiatry*, 27:708–712, October.

FERSTER, E. Z. (1975) "Statutory Summary of Physician–Patient Privileged Communication Laws." Chapter in Allen, R. C. (Ed.), *Readings in Law and Psychiatry*. Baltimore: Johns Hopkins University Press.

GROSSMAN, M. (1977) "Confidentiality: The Right to Privacy Versus the Right to Know." Chapter in Barton, W. E. , and Sanborn, C. J. (Eds.), *Law and the Mental Health Professions*. New York: International Universities Press.

GROUP FOR THE ADVANCEMENT OF PSYCHIATRY (1960) "Confidentiality and Privileged Communication in the Practice of Psychiatry." Report No. 45.

GUREVITZ, H. (1977) "*Tarasoff*: Protective Privilege Versus Public Peril." *American Journal of Psychiatry*, 134:289–292, March.

HETZNECKER, W., AND FORMAN, M. A. (1971) "Community Child Psychiatry: Evolution and Direction." *American Journal of Orthopsychiatry*, 41:350–370, April.

HOLDEN, C. (1976) "Massachusetts Juvenile Justice: De-institutionalization on Trial." *Science*, 192:447–451, April 30.

J.L. & J.R. v. Parham, 412 F. Supp. 112, 117 (1976).

JOINT COMMISSION ON THE MENTAL HEALTH OF CHILDREN (1969) *Crisis in Mental Health: Challenge for the 1970's*. New York: Harper and Row.

KENNEDY, C. (1973) "The Psychotherapist's Privilege." *Washburn Law Journal*, 12:297–316, Spring.

KINDRED, M. (1976) *The Mentally Retarded Citizen and the Law*. New York: Free Press.

KOOCHER, G. P. (Ed.) (1976) *Children's Rights and the Mental Health Professions*. New York: Wiley.

Kremens v. Bartley, 402 F. Supp. 1039 ED Pa., 1975; prob. juris. noted, 96 S. Ct. 1457 (1976).

LIPPIT, R. (1973) "Directions for Change." Chapter in *Social Change and the Mental Health of Children: Report of Task Force VI*. Joint Commission on the Mental Health of Children. New York: Harper and Row.

LOVE, G. H., AND JENITY, G. J. (1974) "Psychotherapy and the Law." *Medical Trial Technique Quarterly*, 20:405–429, Spring.

McGOUGH, L. S., AND CARMICHAEL, W. C. II (1977) "The Right to Treatment and the Right to Refuse Treatment." *American Journal of Orthopsychiatry*, 47:307–320, April.

MEISEL, A., ROTH L. H., AND LIDZ, C. W. (1977) "Toward a Model of the Legal Doctrine of Informed Consent." *American Journal of Psychiatry*, 134:285–289, March.

MILLER, D. (1977a) "The Ethics of Practice in Adolescent Psychiatry." *American Journal of Psychiatry* 134:420–424, April.

MILLER, D., AND BURT, R. A. (1977b) "Children's Rights on Entering Therapeutic Institutions." *American Journal of Psychiatry*, 134:153–156, February.

Mills v. Board of Education, 348 F. Supp. 866 (DDC, 1972).

Morales v. Turman, F. 2d 4603 (5th Cir., No. 74-3436, July 21, 1976), 97 S. Ct. 1189 (1977).

NATIONAL INSTITUTE OF MENTAL HEALTH (1976) *Services to the Mentally Disabled of Selected Catchment Areas in Eastern New York State and New York City*. DHEW Publication No. (ADM) 76-372. Washington, D.C.: Superintendent of Documents, U.S. Government Printing Office.

NEWMAN, M. (1966) "Challenge of Community Child Psychiatry." *Community Mental Health Journal*, 2:281–284, Winter.

OFFICE OF CHILD DEVELOPMENT (1971) *Report of the Conference on the Use of Stimulant Drugs in the Treatment of Behaviorally Disturbed Young School Children*. Washington, D.C.: Department of Health, Education and Welfare.

PAUL, J. L., NEUFELD, G. R., AND PELOSI, J. W. (EDS.) (1977) *Child Advocacy Within the System*. Syracuse, N.Y.: Syracuse University Press.

People v. Leyra (1951) 302 N.Y. 343, 98 NE 2d 553.

People v. Wasker (1958) 353 Mich. 447, 91 NW 2d 866.

POLAK, P. R. ET AL. (1975) "Prevention in Mental Health: A Controlled Study." *American Journal of Psychiatry*, 132:146–149, February.

POLIER, J. W. (1976) "The Rights of Children." Chapter in Westman, J. C. (Ed.), *Proceedings of the University of Wisconsin Conference on Child Advocacy*. Madison: University of Wisconsin–Extension, Health Sciences Unit.

PRESIDENT'S COMMISSION ON MENTAL HEALTH (1978) *Report to the President*, Vol. 1. Washington, D.C.: Superintendent of Documents, No. 040-000-00390-9.

PYFER, J. F. (1974) "The Juvenile's Right to Receive Treatment." Chapter in Katz, S. N. (Ed.), *The Youngest Minority*. Chicago: American Bar Association.

RAFFERTY, F. T. (1976) "Confidentiality, Labeling and the Social Control Function of Psychiatry." Presented at the Annual Meeting of the American Psychiatric Association.

REXFORD, E. N. (1969) "Children, Child Psychiatry and Our Brave New World." *Archives of General Psychiatry*, 30:25–37.

ROTH L. H. (1977) "Involuntary Civil Commitment: The Right to Treatment and the Right to Refuse Treatment." *Psychiatric Annals*, 7:50–76.

Rouse v. Cameron, 373 F. 2d 451 (D.C. Cir., 1966).

SLOVENKO, R., AND USDIN, E. (1966) *Psychotherapy, Confidentiality and Communication*. Springfield, Ill.: Thomas.

STONE, A. A. (1976) *Mental Health and Law*. New York: Jason Aronson.

Tarasoff v. The Regents of the University of California, 118 Calif. Rptr. 129, 529 P. 2d 553 (Calif., 1974)

TULCHIN S. H. (1964) *Child Guidance: Lawson G. Lowrey*. New York: American Orthopsychiatric Association.

WALD P. M. (1976) "The Legal Rights of Children and Treatment." Presented at the Annual Meeting of the American Psychiatric Association.

WATKINS, N. J., AND ROTH, B. A. (1976) "*Kremens v. Bartley*: The Case for the State." *Hospital and Community Psychiatry*, 27:706–708, October.

WEITHORN C. J., AND ROSS, R. (1976) "Stimulant Drugs for Hyperactivity: Some Additional Disturbing Questions." *American Journal of Orthopsychiatry*, 46:168–173, January.

WILSON, J. P. (1978) *The Rights of Adolescents in the Mental Health System*. Lexington, Massachusetts: Lexington Books.

WISCONSIN STATUTES. Chap. 905.05—"Physician–Patient Privilege."

Wyatt v. Aderholt, 503 F. 2d 1305 (5th Cir., No. 8, 1974).

Wyatt v. Stickney, 344 F. Supp. 373, 380 (MD Ala., 1972).

Epilogue

America is puzzled by its children. We feel that we care about children—we respond protectively to those who are abused and spend large sums of money on children generally. Yet we are told we neglect children and trample upon their rights. With justification, we would like to know the facts.

Without question, children fare better today than in previous generations when extreme discrimination against children in the form of "agism" prevailed. From earlier times in which children were barely recognized as more than miniature adults, we have come to appreciate childhood as a period of growth during which personalities and abilities are shaped. Beginning in the last century with the efforts of "child savers" to free children from oppressive labor, we now have reached a time in which we are contemplating ways of assuring them fulfilling childhoods.

Furthermore, this book is an expression of the recognition that strengthening families will improve the lives of children, reduce society's problems and increase both the economic productivity and moral stature of later generations. Although some inevitable conflicts exist between the aims and interests of older and younger generations, it seems clear that America's will is to promote the healthy development of children. The problem lies less in the lack of desire than in finding ways to do so.

The challenge today is to ensure fulfillment of the basic developmental needs of our children. We have considered ways of doing this through identifying those child rearing patterns that have been effective and those that have failed. For a variety of reasons, however, some people despair and conclude that little can be done without further research. We have taken the opposite position that we already know enough but lack concerted efforts to apply that knowledge.

The most important issue is how childhood is conceived. If children are regarded as objects to be shaped by the latest technology, we look to science for guidance in child rearing techniques. On the other hand, if children are seen as the bearers of our culture, we look to culture for values to guide child rearing. Our present dilemma appears to result from reliance on technology for child rearing aims and methods that can really only be defined and articulated by culture. It makes no more sense to base child rearing on technology than it does to base adult living upon the latest experimental findings. We can use science to enhance aspects of our lives but not to provide meaning and purpose.

One of the reasons science has overshadowed culture in child rearing has been the tendency to regard the United States as such a heterogeneous nation that an American culture does not exist. Furthermore, to recognize an American culture has been construed as a denial of the existence of cultural minorities through unwelcome stress on "the majority." The American Bicentennial helped to clear the air as we were reminded of the truly unique American philosophical and political traditions which do form the substrate of an American culture. The existence of that culture is most obvious to those who view America from the outside and least evident to Americans themselves.

One aspect of American culture is its responsiveness to the fruits of technology, but there are more important values that permeate the fabric of American culture as well. In fact, our current concern about children may be a sign that the United States is maturing and examining its own identity. Just as they do for their parents, children are helping America to become aware of its responsibility to provide a "good example" for them. Children do as we do, not as we say. Even worse, without models for identification they become less than human. The dehumanizing tendency of modern technological society not only robs adults' lives of meaning, but erodes the very foundations of humanity as children are deprived of human models.

For the sake of its children and its future, America must articulate ideals for its citizens. The challenge, then, is to define the essence of American life. As individuals find the unique significances of their own personal heritages, there is a parallel need to establish what membership in a pluralistic, but still definable, American society requires. One fundamental characteristic of our social system is its adaptability. For example, at times of national crisis we find that a uniquely American capacity emerges to tolerate differences and maintain collective solidarity. For individual citizens, this national model of stability in the face of ambiguity is precisely the one most needed to ensure competence in personal living.

The evidence presented in this book points to personal competence as the epitome of American living. We have identified the ingredients of personal competence: social skills, self-control, ability to learn, social values, self-identity, self-esteem, and decision-making ability. The enunciation of these qualities provides guidelines in setting child rearing objectives. The failure to articulate them has led to bewilderment and uncertainty in child rearing.

We know that acquiring the ingredients of personal competence depends upon stable parent–child relationships. Gifted individuals may survive and even flourish under adversity during their early lives; however, this is not the case for most children, particularly the vulnerable. We know that each child needs dependable, intimate relationships with adults as models for developing the capacity to relate intimately to other persons, the foundation of gratification in social living. Each child needs intimate relationships with other children to develop self-control and the capacity for cooperative relationships with peers. Children further need to share growth with a variety of adults modeling competent living. When children have had these opportunities to meet their developmental needs, they achieve personal competence.

We also know where we have gone wrong. There is much evidence that disrupted and disturbed parent–child units have not provided models of competence for far too many children. At least 15 percent of our children are handicapped because they have not developed the skills needed for competent living and suffer from a range of maladjustments based upon the lack of self-respect, or respect for others, or both. Another 22 percent of our children are at risk for later social and emotional problems. We know that a variety of personal, family, and social factors interact to convert vulnerability into handicap.

We also know that we have not identified vulnerable children soon enough. We have also inflicted greater disability on many of those whom we have pejoratively and callously labeled. Even worse, we have not provided effective remedies for those we have tried to help. The fragmentation and discontinuity of services for children have made it necessary to call national attention to the disregard of even the most simple human rights of many children.

The intent of this book, however, is not to rebuke America for willful neglect of its children, but to highlight the ways in which we can learn from our mistakes and to point to possible solutions. The fundamental incorporation of the child's point of view into child caring systems, professional practice, and social policies through child advocacy is proposed as a vehicle for conserving the developmental potential of children. In essence, child advocacy is assuming responsibility in varying degrees and ways for meeting the developmental needs of children through both class advocacy and individual advocacy. The aim of child advocacy is to support competent parenting of children. In itself, the problem-solving nature of child advocacy offers a model of competence for children who have experienced adult uncertainty and helplessness.

In promoting the interests of children as a class, the economic cost-benefit aspects of children must be faced. It is evident that the value of children has changed as our society has evolved from stable, rural to mobile, urban based families and from a labor to a technological economy. Children are no longer economic assets to their families. Meanwhile, increases in the cost of raising children cause parents, and the economy generally, to view child rearing as an economic liability in competition with other priorities. Moreover, at the ideological level, there has been a downgrading of the satisfactions of parenthood.

On the other hand, in a less tangible but more important sense, children enrich the lives of adults. Children do not really need specialized expertise from parents. Although technical aid may be required in managing certain children, the day-to-day needs of children, whether they be troubled or not, can be met by well intentioned, competent, and warm persons. To be a parent and raise a child requires more in the way of common sense and less in the way of technical knowledge. People who avoid having or working with children run the risk of missing an irreplaceable aspect of life, namely, the stimulation of growing with them. Unfortunately, many adults encounter seemingly insurmountable barriers to involvement in family living because they are overwhelmed by their own problems or preoccupied with their vocational lives.

From this it follows that promoting the welfare of the family is the most important thrust of class child advocacy. Income maintenance, homemaker services, adequate housing, recreational facilities, and marital counseling to bolster family integrity are vital to the development of children. Family planning is also essential because frequently it is the unwanted child or the additional child who detonates family disintegration as well as becoming its principal victim. For children with mothers in the work force, adequate day care and after-school services are essential if children are to have stimulating environments in which to grow. In general, emphasis upon the realistic rewards of family living is needed to counteract misconceptions about the onerous burdens of child rearing.

Inherent in competent parenting, individual child advocacy is also a professional function of those who work with children. All systems that deal with children have built-in mechanisms that make it possible for professionals to insulate themselves from the tragic and painful dilemmas encountered in the course of their work. The health worker can be absorbed in the treatment of disease, the lawyer in courtroom procedures, the social worker in administrative policies, the educator in the mechanics of teaching, and parents in child rearing techniques. These defenses occur in all systems and are necessary for the homeostasis of each system. They deserve critical analysis, however, because the systems themselves can be self-serving and antithetical to the interests of children.

The challenge is to increase the competence as advocates of professionals who work with children. Those barriers that interfere with the empathic involvement of people in children's lives can be reduced if they are replaced by more effective, mastery enhancing techniques. Child advocacy strives to accomplish this. Through increased knowledge of the developmental needs of children and what to do about them, the helplessness and anxiety generated by apparently overwhelming problems can be reduced and the tendency to deny or avoid them minimized. It is the lack of understanding and sense of helplessness that leads people to turn away from the dilemmas posed by children with problems. There is a pressing need to prepare professionals for advocacy roles based upon knowledge of child development, skills for communicating with children, interdisciplinary teamwork, protection of the rights of children, and coordination of resources for children. Universities bear a special responsibility for developing advocacy training programs at all educational levels.

Although obviously not a panacea, child advocacy offers a means of bringing the voice of the dependent, inarticulate young into a society planned and managed by adults. The current impetus for child advocacy appears to rest upon a broad popular base which can be tapped through calling public attention to what children need at all levels of community life. We do not need new professionals specifically to find children at risk; this can be done by sensitizing people already on the scene. We do not require more research simply to know what children need; our present knowledge can be more broadly disseminated and professionals more effectively trained and deployed. We do not need new people to ensure that services are available; those responsible for planning and developing human services can be sensitized to the needs of children.

Advocacy for children and youth is a field of endeavor ranging from creating a society more conducive to the development of young people to improving the life of a single child. As an essential aspect of working with young people, advocacy skills should be included in the training of all professional disciplines that deal with children and youth.

In a broader sense a social policy committed to conserving our nation's developmental potential through promoting personal competence in developing children and their families is urgently needed. America must place a high priority on child rearing or face an uncertain future. As our nation's largest permanent minority group, our children depend upon us to make that commitment.

Author Index

413

Subject Index

Hampstead profile, 225
Handicapped children, 20 *t*
Harvard Committee, 201
Haziel v. U.S., 289, 292
Health care cost, 335
Health education, 337–41
Health Systems Agencies, 159, 335
Hendricks v. Curry, 325, 332
High school, 200
History of childhood, 30–35
Hobson v. Hansen, 216, 225, 241
Home Observation for Measurement of the Environment, 123–24
Homemaker services, 305, 316
Hospitalism, 398
Hospitalization
    impact on children, 344–45
    voluntary of minors, 386
Hull House, 298
Hyperactive children, 398

Identification, 85, 89
"Illegitimate" children, 261, 312
Immigrant children, 32
Incest, 358, 363
Income maintenance, 36, 151, 305, 329
Incorrigibility, 244, 247, 250, 267
Indian children, 317
Individual differences
    cognitive style, 218–20
        attention control, 219
        compartmentalization, 220
        conceptualizing, 219
        converging thinking, 220
        field dependence, 218
        leveling vs. sharpening, 219
        reflection vs. impulsivity, 220
        scanning, 219
        sensory modality preference, 219
    tactile threshold, 73
    cultural emphasis, 63
    definition of, 72–74
    in education, 218–23
    in intelligence, 221, 225
    in maturational rates, 73–74, 221
    in physical growth, 221
    policy supporting, 154–55
    sex differences, 127
    in temperaments
        difficult child, 11, 221
        easy child, 221
        risk taking, 220
        slow to warm up child, 221
Industrial Revolution, 297
Infancy
    development, 115–17
    screening, 174–75
Informed consent
    and children, 345–51
    in mental health treatment, 388–89
    state statutes, 246–47
Ingraham v. Wright, 207, 241
Inner directed persons, 95
Intelligence, individual differences, 221, 225
Institutional care, 327–28
    of adolescents, 388–89
    dangers of, 397–99
    and juvenile courts, 267
    and psychopathy, 116
    residential treatment, 187
Invulnerable children, 15

J.L. and J.R. v. Parham, 385, 403
Joint Commission on Accreditation of Hospitals, 141, 387
Joint Commission on Mental Health of Children, 35, 37, 45, 51, 156, 376, 379